1950 N

Latin America in the International Economy

Latin America in the International Economy

Proceedings of a Conference held by the
International Economic Association in
Mexico City, Mexico

EDITED BY
VICTOR L. URQUIDI AND ROSEMARY THORP

A HALSTED PRESS BOOK

JOHN WILEY & SONS
New York – Toronto

Published in the United Kingdom 1973 by
The Macmillan Press Ltd

Published in the U.S.A. and
Canada by Halsted Press, a
Division of John Wiley & Sons, Inc.,
New York

Library of Congress Cataloging in Publication Data
Main entry under title:

Latin America in the international economy.

    (International Economic Association publications)
    "A Halsted Press book."
    1.   Latin America—Foreign economic relations—
Congresses.   2.   Latin America—Commerce—Congresses.
I.   Urquidi, Victor L., ed. II.   Thorp, Rosemary, ed.
III.   International Economic Association.
HF1480.5.L385   382'.098   72–13779

ISBN 0 470–89646–9

Printed in Great Britain

Contents

Acknowledgements

The International Economic Association wishes to express its gratitude to the organisations and persons who made possible the publication of this volume.

As to organisations, our thanks go to the Ministry of Industry and Commerce of Mexico, to the Tinker Foundation, and to the Ford Foundation, without whose generous financial support the authors would not have been able to meet and confront each other with their views. Our thanks go also to El Colegio de México which took in charge all local arrangements for the meeting with an efficiency which was much appreciated.

As to persons, the principal debt is, as always, to those who planned the work, to the authors of the various chapters, and to those who have edited the proceedings of the round table at which these chapters were discussed.

Professor Victor L. Urquidi played in fact the most essential part throughout the fulfilment of the project, both as Chairman of the Programme Committee and as the person responsible for the preparation of the meeting in Mexico City. This volume provides the best testimony of the Association's debt to him.

The gratitude of the Association goes also to Mrs. Rosemary Thorp, who acted as *rapporteur* and who has produced the record of the discussion in a very short period of time, as well as to Mrs. Trinidad Warman for her assistance with the task of note-taking.

List of Participants

Dr. Sven W. Arndt, University of California, Santa Cruz, U.S.A.
Dr. Edmar Bacha, Instituto de Pesquisas Economicas è Administrativas, Rio de Janeiro, Brazil
Mr. Carlos Bazdresch, Secretaría de la Presidencia, Mexico City, Mexico
Dr. Rodrigo Botero, Fundación para la Educación Superior y el Desarrollo, Bogotá, Colombia
Professor H. C. Eastman, Department of Political Economy, University of Toronto, Canada
Professor Luc Fauvel, Université de Paris, France
Professor David Felix, Washington University, St. Louis, U.S.A.
Dr. Aldo Ferrer, Instituto de Desarrollo Económico y Social, Buenos Aires, Argentina
Dr. Ricardo Ffrench-Davis, CEPLAN, Universidad Católica de Chile, Santiago, Chile
Dr. Albrecht von Gleich, Institut für Iberoamerika-Kunde, Hamburg, Federal Republic of Germany
Professor Albert O. Hirschman, Harvard University, Cambridge, U.S.A.
Mr. Akio Hosono, U.N. Economic Commission for Latin America, Santiago, Chile
Dr. Jorge Katz, Instituto Torcuato di Tella, Buenos Aires, Argentina
Dr. Wolfgang König, The Catholic University of America, Washington D.C., U.S.A.
Professor Denis-Clair Lambert, Université de Lyon, France
Dr. Rikard Lang, Ekonomski Institut, Zagreb, Yugoslavia
Mr. Santiago P. Macario, U.N. Economic Commission for Latin America, Santiago, Chile
Professor Fritz Machlup, International Finance Section, Princeton University, Princeton, U.S.A.
Dr. Alfred Maizels, U.N. Conference on Trade and Development Secretariat, Geneva, Switzerland
Professor Jean Marchal, Université de Paris, France
Dr. José Antonio Mayobre, Banco Central de Venezuela, Caracas, Venezuela
Professor Alec Nove, University of Glasgow, United Kingdom
Professor Vladimir Pertot, University of Ljubljana, Yugoslavia
Professor Clark Reynolds, Food Research Institute, Stanford University, Stanford, U.S.A.
Mr. Maurice Schaeffer, European Economic Community, Brussels, Belgium
Professor Osvaldo Sunkel, Universidad Católica de Chile, Santiago, Chile
Mr. Luis Szekely, Banco de México, Mexico City, Mexico
Mrs. Rosemary Thorp, Institute of Economics and Statistics, University of Oxford, United Kingdom
Mr. Victor L. Urquidi, El Colegio de México, Mexico City, Mexico
Dr. Adalbert Krieger Vasena, Atlantic Institute, Paris, France
Professor Raymond Vernon, Graduate School of Business Administration, Harvard University, Boston, U.S.A.
Mr. Miguel S. Wionczek, Centro de Estudios Monetarios Latinoamericanos, Mexico City, Mexico

Observers

Dr. David Barkin, Herbert H. Lehman College, City University of New York, U.S.A.

Lic. Carlos Bermúdez Limón, El Colegio Nacional de Economistas, Mexico City, Mexico
Dr. Dimitri Germidis, O.E.C.D. Development Centre, Paris, France
Miss Martha Muse, The Tinker Foundation, New York, U.S.A.
Professor Gustav Ranis, Economic Growth Center, Yale University, New Haven, U.S.A.
Mrs. Trinidad Warman, Universidad Anáhuac, Mexico City, Mexico

Programme Committee
Mr. Victor L. Urquidi
Professor H. C. Eastman
Dr. Rikard Lang
Dr. Alfred Maizels
Professor Clark Reynolds
Professor Osvaldo Sunkel

List of main Abbreviations used

A.I.D.	Agency for International Development
C.E.C.L.A.	Special Committee for Latin American Co-ordination
C.I.A.P.	Inter-American Committee for the Alliance for Progress
C.I.E.S.	Inter-American Economic and Social Council
D.A.C.	Development Assistance Committee of O.E.C.D.
ECLA	United Nations Economic Commission for Latin America
E.E.C.	European Economic Community
EFTA	European Free Trade Area
F.A.O.	United Nations Food and Agriculture Organisation
GATT	General Agreement on Tariffs and Trade
I.B.R.D.	International Bank for Reconstruction and Development (World Bank)
I.D.A.	International Development Association
I.D.B.	Inter-American Development Bank
I.F.C.	International Financial Corporation
I.M.F.	International Monetary Fund
LAFTA	Latin American Free Trade Association
M.I.T.I.	Japanese Ministry of International Trade and Industry
O.A.S.	Organisation of American States
O.E.C.D.	Organisation for Economic Co-operation and Development
O.P.E.C.	Organisation of Petroleum Exporting Countries
UNCTAD	United Nations Conference on Trade and Development

Introduction

External relations have throughout history been seen as a key issue in Latin American development. Recently, however, both the analysis of the implications of that external relationship, and its actual form, have been undergoing a number of significant changes. A discussion of the issue some twenty years ago would have focussed largely on questions of terms of trade, commodity stabilisation, the expansion of intraregional trade, and the better integration into the economy of export enclaves. The 1960s have brought so many new elements into the picture that some effort at assessment and refocus at this point in time appears essential.

First, by the mid 1960s it was clear that a decade or more of import substituting industrialisation in Latin America had brought little relief from the problem of external vulnerability and low levels of development associated with the export economy. If anything, as the recent literature has made clear, external vulnerability is greater and high and increasing levels of un- and underemployment plus low productivity have sharpened income inequality even while a measure of growth has occurred. High rates of population growth in most Latin American countries have compounded the problem and raised doubts as to the sufficiency of the modest growth rates which have been achieved. Further, by the end of the 1960s it was also painfully obvious, with the effective stalemate in LAFTA and serious difficulties in Central America, that integration in the form it had been attempted could provide only part of the answer. At the same time there has been little improvement in the broad social aspects of development in the majority of countries, and a sharpening of social tension has occurred. Despite a number of good programmes in education, land reform, housing and social welfare, these have not sufficed to create a just society. To use a phrase coined by one of the editors in his introduction to the Conference, there may have been some growth but it has been at best 'maldevelopment'.

Over and above this basic situation, the present is a particularly critical period for Latin America as she experiences the repercussions of the international monetary situation and the growing protectionism of the major advanced countries, both in agricultural policy and in restrictions on Latin America's exports of manufactures.

The latter restrictions are all the more significant in as far as by the end of the 1960s the export of manufactures was beginning to emerge, at least in the larger countries, as a key factor not only in the balance of payments but also in the reshaping of the whole industrial structure. Their crucial role springs also from the fact that this is the dynamic sector of world trade, a trade to which Latin America is marginal and in which her share is falling. At the same time during the 1960s the multinational corporation emerged as the dominant vehicle of world trade and as probably the key factor not only in bringing technology but also market access. Increasingly, such corporations penetrated important sectors of Latin American industry, with apparently a two-fold significance for manufactured exports. On the one hand it appeared that they, and perhaps they only, had the key to successful exporting; on the other they clearly, on occasion, set up Latin American subsidiaries only on the firm understanding they would not export. Meantime, despite all the problems, Latin American exports of manufactures quietly moved up to nearly 20 per cent of total exports by the end of the decade, by which time they were rising at an annual rate also of nearly 20 per cent. How indispensable the role played by multinationals in this is far from clear.

What has become clear, however, is that the technology they or their Latin American counterparts have imported has been both costly in the extreme and inadequately adapted to Latin American conditions. How far it can be adapted, how much more cheaply it can be bought and via what institutions, or how far an indigenous and still productive alternative could be generated in its absence, are again imperative issues for investigation in the coming decade.

At the same time a certain element of fluidity has entered the international scene, arising from the challenge to U.S. economic hegemony from Western Europe and Japan and the need for rethinking posed by the international financial crisis, as well as by the crisis in aid policies brought about by the growing disillusion of aid-givers with the results of aid. This makes it all the more important for Latin America to define her own position and actively influence the terms on which she is to be integrated into the world economy.

In response in part to these trends in economic realities, there have been significant developments at the level of analysis. The structuralist approach, which evolved in the 1950s largely out of ECLA thinking, emphasised basic reforms at the same time as it stressed the need for import substitution and an increase in the flow of long-term capital to Latin America, preferably through multilateral mechanisms. A dynamic external sector was seen nevertheless as the determining factor in inducing adequate rates of growth and a higher ratio of domestic savings, thus facilitating the necessary structural changes. However, on the one hand such structural changes proved more or less impossible to bring about given the political obstacles and the lack of a dynamic external sector, while on the other the component of private direct investment in the inflow of capital was far larger than had been foreseen. Direct investment sought both to supply world needs of certain basic products (such as oil and copper) and to take advantage of local markets under import substitution policies. With the increased presence of foreign corporations, the expansion of exports of manufactures which Latin America increasingly recognises as its best hope for a dynamic external sector requires a more complex analytical approach. In particular this must be one where the interplay of political and economic factors is more adequately handled, and where national economic policies include negotiations both with foreign governments and with foreign corporations. The 'dependency' school addresses itself squarely to this question. Where private foreign interests play a large role in the local economy, 'the capacity to negotiate of a country thus penetrated' becomes 'qualitatively different from that of the dominant country; this (is) the nub of dependency' (Sunkel, p. 34 below). The alternative perspective, which has also been considerably developed in recent years, and was the approach espoused by many at the Conference, welcomes foreign investment for its important contribution to growth, employment, taxation, technological advancement, marketing techniques and so forth, and sees the problem as essentially one of bargaining strategy. In contrast to both views (though not necessarily in conflict with the latter), others see the problems supposedly generated by foreign investment as in fact the product principally of misguided industrialisation policies.

There are therefore important new trends to be discerned both in Latin American external economic relations and in recent analysis of the significance of those relations for Latin American development. Given this, both the function and the plan of the Conference followed naturally. First, the problem of 'external dependence' had to be considered and debated both in its entirety and in respect of its components (trade flows, foreign investment, the role of the international financial agencies, the technology transfer problem). As will be seen in the debate below,[1] a main function of the Conference was to contrast the approaches to these topics which we outlined above. Secondly, a crucial aspect of external relations concerns the geographical diversification of such relations. On the one hand diversification *per se* increases bargaining possibilities. On the other, each new relationship raises again the issue of the precise form the relationship is taking and its implications. Given that a number of significant shifts in the geographical pattern of Latin American

[1] See especially the debate on Sunkel's paper and pp. 422–4 below.

external economic relations have been among the trends emerging from the 1960s, the second part of the book falls into place. It examines Latin America's present and future trade and financial relations with the United States, the European Economic Community, the United Kingdom, Japan and Eastern Europe.

Seen as an attempt to crystallise a new focus and new questions, an important part of such a Conference must be the debate. This is why we have presented it at some length, and have taken considerable liberties with it for the sake of coherence. If in the process we have misrepresented anyone, we must beg pardon.

Part 1

The Framework of Economic Dependence : World Trade and Investment

1 The Pattern of Latin American Dependence

Osvaldo Sunkel

UNIVERSITY OF CHILE

Much has been written on Latin America's dependence upon trade, aid, private foreign investment and technological transfers. The structure and trends of foreign trade, the evolution of the terms of trade, commercial policy, the volume, costs and conditions of aid, the amounts, benefits and disadvantages of foreign investment, the obstacles, costs and nature of the transfer of technology: all these are topics that have been subject to extensive empirical and theoretical analysis. Nevertheless, most of the research done has usually concentrated on the independent and separate examination of each of these elements of the economic and financial relations of Latin America with the industrialised countries. This has been both necessary and useful, but it tends to overshadow two very important aspects of the question: first, that there are significant direct relationships among trade, aid, foreign investment and technological transfers, and second, that these variables and their interrelationships are part of a wider system of international economic and political relations.

This paper is a very preliminary attempt to suggest some of the characteristics of that system, at least with respect to the economic relationships among developed countries and the Latin American economies. In this initial effort to understand the global perspective of the pattern of Latin American dependence, I have concentrated almost exclusively on the elaboration of a conceptual framework and its application to the analysis of the interplay between national development and the international system. This approach should bring out the underlying forces and the wider context within which trade, aid, finance, investment and technological transfers take place.

The theories which relate the national development process with the system of international economic relations, and which underlie the interpretation of past and present trends, may be classified in three main groups: the neoclassical theory of international trade, the Marxist theory of capitalistic–imperialist exploitation and the theories of the 'backwash effect' of international trade.

The liberal *laissez-faire* approach is a rather inappropriate basis for analysis and recommendations, because of the highly unrealistic and restrictive assumptions upon which it is based, of which one is particularly damaging. I refer to the identification of the concepts of 'economy' and 'country', which means that countries are conceived as self-contained economic units which exchange products in the international market place. Quite apart from the very partial aspect of international economic relations implicit in this approach, it fails to grasp one of the essential characteristics of the international economy, namely that it is basically made up of international firms which operate simultaneously in various *national* markets, thus constituting an international economic system which penetrates and overlaps with national economic systems.

The Marxist theory of imperialism is based precisely on the recognition of this fact, since it suggests that international monopolies penetrate national economies in search of raw materials and market outlets in order to use their increasing economic surplus and add to it. Nevertheless, the Marxist approach has restricted itself mainly to this aspect of international monopoly capitalism, neglecting an element which seems essential from our point of view: the 'spread' and 'backwash' effects of the international extensions of some national economic systems into other national economic systems, and the influence of these processes on the structural configuration of the underdeveloped economy.

This analysis, which was associated originally with the names of Myrdal, Prebisch, Singer and others, and which has been a central concern in important contributions in recent years, suggests that in the interaction of industrial economies with primary producing economies, the former tend to benefit relatively more than the latter and that this gives rise to cumulatively divergent trends in the development of the two groups of countries. Although there are many different arguments advanced in favour of this hypothesis, they essentially reduce to the following:

(a) the nature of foreign-owned or controlled primary production for export, which tends to be an 'enclave' with little positive effect on the local economy, but substantial positive linkages to the home economy where most procurement, financing, storing, processing, research, marketing and reinvestment take place;

(b) the characteristics of the local economy, which lacks trained manpower, entrepreneurial talent, capital and physical as well as institutional infrastructure, and is therefore unable to respond positively to the potential opportunities of an expanding export activity;

(c) the relative behaviour of the prices of raw material exports and manufactured imports – the worsening of the terms of trade of primary producers – as well as the instability of primary product prices;

(d) the generally monopolistic nature of the primary export activity which, when the firm is foreign-owned, implies an outflow of excess profits.

This approach introduces a most important perspective since it focuses attention on the interaction between the external agents and the domestic economic, social, and political structures. Nevertheless, it is still partial and requires further generalisation and systematisation.

Apart from other considerations, it is partial because it has concentrated its analysis of the differential effects of the interaction between developed and underdeveloped countries exclusively on the primary producing export activities of the latter. One of the results of this bias in the analysis was the conclusion that these countries had to industrialise because industrialisation would result in a cumulative process of self-reinforcing 'spread' effects – Rostow's 'take-off into self-sustained growth'. This seems to have been largely the consequence of a rather mechanical application of the European model of the Industrial Revolution to the Latin American case.

But the model of import substituting industrialisation that has characterised Latin America seems to be something quite different. It is in fact very difficult to understand if, apart from the internal peculiarities of each country, reference is not made to the framework of external links, conditioning factors and pressures that have influenced industrial development so decisively in our countries. In fact, its dynamics and structure and the nature of the productive processes adopted, especially with reference to technology, have been induced to a large extent by external conditions. As a consequence, the development strategy of import substituting industrialisation, which was supposed to free the economy from its heavy reliance on primary exports and foreign capital and technology, has not only failed to achieve these aims, but has in fact aggravated the dependent nature of our economies.

In its initial period, from 1930 to about 1955, it stimulated the development of a significant manufacturing industry and of the corresponding national entrepreneurial class. But subsequently it was taken over to a large extent by foreign subsidiaries, with the result that much of the benefit expected from industrialisation has flowed abroad via growing purchases of current and capital inputs and rising profits, royalty and other financial payments, while at the same time the economy has been increasingly de-nationalised and the

local entrepreneurial class eroded. Furthermore, although the massive penetration of foreign firms may have accelerated global and
especially industrial growth rates, it has also accentuated the uneven
nature of development: there has occurred on the one hand a partial
process of modernisation and expansion of capital-intensive activities, and on the other, a process of disruption, contraction and dis-
organisation of labour intensive traditional activities. Disguised and
open unemployment, the basic sources of marginality, have therefore
been rising and together now account for levels estimated at over
25 per cent. Due to this, and to the fact that the development
strategies pursued aimed at the formation and strengthening of an
urban middle class, income seems at least as heavily concentrated in
the hands of the wealthy as it was twenty years ago, allowing them
consumption levels and patterns similar to those of the middle classes
of developed countries, while both the gap between high and low
incomes in towns and in the countryside, and the urban–rural
differential, appear in most cases to have widened.

The recognition of the fact that industrialisation has not freed
Latin American economies from foreign dependence, but on the
contrary has added new and stronger elements of external control
and influence, while at the same time contributing to the traditional
unevenness of the development process, has led Latin American
economists and other social scientists to go much further in the
analysis of the nature and effects of dependence on the process of
development.

Perhaps the most important new element in such analyses is the
fact that local development and modernisation is no longer seen in
isolation, as had been the case in conventional development theory,
but as part of the development of the international capitalist system,
whose dynamic has a determining influence on local processes.
Therefore foreign factors are seen not as external but as internal to
the system, contributing significantly to shape the nature and functioning of its economy, society and policy. In this way the analysis
links the evolution of capitalism internationally to the discriminating
and marginalising nature of the local process of development,
pointing particularly to the fact that access to the means and benefits
of development is selective, and that rather than spreading wide it
tends to constitute a self-reinforcing process of cumulative privilege
for certain special groups, those more closely linked to foreign
activities.

In other words this approach looks at the capitalist system as a
whole, as a world-wide international system, within which national
economies – nation states – constitute sub-systems not completely
separated from each other but partially overlapping, owing to the

fact that national economies interpenetrate each other through productive facilities, technologies, consumption patterns, private and government institutions, and ideologies. According to this approach, underdevelopment can no longer be seen as a moment in the evolution of a society which has been economically, politically and culturally autonomous and isolated. The present international panorama of countries at different levels of development is not simply an aggregate of individual historical development performances; it is not like a race which started before the Industrial Revolution, and in which some countries reached advanced stages of development while others stagnated or moved more slowly, and therefore are now at more primitive stages. This approach maintains that one of the essential elements of the development of capitalism has been from its very beginning the creation of an international system, which brought the whole world economy under the influence of a few countries. Development and underdevelopment, in this view, are simultaneous processes; the two faces of the historical evolution of the capitalist system, linked to each other in a functional way, interacting and mutually conditioning each other.

The evolution of this global and closely interrelated system over time is what has given rise to the present world panorama of development and underdevelopment; this can be viewed nationally and internationally in terms of two polarisations and the relationship between them. First, a polarisation of the world between countries, with the developed, industrialised, advanced, dominant, central ones on one side, and the underdeveloped, poor, dependent and peripheral ones on the other. Secondly, a polarisation within countries, into advanced and modern social groups, geographical regions and economic activities on the one hand, and backward, primitive, marginal and dependent social groups, geographical regions and economic activities on the other. This internal polarisation exists both in developed and underdeveloped countries, the difference being that in the former, modern and advanced groups, regions and activities prevail, while in the latter the contrary is the case. Thirdly, an important relationship between these two polarisations has emerged in the form of the link between the modern and advanced social groups of both the developed and underdeveloped countries. This arises particularly as a result of the penetration of the underdeveloped economies by the extractive, manufacturing, commercial, technical and financial activities of international firms, which link those groups trans-nationally and produce their close identification in terms of patterns and levels of living.

This international economic system, as any other social system, is simultaneously a system of power, which has historically been organised as a system of domination-dependence, permanently biased in favour of the developed countries and against the under-developed countries. This system has evolved through various historical periods – mercantilism, liberalism or imperialism, and present day neomercantilism – with a succession of substitutions of the hegemonic nation as well as of the instruments of domination which it used. A brief review of each period will help in the understanding of our contemporary situation.

During the age of mercantilism, from 1500 to 1800, the creation of overseas empires (Spanish and Portuguese, Dutch, English and French) played an important role in European economic development and created the basic conditions for development and under-development in most of the territories which were conquered and colonised.

> European expansion...may...be reduced to three types of exploitation of the lands and people with which Europeans came into contact. First and farthest ranging, Europeans continued to penetrate regions where readily available local products had value for European or other civilized markets...Second, in certain tropical and subtropical lands, specially in the West Indies, Europeans reorganized local economies to produce commodities in demand upon the world market. This involved drastic interference with pre-existing social relationships, for European enterprise was based on slavery or other forms of forced labour and sometimes involved massive population transfers. Third, in temperate regions, primarily in North and South America and in the western parts of the Eurasian steppes, European settlements developed from crude beginnings into genuine transplants of a European style of society....[1]

The basic rules of imperial mercantilist policies were the following:

> that trade between the homeland and its colonies should be reserved to the motherland, that this commerce should be carried in ships of the state or of the colonies concerned, that the colonies should buy whatever they could from the production of the homeland, that they should not produce for sale or for distant commerce what could be bought from the metropolitan state, and that they should produce and sell only what the mother country wanted.[2]

These rules were imposed by force by the metropolis on their colonial

---

[1] W. H. McNeill, *The Rise of the West* (Mentor, New York, 1965), pp. 713–14.
[2] S. B. Clough, *The Economic Development of Western Civilization* (McGraw-Hill, New York), 1959, p. 224.

territories, leaving no doubt as to the exploitative nature of the system, and creating in these territories the agrarian and social structures and institutions which have partly survived until today. The golden age of free trade followed, with a huge expansion of international trade, investment and migration, the specialisation of Britain in manufactured goods, and the rest of the world in the production of staples and raw materials. This was a further step in the process of creation of conditions for development in the metropolitan area and for underdevelopment in the periphery.

The international economic system which thus emerged was regulated largely through international markets of goods and the financial market of London, and it functioned so efficiently that when it came to an end after the First World War, Keynes could not help but feel a sense of nostalgia.

What an extraordinary episode in the progress of Man that age was which came to an end in August 1914....The inhabitant of London could order by telephone, sipping his morning tea in bed, the various products of the whole earth, in such quantity as he might see fit, and reasonably expect their early delivery upon his doorstep; he could at the same moment and by the same means adventure his wealth in the natural resources and new enterprises of any quarter of the world, and share, without exertion or even trouble, in their prospective fruits and advantages; or he could decide to couple the security of his fortunes with the good faith of the townspeople of any substantial municipality in any continent that information might recommend.[1]

The same author also gives us the intrinsic economic rationale of this system of international economic relations.

Of the surplus capital goods accumulated by Europe a substantial part was exported abroad, where its investment made possible the development of new resources of food, materials and transport, and at the same time enabled the Old World to stake out a claim in the natural wealth and virgin potentialities of the New.
This last factor came to be of importance. The Old World employed with an immense prudence the annual tribute it was thus entitled to draw....The greater part of the money interests accruing on these foreign investments was re-invested and allowed to accumulate....The prosperity of Europe was based on the fact that, owing to the vast surplus of foodstuff in America, she was able to purchase food at a cheap rate, measured in terms of the labour required to produce her own exports, and that, as a

[1] J. M. Keynes, *The Economic Consequences of the Peace* (London, 1920), p. 9.

result of her previous investments of capital, she was entitled to a substantial amount annually without any payment in return at all.[1]

The age of liberalism and free trade, encapsulated in these quotations and clearly depicted as an implicit structure of domination, turned in the latter part of the nineteenth century into an explicit structure of rival systems of domination. The other European powers, as well as the United States, had their Industrial Revolution too, and also claimed their share of the distribution of the world's natural resources and markets. The golden age of liberalism, *laissez-faire* and internationalism thus became the age of imperialism.

In Latin America, to the agrarian colonial heritage was added specialisation in the large-scale export of staples and raw materials and with it another set of socio-economic and political structures and institutions, including the corresponding new dominant elites, the result of a new situation of dependence and its interaction with the pre-existing structures.

The beginning of the end of *laissez-faire* came with the challenge of British predominance by other European powers and the United States, which sought to establish their own empires or areas of economic and political influence with corresponding mercantilist policies and practices. With the First World War, which was partly a consequence of this rivalry, the breakdown of the international monetary and financial system based on the Gold Standard, the Great Depression and the Second World War, the United States economy developed into the most powerful centre in the capitalist world. When some measure of normality was restored to the international situation, especially after the Korean War, the new economic colossus accelerated its expansion into the economies of both developed and underdeveloped countries, bringing about very substantial changes, notably in the latter. At the same time the United States economy was also changing; government intervention expanded considerably, accelerating growth, reducing cyclical fluctuations and contributing to a remarkable development of science and technology and to bigness and concentration in business.

The multidivisional or conglomerate firm developed, subject to horizontal and vertical integration throughout national and international markets. Specialisation in production was achieved in it by means of the simultaneous control of numerous plants engaged in various lines of production; moreover, a new specialisation evolved between the productive function proper and the planning and management of the conglomerate as a whole. Vast economic, tech-

---

[1] J. M. Keynes, *The Economic Consequences of the Peace* (London, 1920), pp. 19–21.

nological, and therefore political power has also enabled the multi-national corporation, through the control of the marketing and communication processes, to induce consumers and governments to buy the products which it is technologically able to produce in ever-growing quantities; within certain limits it is thus able to plan the development of consumption.

As of 1929, the 100 largest American firms alone controlled 44 per cent of the net capital assets of manufacturing industry. By 1947 and 1962 this percentage had risen to 46 and 57 respectively. The degree of concentration of economic power is indicated by the fact that in 1962 the assets of the 20 largest firms were equal to those of the 419,000 small firms (out of a total of 420,000 firms). One fourth of the net assets belonged to the 20 largest firms; half to the 1,000 largest firms, and the remaining fourth to the other 419,000 firms.[1]

The principal factor in the growing concentration of economic power, even more important than the increase in the size of plants, is the increase in the number of plants belonging to each firm. But this multiplication of the number of plants of each large firm takes place not simply in a single production line, but corresponds to a diversification into a great variety of production lines. In this way, the phenomenon of concentration also assumes the form of a process of conglomeration. This can be observed in Table 1.1.

TABLE 1.1

NUMBER OF PRODUCT LINES OF THE 1,000 LARGEST
U.S. FIRMS

	1950	1962
1 product line	78	49
2 to 15 product lines	354	233
16 to 50 product lines	128	236
More than 50 product lines	8	15

Source: see footnote 1, p. 11.

These institutional developments in the United States are reflected abroad as the new multinational corporations spread throughout the international economy, following a fairly definite pattern: first they export their finished products; then they establish sales organisations abroad; they then proceed to allow foreign producers to use their licences and patents to manufacture the product locally; finally, they buy off the local producer and establish a partially or wholly-owned subsidiary. This is the institutional process behind the great

[1] *Economic Concentration, Hearings before the Subcommittee on Antitrust and Monopoly of the Community on the Judiciary*, U.S. Senate, Eighty-Eighth Congress, second session, U.S. Government Printing Office, Washington, D.C., 1964.

expansion of United States direct private investment abroad during the post-war period shown in Table 1.2.

TABLE 1.2

TOTAL BOOK VALUE OF U.S. DIRECT
FOREIGN INVESTMENT BY AREA AND
ACTIVITY
(Billions of dollars)

Area	1929	1946	1957	1967
Canada	2·0	2·5	8·6	18·1
Latin America	3·5	3·1	8·1	10·2
Europe	1·4	1·0	4·1	17·9
Other	0·6	0·6	4·4	13·1
Total	7·5	7·2	25·2	59·3
Activity				
Manufacturing	1·8	2·4	8·0	24·1
Petroleum	1·1	1·4	9·0	17·4
Mining				
Refining	1·2	0·8	2·4	4·8
Other	3·4	2·6	5·8	13·0
Total	7·5	7·2	25·2	59·3

Source: *Survey of Current Business*, U.S. Department of Commerce.

According to these figures, the greater part of the expansion occurred in Canada, Europe and other countries, but in Latin America the increase has also been very substantial: from 3·1 billion dollars in 1946 to 10·2 billion in 1967. The largest world-wide increase corresponds to manufacturing and petroleum, and this is also the case in Latin America, as can be seen in Table 1.3.

The institutional situation behind these figures is as follows: 80 per cent of U.S. private direct investment abroad was the property of 187 transnational conglomerates, which had over 10,000 subsidiaries in the rest of the capitalist world (including subsidiaries with a minority control of up to 25 per cent).[1] This means an average of 53 subsidiaries per corporation around the world.

When taken globally, it has been estimated that the value of the output of all foreign affiliates of U.S. corporations was a staggering one hundred and thirty billion dollars during 1968. This was four times the U.S. exports of thirty-three billion during that year, showing that the preponderant linkage of the United States to other markets is foreign production rather than foreign trade.

[1] Raymond Vernon, *Report of the Research Project on the Multinational Corporation* (Harvard Business School, 1970).

TABLE 1.3

BOOK VALUE OF U.S. DIRECT INVESTMENT
IN LATIN AMERICA FOR SELECTED SECTORS
AND YEARS
(Millions of dollars)

	1946		1968	
	Value	*Percentage*	*Value*	*Percentage*
Agriculture	407	13·4	*a*	—
Mining, etc.	506	16·6	1,402	12·7
Petroleum	697	22·9	2,976	27·0
Manufacturing	399	13·1	3,699	33·6
Public utilities	920	30·2	627	5·7
Commerce	72	2·4	1,249	11·4
Other	45	1·5	1,057	9·6
Total	3045	100·0	11,010	100·0

Source: U.S. Department of Commerce, Office of Business
Economics, *Survey of Current Business.*

a Included in Other.

Foreign affiliates accounted for 15 per cent of the total production
of 900 billion dollars in the non-communist world ex-United
States. Thus the United States industry abroad has become the
third largest economy in the world, outranked only by those of
the domestic economies of the United States and the Soviet Union.
Moreover, foreign production of American firms has grown by
about 10 per cent a year, i.e. twice as fast as the domestic economies. Multinational corporations are rapidly increasing their
shares of the world's business.[1]

That part of the American economy which is made up of 'a few
hundred technically dynamic, massively capitalized and highly
organized big corporations' is termed the 'Industrial System' by
Professor J. K. Galbraith, who clearly perceives that a system dominated by a few very large corporations is qualitatively different from
the classical conception of the capitalist system consisting of a large
number of small and independent enterprises.

Galbraith's argument is as follows: the tremendous development of
modern technology requires an increase in the capital committed to
production and in the time for which it is committed. The commitment of the time and money tends to be more and more specialised in
a great variety of different tasks. Therefore, requirements of specialised manpower increase greatly, and as specialisation advances,
efficient organisation becomes essential. In order to maximise long

[1] Neil H. Jacoby, *The Multinational Corporation*, School of Business Administration at the University of California, Los Angeles.

run profits and reduce uncertainty and risk, the corporation engages
in planning.

In addition to deciding what the consumer will want and is willing
to pay, the firm must take every possible step to see that what it
decides to produce is wanted by the consumer at a remunerative
price. It must see that the labour, materials and equipment that it
needs will be available at a cost consistent with the price it will
receive. It must exercise control over what is supplied. *It must
replace the market with planning*....The market is superceded by
what is commonly known as vertical integration. The planning unit
takes over the source of supply or the outlet. Where a firm is
specially dependent on an important material or product (such as
an oil company on crude petroleum, a steel company on ore, an
aluminum company on bauxite) there is always the danger that the
requisite supplies will be available only at inconvenient prices....
From the point of view of the firm, the elimination of a market
converts an external negotiation, and hence a partially or wholly
uncontrollable decision, to a matter for purely internal decision...
The size of General Motors depends not on monopoly, or the
economies of scale but on planning. As for this planning – control
of supply and demand, provision of capital, minimization of risk –
there is no clear upper limit to the desirable size. It could be that
'the bigger the better'. The corporate form accommodates to this
need. Quite clearly it allows the firm to be very, very large.[1]

The central nucleus of the international firm is its headquarters,
which is located in the metropolis, and which is the central planning
bureau of the corporation. It is something quite distinct from its
productive activities, which can be classified under three main types –
extractive, industrial and marketing – and which are located also in
the metropolitan country, but with subsidiaries, branches or affiliates
in the peripheral countries. The headquarters consists essentially of a
group of people who plan and decide what, how, where and how
much will be produced and sold, over what period of time. In order
to perform the decision making process rationally, it has developed a
highly efficient system of communications through which the necessary information, personnel, scientific and technological knowledge,
finance and decisions flow.

For the reasons indicated above, and since the expenditures in
research, design and technology have become a major item in the
corporation's fixed cost structure, it has every interest in spreading
these costs over an ever-increasing total output, including the output

    [1] Galbraith, John Kenneth, *The New Industrial State* (Houghton Mifflin,
Boston, 1967). (Emphasis added.)

sold in the metropolitan and overseas markets. Therefore, the capturing of more and more consumers at home and abroad is central to the long-term profitability of the firm. According to Galbraith, in underdeveloped countries the introduction of new consumer goods – cosmetics, motor scooters, transistor radios, canned foods, bicycles, phonograph records, movies, American cigarettes – is recognised as of the highest importance in the strategy of economic development. And he reminds us that, in the golden days, commodities such as tobacco, alcohol, and opium which involved a physical and progressive addiction were considered useful trade goods. It is clear then that this strategy of economic development is really a long-term strategy of maximisation of the international corporation's profits, involving the spreading of its subsidiaries and of a homogenised consumer culture throughout the world.

This analysis leads us to the following tentative conclusion: the capitalist system is in the process of being reorganised into a new international industrial system whose main institutional agents are the multinational corporations, increasingly backed by the governments of the developed countries. This is a new structure of domination, sharing a large number of characteristics of the mercantilist system. It tends to concentrate the planning and deployment of natural, human and capital resources, and the development of science and technology, in the 'brain' of the new industrial system, i.e. the technocrats of international corporations, international organisations and governments of developed countries. This tends to reinforce the relative process of economic, social, political and cultural underdevelopment of the Third World, deepening foreign dependence and exacerbating internal disintegration.

Following the transformations that occurred in the new dominant centres of the capitalist world in the last decades, the system of international economic relations has experienced important institutional and structural changes. As a consequence of these trends, the internal economic, social and political structure of the dependent underdeveloped countries have also experienced fundamental transformations.

The breakdown of the nineteenth-century model of international economic relations opened for Latin American economics the period of import substituting industrialisation. In its earlier stages, our countries were faced with the need of starting almost from scratch to obtain a specialised labour force, highly qualified technicians, entrepreneurs, machinery, raw materials and inputs, financial resources, organisations for marketing, distribution, publicity, sales and credit, as well as the know-how and the technical ability to carry out all these tasks. In the process of industrial growth and diversification, our entrepreneurs have been relying increasingly on the incorporation of these elements from foreign sources, particularly when they moved from elementary manufactures to the more complex sectors of durable consumer goods and basic industries.

But in this increasing reliance on external sources there has been a fundamental shift in the nature of the process of incorporation of foreign inputs. In the earlier decades, entrepreneurs and skilled personnel were obtained by immigration or from other local activities; capital and financing came mainly from public sources, both national and foreign; know-how and technology were obtained through the purchase of licences and technical assistance agreements. All these were procedures which contributed to the formation and strengthening of private entrepreneurship and industry. This meant, in the larger countries of the region, the formation by the middle of the 1950s of a significant manufacturing sector, complete with its entrepreneurial class, professional and technical groups and industrial proletariat, as well as the necessary ancillary government and private financial, marketing and educational agencies. But in recent years there has been a reversal of these trends. Instead of each missing or scarce element being acquired abroad, foreign subsidiaries have penetrated the industrial sector, either buying into existing firms or setting up new ones, and bringing along a *complete* package of entrepreneurship, management, skills, design, technology, financing and marketing organisations. This has been the local counterpart of the institutional transformation in the mature capitalist countries and in the international economy.

As mentioned earlier, the large expansion of the American multinational manufacturing corporation in Latin America gained strength around the middle of the 1950s, and only in the late 1960s did it reach the stage of the wholesale buying up of local firms and integrating subsidiaries and affiliates closely with headquarters and with each other. Table 1.4 gives an indication of these trends.

The large-scale penetration of American subsidiaries into the Latin American economy accounted in 1966 for 35 per cent of total Latin American exports and for 41 per cent of the exports of manufactures. Of the latter, approximately half were exports manufactured in subsidiaries, which provides a clue as to who benefits most from Latin American integration. Moreover, the subsidiary imports represented about 11 per cent of total imports, whereas subsidiary sales represented about 14 per cent of Gross Domestic Product, and nearly one-third of the industrial production of the region.[1] Furthermore, since the rate of expansion of the subsidiaries is substantially higher than

[1] Stacy May, *The Contributions of U.S. Private Investment to Latin America's Growth*, a report for the Council for Latin America, Inc.

that of the host economies, these proportions have been increasing and will continue to do so in the future.

At a more general level, import substituting industrialisation, in the same way as externally propelled primary export growth in the late nineteenth century, constitutes another method of insertion of the underdeveloped economies into the framework of a reorganised world economic system. The new system is formed, as before, on the basis of dominant (developed) economies and dependent (underdeveloped) economies, increasingly linked to each other through the growing transnational interlocking and overlapping of production

TABLE 1.4

OPERATIONS OF 187 TRANSNATIONAL CORPORATIONS
IN LATIN AMERICA
(Number of enterprises)

	1945	1950	1955	1960	1965	1967
U.S. firms with subsidiaries in Latin America	93	113	143	179	185	182
U.S. firms with manufacturing subsidiaries in Latin America	74	90	114	152	175	171
U.S. firms with non-manufacturing subsidiaries in Latin America	19	13	23	27	10	11
Subsidiaries of U.S. firms	452	606	856	1,341	1,813	1,924
Manufacturing subsidiaries	182	259	357	612	888	950
Commercial subsidiaries	73	86	119	198	238	233
Extractive subsidiaries	35	38	43	57	54	56
Other subsidiaries	70	98	166	246	308	338
Subsidiaries with unknown activities	92	125	171	228	325	347

Source: J. W. Vaupel, and Joan P. Curham, *The Making of Multinational Enterprise* (Boston, 1969). Harvard University, Graduate School of Business Administration.

structures and consumer patterns. The new model is operationally structured around the transnational corporation and implies a new form of international division of labour and technoscientific progress. In the plants, laboratories, design and publicity departments, as well as in the planning, decision-making personnel and finance organisations that constitute its headquarters – always located in an industrialised country – the transnational corporation develops:

   (i) new products;
  (ii) new ways of producing those products;
 (iii) the new machinery, equipment and current inputs necessary to produce them; and
 (iv) the publicity needed to create and activate their markets.

In the underdeveloped country, the corporation establishes the subsidiaries necessary for the marketing, assembling or routine production of those goods. As a consequence of this process of internationalisation of production, a new structure of international economic relations is emerging, where trade among national firm Z of country *A* and national firm *Y* of country *B* is replaced by the internal transfers within firm Z among countries *A* and *B*, while firm Y vanishes from the picture. Therefore, the market is gradually superseded by the international firm's plan, market prices and financial flows by accounting prices and flows, local–national by centralised–foreign decision making. The import substituting process of industrialisation has therefore become the corporation's strategy of penetration of foreign protected markets, supported by external public and private credit, international technical assistance and aid, and ideological advice with respect to development policies and strategies.

This last aspect of the new international system merits a profound and careful analysis, since it covers some very important ground: commercial policy, international monetary arrangements, banking and finance, patent legislation, transportation and communication agreements, and the whole paraphernalia of bilateral, multilateral, regional and international policies, agreements, conferences and institutions which have developed mushroom-like since the Second World War, largely to replace the crumbling formal or informal colonial and imperial systems then still in existence. Although this analysis cannot be undertaken here, it should at least be mentioned that in the same way in which government intervention paved the way for business expansion in the national market, the government agencies of developed countries are also increasingly intervening directly and indirectly in 'world markets' – which is really a euphemism for other countries' markets – to support and protect the expansion of their firms. The great extended economic role of the State in the national and international economy is creating what could be called a *superstructure* of international economic relations. This takes essentially two forms: direct, bilateral, government-to-government relationships on the one hand, and on the other, international multilateral economic organisations. The bilateral relationship between a dominant and a dependent country corresponds closely and increasingly to mercantilist practices. The dominant country tries to establish, enlarge and preserve all kinds of exclusive privileges for its business interests, granting in exchange support of various kinds to the local social groups with which it is associated. The instruments of influence in bilateral relationships are well known: tied loans, aid, commercial policy, preferential arrangements with regard to transportation, communications, foreign investment, tariffs and so on. The multilateral relationship consists of a maze of international economic organisations of various kinds, which some would like to set up as a hierarchical system, headed by organisations like the World Bank and the I.M.F., in which developed countries and the multinational business community have a decisive influence. Regional organisations like the O.A.S., which correspond to one hegemonic system, and organisations among the developed countries, like the E.E.C., are kept – for different reasons – independent from outside influence. World organisations where each country counts for one vote are in a rather weak position, much as the organisations among underdeveloped countries of one region (LAFTA or the Organisation of African Unity), while it has not been possible to create a formal organisation of underdeveloped countries (all that exists is the informal '77' within UNCTAD).

The efforts at reorganising the superstructure of international relations so that it corresponds to the transformation in the structure of the world economy have been clearly discernible in the recent plethora of reports on international co-operation. This is not surprising since it should be the function of the international superstructure to provide the ideological rationale and justification of the international system, as well as to lay down the rules of the game and provide the institutional means for policing its implementation. The following quotation constitutes a good statement of these trends by an apologist of the system:

> The international corporation is acting and planning in terms that are far in advance of the political concepts of the nation state. As the Renaissance of the fifteenth century brought an end to feudalism, aristocracy and the dominant role of the church, the twentieth century Renaissance is bringing an end to middle-class society and the dominance of the nation state. The heart of the new power structure is the international organization and the technocrats who guide it. Power is shifting away from the nation-state to international institutions, public and private.... Within a generation about 400 to 500 international corporations will own about two-thirds of the fixed assets of the world.[1]

Finally, let us look at some of the economic effects of this process. In the words of Professor Harry Johnson:

> The corporation... has no commercial interest in diffusing its knowledge to potential native competitors, nor has it any interest in investing more than it has to in acquiring knowledge of local conditions and investigating ways of adapting its own productive

---

[1] A. Barber, 'Emerging New Power. The World Corporation', *War/Peace Report* (October, 1968), p. 7.

knowledge to local factor/price ratios and market conditions. Its purpose is not to transform the economy by exploiting its potentialities (especially its human potentialities) for development... the main contribution of direct foreign investment will be highly specific and very uneven in its incidence.[1]

In other words, the multinational corporation tends to centralise research and entrepreneurial decision-making in the home country. Unless countermeasures are taken, the 'backwash' effects may outweigh the 'spread' effects, and the technology gap may be perpetuated rather than alleviated. Over-reliance on multinational corporations may cause the country to remain underdeveloped.

Hirschman, on his part, has pointed out that direct private foreign investment, by taking over local firms and displacing and undermining local entrepreneurship may be harming the quality of local factors of production. Moreover, given the 'complete package' character of subsidiaries, the foreign contribution may not be complementary but may instead be competitive with local factors of production, retarding or preventing their growth, and therefore leading to a decrease in the quantity of local inputs. His conclusion: 'private foreign investment is a mixed blessing, and the mixture is likely to become more noxious at the intermediate stage of development which characterises much of present day Latin America'.[2] And at the present stage of international business expansion, I would add, when the process of takeovers of local firms of all kinds is at a peak.

Corporate strategy may lead to other negative effects. For example, the process of vertical integration means that the flows of goods, finance, technology, etc. take place increasingly within the firm, even where the country's interests may dictate otherwise. Out of this develops also a tendency not to integrate with local suppliers or to share or adapt their technology as Johnson points out. Furthermore, there is usually a market-sharing agreement between headquarters and the various subsidiaries and affiliates, which means generally that branch plants are not allowed to export. If countries are members of some integration agreement like LAFTA or the Central American Common Market, the presence of subsidiaries in the member countries gives them a great advantage over national firms in using the integration process, further undermining the position of local enterprises.

[1] Harry G. Johnson, 'The Multi-National Corporation as an Agency of Economic Development: Some Exploratory Observations', in Barbara Ward, Lenore d'Anjou and J. D. Runnals, *The Widening Gap: Development in the 1970's* (Columbia University Press, 1971), pp. 244 and 246.

[2] Albert O. Hirschman, 'How to Divest in Latin America, and Why', *Essays in International Finance*, No. 76 (Princeton University, November 1969).

Subsidiaries within one country tend to integrate horizontally, conglomerate among themselves. As these are frequently the largest and fastest growing firms, this means a tendency to greater concentration. Gaining control of finance, credit, markets and publicity means a considerable capacity to influence consumption patterns, to plan consumption, not only of the higher income groups who can afford their goods, but also of lower-income groups by way of the 'trickle down' or 'demonstration' effect, thereby completely distorting their consumption patterns. The control of the commanding heights of the economy also means of course the capacity to influence the allocation of resources of the public sector, frequently in the direction of providing the infrastructure needed for subsidising the expansion of the foreign subsidiary. It also implies the capacity to acquire the command of a significant mass of financial resources, private and public, with which to finance local expansion and foreign remittances, almost without the need of net additional foreign capital inflows. In fact, between 1963 and 1968 only 9 per cent of total funds used by the United States Latin American subsidiaries came from abroad. This, together with their negligible contribution to exports, inevitably leads to a serious balance of payments problem.

Foreign subsidiaries are usually in an oligopolistic position in their respective branches of economic activity, and are therefore able to extract oligopoly profits from the exploitation of consumer and factor markets. As they keep most of their international transactions within the boundaries of the firm, there is a strong tendency to remit excess profits by manipulating the prices, kinds and quantities of their 'external' transactions.

Finally, activities developed by subsidiaries in underdeveloped countries follow a life cycle where at the beginning the foreign firm may make a substantial contribution in capital, skilled personnel, technology, management, etc. But over time the outflow of financial remittances becomes larger than the inflow and the country 'learns' the management and technological skills necessary to run the firm. Its net contribution to the development capabilities of the country becomes then negligible or even negative. Among the various alternative ways of obtaining external co-operation, direct foreign investment in the form of wholly-owned subsidiaries is the one that has the smallest learning effect because it is its policy to try to keep permanently its monopoly of skills and technology. When the technology of the activities in which the firm operates becomes standardised and well known, the subsidiary becomes an 'obsolete' form of foreign ownership from the point of view of its contribution to the resources, abilities and technology of the country.

While these and other negative economic effects illustrate clearly the 'mixed blessing' that foreign private investment represents, it is the socio-political consequences that are of far greater importance and of a much more explosive character.

The massive penetration of foreign subsidiaries into the industrial and related financial, marketing and distribution activities, has fundamentally changed the ownership pattern in most Latin American countries, foreign firms having acquired a dominant position among medium and large-sized firms in many if not all the main sectors and branches of economic activity which are not in public hands. This implies a basic change in social structure and the political power system.

The process of formation of the local entrepreneurial class has been interrupted. The best talents that emerged from local industries are being absorbed into the new managerial class.... National independent entrepreneurship is... restricted to secondary activities or to pioneering ventures which in the long run simply open up new fields for the future expansion of the multinational corporation.... The elimination of the national entrepreneurial class necessarily excludes the possibility of selfsustained national development, according to the pattern of classical capitalist development.[1]

In other words, a significant part of the national bourgeoisie is being transformed into private transnational technocracies and bureaucracies, losing its legitimacy as members of a national ruling class.

But Furtado's observation may be generalised to all groups and social classes to gain a clearer perception of the crisis which is affecting the nation-state in Latin America. At the level of the productive structure, this crisis makes itself felt through the massive and extraordinarily dynamic penetration of the transnational firm with its subsidiaries and affiliates; at the technological level, by the large-scale introduction of highly capital-intensive techniques; at the cultural and ideological level by the overwhelming and systematic promotion and publicity of conspicuous consumption and at the concrete level of development policies and strategies, by the pressure of national and international interests in favour of high-income industrialisation. This so-called modernisation process implies the gradual replacement of the traditional productive structure, which is labour intensive, by another of much higher capital intensiveness. Under these conditions, the process incorporates into the new institutions and structures the individuals and groups that are suited to fit into the kind of rationality which prevail there. But on the other hand,

---

[1] Celso Furtado, 'La concentración del poder económico en los EE.UU. y sus proyecciones en América Latina', *Estudios Internacionales*, Año I, No. 3/4 (Santiago, 1968).

it expels the individuals and groups that have no place in the new productive structure or lack the ability to adapt to it. Therefore this process not only prevents the formation of a national entrepreneurial class, but also limits and erodes the national middle classes generally (including national intellectuals, scientists, technocrats, professionals) and even creates privileged and underprivileged sectors within the working class, adding another serious difficulty to the creation of a strong worker movement.

The crisis of the nation state which has been outlined also affects the main institutions of society: the State, the Armed Forces, political parties, the universities, the Church. These are the social formations which represent in various complex ways the social classes and groups that are being affected by the disintegration process. In certain Latin American countries, the leading groups and classes seem to have accepted dependence and marginalisation as inevitable and necessary ingredients of the process of development and modernisation. An increasing share of the ownership and control of national resources and activities is being turned over to foreign firms and the government apparatus is being put to some extent at their disposal. This means not only the provision of infrastructural investments necessary for their expansion, but also the political and police repression needed to suppress the growing reaction to advancing denationalisation, widening inequality and increasing marginalisation. This development model could perhaps be best described as Dependent State Capitalism.

In other countries, due to the different nature of the pre-existing local conditions and other elements which cannot be analysed here, certain social classes and groups have been able to react to the crisis by attempting to oppose the above-mentioned trends. For this purpose they are trying to regain control over the economy, but this implies, in the first place, taking away the control of the State from the social groups which are more closely associated with the development strategy of Dependent State Capitalism.

Having taken over the control of the State, these groups face the task of correcting the main structural malformations inherited from the historical process of interaction with the international system. This task comprises three essential elements. In the first place, they must transform the agrarian structure, which is at the root of inequality, marginalisation and stagnation; secondly, they must utilise the primary export sector, which represents an underdeveloped country's most important source of capital accumulation, to generate the expansion of basic and wage goods activities; and, finally, they must reorganise the industrial sector, essentially in order to change its orientation away from the satisfaction of the conspicuous consumption of the minority towards the satisfaction of the basic needs of the majority.

In this process of structural reforms and reorientation, many well-established local and foreign interests will be affected. If there are foreign investments in the agricultural sector, they will be affected by agrarian reform. If there are foreign investments in the primary export sector, whether agricultural or mining, they will be affected by the need to control these fundamental sources of foreign financing. If there are foreign investments in the industrial and related sectors, the reorientation of industrial policy will affect foreign subsidiaries. As the present orientation of industrial development has rested to a large extent on the power structures built up by local and foreign interests around the main industrial and commercial monopolies and the banking system, their control is also bound to be taken over by the State, and this will imply nationalisations and renegotiations with foreign interests.

It is interesting to note that international public opinion has more or less become accustomed to the idea that structural reforms are necessary in agriculture, so much so that underdeveloped countries are urged to go ahead with agrarian reform. If foreign interests like those of the United Fruit Co., Grace and Co., etc., are involved, there may be protests but they are considerably attenuated by the recognised need for an agrarian reform. Even in the field of primary export activities it is being accepted that our nations have the right to control one of their most essential resources and activities, and that the policies of foreign subsidiaries do not necessarily coincide with the best long-term interests of the country. It seems, as Hirschman points out, that having arrived at a certain level of industrial and general development, our countries are also beginning to claim the right to reassert their own interests in the field of manufactures, commerce and banking, where foreign penetration is greatest at this time. The conflict of interests with foreign private investment in these sectors will be more or less intense according to whether the country chooses a socialist development path, some rather progressive variety of State Capitalism, or some less well defined and more moderate variety, as in most countries. Whatever the case, the era of 'creating favourable business conditions for foreign direct investment', as a general policy, seems to be coming to an end in most countries. But even then, as is increasingly the case with socialist countries, the possibility of co-operation with foreign firms is by no means excluded, even though there will certainly be little place for wholly-owned foreign subsidiaries or private foreign investment of the traditional kind. A new era is opening of hard bargaining and negotiations, of pragmatic and detailed consideration of specific cases, of weighing the conditions offered by Japan, Europe, the socialist countries and the United States, of building up alliances with countries with similar interests (the Andean Pact, C.E.C.L.A., O.P.E.C.), etc. An era, in short, of the assertion of the national interest of our countries in their international economic relations. The aim is development without dependence and without marginalisation, and to achieve this goal the asymmetrical nature of the present system of international economic relations seems to require a thorough reform. It might be useful if the elements which constitute that system – commercial policy, integration movements, foreign capital, technology transfers, aid, etc. – were examined in the light of the global forces and processes described in this paper.

Discussion of the Paper by Professor Sunkel

Professor Vernon opened the debate by drawing attention to the new perspective the paper offered the conference. With it we were well on our way toward clearing our minds of the problems which had appeared central ten or fifteen years ago, and toward a reshaping of our approach to tackle the critical problems of today. His own comment would in no way take the form of a direct challenge to Professor Sunkel's thesis; rather, he would like to present his own interpretation of the analytic perspective which was necessary to deal with present problems.

As he saw it, the central feature today of contacts between developed and underdeveloped countries was oligopoly. Any given industry was dominated by a number of large uneasy giants, whose primary interest was stability, since they realised the consequences of any untoward act on the part of any one of them. In such a setting, the opportunity for the less advanced country to determine the path which benefited it was large – much larger than under competition or monopoly.

The characteristics of these international oligopolies should be a principal focus of research. He would like to quote a few of the features which had emerged from his own studies. For example, it was very clear that corporations' expansion into Latin America was typically a reluctant response to anxiety, to the need to prevent a rival dominating a market. Further, it appeared that cartel behaviour was peculiarly apolitical: the Soviet Union's participation in the aluminium cartel, or Libya's in oil, turned out to be classic examples of cartel behaviour. Then, no oligopoly should be assumed to be stable in the long run. The typical pattern was rather one where expansion in demand unaccompanied by continuing economies of scale increased the number of members to the point where the oligopoly became unstable. It would be a curious irony if the Chilean takeover of the copper mines created such a situation. And lastly, it appeared we needed to update our picture of international bargaining: the less developed countries were sometimes in fact senior partners in negotiations. O.P.E.C. in particular had acquired such expertise that the oil companies had had to resign themselves to tough bargaining: roughly 80 per cent of gross profit went to the producer countries.

More such detailed analyses of corporate behaviour were needed to provide the groundwork for the new approach he saw as necessary. This had two parts: a descriptive model and a normative model. The elements of the descriptive model he found most satisfying could be well illustrated from a study such as Mr. Wionczek's of the sulphur industry in Mexico: a process of bargaining which began in the 1890s with the invitation to foreign companies to enter, and evolved, with the country developing an ever stronger and more independent position, until nationalisation in the 1960s. This was a dynamic process, to be found in different forms and occurring at different rates in many industries, where the stream of benefits to the recipient country was partly determined by its own energy, initiative, and available skills. The company might strengthen its negotiating position every so often by offering new techniques; when these were exhausted, as in the case of foreign motor vehicle industries in Mexico, the industry might then begin to propose, say, exporting as a response to yet more pressure.

The associated normative model consisted in the problem of what to do to maximise the stream of benefits. He would stress that this was inevitably a situation of dependency: as long as one continued extracting benefits, one was 'dependent' on the source of benefits. One might decide one did not like it and opt for some other route; then the normative model would not apply. However, he would stress that no developing country could avoid the fact that development required some degree of openness. If that was so, then some degree of interdependence had to exist. The smaller the country, the more lopsided the relationship. The choice was only in the form of dependence. It appeared that in very different ways countries such as the Netherlands, Scandinavia and Cuba had found a tolerable form of dependence in terms of self respect and world position.

The major part of the debate which followed was divided between amplification and exploration of the aspect Professor Vernon had focussed on, that of bargaining strategy, and illustration of what emerged as the most widespread general criticism of Professor Sunkel's paper: the extent to which more complex and more detailed analysis was needed and might sometimes lead to rather different conclusions, in particular as to the possibilities of change within the system. Different commentators stressed this both in relation to the behavioural analysis implicit in the paper and to the historical analysis of the role of domestic policy.

First, however, a number of speakers seconded Professor Vernon in his applause for the perspective which the paper offered and a few attempted some further development of the analysis. *Dr. Katz* found the paper particularly useful because it showed that what had normally been called import substituting industrialisation 'constituted yet another way of insertion of the underdeveloped economies into the framework of a re-organised world economic system', and secondly, because it made very clear throughout that economic dependence did not necessarily mean economic stagnation for the dependent nation – a confusion common on the part of much of the Latin American left. *Dr. Macario* was happy to see how the paper integrated a number of elements which were usually treated separately: up to now there had been no real attempt to integrate the multinational corporation into the structure of world trade relations. Trade was still seen very much as a result of decisions by and negotiations between country units; now we were seeing the introduction of a new element: the negotiations of countries with corporations.

Professor Felix proposed a development of the concept of dependency: if it was not to become as 'soft' and rhetorical a concept as 'modernisation' had become, it was essential it should be linked to specific decision taking processes and market behaviour patterns. For example, one area where he saw much scope for careful analysis was the question of market demand formation. Professor Sunkel referred to the multinational corporations'

)duction of new goods. The elements of the analysis could with benefit
pelled out in more detail: what determined receptivity to new goods?
It was partly a question of income distribution, but he suspected it also
had much to do with oligopolistic product differentiation, a game at which
Latin American owned corporations themselves had become increasingly
skilled. Import substitution was continuing, but now the new goods were
locally produced *before* any imports had occurred. There was, he suggested,
an optimum rate of inflow of new goods; the private decisions which
determined the actual rate might well be biased and the biases needed to
be understood and analysed.

Dr. Barkin questioned whether the framework of private enterprise
could permit the achievement of the three goals Professor Sunkel was
proposing: first, changing the structure of production, second, increasing
the surplus available for accumulation, and third, reassigning the surplus
to socially desirable areas. Present patterns of development were based on
duplicating the existing consumption structures of the developed world.
Resources flowed to areas of highest profitability, which tended to be
luxury consumption goods since most governments found it wise and/or
necessary to keep prices down for mass consumption items. Given low
purchasing power and high concentration of income, new private investments were likely to be concentrated in areas satisfying the demands of
upper income groups. It seemed that existing market mechanisms were
unable to deal with the distribution problem of mass consumption goods,
and in fact generally tended to increase existing inequalities. Efforts to
counterbalance these tendencies generally served only to brake the concentration process rather than effectively and permanently redistribute
income. He therefore suggested that if the task was the confrontation of
the problem of increasing marginalisation, then it was essential to abandon
the market. A whole series of industries must be stimulated 'artificially'
(by the State) to supply goods for the masses with insufficient purchasing
power. The surplus generated in high profit industries had to be redirected
to socially desirable zones, by means of a large degree of intervention in
investment decisions by the State.

As he saw it the question was not one of eliminating dependence but
rather of changing its nature. Trade was obviously necessary for most
States, but the nature of the external relation must permit the integration
of marginal groups into productive economic activity; it seemed improbable this could be done within the context of a market economy.

A contrasting view came from *Professor Ranis*, who argued that the
historical association between liberal economic policy and imperialism
should not be confused with causation. While the market was undoubtedly
a handmaiden of imperialism in the nineteenth century, it should not be
assumed that it could not be the handmaiden of national development in
the twentieth century – even in socialist countries.

Other speakers, while welcoming the new insight the paper offered, were
concerned about its level of generality. *Professor Hirschman* said that the
problem with such an insight was that it might itself become a new
paradigm. Seeing phenomena as 'seamless' ideal types with no openings

for change left one in a sense powerless to do anything except attempt to abolish them: in fact in every reality there were contradictory tendencies and so the possibility of change. As activists we must surely try to discern the changes already coming. He would add two to those already mentioned by Professor Vernon: first, the instinctive defence which was taking shape by the emergence of the 'countervailing power' of State-owned corporations, and second, the acquisition of a growing ability to change the rules of the game; this was exemplified in the way multinational corporations in Brazil were being successfully pushed into exporting,[1] and in developments such as the Andean Pact. It was just possible that the multinational corporation might prove to be not the irresistible force which Professor Sunkel's paper suggested, for all his qualifications, but a temporary aberration.

Professor Lambert also distrusted any such overgeneralised view of the world economy. It seemed to him that the paper, which represented a radicalisation of Professor Sunkel's own structuralist thesis, shared the pitfalls of the Centre–Periphery approach. In Europe, especially in France, interpreters of the development of underdevelopment such as Gunder Frank, Samir Amin and Christian Palloix had rejected earlier interpretations of underdevelopment on the grounds that they did not recognise the bipolar character of the world economy. But the principal objection to all such analyses was their oversimplistic view of the world economy: there were in fact many differing degrees of development, different structures, different historical experiences. The overgeneralised world view was particularly dangerous for an economist from the 'Centre' who knew little directly of such differences.

Substance was given to the argument for more detailed and rigorous behavioural analysis by *Dr. Katz*, who set out a number of areas where he saw a need for greater rigour.

First, it did not seem to him that the spread of the multinational corporation followed such a definite pattern as Professor Sunkel indicated. Neither did he find strong evidence to support the idea that there were highly stable and comparable patterns within a given industry. Thus, whereas Ford or General Motors had strongly rejected joint ventures, Fiat and Chrysler had shown the opposite tendency. A similarly unsystematic pattern could be shown to prevail in the electronics industry as well as in various others.

Secondly, Professor Sunkel sketched out a very simple theory in order to account for the expansion of multinational corporations to overseas markets. We were told that 'expenditure on research, design and technology having become a major item in the corporation's fixed cost structure, induces interest in spreading to overseas markets'. Except for pharmaceuticals and electronics, industries in which current R and D expenditure in the U.S.A. came up to around 10 per cent of sales, in most other industries (or countries) R and D expenditure represented a much

---

[1] Fernando Fajnzylber, *Sistema Industrial y Exportación de Manufacturas, Analisis de la Experiencia Brasileña*, ECLA, Nov. 1970 (study done for the Brazilian Ministry of Planning and General Co-ordination).

lower percentage of sales, say 2 or 3 per cent. It was only in the pharmaceutical trade that one frequently heard the argument in the extreme form in which it appeared in the paper, but even here there were strong grounds for disbelieving that the increase of their R and D played a part – let alone the major one – in a corporation's decision to expand overseas. A more elaborate behavioural theory seemed to be needed to explain imperialism in its modern version.

Third, Professor Sunkel argued that the 'so-called modernisation process implies the gradual replacement of the traditional productive structure, . . . limits and erodes the national middle classes generally, . . . and even creates privileged sectors among the working class, adding another serious difficulty to the creation of a strong worker movement'. The point was obviously correct. The problem was, however, that the most serious challenge to the *status quo* seemed to come precisely from privileged trade unions. For example, two unions in Cordoba led a revolt in 1968 which ousted the Minister of Economics. It seemed that a more complex theory of trade union behaviour was needed to account for the impact of monopoly capitalism on the class structure and the social order in general.

Fourth, he found the weakest chain in Professor Sunkel's argument at the point where he said: 'In other countries, and due to different pre-existing local conditions, and other elements that cannot be analysed here, certain social classes and groups have been able to react to the crisis with attempts to oppose the above-mentioned trends.' It was here that one suspected that the model underlying Professor Sunkel's thinking needed yet further elaboration. Presumably what was wanted was something in the form of an explicit mechanism *endogenous* to the model, through which such groups or classes might eventually attain sufficient power in certain Latin American countries. What exactly was the nature of the pre-existing local conditions which made possible such a reaction?

Dr. König made a similar appeal for more conceptual clarity and detailing of the specific characteristics of the system. What was the relative importance of its political and economic dimensions? What was the capacity of the system for change? He found very interesting indeed the statement in the paper that foreign factors absorbed by Latin America could be considered internal to the system. This suggested that the system was highly integrated. If so, then remedial action might have to come from above – e.g. a 'GATT' for multinational corporations as Professor Kindleberger had suggested. But at the end of the paper Professor Sunkel in fact appeared rather optimistic about the possible success of unilateral action by Latin America. He would like to hear him discuss this further.

Further detailed points of interpretation were raised by *Dr. Mayobre*, who thought the paper exaggerated when it claimed that important national entrepreneurial groups in the developing countries became agents and unconditional allies of the multinational corporations, and cited in contrast examples of cases of strong conflict between such groups and foreign corporations, and *Professor Eastman*, who thought Professor Sunkel's use of the term 'expropriation' to describe the purchase of domestic firms by foreign companies was too strong. Domestic sellers received a higher price for their assets than they were worth and the resources involved remained national. It was true that activities changed: for instance, there might be less domestic research. But research was a cost of production, not an output, and less research expense was part of the gain from foreign investment. If society wanted more research, then appropriate science and taxation policies should create it, hopefully in fields not duplicating that already available abroad.

The problem of the precise role to be assigned to domestic policy in generating the condition here described as 'dependency' received considerable attention. *Dr. Krieger Vasena* in particular felt strongly that this was yet another analysis which attempted to blame internal problems on external factors. He thought the paper did not consider the real source of the problems of the so called 'vegetative' industries, which lay in internal policy which had starved them of access to credit. (He felt the term 'vegetative' in itself was partly to blame; governments understood by it that they should abandon such sectors.) He was also critical of the picture the paper presented of a takeover by foreign capital in 1955. Again internal policy was in fact the heart of the problem: the 'desarrollismo' of the 1950s and 1960s had led to industrialisation regardless of costs and efficiency. We were attempting to blame outside factors, in particular the multinational corporation, when this was simply responding to a protectionist policy. And lastly, he found the historical picture of the multinational corporation itself oversimplified. There were many such companies in existence early in the twentieth century, struggling to dominate the world market. Despite their proximity, even a tiny country like Sweden had been able to achieve a remarkable degree of development. All of these points suggested to him that a very careful analysis of the post-war experience of Latin America was needed, to see how far problems which Professor Sunkel attributed uniquely to the multinational corporation in fact arose from peculiar circumstances which need not be repeated.

Professor Ranis supported Dr. Krieger Vasena, arguing that it was important to compare the behaviour of the multinational corporation with that of the large private and public indigenous corporations. This would enable us to see how much of what we called 'anti-social' behaviour was due to something intrinsic to the multinational corporation, and how much was a function of the protectionist environment. Multinational corporations reacted to the environment created by governments. Their subsidiaries in Korea and Taiwan acted very differently, i.e. more desirably, when confronted with 'open' competitive policies, than in Latin America. Even within, say, Mexico, corporations in the interior and at the border behaved differently.

Several speakers developed the bargaining strategy perspective stressed by Professor Vernon. *Dr. Mayobre* had doubts on the appropriateness of the word 'dependence'. Undoubtedly there existed a 'dependence' of underdeveloped upon industrialised countries, which manifested itself in the economic sphere in technology, in capital, in markets and in patterns of consumption. But on the politico-economic plane, it was a question of the negotiating strength of the parties involved – in this case the countries and the multinational corporations. It was rather, as had been said, a situation parallel to a conflict between oligopolies. Certainly we had to consider the appropriate norms for the underdeveloped countries in regard to such relationships – but the interpretation usually given to the term 'dependence' in much of the literature led one, he felt, to ignore the possibilities in such negotiations and the balance of power – which in some cases could be in favour of the underdeveloped countries. The multinational corporations might have capital, technology and market access as weapons, but the fact that they were often in competition with each other provided a gap in their defences. The developing countries controlled access to their internal markets and to natural resources, which could, depending on circumstances, provide them with quite formidable weapons. Sometimes, as in the case of O.P.E.C., agreements among a number of them could strengthen the position of very small producers. In other words, there was a whole area where negotiations might take place and a wide range of possibilities for strengthening the position of the developing countries. Everything depended on national will and capacity to utilise possibilities.

However, both *Mr. Wionczek* and *Mr. Macario* considered that the experience of O.P.E.C. was not translatable to other commodities. *Mr. Wionczek* felt that Latin American nationalism was so strongly related to one's own individual country that this in itself interfered with oligopolistic country groupings for negotiating purposes. *Mr. Macario* saw the core of the policy problem as how underdeveloped countries were to achieve relations of equality with the multinational corporations; he regretted that UNCTAD had been so exclusively preoccupied with measures the developed countries might take. He felt it ought to be possible to introduce more regulations along the lines of those used in Brazil to pressure companies into exporting, and covering matters like local research. The crucial framework within which to do this was that of economic integration. He stressed that the present was a time when the question of restructuring relations with multinational corporations was of enormous importance; the whole international system was being restructured, and developing countries must play a world role now if they wished to avoid a new system which had the characteristics of the old. *Dr. Ferrer* also stressed the importance of examining the problem of dependency within the context of world trade, and added that the present context not only made renegotiation necessary but was even particularly favourable for it. But the real source of capacity to renegotiate lay in internal possibilities of transformation. Redefinition of the rules would only come about if based on a process of national integration.

Further suggestions as to how to explore aspects of the behaviour of the new system we were observing here came from a number of speakers. *Dr. Wionczek* argued for detailed comparative case studies of multinational corporations, in particular of cases of conflict of interest, as for instance I.P.C. in Peru. It would be important not to limit such studies to their economic aspects: corporations were certainly not just economic entities. A particularly interesting aspect to study, he suggested, might be that of the nationality of the corporation, and how if at all this affected its behaviour. He found significant differences, for instance, in the pattern of behaviour of American and Japanese corporations. U.S. firms, for example, strongly preferred complete control of capital in a foreign subsidiary. The Japanese were happy with the minimum percentage of capital necessary to get technical control, and in fact saw this as a defence against the danger of nationalisation.

Dr. Hosono strongly supported this suggestion. There were many Japanese firms which because of the situation in Japan were orientated not to profits, but to the extraction of raw materials essential for Japan, to the point where their behaviour was significantly different from that of the traditional multinational corporation.

Professor Vernon, however, observed that Japanese firms were often bringing products back to a protected home market for domestic consumption. They were thus not concerned with the world market. Might there not come a time when Japan would begin to export to other markets, at which point her corporations might rapidly develop typical oligopolistic behaviour? And Japanese wholly-owned subsidiaries had typically been disastrous, except when located in a Japanese community. This suggested that their preference for minority ownership represented an incapacity to run a wholly-owned integrated operation in a foreign market, which would probably be overcome. Would there then be different behaviour?

Professor Eastman suggested that Professor Sunkel's analysis should be extended to include cases in which the policies of the home country were not supportive of the interests of the multinational firms based within it, but contrary to them and to the interests of the host country. There were recent examples of U.S. pressure on parent firms such that their foreign subsidiaries were restrained from investing, obliged to repatriate profits or prevented from trading with communist countries, when these things were in their interest as well as that of the host country. He stressed that much that was unwelcome in the behaviour of multinational firms was either the result of the policies of one or other of the governments of the countries in question, or could be corrected by appropriate policy. It should also be noted, he said, that discrimination by multinational firms was practised against developed as well as developing countries. Thus, for instance, new knowledge of the behaviour of producers of agricultural machinery had shown that tractor prices were high in high income countries. *Dr. Hosono* supported this with the example of Japan, who, he said, had no negotiating power as against either O.P.E.C. or the multinational petroleum companies – and was now the world's largest oil importer. As a result of such factors M.I.T.I.[1] had frequently precipitated discussion of the problem of the multinational corporation in bodies such as GATT and the O.E.C.D.

Professor Sunkel began his reply by regretting that only a small part of the discussion had in fact concerned his central theme. By way of response he would attempt to clarify this a little further.

First, the alternative to dependency was *not* independence, and certainly not autarky, but a reduction of dependence, the achievement of a more

[1] The Japanese Ministry of International Trade and Industry.

symmetrical relationship. There were many small countries which were less dependent and more open than Latin America, such as Denmark, Switzerland, Holland. Japan was the example *par excellence* of an economy which had avoided the reshaping of its economy by the penetration of foreign interests. Japan's success lay in its own capacity to define its own goals; the existence of M.I.T.I. was no accident. It was remarkable that Latin America paid in royalties a figure of the same order as did Japan, yet the learning process concealed in this could hardly be more different. And an important element in the contrast was the lack of the actual presence of a foreign producer.

Secondly, Dr. Katz had raised the question of the different circumstances which produced different capacities for reaction to dependency. What was needed was not only detailed comparative studies of corporations, as several speakers had rightly stressed, but detailed analysis of different historical contexts. The answer to why Chile should at this moment attempt a socialist experiment, Peru its own unique policy, and so forth, should be related to different internal social structures formed by an historical process. Through such historical analysis one would see how international relations created an economic structure which in turn was important in the formation of internal social structure. Frank in his analysis tended to see all the *bourgeoisie* as integrated into the international system, so one was left merely with a confrontation between internal groups and the proletariat. His own view was more complex: *within* each class there might exist groups aligned with international interests. This had the consequence that the capacity to negotiate of a country thus penetrated by foreign interests was qualitatively different from that of the dominant country; this was the nub of 'dependency'.

Turning to the important point Dr. König had raised on the integration of the system, he said that it was of crucial importance to know whether there was a new system of international relations forming. As yet it was not clear, but he strongly suspected that there was; if so, then Latin America was facing not individual companies, but governments, systems of negotiations, 'Councils of America' and so forth, which would lead increasingly to concerted action, sometimes initiated by companies, sometimes by governments.

Dr. Barkin's comment had stressed the central problem: how to produce for the low income groups, a large proportion of which were still suffering starvation or malnutrition, after twenty years of industrialisation and increasingly close links with foreign corporations – a period which had actually increased existing inequalities. He attributed this failure in part to the form of organisation of the international system and the way in which Latin America participated in it, and in part to the incapacity of political groups in Latin America to change the course of development. But that failure of entrepreneurial and political groups was not of course illogical: they had benefited from the actual course of industrialisation, which had been created by them in their own interests with the collaboration of foreign investors.

2 Recent Trends in Latin America's Exports to the Industrialised Countries[1]

Alfred Maizels

UNCTAD, GENEVA

It is by now a generally accepted axiom of development economics that the sluggish growth in export earnings constitutes a major constraint on the potential for economic growth in the majority of countries in the Third World. Remedial policies designed to achieve a more dynamic growth in exports have been under active discussion in UNCTAD and in other international forums for some years. Though concerted action by the international community remains a vital element in achieving more dynamic growth in the export earnings of developing countries, much also needs to be done by means of devising more appropriate economic and trade policies in the developing countries themselves.

The scope for remedial actions, whether of an international or national character, must be assessed within some analytical framework which attempts to separate the influence of government policies on the flow of trade from the influence of underlying secular economic forces. Such an analysis, particularly as it applies to the trade relations of Latin America with the industrialised countries, is inevitably a difficult and complex task, which falls outside the scope of a brief paper such as this. Nonetheless, it would seem possible to identify some of the major factors at work over the decade of the 1960s, and to assess their quantitative impact on Latin American exports, even if only in a provisional fashion. This is attempted in the following sections, and it is hoped that the analysis provided will assist in the consideration of possible measures to improve the prospects for the 1970s.

MAJOR MARKETS FOR LATIN AMERICAN EXPORTS

As is well known, the United States constitutes by far the major market for exports from Latin America. At the beginning of the 1960s, the United States took some 40 per cent, by value, of all exports from Latin America; by the end of the decade, the proportion had fallen to little more than 30 per cent, but the United States

[1] The views expressed in this paper do not necessarily reflect those of the UNCTAD secretariat.

was still the largest market.[1] What is perhaps not so well known is that, over the decade, Latin American exports have become considerably more diversified as regards market pattern, and that exports to most markets have grown very much more rapidly than those to the United States (see Table 2.1).

TABLE 2.1

TRENDS IN EXPORTS FROM LATIN AMERICA
IN THE 1960s, BY AREA OF DESTINATION

Exports to	Value ($ billion)			Average Rate of Growth (Per cent per annum)
	1959–61[a]	1967–9[a]	Change	
Industrialised countries:				
United States	3·52	3·98	0·46	1·5
Canada	0·15	0·40	0·26	13·6
E.E.C.	1·54	2·50	0·96	6·3
United Kingdom	0·69	0·72	0·03	0·5
Other EFTA	0·29	0·44	0·15	5·3
Other Western Europe	0·15	0·46	0·31	14·8
Japan	0·28	0·66	0·38	11·4
Total	6·62	9·16	2·54	4·1
Other developed market economy countries[b]	0·03	0·04	0·01	2·7
Developing countries:				
Latin America	0·66	1·42	0·76	10·0
Other developing countries	0·86	1·16	0·30	3·8
Socialist countries of Eastern Europe	0·36	0·78	0·42	10·3
Total	8·53	12·55	4·03	5·0

Source: *Yearbook of International Trade Statistics*. United Nations, New York (various issues).

[a] Average of 3 years.
[b] Australia, New Zealand and South Africa.

Among industrialised markets (excluding socialist countries), Latin American exports grew, on average, by over 10 per cent a year to Canada, Japan and to West European countries outside the E.E.C. and EFTA areas. Exports to the United States grew by only 1·5 per cent a year, while to the United Kingdom the rise was a mere 0·5 per cent a year. If, to take a purely hypothetical illustration, exports to the United States had expanded by the *average* rate for

[1] The comparisons in this paper relate to the averages of the years 1959–61, and of the years 1967–9 (1969 being the latest year for which full statistical data were available at the time of writing).

all other industrialised markets, Latin American exports in 1967–9 would have been higher by $1·9 billion (an increase of some 20 per cent over actual exports to the industrialised countries in that period).

As regards other markets, trade among the Latin American countries themselves rose, on average, by 10 per cent a year during the 1960s. This expansion reflected, in part at least, the encouragement to intraregional trade of the liberalisation efforts of the various regional groupings (LAFTA and C.A.C.M.). Yet, even by the end of the decade, the intra- trade of Latin America represented little more than one-tenth of the total. Exports to socialist countries of Eastern Europe also expanded by an average of 10 per cent a year over the period, mainly as a result of Cuban sugar exports to the U.S.S.R. following the break in trade relations between Cuba and the United States. Exports to developing countries in other regions, and to the major primary-exporting developed market economy countries rose by only 3 or 4 per cent a year, reflecting generally competitive, rather than complementary, production structures, as well as inadequate development of infrastructural trade links.

Heavy dependence on the slow-growing United States market was, however, not necessarily associated with poor export performance by individual Latin American countries. Of six countries shipping at least two-fifths of their total exports to the United States, four enjoyed relatively fast export growth during the 1960s. Equally, of the fast export growth countries, some – such as Chile, El Salvador and Guatemala – relied on the United States market for only a minor proportion of their total exports. At the other extreme, one country – Honduras – relying heavily on the United States market, recorded one of the lowest growth rates of all (see Table 2.2).

More relevant to the export performance of individual countries have been the conditions of world demand for their principal export specialities, and their own efforts to improve their competitive position in world export markets. Apart from Argentina, Brazil and Mexico, whose exports are all fairly well diversified, most Latin American countries depend heavily on one, or a few, traditional primary commodity exports, and their relative success or failure in export growth is necessarily related, to a greater or lesser extent, to the rate of growth of world trade in these particular exports. For example, of the 9 countries shown in Table 2.2 as having enjoyed fast export growth during the 1960s, 2 countries have bananas as their main export product, 3 have coffee and 2 have copper. At the other extreme, 3 of the 5 countries with low export growth are heavily dependent on sugar exports.

Nonetheless there is no unique relationship between commodity

TABLE 2.2

TRENDS IN EXPORTS FROM INDIVIDUAL LATIN AMERICAN COUNTRIES IN THE 1960s, DEGREE OF DEPENDENCE ON THE UNITED STATES MARKET AND ON PARTICULAR COMMODITY EXPORTS

	Average Rate of Growth, 1959–61 to 1967–9 (Per cent per annum)	Exports in 1967–9 Total ($ million)	Exports in 1967–9 Propn. to U.S.A. (Per cent)	Principal Exports[a]
Fast export growth				
Panama	16·5	105	71	Bananas (58), petroleum products (20)
Bolivia	14·0	160	41	Tin ore (54), crude petroleum (14)
Nicaragua	12·0	153	30	Cotton (38), coffee (14), meat (10)
Honduras	12·0	170	45	Bananas (47), coffee (12)
Costa Rica	9·5	169	47	Coffee (32), bananas (26)
Guatemala	9·3	231	28	Coffee (33), cotton (18)
Peru	9·2	834	39	Copper (27), fishmeal (23)
Chile	8·7	972	19	Copper (58), iron ore (9)
El Salvador	7·5	207	23	Coffee (43), manufactures (32)
Sub-total	6·3	3,001	32	
Medium export growth				
Mexico	6·4	1,278	57	Manufactures (28), cotton (13), crude fertilisers (7), coffee (6), sugar (6)

Paraguay	6·3	49	22	Meat (29), wood (17), tobacco (9)
Brazil	5·0	1,949	31	Coffee (41), manufactures (8), cotton (7), sugar (6), iron ore (6)
Argentina	4·8	1,482	10	Cereals (25), meat (24), manufactures (12), wool (8)
Ecuador	4·6	197	39	Bananas (50), cocoa (19), coffee (16)
Uruguay	3·7	179	9	Wool, incl. tops (41), meat (33)
Sub-total	5·2	5,134	30	—
Low export growth				
Colombia	2·5	559	42	Coffee (63), manufactures (10)
Venezuela	2·3	2,878	33	Petroleum, crude and products (93)
Haiti	1·9	36	—	
Dominican Republic	1·5	168	88	Sugar (52), coffee (11)
Cuba	1·2	681	0	Sugar (85), tobacco (4)
Sub-total	2·4	4,322	—	

Sources: *Yearbook of International Trade Statistics*, and *Monthly Bulletin of Statistics*, United Nations, New York: *International Financial Statistics*, I.M.F., Washington; national trade statistics.

* Figures in parentheses relate to percentage of total exports from country listed in 1968 (1967 for Peru, Dominican Republic and Cuba; 1966 for Chile).

pattern and export growth, since the competitive position of different producing countries, and consequently their respective shares of the world market are continually changing. Countries which can diversify into new products for which world demand is relatively dynamic, or can redirect their exports towards relatively expansionary import markets, can achieve significantly faster export growth than countries continuing to depend on traditional slow-growing markets.

Over the past decade the changing pattern of demand, by commodity group and major industrialised market, for Latin American exports has indeed been a complex one (see Table 2.3). Over the whole period (i.e. from 1959–61 to 1967–9), the European Economic Community accounted for almost 40 per cent of the value of the export growth in all Latin American exports, though at the beginning of the decade the Community took only 23 per cent of total exports to the industrialised countries (Table 2.1). The Community's major contribution was in the food, beverages and tobacco group, in which it accounted for over one-half of the expansion in Latin American exports, while for raw materials and non-ferrous metals it contributed about two-fifths of the total expansion. Other Western Europe accounted for between one-fifth and one-quarter of the growth in Latin American exports in these three commodity groups, while for raw materials one-half of the total expansion represented additional shipments to Japan.

The United States, Latin America's largest single market, contributed less than one-fifth of the expansion of the region's exports over the decade.[1] For manufactured goods, however, the United States market accounted for over one-half the increase while for non-ferrous metals and fuels the United States contributed about one-quarter of the increase. For food, beverages and tobacco, however, only one-seventh of the growth in Latin America exports over the period went to the United States, while for raw materials exports to the United States actually fell off in value terms.

TRADE FLOWS AND ECONOMIC GROWTH

These very different rates of growth in commodity imports from Latin America into the various industrialised market economy countries are the resultant of a number of underlying economic forces. It is important to attempt to quantify these, so far as possible, so as to provide some objective basis for assessing prospects for the future, as well as possible remedial policies.

[1] Editors' note: the differences between the figures in this paragraph and those given by Reynolds in his paper in this volume are discussed in footnote 2, page 244, of Reynolds' paper.

TABLE 2.3

TRENDS IN EXPORTS FROM LATIN AMERICA IN THE 1960s BY MAJOR COMMODITY GROUP TO THE PRINCIPAL INDUSTRIALISED COUNTRIES
($ billion)

	Food, Beverages and Tobacco[a]	Raw Materials[b]	Non-ferrous Metals[c]	Fuels[d]	Manufactures[e]	Total
Exports in 1959–61	3·13	1·40	0·54	1·40	0·15	6·61
Exports in 1967–9	4·05	1·83	1·01	1·81	0·44	9·15
Change	+0·93	+0·43	+0·47	+0·42	+0·29	+2·54
(% change per annum)	3·3	3·4	8·2	3·3	14·3	4·1
Contribution to change (per cent)						
Exports to:						
United States	14	−10	26	23	54	18
Canada	0	2	0	58	1	10
E.E.C.	55	38	38	9	28	38
Other Western Europe	24	21	23	4	12	19
Japan	7	49	13	6	5	15
Total	100	100	100	100	100	100

Source: *Monthly Bulletin of Statistics*, United Nations, New York.

[a] *S.I.T.C.* 0 and 1.
[b] *S.I.T.C.* 2 and 4.
[c] *S.I.T.C.* 68.
[d] *S.I.T.C.* 3.
[e] *S.I.T.C.* 5–8 (except 68).

One major factor to be considered is clearly the rate of economic growth in the industrialised countries themselves. It has often been remarked that the major contribution which developed countries can make to expand the market for the exports of developing countries is to ensure that their own economies grow at a reasonably rapid rate. However, the relationship between economic growth in developed countries and their commodity imports from developing countries – and particularly imports from one region, such as Latin America – is not a simple or direct one.

Over the period under review, the average growth rate of G.N.P. (in real terms) did in fact vary substantially from one industrialised country to another. For the United Kingdom, the slowest-growth country in this group, the average growth rate of G.N.P. was 3 per cent a year, while for Japan, at the other extreme, the G.N.P. growth rate was almost 11 per cent a year (see Table 2.4). For all these countries, however, consumption of bulk foods and beverages rose more slowly than G.N.P. This reflected, in part, the fact that as real incomes rise the proportion spent on bulk foods, such as cereals, sugar, and beverages tends to decline; and also the fact that at higher income levels the proportion of expenditure devoted to distributive services, including packaging and advertising, increases. For all the industrialised countries included in Table 2.4, consumption of foods and beverages[1] rose, on average, at only 2·9 per cent a year, compared with an increase of 4·9 per cent a year in real G.N.P.

Total imports of foods and beverages rose, on average, by about the same rate as domestic consumption, though there were wide variations as between the different industrialised countries. The outstanding feature of the situation, however, was that (apart from the E.E.C. area), imports from Latin America increased at a substantially lower rate than did total imports. Indeed, for both the United States and the United Kingdom, the volume of food and beverage imports from Latin America at the end of the decade was lower in absolute terms than at the beginning.

As regards industrial materials, the volume of consumption of the major bulk agricultural and mineral raw materials rose, on average, by very nearly the same rate as the index of industrial production (5·5 as against 5·8 per cent a year). The volume of raw material imports into these industrialised countries, however, rose by only some 3½ per cent a year, while raw material imports from Latin America rose by only 3 per cent a year. Again, large differences can be discerned in the experiences of individual import markets, but

---

[1] The foods, beverages and industrial materials included in Table 2.4 represent approximately 80 per cent of the value of all primary commodity exports from Latin America to O.E.C.D. countries.

ECONOMIC GROWTH IN SELECTED INDUSTRIALISED COUNTRIES: 1959–61 TO 1967–9

	Rates of Growth[a] (Per cent per annum)				Elasticities[c]		
	G.N.P. or Industrial Production[b]	Consumption	Total Imports	Imports from Latin America	Consumption	Total Imports	Imports from Latin America
Food and beverages[e]							
United States	4·7	2·8	1·4	−1·4	0·60	0·30	−0·30
Canada	5·1	3·6	4·0	0·6	0·71	0·78	0·12
E.E.C.	5·2	3·2	3·9[d]	5·0	0·62	0·75[d]	0·96
United Kingdom	3·0	0·9	0·6	−9·3	0·30	0·20	−3·10
Japan	10·8	4·2	11·3	6·9	0·39	1·05	0·64
Total	4·9	2·9	3·2	0·6	0·59	0·65	0·12
Industrial materials[f]							
United States	5·4	5·0	2·9	−1·7	0·93	0·54	−0·31
Canada	6·4	6·7	4·9	14·0	1·05	0·76	2·19
E.E.C.	5·6	5·0	3·1[d]	3·6	0·89	0·55[d]	0·64
United Kingdom	3·0	1·8	−0·2	2·1	0·60	−0·07	0·70
Japan	13·4	10·5	9·3	10·2	0·78	0·69	0·76
Total	5·8	5·5	3·6	3·0	0·95	0·62	0·52

Sources: *Foreign Trade Statistics, Series C* and *Main Economic Indicators*, O.E.C.D., Paris; *Production Yearbooks* and *Trade Yearbooks*, F.A.O, Rome; publications of international commodity bodies; national statistics.

[a] Valued at 1959–61 export unit values.

[b] G.N.P. for food and beverages; industrial production for industrial materials.

[c] Ratio of consumption or import growth rate to growth rate of G.N.P. (for food and beverages), or of industrial production (for industrial materials).

[d] Excluding the intra- trade of E.E.C. countries.

[e] Wheat, maize, rice, beef and veal, sugar, bananas, oranges, vegetable oilseeds and oils, pepper, coffee, tea and cocoa.

[f] Cotton, wool, sisal and abaca, jute, rubber, tobacco, tropical wood, copper, iron ore, lead, zinc, tin, bauxite and manganese ore; man-made fibres and synthetic rubber.

only one country – the United States – imported a smaller volume of raw materials from Latin America at the end, than at the beginning, of the decade.

Expressed in terms of elasticities,[1] it would appear that while the total import elasticity for food and beverages was positive for each of the industrialised countries, for imports from Latin America, the elasticities were negative for both the United States and the United Kingdom, while only for the E.E.C. area did the elasticity approach unity. For industrial materials, again, there were wide divergences among the various import markets, the elasticity for imports from Latin America being exceptionally high (over 2) for Canada, between 0·6 and 0·8 for the E.E.C., United Kingdom and Japan, but once again negative for the United States.

What were the factors behind these very different trends in imports from Latin America during the 1960s? Are these factors likely to continue to operate in the 1970s? To what extent are they susceptible to modification by government intervention? Answers to these and related questions would be very relevant to any assessment of the outlook for the commodity exports of the Latin American countries over the coming decade.

CONSTRAINTS ON EXPORT GROWTH

The fact that imports from Latin America have grown much less rapidly than G.N.P. or industrial production in the industrialised countries indicates that countervailing, constraining, factors were at work. As regards food and beverages, exports from Latin America are fairly heavily concentrated, in terms of value, in a limited range of commodities. Coffee, the major export item, accounted in 1967–9 for some 40 per cent of all Latin America's export earnings from food, beverages and tobacco. The constraining factors must clearly be sought in terms of the highly specialised basket of foods which Latin America offers for export. Though much the same generalisation holds for raw materials, there is an additional constraint here of major proportions, namely, the displacement of traditional natural materials by synthetics produced in the developed importing countries.

Taking the same period as before, the volume of major industrial materials consumed in the main industrialised market economy countries, including both natural and synthetic materials, rose by over 50 per cent, whereas both total imports and imports from Latin America rose by only about 30 per cent (see Table 2.5). This divergence in growth rates indicates that the development of the synthetic materials industries in the industrialised countries has proved to be

[1] For definition, see footnote *c* to Table 2.4.

a major constraining element in the demand for imported natural materials, including those originating in Latin America.

Apart from the influence of the rate of economic growth in the industrialised countries, and the displacement of natural by synthetic

TABLE 2.5

CONSUMPTION AND IMPORTS OF MAJOR
COMMODITIES IN THE INDUSTRIALISED MARKET
ECONOMY COUNTRIES: 1959–61 AND 1967–9
($ billion at 1959–61 prices)

	Food and Beverages[a]	Industrial Materials			
		Agricultural Materials[b]	Ores and Metals[c]	Synthetic Materials[d]	Total
Consumption					
1959–61	29·74	8·44	5·33	3·59	17·36
1967–9	37·28	8·76	7·70	10·08	26·54
Change	+7·54	+0·32	+2·37	+6·49	+9·18
(% change)	+25·00	+4·00	+44·00	+181·00	+53·00
Total imports[e]					
1959–61	7·21	4·60	3·03	0·26	7·89
1967–9	9·27	5·10	4·62	0·78	10·50
Change	+2·06	+0·50	+1·59	+0·52	+2·61
(% change)	+29·00	+11·00	+53·00	+200·00	+33·00
Imports from Latin America					
1959–61	2·58	0·66	0·85	—	1·51
1967–9	2·72	0·76	1·15	—	1·91
Change	+0·14	+0·10	+0·30	—	+0·40
(% change)	+5·00	+15·00	+35·00	—	+27·00

Sources: *Foreign Trade Statistics*, Series C, OECD, Paris; *Production Yearbooks* and *Trade Yearbooks*, FAO, Rome; publications of international commodity bodies; national statistics.

[a] Wheat, maize, rice, beef and veal, sugar, bananas, oranges, vegetable oilseeds and oils, pepper, coffee, tea and cocoa.
[b] Cotton, wool, sisal and abaca, jute, rubber, tobacco and tropical wood.
[c] Copper, iron ore, lead, zinc, tin, bauxite and manganese ore.
[d] Man-made fibres and synthetic rubber.
[e] Excluding intra- trade of EEC.

materials, a number of other factors have to be considered. One is that, as already indicated, a rising level of real income is associated with shifts in the commodity pattern of demand, and such shifts may well affect adversely the demand for those products exported by Latin American countries. Another factor is that all industrialised countries protect their domestic production of primary and processed products, to a greater or lesser extent, against competition from imports, and changes in the degree of protection will influence the demand for supplies from external sources. Finally, within the total imports of similar or competing commodities, the share held by Latin American countries may change significantly, in one direction or the other, as a result of changes in the relative competitive position of different exporting countries, or of changes in preferential trade barriers.

With so varied and complex a series of factors at work, the relative importance of each factor varying from one industrialised country to another, it is not practicable to measure the net effect of each at all precisely. However some approximate quantitative estimates can be made of the relative importance of these different factors. The estimates, which are summarised in Table 2.6, relate to the same commodities and import markets that were included in Tables 2.4 and 2.5. For each import market, the change in the value of imports from Latin America (at constant 1959–61 prices) over the greater part of the 1960s has been subdivided to indicate the approximate quantitative effect of each of the relevant factors[1].

For food and beverages, the results of this calculation show that the principal factor operating during the 1960s to hold down the rate of growth of exports from Latin America was the relative displacement of these exports by competing imports from other sources. In total, this factor offset about two-thirds of the expansionary effect of the growth in demand for Latin American export specialities in the industrialised countries. Putting the point in another way, it can be estimated that, had the Latin American countries retained their share of the import market in the industrialised countries, the rate of growth in the volume of exports of food and beverages from Latin America from 1959–61 to 1967–9 would have averaged 2·5 per cent a year, rather than the 0·6 per cent a year shown in Table 2.4.

The biggest single element in the deterioration in Latin America's competitive position in the import market of the industrialised countries resulted from the expansion of exports of *robusta* coffee from African producing countries.[2] Other factors of some importance were the cessation of Cuban sugar exports to the United States following the diplomatic break between these two countries, and the decline in Argentine beef exports to the United Kingdom, resulting mainly from sanitary regulations.

The other major factor in Latin America's food and beverage exports was the marked shift in consumption patterns in the United States, which had a particularly adverse effect on import demand for

[1] See appendix at end of this chapter for explanation of the method used.
[2] The switch to African coffees accounted for some $160 million of the notional loss of $195 million shown for the United States market.

TABLE 2.6

FACTORS INFLUENCING CHANGES IN COMMODITY
IMPORTS INTO SELECTED INDUSTRIALISED
COUNTRIES FROM LATIN AMERICA: 1959–61 TO 1967–9

	U.S.A.	Canada	E.E.C.	U.K.	Japan	Total
		($ million at 1959–61 prices)[a]				
Food and beverages[b]						
1. Growth in total consumption	360	25	200	15	40	640
2. Change in pattern of consumption	– 300	– 5	95	—	95	– 115
3. Displacement of imported by domestic products	– 15	—	55	– 10	– 10	20
4. Competition between Latin America and other external suppliers	– 195	– 15	– 20	– 130	– 55	– 415
Total change	– 150	5	330	– 125	70	130
Industrial materials[b]						
1. Growth in total consumption	270	5	230	30	270	805
2. Change in pattern of consumption of natural materials	– 65	5	– 20	—	– 45	– 125
3. Competition between natural and synthetic materials	– 60	– 10	– 155	– 50	– 140	– 415
4. Displacement of imported by domestic natural products	– 30	—	30	10	60	70
5. Competition between Latin America and other external suppliers	– 185	15	75	50	115	70
Total change	– 70	15	160	40	260	405

Sources: As for Table 2.5; see appendix for method used.

[a] Figures round to nearest $5 million.
[b] See Table 2.4 for definitions.

coffee. Whereas coffee consumption accounted in 1959–61 for 6·2
per cent of the value of United States consumption of all foods and
beverages covered in Table 2.6, by 1967–9 the proportion had
declined to 4·3 per cent. The shift in the pattern of United States
consumer demand into livestock products, fresh fruit and fruit
products and polyunsaturated vegetable oils had little beneficial
impact on the export basket offered by Latin American producers.

There were, however, some shifts in consumption patterns which
were favourable to Latin America. In both the E.E.C. and Japan,
there were relative shifts towards greater consumption of coarse
grains, coffee and bananas, but these were not sufficient to offset the
impact of the shift in United States consumption patterns mentioned

above. On balance, the net effect of changes in consumption patterns offset almost one-fifth of the expansion in demand for Latin American exports of food and beverages arising from increased consumption in the industrialised countries.

Changes in the degree of import-substitution (i.e. the displacement of imported by domestically produced foodstuffs) were, on balance, a relatively minor factor during the 1960s. However, the substitution of relatively high-cost production of beet sugar for cane sugar exports from developing countries – including Latin America – continued on a substantial scale, but this was rather more than offset, as regards Latin American exports, by a greater dependence by the E.E.C. countries on imports of coarse grains and of beef and veal.

By contrast, the major adverse influence on Latin American raw materials exports was the encroachment of man-made fibres on the markets for cotton, wool and sisal (including henequen). According to the estimates in Table 2.6, the adverse impact of the competition with man-made fibres offset over one-half of the growth in demand for the principal industrial materials exported from Latin America. The sharpest adverse impact on the markets for the natural fibres occurred in the E.E.C. and Japan, but there were adverse effects in all the other industrialised countries also.[1] Changes in the pattern of demand for the various natural industrial materials were also generally adverse for Latin America, offsetting about one-sixth of the growth in total consumption. The principal pattern changes were the relatively slow growth in demand for certain mineral ores (lead, tin and manganese), and for natural textile fibres and tobacco.

Unlike the position for foods and beverages, the displacement of imports of industrial materials from Latin America by those from other external suppliers was, on balance, relatively small during the 1960s. The major change was the rapid growth in iron ore supplies from Australia into the United States (Latin America also lost some share of the United States import market for copper, zinc and manganese ore); but these adverse factors were more than offset by gains in market shares in Japan (due mainly to shipments of iron ore under long-term contracts), in the E.E.C. (raw cotton) and in the United Kingdom (raw wool and raw cotton).

PROSPECTS FOR THE 1970s

What are the prospects for an accelerated rate of growth in Latin American exports to the industrialised countries over the current decade? Are the trends discernible during the 1960s likely to con-

[1] A small allowance has also been made in Table 2.6 for the substitution of plastic materials for tropical timber in certain end-uses.

tinue, or can they be significantly modified by policy changes in both Latin American and industrialised countries?

As regards manufactures, the introduction of the Generalised System of Preferences (G.S.P.) negotiated in UNCTAD should provide new market opportunities, and new incentives, for Latin American countries, along with other developing countries, to expand further their exports of such products. Unfortunately the United States – Latin America's largest market for manufactures – has not yet ratified its G.S.P. proposals. Even with all current G.S.P. proposals in operation, however, a number of important non-tariff barriers to trade will remain, and increasing international efforts will be needed to provide a commercial policy environment conducive to a more rapid growth in exports of manufactures from developing to industrialised countries.

It still remains true, however, that the majority of Latin American countries are heavily dependent on primary commodities for the bulk of their export earnings, and this position is unlikely to change significantly during the current decade at least. One conclusion which follows from the analysis of trends in the 1960s is that even a rapid economic expansion in the industrialised countries may not, in itself, be a sufficient condition for a sustained growth in demand for the primary commodity exports of Latin America.

In the foods and beverages group, conscious efforts to improve the competitive position of Latin American products in the markets of the industrialised countries would seem to be one essential condition for accelerated export growth. To the extent, however, that demand patterns are shifting away from Latin American products, or Latin American varieties of products, it might also be necessary to consider the advisability of diversification into activities producing commodities, manufactures or services with more dynamic demand prospects.

For the temperate-zone foods, however, a major constraint on the flow of international trade results from the protection of high-cost production in the industrialised countries. Such protection is often a consequential effect of domestic policies designed to provide a minimum level of real income for the rural community, but it also results in a limitation of the market opportunities for many of the traditional export products of developing countries. As far as Latin American exports are concerned, sugar, vegetable oilseeds and oils, tobacco and cereals are probably the commodities most affected. Though there appears to have been no net loss incurred during the 1960s by any additional import-substitution in food supply in the industrialised countries (see Table 2.6), it nonetheless remains true that a reduction in domestic price support policies would allow for a significant expansion in competing imports from lower-cost sources in developing countries.

As regards the industrial materials group, the main constraint on the growth of Latin American exports over the past decade, as indicated in Table 2.6, has been the intensified competition between natural and synthetic materials, particularly in the fibres field. The production of synthetic materials has been a particularly dynamic element in the economic growth of the industrialised countries over the past two decades, though it has only recently become recognised that such production may involve heavy social costs, particularly as regards the pollutive effects on the environment of synthetic effluents.

The rapid expansion of the synthetic materials industries has involved very large expenditures on research and development. To meet the growing challenge of synthetics, the developing countries producing competing natural products need to mount a far larger, and co-ordinated, research and development effort to improve the competitive position of their exports, by developing new end-uses for them, by improving the technical characteristics of their products, and by improving productivity and reducing costs of production. For most natural products facing competition from synthetics, the individual research efforts of particular developing countries must inevitably remain inadequate to the task. What is needed is a world-wide research and development programme in which the producing countries of all the developing regions can fully co-operate.

PRICE ASPECTS

The above analysis has been conducted essentially in quantitative terms. This is a useful device for focussing on the underlying 'real' factors at work. But it tends also to obscure the importance of the price aspects of trade flows. As already mentioned, the competitive position of Latin American exports in the world market will inevitably play a major role in the future evolution of the region's internal trade, and Latin American productivity and export prices are an essential aspect of the competitive position.

There is, however, another aspect of the price question which merits serious consideration. For those commodities for which demand is price-inelastic in the markets of industrialised countries, and which are produced wholly or mainly in developing countries, the latter can improve the level of world prices, and consequently the rate of growth in their export earnings, by joint action to regulate the rate of increase in total supplies coming on the world market. Joint action of this type is in operation for coffee, in the content of a formal commodity agreement, while similar, though informal, export quota arrangements exist for sisal and tea. The draft international cocoa agreement, now under negotiation in UNCTAD, also contains provisions for price stabilisation.

The recent series of agreements on taxes and royalty payments between the international petroleum companies and the governments of the producing countries provide another kind of example of the need strongly felt by developing countries to improve the prices received for their major export products. There seems little doubt also that, in the coming decade, many developing countries will make further efforts to improve their share of the profits earned by international companies operating within their territories, particularly those engaged in the more dynamic mineral sectors.

APPENDIX: Calculation of elements affecting changes in commodity imports from Latin America into industrialised countries.

1. The change in the value of imports, at constant prices, of an individual commodity i from Latin America into a given industrialised country j from period 0 to period 1 can be defined as:

$$\Delta M_{ij} = M_{ij \cdot 1} - M_{ij \cdot 0} \tag{1}$$

Summing over n commodities, this can be written as:

$$\sum_{i=1}^{i=n} \Delta M_{ij} = \sum_{i=1}^{i=n} m_{ij \cdot 1} C_{ij \cdot 1} - \sum_{i=1}^{i=n} m_{ij \cdot 0} C_{ij \cdot 0} \tag{2}$$

where C_{ij} represents domestic consumption of i in country j, and m_{ij} is the proportion of consumption met by imports from Latin America.

2. The right-hand side of (2) can conveniently be divided into two elements representing, respectively, the influence on imports from Latin America of the change in domestic consumption of the relevant commodities, and the influence of the change in the proportion of consumption met by imports from Latin America:

$$\sum_{i=1}^{i=n} \Delta M_{ij} = \sum_{i=1}^{i=n} m_{ij \cdot 0} (C_{ij \cdot 1} - C_{ij \cdot 0}) + \sum_{i=1}^{i=n} C_{ij \cdot 1} (m_{ij \cdot 1} - m_{ij \cdot 0}) \tag{3}$$

3. The first element on the right-hand side of (3) can also be regarded as the net effect of three distinct factors, namely:

(a) The effect of the overall growth in domestic demand for the group of commodities in question (for example, in the case of industrial raw materials, this factor would reflect the growth of industrial production as a whole);
(b) the effect of changes in the commodity pattern of demand for natural commodities; and
(c) the effect of the displacement of natural by synthetic materials.

These three factors can be expressed, respectively, as follows, using the same notation as above:

$$\sum_{i=1}^{i=n} m_{ij\cdot 0}(C_{ij1\cdot} - C_{ij\cdot 0}) = \sum_{i=1}^{i=n} m_{ij\cdot 0}C_{ij\cdot 0}\left(\frac{\displaystyle\sum_{i=1}^{i=n} C_{ij\cdot 1}}{\displaystyle\sum_{i=1}^{i=n} C_{ij\cdot 0}} - 1\right) +$$

$$\sum_{i=1}^{i=n} m_{ij\cdot 0}\left\{C_{ij\cdot 1} - C_{ij\cdot 0}\left(\frac{\displaystyle\sum_{i=1}^{i=n} C_{ij\cdot 1}^*}{\displaystyle\sum_{i=1}^{i=n} C_{ij\cdot 0}^*}\right)\right\} +$$

$$\sum_{i=1}^{i=n} m_{ij\cdot 0}C_{ij\cdot 0}\left(\frac{\displaystyle\sum_{i=1}^{i=n} C_{ij\cdot 1}^*}{\displaystyle\sum_{i=1}^{i=n} C_{ij\cdot 0}^*} - \frac{\displaystyle\sum_{i=1}^{i=n} C_{ij\cdot 1}}{\displaystyle\sum_{i=1}^{i=n} C_{ij\cdot 0}}\right) \tag{4}$$

Where $\sum_{i=1}^{i=n} C_{ij}^*$ represents the value of consumption of natural commodities only, whereas $\sum_{i=1}^{i=n} C_{ij}$ represents the value of consumption of both natural and synthetic products.

4. The second element on the right-hand side of (3) can also usefully be sub-divided, since m_{ij} (the proportion of consumption met by imports from Latin America) is itself a combination of two factors, namely the proportion of total imports in consumption (r), and the proportion of imports from Latin America in total imports (s). Thus, this second element on the right-hand side of (3) can be rewritten as:

$$\sum_{i=1}^{i=n} C_{ij\cdot 1}(m_{ij\cdot 1} - m_{ij\cdot 0}) = \sum_{i=1}^{i=n} s_{ij\cdot 1}C_{ij\cdot 1}(r_{ij\cdot 1} - r_{ij\cdot 0})$$

$$+ \sum_{i=1}^{i=n} r_{ij\cdot 0}C_{ij\cdot 1}(s_{ij\cdot 1} - s_{ij\cdot 0}) \tag{5}$$

In this formulation, the first term on the right-hand side of (5) represents the effect of import-substitution, i.e. the effect on imports from Latin America of the growth of domestic production of competing natural products in the industrialised countries. The second term represents the effect of changes in the competitive share of Latin American countries *vis-à-vis* other external sources of supply of imports into the industrialised countries.

5. The original change in imports from Latin America, as shown in (2) can thus be divided into five separate elements, namely the three on the right-hand side of (4), plus the two on the right-hand side of (5). Alternative formulations can also be devised, using different weighting systems, but it is unlikely that these would affect the results to any significant extent.

Discussion of the Paper by Dr. Maizels

In the absence of Dr. Maizels, the paper was introduced and summarised by *Dr. Mayobre*, who stressed that the important contribution of the work was its quantification of the importance of the different factors explaining export trends in different markets. Commenting on the conclusions Dr. Maizels drew from the analysis, he tended to emphasise even more strongly than the paper did the problems to be anticipated, from synthetics in the case of industrial materials and from protection in food products, especially in the E.E.C. and the more so once the United Kingdom entered. On exports of manufactures, the slow but positive response UNCTAD had been obtaining had now been put in jeopardy by the U.S. import surcharge. The tendency in the underdeveloped countries had been as he saw it to rely very heavily on UNCTAD obtaining preferences: he thought it essential that such efforts should be combined with a far stronger effort in the sphere of domestic industrial policy, to create on the supply side conditions which would make possible industrial exports. In his own view the great problem of the next few years would be the growing protectionism Latin America would face.

Professor Vernon found the paper extremely helpful, but from the policy point of view only a beginning and unsatisfactory in certain crucial respects. This derived from the fact that the paper asked how far changes in exports could be explained by price and income elasticities on the demand side. These variables were outside the reach of Latin American policy, whereas there were other factors that were within the reach of policy and thereby of greater interest; supply conditions, and the question of information. He would like to suggest that the latter in particular was of overwhelming importance. Many studies of trade patterns assigned a large role to distance and to preference, but were these not in fact surrogates for information flows? He found that the distance variable worked where it should not, where distance added no cost, and the preference variable where there was no actual preference. He thought that Japan's decision not to go for protection, but rather to make a major investment in information explained much of her changed export pattern, in combination with her undertaking to change supply conditions. All the conditions that existed now on the Mexican frontier zone had existed for a long time, without giving rise to much trade; it was the development of an information grid which was crucial for the expansion of trade. This was where the multinational corporations could play a positive and important role.

Dr. Katz took up the point about information: this was a clear case, he said, where the market did not generate the optimum flow, since the returns from investment in information were not fully appropriable. It was therefore essential that the State should intervene in this area. *Professor Nove* and *Professor Felix* both felt that the role of information was important, although the latter believed that in instances of considerable success such as Taiwan and Korea their special relationship to the United

States was still more important. Professor Nove thought the point was particularly applicable to manufactures. Much might be done by joint marketing and by joint government-sponsored information services. Thus hardly anyone in Scotland had ever seen a Mexican consumer good; there might be many potential opportunities which it was beyond the ability of individual firms to identify or to take.

Mr. Macario strongly supported Professor Vernon's criticism of the paper for its emphasis on external factors and neglect of internal factors such as supply capacity, exchange rate policies, inflation, infrastructure deficiencies and others. Anticipating a later discussion, he found Dr. Maizels and Professor Reynolds alike in their stress on external factors, the former on the evolution of markets, the latter the evolution of comparative advantage. Both factors were clearly important but not as important as the papers suggested.

Further, in regard to the external factors themselves, he would himself have analysed them rather differently. He saw the policy of the developed countries as far more important than Dr. Maizels suggested. Then the paper analysed the effect of income growth on demand; he felt this needed a closer examination, since what mattered was not only the amount of growth but its form; thus for example it was of great significance that the particular strategy of growth Japan was embarked on included an agricultural policy which was making her into a large food importer (in contrast to E.E.C. strategy, for instance). Then it was important to make clear that there were certain products where no matter how fast the developed economies grew, Latin American exports would not rise, either because of saturation or substitution, as was the case, for example, with coffee.

Dr. Katz pointed out that on the demand side the paper made no reference to the possibility of diversifying markets, for example increasing sales to Eastern Europe. Second, among the factors on the supply side which should be mentioned, he would like to bring up the question of local policy on technology. A good example was the change in the structure of sales of Argentine beef, from chilled beef to a semi-manufactured product. This had required a major technological development, which tended to confirm the correlation Professor Vernon's work had found between exports of manufactures and local research and development. In this kind of technological evolution, the support, or lack of it, available in the policy of the country concerned could be crucial.

Professor Hirschman said that the very clear statistics the paper was offering us enabled us to dispose neatly of certain widely held beliefs. For instance, it was no longer possible to say that Latin America had done badly in exports of manufactures. In fact the degree of success was remarkable in view of the numerous biases against such exports implicit in the strategy of industrialisation. A combination of inflation and an overvalued currency was extremely unpropitious for manufactured exports; much of the stagnation of the 1960s could, he thought, be traced to attempts to get away from such a system. Another belief he himself had held which Table 2.6 showed to be wrong was that displacement of imported by domestic products would far outweigh competition from other suppliers as a factor explaining the slow growth of exports of food products. A large element in this, incidentally, was apparently coffee: was it permissible to ask whether it was actually to be deplored that Latin America should give way to Africa? *Mr. Urquidi* added that what had impressed him in Table 2.6 was the enormous importance of competition from synthetics, even – in fact, especially – in the case of Japan. *Professor Hirschman* agreed, and wondered if we might not now seriously consider placing controls on this kind of technical progress, since we were becoming so much more aware of the accompanying problem of pollution.

Professor Nove then turned to the criticisms made of the paper, and commented that it seemed unreasonable to accuse Dr. Maizels of not doing the impossible. To study in detail the trade opportunities of every country, in order to serve as a policy guideline, would require years of work and a number of volumes. However, it was certainly true that aggregates were not useful for practical purposes. Thus the apparently weak performance of Latin American exports in Great Britain were in fact the result of two factors: a decision by oil companies to sell less Venezuelan oil in the British market, and a reduction in purchases of beef from Argentina because of fear of foot and mouth disease. Neither had anything to do with elasticities.

Dr. Ferrer seconded Professor Nove's defence: the comments people had been making were all sound points in themselves, but he could not consider them criticisms of the paper. The point that Dr. Maizels was trying to make was that quite apart from domestic policies there were certain tendencies to be observed in our markets – in particular an inevitable tendency towards a declining share in trade in the absence of countervailing policy. Developments in trade could not be fully comprehended unless such underlying trends were taken into account. Of course, the crucial issues for Latin America lay in areas within reach of policy, but this had to be seen in the context of external trends.

Having said that, he wanted himself to turn to internal policy. As he saw it, the problem of the external bottleneck had its roots deep in industrialisation policy. It was misleading to talk of exports of manufactures as if their key significance was that they would directly help the balance of payments. They would, but their real significance went deeper: they could provide the means also of moving towards a better industrial strategy for Latin America. Many Latin American countries had diversified considerably in recent years and basic industry was now a significant component of the total. But such industry was desperately in need of expanding markets and product specialisation, and it was here that exports could provide the key.

Dr. Mayobre supported the defence of Dr. Maizels, and added that in Professor Vernon's example of Japan, information may have been important but it had to be accompanied by capacity to compete in terms of costs.

He then commented on Professor Nove's reference to exports. Professor Nove had referred to their poor performance in the United Kingdom market for reasons which he assumed had nothing to do with elasticities. In fact there were three main reasons as he understood it: first, the Middle

East and North Africa had lower production cost; second, reserves in the West were relatively low and companies in adjusting sources of supply had an eye to conservation of resources for the future; third, in terms of security from nationalisation, the Middle East at present looked preferable to Latin America.

Dr. Maizels subsequently responded in writing to the discussion. He said he very much regretted having been unable to participate personally, in particular in the discussion of his paper. He would like to begin by saying that he was in complete agreement with the point made by many speakers that trends in Latin American exports must be explained by factors on both the demand and supply sides of the market. However, to interpret the method of analysis which he had used as emphasising the demand factors to the neglect of those on the supply side – as did Professor Vernon and Mr. Macario – was to misunderstand the nature of the statistics presented.

The analysis summarised in Table 2.6 was purely an *ex post* calculation which sought to distinguish the main elements of the change in the volume of Latin American exports of primary commodities during the decade of the 1960s. Each element distinguished was itself the result of changes in supply and demand, including their mutual adjustment in the world market. In other words, this kind of *ex post* statistical manipulation of the trade figures was essentially neutral, in the sense that, by itself, it told us nothing about the underlying causal forces which were operating. What was necessary, therefore, was to interpret the statistical results in the light of other information about changes in market forces.

For example, changes in the level of consumption, and in the pattern of consumption, were clearly the result of price changes, as well as of specific demand factors such as changes in consumer tastes, population and real income changes. These price changes were, in turn, partly influenced by economic events in the producing countries – in this case, in Latin America – as well as by those in the consuming countries. Again, changes in trade patterns attributable to the changing competitive position of Latin American and other external suppliers to the United States market (the last element distinguished in Table 2.6) were predominantly influenced by relative productivity and cost changes.

On the other hand, it could reasonably be assumed that marked changes in the ratio of imports to domestic production of those competing primary commodities in which Latin America had a comparative advantage reflected essentially changes in the degree of protection to domestic agriculture afforded by Government support policies in the industrialised countries. Similarly, changes in trade attributable to the expansion in the output of synthetic substitutes could reasonably be interpreted as reflecting changes on the demand side of the market. Even in this case, however, it could be argued that policies in the countries producing the natural materials being displaced by synthetics should have been more positively directed to cost reduction and to improving the technical characteristics of the natural materials, in order to slow down the rate of displacement of these materials by synthetics.

As regards Professor Vernon's point about information, he would agree with Professor Nove that this point was particularly applicable to trade in manufactures. He did not, however, believe it to be of importance as regards trends in trade in primary commodities, the subject with which his paper was essentially concerned.

3 The Role of World Trade Policy: a Latin American Viewpoint

Santiago P. Macario[1]

I. THE DEVELOPING COUNTRIES IN WORLD TRADE

The economic development of any country is essentially its own responsibility and must basically depend upon its own economic policy and internal efforts. There are, however, considerable limitations both on a country's freedom of decision and action in the field of economic policy and on the effectiveness of its actions – particularly in respect of external trade policy. Such restraints are an inevitable result of the interplay of international economic relations; they imply limitations to national sovereignty at the economic, and therefore also at the political, level, at least *vis-à-vis* the exterior.

Therefore, however important and decisive the economic policy and internal efforts of a country may be, its economic development will also be affected, to a greater or lesser extent, by its economic relations with the rest of the world, and thus by circumstances that are more or less beyond its control. A further and more important consideration is that, even if a country carries out what it believes to be the best trade policy in a given context (i.e. the one that seems most likely to achieve the objectives of its economic development policy), the effectiveness of this policy will to some extent be determined, and therefore limited, by these external factors.

This may seem platitudinous; yet, as a key fact of world trade policy and relations, it is worth bearing in mind. Its real significance, however, lies in the fact that there are wide differences in the limitations on the freedom of decision and effective action of various countries in the field of foreign trade policy, as well as in the extent to which each country is able to influence world trade policy and relations. The relative economic power of a country (and of course its ability to use it) is the main determinant of its bargaining power; it thus also determines the extent to which it can effectively exercise economic independence and sovereignty, and its capacity to influence outside economic events and policies. Moreover, *ceteris paribus*, its

[1] The author is head of the Trade Policy Division of the U.N. Economic Commission for Latin America. However, the opinions expressed in this paper are not necessarily those of ECLA's secretariat nor do they in any way commit the organisation for which he works.

economic power increases in so far as it is able to make world economic relations work in its favour.

World trade policy and relations are thus to a large extent shaped by a handful of economically powerful countries – or at least influenced to a much greater degree by them than by other countries, in particular the underdeveloped nations. This being the case, it is inevitable that world trade policy and the structure of international economic relations will respond much more closely to the interests of the former than of the latter.

At the same time, particularly since the end of the Second World War, there has been a continuous and substantial decline in the developing countries' share in world trade: Latin America's share, for instance, has fallen from about 11 per cent in the early 1950s to only 5½ per cent in the late 1960s. The situation described above is in part responsible for this decline, which in turn involves a corresponding decrease in the developing countries' ability to influence the working of the international trade system. The developed countries, on the other hand, because of the growing importance of their mutual trade, concern themselves increasingly with this trade and the problems associated with it while giving less and less attention to the trade problems of the developing countries, so that their support for a programme of international economic cooperation favouring the latter is often merely lip service.

THE SOURCES OF INEQUALITY

The basis of this unequal structure, as far as trade relations between the developed and developing countries are concerned, is the traditional scheme of the international division of labour. Its effects are, moreover, aggravated by the manner in which the scheme is operated via the trade and investment policies of the industrial countries.[1] According to this scheme the developing countries specialise in the production and export of primary goods. These they supply to the developed countries from whom in turn they import manufactured goods. Since primary goods are at a serious disadvantage *vis-à-vis*

---

[1] Although these policies were a typical and essential feature of the colonial system, they were also widely and successfully applied to 'politically independent' underdeveloped countries, such as those of Latin America. Moreover, they are still being applied today, even after the system has practically disappeared as a political entity, at least in theory. In practice, the economic dependence of the developing countries (whether newly 'independent' or not) and the consequent limitations on their effective economic sovereignty is one of the main causes of political dependence.

manufactured ones,[1] both with regard to production and trade, the scheme is strongly biased in favour of the developed nations.

It is true that the disadvantages of primary products *vis-à-vis* manufactured ones are largely due to the nature of their respective production processes. But the situation is not improved by the fact that primary commodities are traded internationally under conditions approaching perfect competition, whereas trade in manufactured goods is carried out under quite different conditions. Furthermore, both world trade policy and the domestic agricultural policies of the developed countries tend if anything to worsen the already unfavourable situation.

Thus, the basic aim of the agricultural policies of most developed countries is, through government intervention, to increase the income of their rural population so that their farmers can enjoy an adequate standard of living, comparable to that of the industrial sector, and certainly much higher than would result from the free operation of market forces. However, these policies frequently include import restrictions and lead to increasing self-sufficiency and the production of surpluses, which are disposed of by exporting them with the aid of heavy subsidies; such practices seriously distort world markets for agricultural products. Besides restricting or denying access to the markets of the developed countries, these policies tend to increase competition in world markets and depress agricultural prices. In the case of the E.E.C.'s Common Agricultural Policies, they also, in respect of imports subject to a 'variable levy', create a situation of serious uncertainty as to the actual import charge that will be applied on each occasion. Similar policies are often adopted by the developed countries for other non-agricultural primary products (namely fisheries, mining).

Of the many problems which beset world trade in primary products, the most serious is that of their price in world markets. This is the chief – but by no means the only – cause of the very inequitable distribution of the benefits derived from international trade. Commodity prices are generally characterised by their low level, frequent and pronounced short-term fluctuations, and a secular tendency to deteriorate in relation to industrial prices.

Further, in the case of some commodities produced and/or exported by foreign firms, such as bananas, most minerals and,

---

[1] Those disadvantages which spring from lack of control over production and prices, the nature of demand, its instability, the low level of value added, the small impact of exports on economic activity, and so forth, are quite well known, and need not be dealt with in detail here. A further less widely acknowledged disadvantage is that while it is normal in trade in primary goods for the importing country to play the dynamic role, the reverse is true in trade in industrial products.

formerly, also petroleum, only a small proportion of the world price goes to, or remains with, the producing country. This, with the generally low international prices of primary products, means not only low remuneration and a low standard of living for the labour force, but also a relatively small foreign exchange income for the exporting country. Given also the sluggish growth of world demand for most primary products, these factors result in an insufficient import capacity, the latter being one of the major bottlenecks limiting their rate of economic development.

A number of economists, particularly in the United States and other industrialised nations, deny the existence of any statistical evidence of declining terms of trade for primary commodities in relation to manufactured products. It is true that the results for any given period will vary considerably, and may even show an improvement in the terms of trade for primary products according to the year used as a base. Nevertheless, the existence of a secular downwards trend is in fact proven by the agricultural policies of the developed countries themselves. For as we have said, prices of primary products, especially in agriculture, when left to the free operation of the price mechanism, tend to be too low to give farmers and other primary producers sufficient purchasing power with respect to the articles they buy to enable them to enjoy an acceptable standard of living.

Thus in most cases (especially in the U.S. and the E.E.C.), the key element in agricultural policy is a programme of price support for certain commodities. In the United States, the level of price support is almost always expressed in terms of 'parity prices', which are measures of the different commodities' purchasing power, or the prices at which commodities must sell in order to have the same purchasing power as in the base period.[1] The concept of parity prices, though not explicitly stated, is implicit in the Community's Common Agricultural Policy. This is also true of the United Kingdom's deficiency payment system (which is being replaced by one of outright price support) and of the agricultural policies of other developed countries.

This decline, and frequent fluctuation, in the prices of agricultural and most other primary commodities under conditions of free competition is as characteristic of the international economy as of the

---

[1] The Agricultural Adjustment Act of 1933 declared that it was to be the policy of Congress to 'establish prices to farmers at a level that will give agricultural commodities a purchasing power with respect to articles that farmers buy, equivalent to the purchasing power of agricultural commodities in the base period'. For about a third of the commodities the base price was – and still is – the average of monthly prices over the 5 years between August 1909, and July 1914. For the other two-thirds, the base prices are averages of seasonal averages over various periods, namely, 1919–29 or some portion thereof, 1934–9, and 1936–41.

national. Yet apart from international agreements negotiated for a few commodities, and some other partial measures such as the compensatory credit system of the International Monetary Fund (aimed at compensating for some of the effects of price instability on the export earnings of developing countries),[1] this question has been ignored in international trade policy (see Section II below).

This situation clearly benefits the developed nations, for it means that they have a cheap supply of foodstuffs and industrial raw materials while selling relatively expensive manufactured products to the developing countries. They thus reap most of the benefits of the international division of labour. The transfer of resources from the developing to the developed countries which this situation implies has undeniably been an important factor in the economic development and accumulation of wealth by the latter.[2]

[1] Another very significant exception is the success of the members of the Organisation of Petroleum Exporting Countries (O.P.E.C.) in appreciably increasing their share of the benefits derived from the production and marketing of petroleum. While this is not strictly an exception to world trade policy as such (in the sense of a generally accepted set of principles and rules), it is an exception to the way world trade relations are normally conducted. Though reversing the usual situation of developing countries in world economic relations, it actually confirms the manner in which these relations become structured, and where the fundamental factor is *bargaining power.*

It should also be mentioned that the International Development Strategy for the Second United Nations Development Decade, adopted by the General Assembly in November, 1970, does include among its recommended policy measures on international trade a provision (paragraph 24) to the effect that before the Third UNCTAD an effort should be made to agree upon a set of general principles for a price fixing policy for primary products. One of the main objectives proposed for the policy was that it should guarantee stable, remunerative and equitable prices in order to increase the receipts from exports of primary products by developing countries. So far as is known, however, no action has yet been taken on this, even though it is already a year since the resolution on Strategy was adopted.

[2] The Comptroller-General of the United States, in his Report to Congress on *Foreign Aid Provided through the Operations of the United States Sugar Act and the International Coffee Agreement* of October 23, 1969, takes precisely the opposite position, claiming that as a consequence the United States (and, in the case of the Coffee Agreement, other developed countries) pay a higher price for imported sugar and coffee than they would on a free market, or if the Coffee Agreement did not exist. According to him, this implies a transfer of resources from the U.S. and from other developed countries to the developing nations from which these imports are derived. He estimates this 'transfer' at between $290 and $342 million annually for the period 1965–7 in the case of sugar, and at $314 million (1964–7 annual average) in the case of coffee imported by the U.S. The latter figure rises to $600 million if the other importing countries are included. In 1967 Latin America would have received about 63 per cent of the amount transferred in the case of sugar, and 66 per cent in the case of coffee. These transfers are, in the opinion of the Comptroller-General, a form of financial assistance given to the developing countries, and should be considered part of the regular

The low costs and prices characteristic of developing countries result not from high productivity but mainly from a superabundance of unskilled labour available at very low wages. Sometimes the developed countries object to a substantial increase in the world price of a primary commodity; this happened in the United States when coffee prices reached relatively high levels in 1954 and again in 1970. Nevertheless the fact that they benefit from the cheap labour of the developing nations does not prevent them, especially the United States, from imposing heavy restrictions against imports from 'low-wage' countries when these imports compete with domestic production. In justification, they invoke 'market disruption' or the need to protect their workers' standard of living against the 'unfair' competition of cheap foreign labour, that is, against what is now being called 'social dumping'.

Thus it is that developed countries preach free trade and competition, which they certainly practise – up to a point – so long as it does not seriously interfere with their interests. But when they find that free trade and competition from imports threaten some domestic economic activity, they seldom hesitate to protect it by whatever restrictions may be most effective (usually by non-tariff controls). This they do, regardless of how uneconomic the activity is, or how costly its protection may be for themselves or other countries, in terms of non-optimal resource utilisation at the domestic and international level.[1]

---

aid contributed by the U.S. As such, it would be subject to the same control by Congress (authorisation, control over its use, etc.).

The Comptroller-General's case is implicitly based on the assumption that free world market prices for commodities are 'just' and 'equitable', and that consequently higher prices imply a transfer of resources from the importing to the exporting country. But this assumption begs the whole question of what are 'equitable',and 'remunerative' prices for primary goods. Moreover, it questions the social and economic justifications for the agricultural policies of the U.S. and other countries, as well as the provision for the establishment of a price policy for primary products contained in the General Assembly's resolution on the International Development Strategy for the Second Decade. It also questions one of the basic objectives of international commodity agreements or of any other arrangement whose aim is to fix or raise prices above the free market level. The Comptroller-General's position with regard to the operation of the International Coffee Agreement should of course hold good for any similar arrangement.

[1] In his Report, *Inflation – The Present Problem* (December 1970), the O.E.C.D.'s Secretary General estimates that direct public expenditure by 11 O.E.C.D. countries in 1968 or 1968–9 in connection with their agricultural assistance policies amounted to $14 billion – about 1 per cent of their aggregate G.N.P. But this expenditure is only part of the total cost of agricultural protection. Another very important component is the cost to the consumer in the form of higher prices. Thus, in a report by a panel of experts on the *Future for European Agriculture* (The Atlantic Institute, Paper No. 4, 1970), the total cost to the E.E.C. countries of the Community's Common Agricultural Policy, during the latter part of the

The countries relatively most affected by such restrictions are usually the developing ones, since in the case of manufactures restrictions are heavier and more frequently imposed upon products of special interest to them – such as textiles, leather manufactures and other exports derived from relatively simple, labour-intensive industries in which the developing countries are more likely to enjoy a competitive advantage. Moreover, these industries are generally the first to develop in the process of industrialisation. For this reason they are the older, more traditional, less efficient and therefore less competitive industries in the developed countries. Consequently, such restrictions have become a rather common feature of world trade policy and are in fact 'legitimated' by the safeguard clauses and other provisions of GATT. They form a considerable obstacle to the development of manufactured exports from developing countries, and therefore to any change in the structure of world trade.

This situation seems particularly unjust in that the restrictions are in most cases applied as a consequence of problems caused by the rapid growth of imports, not from developing countries, but from other developed ones. Frequently, however, it is the exports of the former that are most affected. This is also the case with the restrictive trade measures adopted by developed countries as a result of other problems and conflicts of interest in their reciprocal economic relations (as, for example, with the measures taken by the United States in August 1971). Yet it is much more difficult for developing than for developed countries to adjust their exports of manufactures to new restrictions and other changes in international economic relations. This is because their exports are not sufficiently flexible, being relatively slight, often precarious, and with small profit margins. Also they are less well established than those from developed countries, and less capable of entering new markets.

In this connection it should be pointed out that as far as international trade policy is concerned the most serious obstacle to the development of manufactured exports from developing to developed countries generally lies not in the existing (usually tariff) restrictions on access to the latter's market but in the lack of continuity in the conditions of that access; in other words, in the modification of the *status quo* through the imposition of new, usually non-tariff (and

1960s, is estimated at between $11 and $13 billion. Of this figure about $5 billion represents net direct government expenditures in 1969–70, and $6 to $8 billion the cost to the consumers in the form of higher prices in 1967. The cost of industrial protection, though less obvious, is also very high. The above-mentioned Report by the O.E.C.D.'s Secretary General estimates that the total cost of non-optimal resource utilisation in the engineering sector alone exceeds $50 billion annually (direct government aid, the cost of indirect intervention, other forms of market protection and the resulting structural backwardness).

increasingly hidden) restrictions. This is a rather common occurrence – in spite of the legal and political commitments to the contrary which will be discussed below.

The developing countries' position in world trade has also deteriorated considerably as a result of the changes that have taken place in the structure of world trade relations and policies during the post-war period, particularly during the 1960s. These changes show little sign of abating; some of them – including several potentially very harmful to the long-term interests of the developing countries – threaten to become much more pronounced as a result of the enlargement of the E.E.C.

Changes that deserve special mention are: the declining importance of tariffs, and the increasing use of non-tariff restrictions, especially hidden, administrative ones; the expanding share of manufactures in world trade, with a corresponding decline in the relative importance of trade in basic commodities (while at the same time an increasing proportion – already well over 50 per cent – of the latter is carried on by the developed countries); the growing importance of multinational (or transnational) corporations both in world production and trade, and their growing influence on these areas, notably on the development of production and exports of manufactures in developing countries. The power and international scope of these corporations give them the means to evade or circumvent the norms, rules and regulations traditionally applied to international trade and financial transactions. However, the most significant and potentially the most harmful changes for the developing countries are those resulting from the proliferation of preferential trading areas or arrangements, particularly between developed and developing countries. The most glaring example of this is the association of Mediterranean and African countries with the E.E.C., now in the process of considerable expansion as one of the consequences of the enlargement of the Community; it may eventually include over fifty developing countries. But we may also seriously anticipate that in reaction to the preference system of the enlarged E.E.C., similar preferential trading areas may emerge between the United States and some Latin American countries, and between Japan and some Asian countries.

One important effect of the expansion of the preferential trading areas is the erosion of the most-favoured-nation principle – the cornerstone of GATT; much more significant, however, is the fact that this expansion is giving a decisive impetus to the process of regionalisation and verticalisation in trade and other economic relations between the developed and the developing countries. In other words it is crystallising the division of the world into spheres of influence, and leading inevitably to a much greater dependence on the part of the developing nations.

Another fundamental change in the structure of world economic relations, closely associated with the process mentioned above, is the formation and expansion of the European Economic Community itself. Once the present enlargement is completed, this will represent over 40 per cent of world trade (nearly 50 per cent for the free-trade zone in industrial products being negotiated with non-candidate EFTA countries, which, through the existing association of other European countries with the Community, will cover virtually the whole of Western Europe). The economic power of the enlarged Community will thus be greatly magnified, so that it will be in a position to play a dominant role in world trade relations and policy. In fact, there will be a far greater concentration and polarisation of world trade and economic power in just three major economic centres: the United States, the enlarged E.E.C., and Japan.

AID AS A MEANS OF REDRESSING THE BALANCE

It could be argued that the unequal situation we have here described is, to some extent, redressed by development assistance aid, a post-war phenomenon which came into its own during the second part of the 1950s, and which is usually presented as constituting a large-scale transfer of resources from the rich to the poor countries, in order to promote the modernisation and economic development of the latter.

The key question, however, is: to what extent does this 'aid' genuinely result in a permanent and effective transfer of resources? To what extent, in fact, can it legitimately be considered as aid? This in turn depends upon the extent to which its basic purpose is really to assist the economic development of the recipient country rather than serve the economic, political or military interests of the donor. Of course, there is no reason why 'aid' should not serve these interests too; but they should be by-products, rather than primary objectives.

Thus foreign private investments cannot be considered as aid, since no matter how much they may contribute to the country's economic development, their basic motivation is simply to make a profit, and the investment would certainly not be made unless there was a reasonable expectation of doing so. Furthermore private investments are never considered aid when they are made in another developed country, even though they normally contribute to that country's economic development.

The same considerations apply to private credit and loans (such as suppliers' credit) to developing countries, and to a substantial portion of public or government 'aid', especially bilateral aid. Much of this is really just export or supplier's credit; it is, in fact, one of the principal instruments of export promotion (as, for example, export financing by the Eximbank). Sometimes, it may even be very costly for the recipient countries, as in the case of the tied loans made by A.I.D. (At least this was so until the requirement of 'additionality' was discontinued in 1969. This requirement, plus several others normally applied in A.I.D. loans to Latin America, increased the cost of the goods bought with these loans by about 30 per cent.) In other cases, development aid is politically motivated, and has considerable political implications for the recipient country.

In conclusion: development assistance aid results in an effective transfer of resources only in the case of grants, donations, non-repayable loans, untied bilateral loans and loans from international or regional financial institutions, in so far as these are given under more favourable conditions than could be obtained in the international financial markets.[1]

THE ROLE OF DOMESTIC POLICY

We are forced to conclude then that world trade policy and the structure of international economic relations, far from taking sufficient account of the interests of the developing countries, are heavily weighted in favour of the interests of the developed ones. Many of their features have a negative effect on the economic problems which beset most of them in their external sector. This is not to imply, however, that these problems are exclusively or even mainly due to such external factors, or that the developing countries bear no part of the blame for them. On the contrary, the problems are very much the responsibility of these countries themselves, especially in the case of the larger and more industrialised nations, since they are a consequence of the very inadequate, and at times irrational, internal economic policies pursued by them, particularly in their policies of industrialisation. The excessive emphasis placed on industrialisation at all costs, based on indiscriminate import substitution through rather extreme and irrational protectionist policies with a heavy anti-export bias, together with very inadequate foreign trade

[1] Concerning the rationale of development assistance, see John Pincus, *Trade, Aid and Development: The Rich and Poor Nations* (McGraw-Hill, 1967), particularly pp. 13–14; and Robert Asher, *Development Assistance in the Seventies – Alternatives for the United States* (The Brookings Institution, Washington, D.C., 1970). See also Patricia Blair, 'The Dimensions of Poverty' in *International Organization* Vol. 23 (summer 1969), on the humanitarian or ethical considerations of such assistance.

policies, are the main reasons why these countries have, with few exceptions, been incapable of developing substantial exports of manufactures. In some cases, they have not even been able to maintain their traditional exports, either because of supply problems, or because of an inability to adapt to the changing conditions of world markets and trade.

Thus, the majority of developing countries (and this is particularly true for most of Latin America) lack any systematic, integrated, and coherent foreign trade policy responding to rationally defined objectives in the context of a properly programmed policy of economic development. Their trade policies are short-term, and non-autonomous, generally consisting of isolated measures adopted in response to short-term considerations and to the usually powerful vested interests of the export sector. The chief preoccupation of any long-term trade policy is usually the defence of traditional exports to traditional markets. Moreover, it is a passive policy, lacking flexibility and unable to adapt to the changing conditions of world trade relations. Inadequate both in formulation and implementation, an important feature of it is normally the maintenance of highly unrealistic exchange rates which are grossly overvalued as far as the export of manufactures is concerned.

The best evidence for the validity of these assertions is provided by those few developing countries which have adopted a development strategy based on export-oriented industries, with a systematic, integral, coherent and well-co-ordinated set of measures both at the internal and at the external levels; for these are the ones that have been able to develop a substantial and rapidly growing export of manufactures. The most eloquent and successful example of this in Latin America is Brazil.

II. THE PRINCIPLES AND RULES FOR WORLD TRADE RELATIONS IN THE POST-WAR PERIOD: THE ROLE OF GATT AND UNCTAD[1]

(i) THE ROLE OF GATT

The principles and rules that have regulated world trade relations during the post-war period are primarily those embodied in the General Agreement on Tariffs and Trade (GATT), a legal code of 'good conduct' drawn up in October, 1947. In order to apply these measures pending the ratification of the Havana Charter, the code was put into effect in the form of the Protocol of Provisional Applica-

---

[1] The following two sections were added after the Conference, and will be expanded in a forthcoming article.

tion[1] which incorporated many of the commercial policy provisions of the draft charter of the International Trade Organisations as well as most of the amendments referring to trade policy added to that draft charter at the 1948 Havana Conference. The charter itself was never ratified because of the United States' refusal to do so, and the General Agreement continued to fulfil on a 'provisional' basis the trade policy role that had been assigned to the ITO.[2]

The basic principles and rules included in GATT responded primarily to the interests and position of the United States. At the end of the 1940s, the United States had an almost total hegemony in world trade, and thus benefited from this trade being free and non-discriminatory, as, to a lesser extent, did the other main trading countries of the time, particularly the United Kingdom. Thus the two fundamental principles of GATT are precisely those of the most-favoured nation and non-discrimination, with the tariff as the only 'normal' import restriction. Quantitative and other non-tariff restrictions are prohibited, except temporarily in case of balance of payments difficulties. On the other hand, in its original form and for most of its life, the GATT incorporated practically none of the few provisions of the Havana Charter (such as those on international commodity agreements)[3] which took account of the special situation and problems of the less developed countries.

Furthermore, the basic principles and rules were subject to exceptions that also reflected primarily the interests of the United States and the other original signatories of the Protocol of Provisional Application. Thus, the same Article I that established the most-

[1] Signed originally by the United States, Canada, the United Kingdom, France, Belgium, the Netherlands, Luxembourg and Australia.

[2] This provisional application is one of the main weaknesses of the GATT. On this subject, and more generally for a legal analysis of the General Agreement, see K. W. Dam, *The GATT Law and International Economic Organization* (The University of Chicago Press, 1970), and J. H. Jackson, *International Trade and the Law of GATT; a Legal Analysis of the General Agreement on Tariffs and Trade* (Indianapolis, 1969).

[3] As stated above, the General Agreement included most of the trade policy measures of the Havana Charter, but not its substantive chapters dealing with 'Employment and Economic Activity', 'Economic Development and Reconstruction', 'Restrictive Business Practices' and 'Inter-Governmental Commodity Agreements', nor any of the Charter's organisational or procedural provisions. It should be remembered that, as Dam says (*op. cit.*), 'The GATT can trace its origin to the work of a number of United States Department officials during World War II' and 'it contains most of the provisions on commercial policy supported in the 1940s by United States Department of State Officials. The General Agreement is therefore a sufficiently direct expression of United States views on the appropriate form of concerted international action in the commercial policy area that it cannot be understood without an examination of those views.' (pp. 10 and 12).

favoured nation principle includes exceptions in favour of the preferential systems in force in 1947, such as those of the Common-wealth, the French Union, the Benelux countries with their dependent territories, and those between the United States and Cuba and the Philippines. Similarly, an exception is made to the rule against the use of quantitative restrictions (Article XI) in order to permit the United States to continue to support domestic agricultural prices at higher than world market levels. The 1955 reform later complemented this by excepting primary products from the prohibition against direct or indirect export subsidies that would result in export prices lower than the price charged to domestic consumers (Article XVI, Section B). In other words, these subsidies are permissible in the case of exports of primary products. These articles constitute the 'legal' basis, in terms of the GATT rules, for the agricultural protectionist policies of most developed countries, and for their export of heavily subsidised agricultural surpluses.[1]

It should also be pointed out that in addition open or disguised violations by the developed countries of many basic GATT pro-visions are becoming increasingly frequent. For example, in the case of the escape or safeguard clause of Article XIX which allows emergency action on imports in cases of 'market disruption' the procedure for such emergency action provided in the same article is very seldom, if ever, complied with. Also frequently abused by the United States, and even more so by the European Economic Com-munity, are the exceptions contained in Article XI mentioned above, in favour of agricultural production and exports; another case is the subsidisation of exports of non-primary products such as synthetic fertilisers.

Perhaps the most significant violation occurred during the late 1940s and early 1950s, when the United States Congress refused to comply with the GATT provisions on agriculture by approving modifications to Section II of the Agricultural Adjustment Act according to which the President of the United States had to impose higher duties or quantitative restrictions on imports of agricultural products if such action was required in order to implement the Act. In this section, it was further laid down that no trade agreement or other international agreement in which the United States participated could be applied in a manner inconsistent with the provisions of that section. To regularise the situation, the United States requested, in

---

[1] This exception suits the cost and price structure of developed countries, reflecting the relative efficiency of primary *v.* manufacturing production; but developing countries have an opposite price structure (i.e. their industrial production is less efficient than that of primary products). They would thus need to be allowed to subsidise exports of manufactures.

1955, a waiver authorising it to apply the provisions of her Agricultural Adjustment Act; and the Contracting Parties had no alternative but to grant it, in order to end a flagrant violation of GATT, thus giving the United States ample freedom to protect its agriculture. This privileged situation made other large countries unwilling to comply with GATT provisions on trade in agricultural products. This has been the major obstacle to the liberalisation of such trade, as was the case in the Kennedy Round, in spite of this having been a declared objective of these negotiations.

Until the new Part IV was incorporated in 1965, the only GATT provisions specifically related to the special problems of developing countries in international trade were those of Article XVIII, on 'Governmental Assistance to Economic Development'. Here the contracting parties recognise that it may be necessary for less developed members 'in order to implement programmes and policies of economic development designed to raise the general standard of living of their people, to take protective or other measures affecting imports, and that such measures are justified in so far as they facilitate the attainment of the objectives of this Agreement', and that they

> should enjoy additional facilities to enable them (a) to maintain sufficient flexibility in their tariff structure to be able to grant the tariff protection required for the establishment of a particular industry and (b) to apply quantitative restrictions for balance of payments purposes in a manner which takes full account of the continued high level of demand for imports likely to be generated by their programmes of economic development.[1]

However, the 'additional facilities' here mentioned are limited in scope. First, they concern only import restrictions imposed for protectionist or balance of payments purposes, and secondly, they do not go much further than the measures available to any contracting party, whether developing or developed: increases in duties for protective reasons, subject to negotiations with other contracting parties when the increase affects an already existing concession (see, *inter alia*, Articles XIX and XXVIII), and recourse to quantitative restrictions to safeguard the balance of payments, as provided under Article XII. In fact, the 'additional facilities' consist mainly in the following. First, somewhat more liberal procedures are established, at the same time as a more sympathetic and expeditious application

---

[1] In paragraph 8 of Article XVIII the contracting parties recognised that developing countries 'tend, when they are in rapid process of development, to experience balance of payments difficulties arising mainly from efforts to expand their internal markets as well as from the instability in their terms of trade' – a limited but significant admission in the light of views then generally held, as will shortly be seen.

of such procedures is looked for. Second, developing countries may have recourse to protectionist measures not consistent with other provisions of the General Agreement when none of these suffices (but subject to a process of prior notification and to a waiting period in addition to negotiations with other contracting parties if a modification or withdrawal of concessions is involved). Third, they may restrict imports for balance of payments reasons not only in order to safeguard their external financial position, but also 'to ensure a level of reserves adequate for the implementation of [their] programme(s) of economic development'.[1]

It must nevertheless be acknowledged that the provisions of Article XVIII have been applied quite liberally, since in practically all cases the requests made under them by the developing countries (including several Latin American ones) have been readily granted. In fact, such countries have in general been allowed to do very much as they please concerning the use of tariff and non-tariff restrictions on imports for protectionist or balance of payments purposes. Further, those provisions, however limited in scope, do constitute significant departures from the conventional theory of international trade on which the General Agreement – as well as the Havana Charter – was mainly based. Moreover, the resolution adopted by the U.N. Economic and Social Council at its first meeting (February 1946) calling for an International Conference on Trade and Employment (the Havana Conference) included, among the topics it suggested as a basis for the work of the Preparatory Committee established to elaborate an annotated draft agenda and a draft convention for the Conference, 'the need to take into account the special conditions which prevail in countries whose manufacturing industry is still in its initial stages of development'. However, at that time no adequate appreciation existed of what those special conditions were or of their implications – or, consequently, of the special measures needed. As for the developing countries, they were still far from having defined their aspirations or articulated their position, and their demands for special treatment did not go much further than that provided by Article XVIII. Thus, at the meetings of the Preparatory Committee several developing countries, notably Brazil and Chile, pressed for some general exceptions for such countries to the most favoured nation treatment, but what they were referring to were

[1] In paragraph 3 of Article XVIII it is stated that 'the contracting parties finally recognize that, with those additional facilities which are provided for in Sections A and B of this Article, the provisions of this Agreement would normally be sufficient to enable contracting parties to meet the requirements of their economic development', some special procedures being laid down in Sections C and D to deal with exceptional cases. In the light of subsequent developments, this affirmation appears a rather extreme example of wishful thinking.

mainly exceptions that would allow new preferences between neighbouring developing countries.

The situation evolved very significantly during the 1950s, as a result both of the pioneering work done by some economists (particularly Prebisch in ECLA from 1948 on), and of the trends in international trade, which laid bare the inadequacies both of conventional trade theory and of the trade policy embodied in the GATT provisions. The contracting parties of GATT became increasingly concerned with certain of those trends, particularly with the failure of the exports of developing countries to expand at a rate commensurate with their growing import needs, with the instability in the prices of primary products and therefore in the export earnings of primary producers and with the prevalence of agricultural protectionism; this led to the appointment, at the Twelfth Session of the Contracting Parties (November 1957) of a Panel of Experts to carry out 'an expert examination of past and current international trade trends and their implications', with special reference to the factors referred to above.

The Report of the Panel, *Trends in International Trade* (also known as the Haberler Report) published in October 1958, had as one of its main conclusions the acknowledgement that 'the present rules and conventions about commercial policy are relatively unfavourable' to primary producing countries. This constituted a turning point in the history of the GATT, initiating a process of reorientation which, stimulated by the activities of UNCTAD, culminated in the addition in 1965 of a new Part IV, on 'Trade and Development', to the text of the General Agreement.

This Part IV is, to a large extent, complementary to Article XVIII: this had dealt with the special needs of developing countries concerning restrictions on imports, while Part IV gives ample recognition to the particular export problems of those countries as well as to the vital part that export earnings play in their economic development. Thus, it acknowledges the need

to provide in the largest possible measure more favourable and acceptable conditions of access to world markets for [primary] products, and whenever appropriate to devise measures designed to stabilise and improve conditions of world markets in these products, including in particular measures designed to attain stable, equitable and remunerative prices, thus permitting an expansion of world trade and demand and a dynamic and steady growth of the real export earnings of these countries so as to provide them with expanding resources for their economic development, as well as the 'need for increased access in the largest possible measure to markets under favourable conditions for processed and manufactured products currently or potentially of particular export interest to less developed contracting parties', in order to promote the diversification of the structure of their economies and avoid their excessive dependence on the exports of primary products (paragraph 4 and 5 of Article XXXVI).

Unfortunately, the provisions contained in Part IV are not commensurate with the needs we have outlined above or with other principles and objectives stated in Article XXXVI. In Article XXXVII the developed contracting parties commit themselves to

(a) accord high priority to the reduction and elimination of barriers to products currently or potentially of particular export interest to less-developed contracting parties, including customs duties and other restrictions which differentiate unreasonably between such products in their primary and in their processed forms; (b) refrain from introducing, or increasing the incidence of, customs duties or non-tariff import barriers on [such products]; and (c) (i) refrain from imposing new fiscal measures, and (ii) in any adjustments of fiscal policy accord high priority to the reduction and elimination of fiscal measures, which would hamper, or which hamper, significantly the growth of consumption of primary products, in raw or processed form, wholly or mainly produced in the territories of less-developed contracting parties, and which are applied specifically to those products.

But these are far from being firm commitments. For one thing, their implementation is in no sense obligatory, since all the developed countries have agreed to is to give effect to them 'to the fullest extent possible – that is, except when compelling reasons, which may include legal reasons, make it impossible'. The conditions under which recourse to such a vague, all-embracing escape clause would be justified appear almost impossible to ascertain. Secondly, nothing is said as to when or by how much the barriers to trade or internal taxes would be reduced; in other words, there are no specific targets or action programmes, so that even without the above-mentioned reservation it appears impossible to enforce, legally or otherwise, the effective implementation of the provisions.

The implementation of provision (b) above, the 'commitment to maintain the *status quo*' or 'standstill', is particularly affected by the overall escape clause, which in this case operates through the most important escape clause of the General Agreement, that of Article XIX, providing for 'emergency action on imports of particular products', and which authorises a contracting party to suspend in whole or in part obligations incurred under the Agreement or to withdraw or modify concessions in respect of any product, the imports of which have increased or take place under such conditions as to cause or threaten to cause serious injury to domestic producers of like or directly competitive products – a situation commonly characterised as 'market disruption'.

This escape clause has a far-reaching character, for its use is subjected to only minor conditions: that the market disruption problems should be caused by the increase in the quantity or other features of imports of the product in question; that the emergency action on those imports should be taken only to the extent and for such time as may be necessary to prevent or remedy the injury, and that consultations should be held among the interested contracting parties. But even these minor conditions have been increasingly disregarded by some developed countries – particularly the United States – which have invoked this escape clause to protect domestic industries from external competition even when imports have little or nothing to do with the problems that those industries face (as, for instance, when imports represent a very minor share of total domestic consumption), and the origin of those problems is to be found mainly in domestic problems, or when it is only a few marginal firms that are injured or threatened. Furthermore, the emergency action is taken without seriously attempting to limit its extent and duration (the restrictions often becoming a permanent fixture) or putting sufficient emphasis on domestic adjustment measures. Moreover in most cases the industries on behalf of which the emergency action[1] is taken are labour-intensive and traditional, such as textiles, shoes and other leather manufactures – that is, precisely the ones most likely to be first established in the developing countries and to be at a point where exports are a possibility.

The use of this escape clause, and the lack of any means of adequately controlling its use, as well as the indiscriminate application of the restrictive measures to imports from developing countries even when, as in most cases, such imports have not contributed significantly to the market disruption situation,[2] render inoperative the 'standstill' commitment of Article XXXVII. For reasons which have been explained before (see page 64 above), this lack of continuity in access is particularly harmful to the export of manufac-

---

[1] Such restrictions may take the form of the imposition of 'voluntary' limitations on exports – an increasingly common practice on the part of the United States.

[2] A similar situation arises when the import restrictions are applied for balance of payments problems, as was the case with the import surcharge introduced by the United States in August 1971.

tures from developing countries. In fact, the effective implementation of that commitment would be much more significant as a measure to promote such exports than the reduction or elimination of existing duties and other import restrictions on those products by developed countries, since for most of these the level of the duties is relatively low, and non-tariff restrictions are seldom used – the main exceptions being usually the restrictions imposed under 'market disruption'.

It is true that this Article also establishes a consultation procedure, to be followed whenever any interested contracting party considers that effect is not being given to any of the above-mentioned provisions. But even though it must be recognised that the developing contracting parties have not really tried to make effective use of such procedure, it is doubtful whether it would yield significant results, for the final judge of whether a developed country has complied with the provisions of that Article 'to the fullest extent possible' is this country itself. In fact, as indicated above the absence of specific targets or action programmes makes any effective periodical evaluation an impossible task, since it would require an examination product by product, country by country, to ascertain whether each developed country has actually reduced duties and internal taxes 'to the fullest extent possible'. Thus although the Trade and Development Committee of GATT undertakes periodical examination of the implementation of Part IV of the Agreement, the elements for this examination go no further than presenting a list or inventory of the reduction in duties (and, very seldom, of internal taxes) made by different developed contracting parties in favour of the above-mentioned products, and the evaluation is limited to some general complaints on the part of the developing countries to the effect that the commitments are not being complied with adequately, and counterclaims on the part of the developed countries insisting they have done as much as they could.

Consequently, although Article XXXVII is entitled 'Commitments', its provisions concerning the actions which the developed countries have agreed to undertake in favour of the developing countries do not constitute real commitments except in a general political sense; they are in fact nothing more than declarations of intent. This is precisely how the developed countries view them, for in spite of the contractual character of the General Agreement they deny that such provisions are legally binding. This much, furthermore, seems to be implied by the last paragraph of Article XXXVI, in which it is stated that 'the adoption of measures to give effect to [the principle and objectives listed in this Article] shall be a matter of conscious and purposeful effort on the part of the contracting parties both individually and jointly'.

Another very important field in which, according to the provisions of Part IV, the contracting parties should have acted but have done practically nothing so far concerns the prices of primary products in world markets, which we discussed above (see pages 60–3). Although there are no 'commitments' in Part IV concerning this question, it is included among those on which the contracting parties have agreed to take joint action (paragraph 2(a) of Article XXXVIII). But the developed countries have strongly refused even to consider seriously any proposal to implement this provision, the 'conscious and purposeful effort' on their part having gone no further than the acceptance of some price stabilisation measures in the context of the international agreements adopted for a very few products – coffee, tin, sugar – this last, however, without the participation of the European Community. One of the main obstacles to the conclusion of an agreement on cocoa has been the United States' insistence that the price should be stabilised within a range a few cents below that proposed by the producing countries. As for the international wheat agreement, all the provisions in it which concerned price stabilisation were eliminated when it was last renegotiated.

Up to now, the only provision of Part IV that has in fact been implemented[1] is that of paragraph 8 of Article XXXIV, which states that 'the developed contracting parties do not expect reciprocity for commitments made by them in trade negotiations to reduce or remove tariffs and other barriers to the trade of less-developed contracting parties'. According to the complementary notes, this means that developing countries 'should not be expected, in the course of trade negotiations, to make contributions that are inconsistent with their individual development, financial and trade needs, taking into consideration past trade developments'.

This provision embodies the so-called 'principle of non-reciprocity' – at least partially, under the form of 'relative reciprocity'. In fact it has been applied more liberally than the scope of its wording, since the developed countries have not, in general, demanded any reciprocity for concessions they have granted or extended to the developing ones. On the other hand, however, there have not so far been many such concessions – except under the system of generalised preferences; that is, not much has been done by the developed

---

[1] The establishment by a number of developed countries (the main exception being so far the United States) of a system of generalised preferences for manufactures and semi-manufactures from developing countries does not constitute, except in a loose sense, an application of the provision concerning the reduction and elimination of barriers to the trade of products of particular export interest to these countries; since under this system duties (but not other import restrictions) are totally or partially suspended only temporarily, often within a quota.

countries to make the principle of non-reciprocity relevant.

This analysis leads to the conclusion that for all the recognition given in GATT to the special trade and development problems of the developing countries, the results obtained so far have been disappointing, commensurate with neither the effort nor the expectations of those involved. A major reason has been that the developed countries with few exceptions have acted only marginally and sporadically on the different measures to which they are committed, refusing to accept commitments concrete enough to ensure the effective implementation of measures they were willing to agree to in principle. Meanwhile the position of the developing countries in world trade and other aspects of the world economy has continued to deteriorate.

This situation largely reflects the fact that the special provisions in favour of the developing countries added to the General Agreement have not substantially modified its nature and operation; since even with such provisions, the principles and rules embodied in this Agreement, and particularly the procedures established to enforce or put them into effect, are still far from satisfactorily remedying the main failure of the GATT (at least from the point of view of those countries): the failure to compensate adequately for the substantial difference between the bargaining power of the developed and of the developing contracting parties.

Given such inequality, the main objective of the 'law' of international trade cannot be merely the orderly conduct of trade relations, but rather the establishment of a just order. To achieve this, its principles, rules and procedures must be such as to offset the imbalance in bargaining power which we have described as well as compensating for the other factors examined above which, under the free working of market forces, put the primary exporting countries at a great disadvantage. In the last analysis, this would mean applying to international economic relations very much the same economic and social principles as are applied domestically by most industrialised countries – particularly in respect of their own farmers and other primary producers.

Thus the GATT, being basically a negotiating forum, should ideally be structured in such a way that the result of negotiations did not depend, as it does now, on the bargaining power of the contracting parties. On the contrary, the negotiating process should be made independent of this factor, by subjecting it to appropriate pre-established fixed principles and rules.

(ii) THE CONTRIBUTION OF UNCTAD

The United Nations Conference on Trade and Development, held in Geneva in 1964, represents the most significant effort made so far to deal with the problems of the developing nations by evolving a better system of international economic co-operation. 'UNCTAD' was subsequently given permanent status as an organ of the General Assembly of the United Nations, with the functions of promoting international trade, formulating principles and policies on this and related fields and making proposals for their implementation, with a view to accelerating the economic development of the developing countries.

Since the Conference as such meets only every four years (New Delhi, 1968 and Santiago, Chile, April–May 1972) its functions are performed in the interim by the Trade and Development Board, a permanent organ of the Conference which meets twice a year.

UNCTAD has undoubtedly made a most valuable and decisive contribution – particularly at its first session – to the identification of the problems affecting the trade of developing countries, as to the principles that should govern world trade relations and the specific measures which could contribute to effective solutions. Unfortunately, the practical achievements of the Conference, while a little less meagre than those of GATT, have still fallen far short both of needs and of expectations. In particular, almost none of the excellent recommendations adopted at UNCTAD I, and in part reiterated in New Delhi,[1] have been reflected in systematic action on the part of the developed countries. Some measures have been adopted – such as reducing duties on a few products of special export interest to developing countries – but these have been isolated cases, usually concerning products of minor importance, or being merely the by-product of concessions negotiated among developed countries in their own interest.

The fundamental point is that such measures as may have been adopted represent only quantitative, not qualitative changes, and that they do not add up to any substantial modification in the structure of international economic relations. Indeed, as we have seen, this structure has become even less favourable to the interests of the developing countries. In short, the basic objectives of UNCTAD are still very much in the realm of aspirations.

---

[1] Concerning, for example, a wide range of measures to be adopted by the developed countries in favour of primary and manufactured products of special export interest to the developing countries, and measures on commodity agreements, on the gradual abolition of discriminatory preferential agreements, on subsidies to exports, guidelines for international financial co-operation, and so on.

THE ATTITUDE OF THE DEVELOPING COUNTRIES

In reviewing the reasons for the relative ineffectiveness of UNCTAD, it must first be made clear that the developing countries themselves do not act in a manner conducive to an efficient utilisation either of its periodic sessions or its permanent machinery.

Thus for example, it became clear during the preparatory sessions preceding UNCTAD II that serious concern was felt over the unsatisfactory progress made in implementing recommendations already adopted, and that the next session should be 'action-oriented', adopting a selective agenda so as to concentrate its attention on a limited number of fundamental and specific subjects, in order to arrive at practical concrete measures which might be effectively implemented. Yet for all this these 'basic objectives' were soon diluted by the addition of many which were much less concrete, while individual countries would insist on the inclusion of some particular question in their own interest, regardless of its relative importance or feasibility. Consequently, the Conference found itself with a hopelessly overburdened agenda, within which an assignation of priorities could not even be attempted. In the event, very little attention was given to the means for the effective implementation of the recommendations adopted in UNCTAD I. And furthermore, despite the pre-Conference meetings and the adoption of the Charter of Algiers, more time was spent by the developing countries in negotiating among themselves at the Conference than in negotiating with the developed countries.[1]

This last fact reflects in part the danger of the piecemeal approach which UNCTAD has so far adopted. The more specific is each proposal, and the more proposals there are, the more difficult is the reconciliation of divergent interests, while since each proposal is dealt with individually the possibility of reconciling conflicts by means of integrated solutions is greatly diminished. The developed countries are able to deal with each issue separately from the general 'political' or 'moral' commitments they have subscribed to. Their bargaining position is thus strengthened.

To explain the developing countries' inability to act in a more effective manner, not only in UNCTAD but in their international economic relations in general, we must look to their level of economic

[1] For a valuable and frank evaluation of UNCTAD and the UNCTAD machinery, see the report by the former Secretary General of UNCTAD, Raúl Prebisch, 'The Significance of the Second Session of the United Nations Conference on Trade and Development' (TD/96/Rev. 1., New York, 1968). It is most regrettable that this report was never given adequate consideration by the governments involved.

development. Underdevelopment is both the cause and the result of a relative lack of officials with adequate expertise and continuity in office. It is also, most importantly, as we have said above, character- ised by a limited capacity to focus on medium- and long-term objectives, and thereby put into perspective and face up to, in particular, the vested interests of the producers and exporters of traditional export products.

It is precisely such vested interests, and the link of those interests to specific developed countries, that lie at the root of most of the conflicts between the developing countries themselves within UNCTAD. The influence of these groups is such that they are typically able to determine the course of trade policy, or at least are able to oppose any compromise harmful to their interests but without which no long-term solution to these conflicts is possible.

This situation is closely related to another fundamental factor which conditions the attitudes of the developing countries in UNCTAD and elsewhere: their economic dependence on the indus- trialised countries. The structure of external economic relations is built around such dependence and assumes its continuity, while conversely the maintenance of the situation of external dependence is an essential requisite for the continuation of the *status quo* and the protection of vested interests.

As long as such interests have a predominant influence in the trade policy of the developing countries, it is most unlikely that they will seriously tackle, in UNCTAD or elsewhere, the fundamental defects of the structure of international economic relations. They are happy to reiterate complaints and submit endless joint declarations and proposals for action – but lack the will power to go beyond and engage in a systematic action to get recommendations effectively implemented.

THE ATTITUDE OF THE DEVELOPED COUNTRIES

We have dealt first with the responsibility of the developing countries for the meagre results which UNCTAD has so far produced, on the grounds that these are the countries most interested in its successful operation. But in the last analysis it is the position of the developed countries that is the decisive factor. Without a sufficiently flexible position on their part, it is most unlikely that UNCTAD could produce substantially better results even if the other shortcomings we have discussed could be overcome. It is in this sense that if we are to single out one factor as that mainly responsible for the unsatisfactory progress to date in evolving a more effective system of international economic co-operation, we should look to the attitude of the developed countries. This position, at both UNCTAD I and II (as in practically all similar occasions), has been in striking contrast to the moral, political and even legal commitments they have appeared to accept.[1] In practice at UNCTAD I and II they showed themselves unwilling to make any but the most minimal concessions. Any text involving precise commitments was smothered with reservations and subjected to generous safeguard clauses. Their position, especially in UNCTAD II, was characterised by a lack of flexibility, springing, as Prebisch argued in the Report mentioned above, from the 'group system' which characterises the functioning of UNCTAD.[2]

The developed countries usually account for their predominantly negative position by referring to special difficulties in the international monetary system, or to an unfavourable domestic situation, or to the impossibility of agreeing on burden sharing, or in the case of the E.E.C. to the limitations on community action while that community is still incompletely formed. Further, they tend to argue that some other forum, such as GATT or the I.M.F., is more appropriate than UNCTAD for dealing with some specific issue. But while there are certainly limitations at a particular moment on what the developed countries can accept, the fundamental explanation of their unwillingness to give effect to more than a bare minimum of concessions is to be found elsewhere. Basically, the problem is one of political will. In spite of all the declarations made, public opinion in the major industrial countries is not sufficiently informed or conscious of the problems faced by the developing countries, or of the key role the developed countries would have to play in their resolution.[3]

---

[1] See, for instance, the comments made above concerning the application of the provisions of Part IV of GATT.

[2] Prebisch, *op. cit.*, p. 12. He points out here some of the major shortcomings of this system – in particular the use of unanimous group decision in an attempt to strengthen solidarity. 'The result was obvious: the group of developed countries tended to agree, in response to the requests of the developing countries, on the lowest common denominator. The dynamic drive of some delegations of the developed countries . . . was thus lost. As for the group of developing countries, frequently it had to agree to the maximum demands of some of its members. And in these attempts to arrive at full unanimity, it was enough that one or a few countries inside the group had a dissenting attitude to unduly delay or even paralyse not only the decisions of the group but also the progress of the whole Conference.' He adds: 'Another shortcoming concerns the ability to negotiate. In addition to the large membership of negotiating bodies, group discipline often may have prevented useful inter-group communications among representatives whose experience and knowledge could have facilitated in proper time the search for compromise agreements.'

[3] See Prebisch, *op. cit.*, p. 1. Also, on this and other factors behind the ineffectiveness of UNCTAD, see J. S. Nye, 'La UNCTAD bajo Prebisch: la estructura de influencia', *Foro Internacional*, Vol. XII, no. 3, El Colegio de México. (Reprinted in R. Cox and H. Jacobson, *The Anatomy of Influence* (New Haven, Yale University Press, 1971).)

While these comments are broadly applicable to all, there are of course differences among developed countries. Among the developed market economies it is typically the larger and more advanced (the U.S., the E.E.C., Japan and, to a lesser extent, the U.K.) that are least willing to commit themselves – despite their apparently greater capacity, in terms of wealth. Precisely because of their great economic and political power, which entails wide interests and significant influence, their governments are subjected to much greater demands and pressures than those of other countries, from both internal and external sources. Whereas the smaller countries (Scandinavia, Holland, to a lesser extent Belgium and Austria), whose governments are not subjected to so many powerful pressures and where public opinion is both proportionately better informed and more effective (being closer to the decision centres), show in general a more positive attitude and greater readiness to act.

More specifically, the relatively negative attitude we find characteristic of the developed countries appears to spring from a number of factors, of which two appear of particular significance. First, the more powerful developed countries wish to remain masters of their potential concessions, in order to use them subsequently as instruments of pressure and negotiation.[1] Second, a serious obstacle to a more favourable attitude arises from the threat to employment in specific industries implied by increased imports – or rather, from the failure of the developed countries to take adequate measures to facilitate the process of adaptation. Only Canada and the United States have gone so far as to adopt programmes of adjustment assistance linked to imports. But even these measures are still far from adequate.

III. CONCLUDING REMARKS AND SUGGESTIONS

As we have seen in the preceding pages, when either GATT or UNCTAD is assessed in terms of its efficacy in fulfilling the main functions assigned to it, the conclusions are inescapably discouraging, since more than a decade of action in the fields of trade and development assistance has produced very limited results. We have stressed that the few measures of any importance adopted have been quantitative rather than qualitative, with minor exceptions,[2] and do not add up to a substantive change in the desired direction. They have

[1] This became particularly clear in UNCTAD III, as is described in the post-script to this chapter.

[2] For example the acceptance by the developed countries (in practice rather than formally) of the principles of non-reciprocity and of preferential treatment in regard to the developing countries.

not even been enough to compensate for the adverse effect on the developing countries of the unfavourable trends in world trade policy of recent years and the changing structure of international economic relations. Thus as we have seen the net result has been a further deterioration in the position of the developing countries, and in particular a substantial evolution in centre-periphery relations, with an increasing satellisation of the developing countries around the four main poles: the United States, the E.E.C., Japan and the Soviet Union (though in the case of the latter with a somewhat different structure).

However, this evaluation should not be assumed to lead to the conclusion that all such efforts at restructuring world trade relations are of no avail. On the contrary, the intention is a positive one. First, it is urgent to dispel the dangerous complacency which appears prevalent regarding particularly the evaluation of each succeeding session of UNCTAD. And second, and most important, the fundamental objective of the analysis is to stimulate a more purposeful search for a more effective approach.

Along what lines, then, should a more adequate approach be sought? We have stressed repeatedly in the above pages that in the last analysis the problem is one of pressure, that is, of bargaining power. The fundamental question, then, becomes how to modify sufficiently the unequal power relation. The accomplishment of this has to be primarily the task of the developing countries themselves; unfortunately, it is a task that is far from easy to carry out, particularly since it demands a profound change in the manner in which these countries usually formulate and implement their policies.[1]

Thus, the most obvious way in which the developing countries could substantially increase their bargaining power is by effective joint action, aimed basically at *en bloc* negotiations over markets and natural resources. Such action would require, of course, that they should first obtain real control over their resources – in which respect as well joint action would be essential. Should they succeed, they could proceed, as the O.P.E.C. countries have done, to negotiate substantially more favourable terms on access to markets, prices, participation in profits. They would also be in a position to retaliate effectively against developed countries in the case of non-compliance. In short, they would be able to exert the pressures necessary to counteract other pressures which at present block the emergence of the political will in the developed countries necessary for them to play their part in the resolution of the development problem.

While such a proposal may sound utopian in regard to the whole group of developing countries, it becomes much more feasible if

[1] See the discussion on pp. 80–1 above.

considered first in regard to regional action, and second at the level of individual commodities.

In respect of the first, the arguments in its favour stem from the greater coincidence of interest among countries of a given region, and from the fact that some machinery already exists (notably in Latin America). There would of course remain serious obstacles, the chief of which are the lack of concern of most developing countries with long-term objectives, reflecting the dominance of particular pressure groups, and their excessive preoccupation with 'national sovereignty'. It has to be recognised that in the present situation of economic and to some extent also political dependency, such sovereignty is largely fictitious and that it is only by relinquishing a part of it (preferably in the context of an integration scheme) that they will be able to exercise some degree of effective sovereignty. All this implies political decisions difficult to accomplish given the existing political machinery, and in particular the strength of narrow parochial interests – but essential to the achievement of bargaining power.

The second type of joint action, in respect of individual commodities, may well prove more feasible than regional joint action on all fronts. The developing countries must learn to exploit the bargaining power implicit in their possession of natural resources urgently needed by the developed countries (the more so as concern for the environment limits the production and use of synthetics). To this end the technique of the producers' cartel must be extended to other commodities, using the experience of O.P.E.C. It is true that the strategic nature of petroleum makes it something of a special case, and obviously the extent to which a cartel formed for a given commodity will improve the negotiating position of the exporting countries will depend on a number of factors such as the price-elasticity of supply and demand for the product, the degree of dependence of developed countries upon imports, and the availability of substitutes. But the commodity does not have to be 'strategic' or even essential: bananas, coffee or cocoa could do as well as copper, iron ore or bauxite, since what is really significant in the case, say, of bananas is the existence of a few multinationals with large investments in the producing countries and in transporting and marketing which they would not willingly relinquish.

The problem of the stimulus to production represented by success in achieving better prices could be handled by negotiating a pricing policy based not on increasing actual world prices, but on 'price compensation agreements', whereby a standard price and the amounts to be traded would be fixed for each commodity; the developed countries would then compensate the developing countries, through contributions made to a development fund for the difference between the actual value of their imports and the value it would have had at the reference price.[1]

The key problem, again, would lie not in the technicalities but in the developing countries themselves. Such joint action would demand a discipline and basic political decisions very difficult to obtain.

In the near future two major events will take place that are fraught with both challenges and opportunities for the developing countries: the enlargement of the E.E.C., and the trade negotiations scheduled to start in 1973 (as well as the negotiations for the reform of the international monetary system). How those countries face these challenges will largely determine the structure of international economic relations for years to come, as also the role that developing countries will play, as well as whether the deterioration of their relative position in world trade and income will accelerate or be reversed.

POSTSCRIPT: UNCTAD III[2]

The record of UNCTAD III, held in April–May 1972, has only served to strengthen the conclusions of this paper. Each criticism made above on the preliminaries to and proceedings of UNCTAD II can be repeated of UNCTAD III. We saw evidenced the same proliferation of resolutions, the same lack of a concrete strategy aimed at effective implementation, the same conflicts among developing countries, the same lack of flexibility on the part of the developed countries; in fact if anything changed it was for the worse, in that there was a noticeable hardening in the attitude of the developed countries, partially resulting from the serious deterioration in world economic conditions and partially from a desire to retain a strong bargaining position in view of the coming negotiations on international monetary problems and in 1973 on trade. As suggested above this seems to have been a powerful motivation to hold back concessions in order to use them as weapons at a later date, particularly with respect to the major countries' spheres of influence.

Consequently agreement on the few resolutions adopted unanimously by the Conference was obtained only after the developing countries retreated considerably from their original demands, so that the resolutions in question are generally innocuous, mostly limited to requests to the Secretariat or some other organisation to initiate or speed up studies, or calling for further consultations, or some such

---

[1] Professor J. E. Meade made a fairly similar but less ambitious proposal in the document he prepared for UNCTAD I, on 'International Commodity Agreements' (*Proceedings*, Vol. III, pp. 454–6).

[2] Added in the revision of the paper.

indefinite measure. On other important matters no resolution could be adopted, or if it was, it was with the abstention or negative vote of some or most of the developed countries. Such was the case for the resolutions on the much-vaunted Charter of Economic Rights and Duties (19 abstentions), on the principles that should govern world trade policies and relations (18 abstentions, 15 votes against), on the role of the I.B.R.D. in price stabilisation (13 abstentions, 2 against), on requesting a study of marketing and distribution systems for commodities of interest to developing countries (4 abstentions, 16 against), on the debt servicing burden (17 abstentions, 14 against), *et cetera*.

Further, and very seriously, with only two exceptions discussed below, the developing countries appeared little concerned about the important changes in the structure of international economic relations which are currently taking place or which can be anticipated in the near future.

The major exception to this was related to the international monetary situation: during UNCTAD III the developing countries strove hard to secure effective participation in the reform of the international monetary system and the establishment of a link between special drawing rights and development finance, as well as the co-ordinated consideration of trade, finance and monetary questions under the aegis of UNCTAD. But the developed countries (particularly the United States) were strongly opposed; in fact, the resolution finally adopted was in important respects a step backwards relative to Resolution 32(II) adopted at UNCTAD II.

The second refers to the multilateral trade negotiations which the market-economy countries agreed in March 1972 to initiate in 1973 in the framework of GATT. At UNCTAD III the developing countries pressed for the adoption of a resolution recommending a number of principles which should govern the negotiations. The resolution which was eventually passed did give UNCTAD some participation in the preparatory arrangements for the negotiations. However, no formal joint machinery was created, and in respect of the key issue the resolution fell well short of its objective, since it simply drew attention to the principles as representing the developing countries' views, rather than adopting them.

4 The Role of World Trade Policy: the View from the Advanced Countries

Sven W. Arndt

UNIVERSITY OF CALIFORNIA, SANTA CRUZ

More than two decades of aid projects and alliances have brought the idea of development through foreign assistance to the nadir of its popularity. Soaring promises and expectations have given way to growing criticism, cynicism and disappointment. The stunning lesson of recent history is not that economic progress has been lacking, but that whatever progress has occurred has been so very much less than the grandiose predictions that seemed to accompany every launching of every new project.

Disenchantment with traditional concepts of economic aid is remarkably widespread; and while much of the criticism is undoubtedly as unthinking as was the ready support of an earlier age, the disillusionment is too pervasive to be readily dismissed as a mere fad. In developed countries the declining belief in the efficacy of aid as an engine of economic development is best typified by the burgeoning hostility of the United States Congress to continued American foreign assistance programmes, while the less developed countries have expressed their disillusionment in the massive, and often uncritical, enthusiasm which they have lavished upon the concept of discriminatory trade preferences.

The problems which currently beset the traditional programmes of economic aid are not unique; rather they are symptomatic of the general disarray within the global economic system, whose major institutions are in a state either of serious disrepair or of collapse. In the quarter century since the Second World War an international economic system has been constructed whose primary characteristic is a general absence of the free play of market forces. The guiding principle has been orderly intervention – or disorderly intervention designed to create order – in all markets, be they markets for goods, currencies or capital. It is a world in which adjustment occurs in consonance with a welter of non-co-ordinated policies, but in which every policy maker tends nevertheless to assume that his policies are superimposed on an otherwise unimpeded system.

In this world a wide variety of policy instruments are manipulated for sundry purposes by an equally wide variety of players, where indeed players seem to have had more free play than has been accorded those mythical market forces of classical economics. The question is whether all of this has added up to a symphony? One has to conclude that the answer is no. The observable state of the world economy resembles rather more the nervous exhaustion that follows upon excessive exposure to cacophony. The remarkable fact of our age is that independent and decentralised decision-making bodies have acted virtually at will without paying much heed to the global effects of their 'price-making' interventions. In a closed world economy, oligopolistic firms and governments have systematically ignored the actions of other oligopolists. Not only do nations claim sovereignty over matters of economic policy, but they act as if they believed that theirs was the sovereign power to guarantee the success of their policies. In terms of our musical analogy, each player not only asserts his unchallengeable right to toot his horn as he may choose, but rests secure in the belief that the end result will be shaped by the modulated puffs of air which stir his instrument.

Economic development is assumed everywhere to require the visible hand of the policy maker, which may indeed be so; but everywhere the policy universe is taken to be the nation-state, and in a supremely interdependent world economy that probably is not the case. In the following pages we examine the problem of economic development, and the role therein of the advanced countries, from the perspective of the world economy as a closed policy system.

I. ECONOMIC DEVELOPMENT AS AN EXTERNALLY-CONSTRAINED PROCESS

To be concerned about the role of advanced countries in the process of industrialisation and development in the rest of the world is to view that process as being responsive to forces external to the country in which it is to take place. This attitude is critical, for example, in export-oriented models of economic growth, and it is at the core of traditional trade theory.[1] According to the dynamic postulates of orthodox trade theory, both the quantitative and the qualitative characteristics of a country's comparative advantage are subject to change over time. From the global perspective this implies that comparative advantage in the production of a commodity will tend to shift among countries as social, economic, technological and cultural pressures operate. On the assumption of an efficient and essentially competitive international economic system, given industries will emerge in some countries as they decline in others, while still other countries will witness the birth of altogether new economic activities.

[1] But the usefulness of external influences is by no means universally accepted. See, for example, H. W. Singer [12].

Adjustment to these evolving patterns is seen by the theory to follow the dictates of an essentially free market mechanism, the operations of its laws being sufficient to ensure the optimal allocation of the world's scarce resources for the world's benefit.

In the context of economic development this means that abundant and inexpensive labour will create in backward countries the conditions for competitive production of a variety of standardised manufactured and semi-manufactured products such as textiles, motor vehicles, electrical components, machine parts, and so forth.[1] In established countries, on the other hand, highly skilled populations, massive accumulations of capital and institutionalised approaches to risk taking will provide the conditions for advanced-technology activities. The growing contemporary preoccupation with the so-called post-industrial age, which is universally assumed to arrive first in the United States and in Western Europe, and the advent of which will transfer the sources of supply of the standard bread-and-butter products of the Industrial Revolution era to the nations of the Third World, is an expression of a widespread faith in the laws expounded in the traditional theory.[2]

The critical premise of that theory concerns the efficiency and smooth functioning of the adjustment mechanism as it allocates and reallocates the world's productive resources. This premise, together with virtually all other important characteristics of the orthodox

[1] This process has been examined, notably by R. Vernon [15], who stresses the standardised nature of these products and their large-scale markets and low requirements of entrepreneurial initiative and risk-bearing.

[2] According to the dynamic of traditional trade theory, the United States should now or in the near future begin to de-emphasize production of a wide variety of standardised products, and turn to the production and sale abroad of high-technology products and, to an increasing extent, of services as well. In a fundamental sense, this is the only way in which industrialisation can be spread around the globe, assuming that such spreading is in fact feasible and desirable. Yet by all indications, the United States is engaged in a concerted effort to impede and slow down the reallocation of the world's production and investment in that direction. Among the many instances, imposition on Japan and, more importantly, on other Asian nations of 'voluntary' export quotas stands out as a warning signal. In a broader sense, the entire international component of the President's New Economic Policy of 1971 seems heavily directed at preventing the growing importation of standardised industrial products into the United States.

As a wealthy and affluent nation, the United States should undoubtedly make real transfers to other countries, but the composition of that surplus must be allowed to change. It should probably be that the world's output of automobiles should increasingly come from less advanced countries, while the United States shifts its energies and its talents to other pursuits. The short-term economic and political implications, however, of a declining auto industry will undoubtedly serve for some time to compel American leaders to exert all efforts to prevent the international reallocation of production. For an interesting essay on this subject, see Krause [7].

trade model, has of late been adopted by the proponents of trade preferences whose most eloquent spokesman, Raúl Prebisch, is also the architect of the original UNCTAD proposal [10]. The trade preference argument is a second-best argument; inasmuch as it proposes that developed nations grant trade concessions which discriminate against other developed countries, it violates the conditions of Pareto optimality.[1] It is consistent with the spirit of classical trade theory, however, in that it views the existence of tariff barriers in developed economies as an obstacle to the optimal allocation of the world's resources, in general, and to the opportunity for industrialisation of the Third World in particular.

The principal weakness of the classical model is its assumption of atomistic competition and of relatively frictionless adjustment. While the possibility of rigid factor prices and of immobile factors was raised long ago by Haberler [5], and while there has emerged recently a growing literature on the international effects of domestic distortions,[2] these considerations have not been integrated into the basic trade model. The reason for this omission is the feared destruction of the theory's simplicity, elegance and definitiveness, which would be the consequence of abandoning its essential policy neutrality and its orientation toward free market mechanisms.

If one views the world, on the other hand, as thoroughly infested with distortions of the sort associated with externalities, monopolies, costly and biased information, and complex governmental interventions, then economic development becomes a question of the extent to which existing policies in the world impede or support economic progress, and of the availability of policy alternatives which might more effectively contribute to the objectives at hand while interfering minimally with other goals. In the true sense of second-best, it does not necessarily follow in a closed system in which semi-autonomous decision agencies manipulate specific controls in the pursuit of specific targeted values of specific state variables, that discriminatory trade preferences will be more productive of economic development than any other set of policies including those traditional favourites, foreign aid and assistance.

The focus is thus on the world as a self-contained policy system rather than a system of free markets. In a policy system as much as in a market system, nature abhors a vacuum. In a market system, changes in one market reverberate through the system until consistent responses have produced a new state of balance; this is the

---

[1] Harry Johnson [6] has ably dealt with the relevance of this criticism in a world in which common markets, free-trade areas and the GATT rules themselves have introduced and perpetuated far-reaching distortions in many markets.

[2] See, for example, Bhagwati and Ramaswami [2].

essence of the process of adjustment upon which the elaborate edifice of economic theory has been constructed. In a decentralised policy system, a shift in one policy sets in motion analogous forces of adjustment, but the adjustment path and the achievement of the objective which gave rise to the initial policy change depend upon the extent to which the response of the entire policy system may be characterised as sympathetic or antithetic. The system's sympathy is closely related to the hierarchical structure of the control and target variables which enter into the objective functions of the decision makers. From the perspective of a single decision agency the system's sympathy is at best tenuous and the potential for policy conflict correspondingly high.[1]

A SIMPLE POLICY MODEL

In a closed economy, market equilibrium requires the identity of supply and current absorption. For the sake of simplicity we ignore past accumulations of goods, so that we may substitute current output for supply. The level of current absorption (A) may be viewed as a function of variables, some of which are controlled by the authorities while others are not. In a two-control model we write

$$A = \beta_{11}a_1 + \beta_{12}a_2 + u_1 \tag{1}$$

where the a_1 are the controls or policy instruments and u_1 represents the stochastic effect of the uncontrolled variables. The current level of output (Q) may be similarly related to controls and other variables[2]

$$Q = \beta_{21}a_1 + \beta_{22}a_2 + u_2 \tag{2}$$

In equilibrium,

$$A = Q \tag{3}$$

The control variables have for convenience been grouped into two broad classes, one having the primary impact in the monetary sector and consisting of *specific* policies such as bank regulation and interest ceilings, and *general* instruments such as open-market operations; the other containing policies whose primary impact is on expenditure and production and consisting of specific as well as general fiscal and budgetary instruments.

While equations (1) and (2) relate production and absorption

---

[1] In two interesting studies, R. N. Cooper [3] and D. E. Roper [11] have recently examined the implications of decentralised decision processes for efficient and conflict-free short-run stabilisation policy.

[2] For most of the discussion the distinction between actual and potential output is ignored.

directly to controls, the exact nature of the relationships may involve a number of intermediate variables. Thus, absorption is affected by variations in income, in interest rates and in price levels, while output varies in response to changes in factor inputs, which in turn vary with prices and factor rewards. Thus

$$A = A(Y, i, P) \tag{4}$$

$$Q = Q(N, K) \tag{5}$$

The effect β_{ij} of control variable a_j consequently summarises or aggregates a variety of impulses, as indicated by the equations of change

$$\frac{\mathrm{d}A}{\mathrm{d}a_j} = \frac{\delta A}{\delta Y} \cdot \frac{\mathrm{d}Y}{\mathrm{d}a_j} + \frac{\delta A}{\delta i} \cdot \frac{\mathrm{d}i}{\mathrm{d}a_j} + \frac{\delta A}{\delta P} \cdot \frac{\mathrm{d}P}{\mathrm{d}a_j} + \frac{\delta A}{\delta a_j} \tag{6}$$

$$\frac{\mathrm{d}Q}{\mathrm{d}a_j} = \frac{\delta Q}{\delta N} \cdot \frac{\mathrm{d}N}{\mathrm{d}a_j} + \frac{\delta Q}{\delta K} \cdot \frac{\mathrm{d}K}{\mathrm{d}a_j} + \frac{\delta Q}{\delta a_j} \tag{7}$$

Unlike the free market system in which A and Q respond to the impersonal forces of the market, we are dealing with a world in which the time paths of A and Q are critically determined by the a_j. Indeed, equations (6) and (7) suppress a problem which is pervasive in policy planning and which pertains to the lag structure and to reaction speeds inherent in the adjustment process. The β_{ij} of equations (1) and (2) are uniquely determined only for unique time periods, so that the temporal dimensionality of the policy system is uniquely related to the time horizon of the economic plan.[1]

When governments intervene in the economic system, they do so with a view to achieving certain social ends. In the standard Keynesian model of short-term stabilisation, capacity is assumed fixed and demand is managed in order to attain targeted levels of employment, prices and external payments. In a medium-term development plan, on the other hand, effective supply management plays a critical role. In both cases, the historical development of the theoretical argument has been based on single-country models, in which the representation of societal economic goals in terms of fixed targets based on the work of Tinbergen [14], Meade [8], and Mundell [9], and of variable targets based on Theil [13], has gained prominence.[2]

In following Theil, we assume that the authorities minimise the expectation of a social loss function of the following general type

$$E\{L(a, x)\} = E\{\Sigma w_i (x_i \widetilde{\mathcal{E}} x_i^*)^k\} \tag{8}$$

---

[1] We shall, however, abstract from the difficulties inherent in defining a single time horizon in the context of decentralised decision making.

[2] For a discussion and comparison of these approaches, see Fox, Sengupta and Thorbecke [4].

where the x_i and x_i^* are actual and targeted values, respectively, of state variables and where w_i are weights representing the hierarchy of goals and objectives.[1] In a highly centralised decision system, the 'authorities' may be identifiable as a single agency in whose hands rests the power to establish the hierarchy of goals and to allocate controls in accordance with that hierarchy. In a decentralised system of the sort which characterises most developed countries and which is the world economy, a number of decision agencies will each be charged with responsibility for one or more specific state variables and will be empowered to exercise control over one or more specific instrument variables. In these cases, selection of the final set of targets (x_i^*) and determination of the relative importance of each target (w_i) are functions of a process of policy bargaining in which the political power of the constituencies which each agency serves is vital.

II. THE WORLD ECONOMY: A CLOSED SYSTEM OF DECENTRALISED DECISION PROCESSES

In the present section we examine some implications for a closed policy system of a scheme of trade preferences. We suppose that the world may be divided into two blocks or 'countries', one under-developed (U), the other (D) developed in the main, but consisting of an advanced, industrialised component (D_1) and of a backward component (D_2), where the latter has the important characteristic of containing those industries and economic activities which compete directly with the industries in U whose products are to be admitted into D under trade preferences. We assume further that the world is initially in equilibrium such that D_1 produces more than it absorbs, leaving an excess of current output for transfer to country U, which thus absorbs more than it currently produces. In D_2, on the other hand, current production and current absorption are assumed to be in balance. We wish to examine the effects of trade preferences under (i) conditions in which a classical mechanism of adjustment operates in relatively unfettered markets, and (ii) conditions in which the adjustment process is policy-constrained.

CLASSICAL ADJUSTMENT

According to traditional trade theory, a tariff impedes the efficient allocation of world resources and thus reduces world welfare. By

---

[1] While targets enter the function as unique values, it is possible to replace them with ranges of values and to redefine the weights accordingly. Moreover, some or all of the control variables may be subject to constraints which effectively reduce acceptable values to a subset of all possible values.

changing the terms of trade and by altering relative factor rewards the tariff can also be shown to disturb the existing distribution of world product among countries and among factors of production.

From the global perspective of efficient resource allocation in a world of unencumbered markets the optimum solution is the free-trade solution. In proposing discriminatory trade preferences, supporters of the scheme have made substantial use of the infant industry argument for tariff protection, where the protection in this case is of the products of young industries in developing countries from competition by similar products of developed countries in the markets of other developed countries. We shall focus our attention on the effects in the preference-granting country of cheaper imports.

It is clearly intended that imports from country U will replace domestically produced goods by means of price competition. The stress is on conquering markets serviced by established but relatively inefficient and protected domestic producers. Assuming that markets are uncontrolled and resources are mobile within country D, the removal of protection will cause the affected industries to decline and to release factors of production for absorption elsewhere in the system. Returns to the factors used abundantly in the declining industries will fall relatively. Consumers in country D will benefit from the decline in import prices, realising a gain in real income which will enable them not only to increase their intake of all goods, but which may induce them to 'spend' some of the gain by increasing their aid to country U. Such benefits would accrue to country U over and above the gains from stimulation of its export industries and from forward and backward linkages associated with expansion of the export sector.

POLICY-CONSTRAINED ADJUSTMENT

We now drop the assumption of resource mobility, supposing instead that labour is largely immobile and that the authorities in country D are committed to maintaining some minimum level of income for each individual. We further suppose that the authorities take responsibility for maintaining 'full employment' in the economy.

The removal of protection introduces the competition of cheaper imports. If domestic factors employed in import-competing industries accept lower returns in preference to idleness, the available market for imports will remain limited as long as domestic producers are able to effect reductions in factor prices. The government in D may facilitate this retrenchment by providing income subsidies to workers whose wages decline. In imposing this burden on the rest of country D, the authorities may plausibly argue that to let an industry die altogether would impose a still heavier burden on society at large. There exists an evident conflict here between country D's goal of fostering economic development abroad and its goal of maintaining standards of living and full employment at home.

If labour unions or minimum wage laws or other constraints prevent factor returns from falling in import-competing industries, resources will be made idle. Since those industries are by assumption located in D_2, output and income in D_2 will decline, a chain of events to which the authorities in country D respond with income transfers from D_1 to D_2. These transfers have the effect of shifting part of the burden of the policy of tariff concessions to D_1, with the result that in addition to its transfer of goods to country U, region D_1 is now called upon to come to the aid of region D_2 as well. The simplest means of achieving the domestic transfer is for country D to cut its foreign aid and to channel the goods thus released to D_2. If country D is not prepared to curtail its foreign assistance, it must introduce policies which would increase current output at unchanged levels of D_1-absorption, or policies which would reduce levels of absorption in D_1 at current levels of output.

The policy of trade preferences has thus come into conflict with society's other goals, specifically its goals of income maintenance and full employment. Introduction of one policy disturbs the policy equilibrium and elicits changes in all other policies or in the settings of other policy instruments. Whether and to what extent the policy of trade preferences achieves its intended result depends importantly on the means by which country D attempts to achieve its goals of income maintenance and full employment. Some of the many policy mixes which might be adopted are considered below.

(a) As we have seen, foreign aid may be reduced in order to provide relief at home. The adverse effects of reduced aid on economic development in country U must be set against the positive effects associated with expanded export production. If the original aid recipients in U are not also those who benefit from export expansion, the net welfare effect on U is difficult to ascertain without resort to interpersonal welfare comparisons, but the new situation may be compared to the old by considering the compensating transfers which would be required between the gainers and the losers. The situation becomes more complex when U is assumed to be a block of developing countries with various backgrounds, different resource endowments, and diverse development rates. In the competition for country D's markets, the competing countries will have varying degrees of success. Those who possess a comparative edge will outmuscle the rest and thus reap relatively greater benefits from the policy of trade preferences. Unless one is willing to assume that all underdeveloped countries who may be entitled to preferences are equally qualified to produce the goods involved, a process of natural selection among them will inevitably develop. Under these conditions, a uniform reduction in country D's foreign assistance programme will hurt some countries more than others, and there does not exist a ready mechanism for effecting compensatory transfers among countries. Recognition of this danger may lead authorities in countries lacking comparative advantage in certain commodities to nevertheless push investment in relatively inefficient industries and thus contribute to the inefficient use of the world's resources.

(b) The foreign aid objective may be considered too important to be sacrificed, perhaps because the agency in control of foreign aid possesses powerful allies in the country's legislature. As an alternative method of facilitating the subsidy to D_2, the authorities may tax consumption in D_1. This will have adverse repercussions for country U if it reduces demand in D for consumption goods exported by country U. Of course, in the absence of income transfers within country D there would have occurred a cut in overall demand as a consequence of declining incomes in D_2. Moreover, whatever the changes in overall demand, the composition of demand is likely to be changed as well.

Thus the tax-cum-subsidy policy of income maintenance in D touches country U at several points. Incomes having declined in the former country, total expenditure and expenditure on goods produced in country U will also decline. But if the income elasticities of demand differ as among goods exported by country U, or by the several countries which may compose the underdeveloped world, the producers of these goods will feel the decline in D with different intensity. Analogous changes in the demand for various classes of goods will result from any changes in the overall composition of expenditure which follows the income transfer within country D. These adverse repercussions of the tax-cum-subsidy policy of income maintenance must be set against the beneficial consequences of the policy of tariff preferences. Unless the benefits and the costs are assumed to be uniformly distributed, the net benefit which accrues to individuals or to regions or to countries within U may vary substantially, leaving some worse off while the welfare of others improves.

(c) The authorities may tax corporate income, thus reducing domestic private investment and replacing it with public 'investment' in income maintenance. Such programmes tend to reduce growth in productivity and in output and thus diminish, among other things, country D's future ability to expand its foreign aid.

It is interesting to note, moreover, that from a global perspective the proportion of world product which must go to support idle individuals may increase as a consequence of the tariff concessions. If we suppose that the enlarged output of exports in U is achieved in part by introducing previously unemployed labour into the active work force, the granting of trade concessions reduces the pool of idle resources and in so doing also reduces, at least initially, the quantity of public resources devoted to life and income maintenance. At the same time, declining industries in D release labour into idleness and thus increase the quantity of resources devoted to life and income maintenance there. Now, it is probable that a given quantity of output will be produced in U with a greater proportional input of labour than had been the case in D_2; but due to the higher standard of living which is likely to prevail in the backward sector of country D, the per unit burden of income maintenance is doubtless higher in that country. It follows that, for given production functions and resource endowments, the quantity of world resources devoted to income maintenance is more likely to increase in consequence of discriminatory trade preferences as the differences increase in living standards between the two countries.[1]

The preceding discussion has assumed that immobile resources in country D's declining industries are banished to idleness as imports replace domestic products. If the authorities in country D are committed to the societal goal of full employment, the aforementioned income support policies cannot be more than interim policies. Over the longer term, employment-creating policies must be devised. Resources will be used up as attempts are made in country D to return idle factors to active employment. Job training programmes draw resources from other projects some of which may cause immediate withdrawals of resources from country U. If incentives are offered to private industry to create jobs in D_2, the result may be less foreign investment in U, particularly as it is likely that investment opportunities in D_2 and in U will be highly substitutable. If general fiscal policies are initiated in the hope of increasing the level of aggregate demand and thus creating incentives for resource mobility, the uneven impact of demand-management policies can create inflationary pressures in some of D_1's industries and markets before substantial inroads are made into unemployment in D_2. In these conditions, country U will suffer from the higher prices which it must pay for its imports from D, even as it will benefit from demand shifts toward its goods. If as a consequence of these adjustments, the

---

[1] The burden on world resources is bound to increase if the labour made idle in D_2 becomes truly idle, whereas the formerly 'idle' individuals in country U were drawn from the agricultural sector where they may have made seasonal contributions to output.

overall balance of payments in *D* develops a deficit, the monetary authority may respond by raising interest rates, and any such increase in the cost of borrowing is detrimental to country *U*.

The conclusion which emerges is clear: it is not in general possible to evaluate the role which the developed country may play in the growth plan of the backward country except by reference to a complete policy system. This is true for trade preferences, where subsidiary and induced policy changes may support or impede the initial

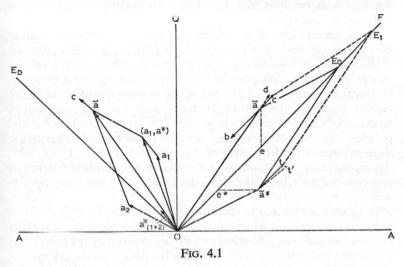

FIG. 4.1

favourable impact of trade concessions. This is true of traditional foreign aid programmes, whose undistinguished record may be traced in part to the fact that the goal of development abroad has always stood substantially outside the main goal structure of donor nations and thus has tended to exist not as an integrated component of the policy plans in those countries, but rather more often as an afterthought or a separate factor.

III. SOME GENERALISATIONS

The arguments of the preceding section may be illustrated with the aid of the above simple geometrical construction, which lends itself also to the extraction of a number of generalisations. In the left quadrant of Fig. 4.1, the impact of world economic policies on country *D*'s total output (*Q*) and total absorption (*A*) is indicated by several vectors. The vectors a_i represent the domestic effect of domestically designed policies, while the vector $a^*_{(1+2)}$ represents the net effect on country D of the policy vectors $\mathbf{a}_1^*$ and $\mathbf{a}_2^*$ (not drawn) of country U. In an open economy, the domestic effects of external policies must clearly be taken into account, with the implication that the open economy equivalents of equations (1) and (2) are given by the following:

$$A = \beta_{1i}\mathbf{a}_i + \beta_{1j}\mathbf{a}_j^* + u_1 \qquad i = 1, \ldots, m \qquad (9)$$
$$Q = \beta_{2i}\mathbf{a}_i + \beta_{2j}\mathbf{a}_j^* + u_2 \qquad j = m+1, \ldots, n \qquad (10)$$

Analogous expressions may be written for country U's absorption (A^*) and output (Q^*).

In the general case, the number of policies and thus the number of vectors will be large; for reasons of convenience, however, we shall assume that vectors $\mathbf{a}_1$ and $\mathbf{a}_2$ express the net effect of two classes of policies, respectively. The first vector may, for example, represent the net effect of policies in the monetary sector, while the second indicates the thrust of fiscal and budgetary measures. Alternatively, the vector $\mathbf{a}_1$ may be taken to represent 'domestic' policies, with vector $\mathbf{a}_2$ cumulating the impact of policies in the 'foreign' sector. Under a fixed exchange rate, for example, an inflationary monetary policy would tend to increase absorption faster than domestic output, while a tariff or a devaluation will have the opposite effect.

Some care is required in the interpretation of policy vectors, inasmuch as the response of output and absorption to policy stimuli is rarely instantaneous. The effect of a policy as given by the dimension of a vector will thus vary not only with the dosage of the policy, but also with the time horizon for which the analysis is defined. The slope of a vector will similarly be a function of time whenever the lagged response of output differs from that of demand. Moreover, while equations (9) and (10) specify and vectors $\mathbf{a}_i$ reflect strictly linear relationships among controls and target variables, nonlinear relationships accommodating varying degrees of scale effects with differential impacts on A and Q may be more realistic.[1]

The combined effect of domestic policies and external forces may be ascertained by construction of the appropriate rectangle and is given by the vector $\tilde{\mathbf{a}}$, which is reproduced in the right panel together with an analogously defined policy vector $\tilde{\mathbf{a}}^*$ for country U. The equilibrium condition in the present case is that world absorption (A_w) equals world production (Q_w):

$$A_w = A + A^* = Q_w = Q + Q^* \qquad (11)$$

In Figure 4.1, country D's excess output is exactly offset by the other

[1] For an application of this approach to stabilisation policy in an advanced open economy, see Arndt [1].

country's excess absorption ($e\tilde{a} = e^*\tilde{a}^*$), so that world equilibrium is established at E_0.

The classical mechanism of adjustment in response to the introduction of trade preferences may be briefly indicated. On the assumption that country U has supplies of idle labour and that the period of analysis is of sufficient duration to permit some capital formation, the opening of new markets for the country's exports will generate a multiple expansion of output and absorption. If we suppose that the total quantity of aid which country U receives during the period remains unchanged from earlier levels, absorption can increase at most by as much as the expansion in domestic product.[1] The uniform expansion of country U's economy is shown by the vector $\tilde{a}^*t$ which possesses slope of unity.

In country D, trade concessions introduce the competition of low-priced foreign imports. If domestic producers of substitute products are unable to adjust to these pressures due to constraints imposed by factor immobility and factor–price rigidities, output and absorption will decline along a vector such as $\tilde{a}b$. That vector will have a slope of unity if the burden of adjustment to the decline in output falls entirely on domestic absorption. It will have a slope greater than unity if part of the burden of adjustment falls on foreign aid. Thus, if the original ratio of output to absorption is to be maintained, i.e. if the system is to move along $O\tilde{a}$, the quantity of output available for transfer to country U must decline correspondingly. Under the relatively efficient adjustment assumed by traditional trade theory, however, the resources released by import-competing enterprises will be absorbed elsewhere. Since by assumption this reallocation of resources will proceed in accordance with the imperatives of comparative advantage, the result will be a more efficient allocation of the country's resources and thus a greater total output than that given by the point $\tilde{a}$. This efficiency-related increment in output may be absorbed entirely at home, in which case the country moves along vector $\tilde{a}c$ with its slope of unity, or some part of the gain may be allocated to country U, in which case the movement is along vector $\tilde{a}d$, with a corresponding relocation of vector $\tilde{a}^*t$ to $\tilde{a}^*t'$. In global terms the improved allocation of world resources will have increased output to a point such as E_1, an outcome consistent with the predictions of orthodox trade theory.

CONSTRAINED ADJUSTMENT

We turn now to the case in which the presence of constraints prevents

[1] This is not to argue that the entire new output of domestic goods will be absorbed domestically.

smooth adjustment in D's economy to the removal of trade barriers. In Fig. 4.2, vectors $O\tilde{a}_1$ and $\tilde{a}_1\tilde{a}_2$ represent the net effect on output and absorption of existing policies in sectors D_1 and D_2 of the developed country, while $O\tilde{a}^*$ is analogously defined for country U.

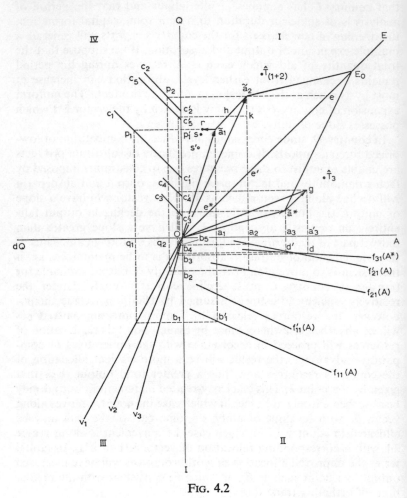

FIG. 4.2

The unitary slope of the vector $\tilde{a}_1\tilde{a}_2$ reflects the assumption that output just equals absorption in sector D_2, so that all of the first sector's excess production accrues to country $U(e'\tilde{a}_2 \Leftrightarrow e^*\tilde{a}^*)$. The world is initially assumed to be in policy equilibrium at E_0.

The remaining panels illustrate some particular features of that equilibrium. Thus in country D's advanced sector, an absorption level of Oa_1 is assumed to be divided between Ob_1 of investment, that allocation being determined by the investment demand function $f_{11}(A)$, and the remainder distributed among other forms of absorption.[1] In quadrant III, the incremental investment/output ratio (v_1) shows the rate at which investment is transformed into new output (dQ). Investment outlays of Ob_1 give rise to Oq_1 of new output, and the addition of new output to total previous output is facilitated by the translator functions in the fourth panel. Thus the function c_1c_1' indicates that the combination of accumulated capital stock and current investment are capable in conjunction with other factors of generating a total output of Op_1' in sector D_1. As capital formation continues in future periods and as other factors of production are augmented, the translator function will shift upward.[2]

The removal of tariff protection in country D causes the demand for U-exports to rise and for D_2-output to fall. The expansion in country U's exports produces during the planning period a multiple expansion in output and absorption, which we assume to be represented by the vector $\bar{a}^*g$. As a consequence of the growth in demand, total investment in country U is assumed to be given by point d on the investment demand schedule $f_{31}(A^*)$. Prior to the boost in export demand, total absorption in country U was a_3, with an amount a_3d' devoted to investment. The contribution to output made by that investment is indicated by the incremental investment/output curve v_3, while translator function c_3c_3' establishes the resulting total output at $\bar{a}^*$. As a consequence of the growth in export demand and the related expansion in investment, the translator function shifts to c_4c_4', where it is noteworthy that the shift of the function will be greater, the greater is the flow of idle labour into productive employment. For underdeveloped economies this type of labour migration represents an important source of productive capacity.

The success of trade preferences in raising production and absorption in country U is a function of several variables among which the

---

[1] The scales along the OA and OI axes are clearly different, and the proportions shown in the figure are not intended to reflect real world shares.

It should be noted that the diagram deliberately suppresses many specifics of the global equilibrium. Thus, it is assumed that the equilibrium level of absorption Oa_1 may be traced to detailed behavioural functions of the types suggested in equations (1)–(10).

[2] Thus points of intersection with the Q-axis of translator functions may be interpreted as giving levels of output which prevailed prior to present investment. It follows that with a given level of capital formation, an augmentation of the active labour force – as when export expansion induces a flow of labour in country U from agrarian into industrial occupations – will shift the translator curve upward, thus giving rise to a greater output level.

magnitude of the initial expenditure injection is only one. The manner in which the domestic policy system is capable of diverting absorption into capital formation, and the extent to which it combines additions to the capital stock with other factors of production will have a critical bearing upon the final result. Policies which raise the slope of the investment demand function, for example, will produce greater ultimate growth of output.

What is beneficial for country U, however, may work to the disadvantage of sector D_2 of the advanced country. There the consequences of the freeing of trade are unemployment, reduced output and diminished absorption. The contraction of that sector's economy need not, however, proceed along vector $\tilde{a}_2\tilde{a}_1$, provided that the authorities in D are committed to some form of income maintenance. We suppose that this commitment is fulfilled by the transfer of income subsidies from tax revenues collected in D_1, and that as a result of these public transfers the original level of absorption is maintained in D_2, although production falls to the level indicated by k. The decline in production is brought about by two developments, the first being the dismissal of workers as shown by the downward displacement of the translator curve c_2c_2' to c_5c_5', the second being the reduced profitability of capital formation in that sector as indicated by the displacement of the investment demand schedule from $f_{21}(A)$ to $f'_1(A)$.

In the advanced sector of country D the repercussions of the foregoing disturbances depend on how the authorities elect to finance the income transfer to D_2. Among several alternatives, aid payments may be switched from U to D_2, with the consequence of causing policy vectors $O\tilde{a}^*$ and $O\mathbf{g}$ to rotate in a counterclockwise direction and thus of cancelling some of the gains which countries hope to achieve through trade preferences. The adverse effects of any aid reduction will be magnified if that reduction necessitates cuts in investment in country U, that is to say, if it leads to an upward displacement or an adverse rotation of the investment demand schedule, $f_{31}(A^*)$.

If the authorities resist the temptation to cut foreign aid, they must devise some alternative means of reducing absorption in D_1 in order to maintain absorption in D_2. Suppose that absorption through consumption is reduced in D_1. The geometric interpretation of this policy decision is a counterclockwise rotation of the vector $O\tilde{a}_1$ as indicated by the arrow emanating from $\tilde{a}_1$. With lower levels of absorption should come lower levels of investment (along $f_{11}(A)$, which is here assumed constant, but which may shift upward under pressure of adverse expectations, for example), which, in turn, imply lower levels of output. Instead of reaching points like r, therefore, the economy tends to move in the direction of s (the terminal point of the new but undrawn policy vector). If the point s lies to the right of a line (not drawn) with slope of unity through point r (which indicates the amount by which absorption in D_1 has to decline at unchanged output level given by $\tilde{a}_1$ in order to maintain absorption in D_2 at its original level), the policy will have failed to generate the desired magnitude of income transfer.

The cost to sector D_1 of preferential tariff reduction is compounded if the income transfer is taken out of investment expenditures, in which case the investment demand schedule shifts upward to $f'_{11}(A)$, thus reducing still further the level of output in D_1 and leading the system still further into unemployment in the direction of points like s'. It can be seen that the increasing severity of repercussions in country D – the degree of severity being in part a function of the policy mix which accompanies the original policy of reduced protection – diminishes the ultimate expansion in world production and may, indeed, lead to a net decline in world output from the level indicated by point E.

We are able to conclude from the foregoing analysis that in the global policy system as it has been described here, the efficacy of a change in one of several policies cannot be properly evaluated except in a general policy-system context. We have seen that a shift or rotation in one policy vector shifts the impact of all. Moreover not only must policies be consistent with respect to a given target, but the target structure requires an analogous internal consistency. Thus, if country D elects to pursue a particular target ratio of absorption to output, as indicated, for example, by point $\hat{T}_{(1+2)}$ and expressed by the loss function (equation 8), such a decision effectively constrains the range of choices of A/Q ratios available to U. This mutual dependence of targets is particularly evident when targets are fixed and single-valued, but it holds as well for economic targets specified in terms of ranges.

Inasmuch as targets $\hat{T}_{(1+2)}$ and $\hat{T}_3$ are two-dimensional, containing both output and absorption objectives, and inasmuch as achievement of such goals is a function of economic policies at home and abroad, any attempt by one of the countries to minimise its own loss function must take account of the global effect of the second country's control settings.

In an interdependent policy system, the introduction of a new economic target or the pursuit of an existing target by means of a new mix of policies disturbs the entire system. When the perturbation occurs in the context of decentralised decision making, it is likely to evoke a series of secondary and tertiary policy responses, some of which may impede achievement of the objective at hand while others facilitate that achievement. Consequently, it is in general impossible to evaluate the efficacy of the chosen instrument with which the objective is to be achieved except in terms of the policy system as a whole. It follows further that the efficacy of any country's policy mix is affected by the constellation of policies in existence elsewhere. These considerations add up to a strong argument in favour of multinational policy co-ordination, where policy bargaining may increase the efficiency of allocation of world policies to world targets, although countries may fail even after policy co-ordination to attain their original objectives.

REFERENCES

[1] S. W. Arndt, 'Macroeconomic Policy Planning in an Open Economy', in E. Claassen and P. Salin (eds.), *Stabilization Policies in Interdependent Economies* (Amsterdam: North-Holland Publishing Co., 1972).

[2] J. Bhagwati and V. K. Ramaswami, 'Domestic Distortions, Tariffs, and the Theory of Optimum Subsidy', *Journal of Political Economy*, LXXI (Feb. 1963).

[3] R. N. Cooper, 'Macroeconomic Policy Adjustments in Interdependent Economies', *Quarterly Journal of Economics*, LXXXIII (Feb. 1969).

[4] K. A. Fox, J. K. Sengupta and E. Thorbecke, *The Theory of Quantitative Economic Policy* (Chicago: Rand McNally, 1966).

[5] G. Haberler, 'Some Problems in the Pure Theory of International Trade', *Economic Journal*, LX (June 1950).

[6] H. G. Johnson, 'Trade Preferences and Developing Countries', *Lloyds Bank Review*, No. 84 (April 1967).

[7] L. Krause, 'Why Exports Are Becoming Irrelevant', *Foreign Policy*, No. 3 (Summer 1971).

[8] J. E. Meade, *The Theory of International Economic Policy*, Vol. 1: *The Balance of Payments* (London: Oxford Univ. Press, 1951).

[9] R. A. Mundell, *International Economics* (New York: Macmillan, 1968).

[10] R. Prebisch (Report of the Secretary-General of the UNCTAD), *Toward a New Trade Policy for Development* (Geneva, 1966).

[11] D. E. Roper, 'Macroeconomic Policies and the Distribution of the World Money Supply', *Quarterly Journal of Economics*, LXXXV (Feb. 1971).

[12] H. W. Singer, 'The Distribution of Gains between Investing and Borrowing Countries', *American Economic Review*, XL (May 1950).

[13] H. Theil, *Optimal Decision Rules for Government and Industry* (Amsterdam: North-Holland, 1964).

[14] J. Tinbergen, *On the Theory of Economic Policy* (Amsterdam: North-Holland, 1952).

[15] R. Vernon, 'International Investment and International Trade in the Product Cycle', *Quarterly Journal of Economics*, LXX (May 1966).

Discussion of the Papers by
Mr. Macario and Dr. Arndt

Dr. Krieger Vasena considered that, contrary to the impression Mr. Macario gave, Latin American countries had successfully begun trading manufactures. He saw the key element in the expansion of such trade as being co-ordination among Latin American countries; for this reason C.E.C.L.A. (the Special Commission for Latin American Co-ordination) was an important recent development.

He thought a crucial point Mr. Macario made concerned the role of internal policy in external trade problems. He could not stress enough that the solution of all external problems would not lead to a major expansion of exports of manufactures, unless internal problems reducing efficiency were tackled. The present inclination to propose delay till the external crisis was solved was disastrous.

Turning to Dr. Arndt's paper, he felt that it went into depths in an important problem and that the author's analysis showed up how poor a case Latin America had made for herself by treating preferences as a gracious concession. His own view was that the developed countries must deliberately create the type of situation which would have come about with a free market, i.e. certain sectors of production would have to be abandoned altogether as development proceeded. But this required much policy machinery, of which there was no sign. His own approach to the E.E.C. offices on the subject had been met with amazement — yet as he saw it labour shortages would eventually force the E.E.C. to deal with the problem. The United States was no more sensitive; the surcharge in fact revealed a regression in thinking on such matters, despite the growing concern with the environment, which logically ought to lead to a rethinking of industrial policy. He was curious about the case of Sweden – an example of a country which had deliberately abandoned textile production early in the century, and appeared to have done very well.

A number of speakers were concerned with the perspective that Dr. Arndt's analysis offered. *Mr. Urquidi* said that Dr. Arndt had rightly pointed out in his paper that a competitive free international market was no longer satisfactory for solving the problems of the less developed countries and that we lived instead in a 'system of policies' – policies and counter-policies – which had a great potential for conflict. But it was important to insist on long-term policies instead of the short-term measures that characterised most trade policy discussions. And such long-term policies had to evolve within a broader framework relating to the development of the world as a whole. It was necessary to formulate long-range objectives concerning: (a) levels of basic consumption and welfare, (b) desirable population growth, (c) use and possible exhaustion of natural resources, (d) pollution and deterioration of the environment, (e) correction of gross inequalities. International trade policy should be an instrument of world development — we should start thinking of 'post-UNCTAD' policies. Latin America should define its prospective role within these

overall objectives and seek changes in policies in favour of the less developed
countries, remembering of course that although domestic efforts were
essential, their interaction with suitable international co-operation was no
less important.

Dr. Bacha thought that it was more important to focus on the consequences for *U* of alternative policies, rather than, as Dr. Arndt did, on the
consequences for *D*. Attempting to develop this aspect, he contrasted
preferences leading to expanding trade with their alternative, aid, from the
point of view of the recipient country. His own position, he said, was
distinct from both the neo-classical vindication of aid and the two-gap
model, which equated trade and aid. This third position started from the
fact that less developed countries strongly desired industrialisation.
Foreign aid, by providing foreign exchange, allowed the less developed
countries to develop home market oriented industries in which they did
not have a comparative advantage. Basically, this was because they lacked
knowledge of the most efficient production techniques. These techniques,
as a rule, were monopolised by foreign enterprises. Thus, domestic production of these goods was either inefficient or in the hands of foreign corporations. Hence, foreign aid allowed a misallocation of domestic resources
and/or created conditions for the inflow of foreign enterprises, tending to
denationalise the economies of the less developed countries.

The opportunity to export, on the other hand, did not provide free
additional foreign exchange resources, but required the deployment of
domestic resources in export industries. Assuming that the preference for
industry of the less developed countries was strong enough, the traditional
primary exporting sectors would be discriminated against, thus providing
the opportunity for the expansion of manufactured exports. These products,
of course, were those in which the less developed countries had a comparative advantage within the industrial sector. Hence, generally they could
be developed by domestically owned firms.

So, foreign aid provided additional resources for the less developed
countries. But this allowed an inefficient allocation of domestic resources
and/or resulted in denationalisation of the industrial sector of the developing countries' economies. By contrast, the trade opportunity did not
generate free resources, but required deployment of domestic resources in
the most efficient industrial sectors, under the command of domestic
entrepreneurs. Thus, both from an economic and a political point of view,
trade was preferable to aid.

The case for trade not aid was supported by *Dr. Ffrench-Davis*: as Dr.
Arndt said, in theory, to reduce a distortion by granting a tariff preference
in a world of imperfections was not necessarily to move closer to the
optimum, since the effect on resource allocation of a reduction in one
distortion depended on the indirect effect on the other existing distortions.
However, analysing the whole gamut of distortions as they existed in Latin
America, he believed that one could state that tariff preferences for developing countries in the present situation would represent on balance a move
towards the optimum, both from their point of view and from the
world's.

Further, if there were to be a reduction in aid to compensate, then it was probable that the reduction in aid would be directed against the countries achieving the expansion in exports: hence it became a matter for the U in question of balancing the eventual loss in aid, suitably discounted, against the gains from an increase in trade. At present the latter looked the more promising, even without introducing dynamic considerations such as the increase in foreign investment that trade opportunities would bring but aid would not.

Professor Ranis said that it was hard to resist Dr. Arndt's call for a general equilibrium framework, and it was as well to be reminded to be precise about objectives, instruments and constraints. Nevertheless, the question arose as to how useful such a policy model was when our understanding of the behaviour of the systems involved was still so poorly specified, i.e. if we rushed into policy before we knew the important elements in a descriptive or analytical model we might suffer from 'empty policy systems' and misplaced concreteness. For example, why was D divided into D_1 and D_2, while U, which was much more dualistic, was not subdivided? Then conclusions which might hold in a two-country case might not hold in a world with many U's in which each could trade with the others as well as with the D's. Similarly, in the case where D used taxes for adjustment assistance (while maintaining foreign aid), the effect on D's income and thus on U's exports which Dr. Arndt mentioned was only a third-order effect. The relative impact on U of alternative Keynesian full employment policies in D seemed much less important to him than other aspects of the framework of interactions presented. For example, while, as Mr. Bacha pointed out, aid was preferable to trade in the static case, since it entails zero resource cost, trade might have much more important dynamic effects in both D and U. Adjustment plus trade, with policies in both D and U ensuring flexibility over time, was the essence of the problem. To ensure such flexibility required a policy mix which permitted the less developed countries to move out of import substitution at some point in their development and into a continuously changing export oriented regime. It should be recalled that Japan had a short and not very severe period of import substitution historically and yet retained a flexible outward oriented policy permitting a move from natural-resource-intensive to labour-intensive to skill- and capital-intensive output mixes over time. Policies which permitted entrepreneurs to adjust to the changing factor endowment in this fashion were, he assumed, another proxy for what Professor Vernon had called 'information'. He did not believe J.E.T.R.O. was responsible for Japanese success – even though socialised market research could be helpful. Nor was their 'client status' (Professor Felix's suggestion) responsible for the more recent success, along similar lines, of Korea and Taiwan. The move from mushrooms to asparagus to electronics in Taiwan was based on entrepreneurs taking advantage of changing factor endowments, not State Department orders to U.S. businessmen. It was of course true that both Korea and Taiwan received a substantial volume of foreign aid, but here again, since we were constantly being told that aid harmed domestic capital formation, this indicated only that aid could help when the domestic policy setting was good, and could hurt in helping to perpetuate an unfavourable policy setting.

Dr. Katz found Dr. Arndt's paper useful for its illumination of the set of constraints and potential trade-offs which the policy maker might face. It provided the logical infrastructure to Dr. Maizels' paper: thus according to the latter the major reason for the slow rate of growth of Latin American food exports over the 1960s was their displacement by competing imports from other sources; such a situation was described by Dr. Arndt when he stated: 'The situation becomes more complex when U . . . is assumed to be a block of developing countries with various backgrounds, different resource endowment, etc. In the competition for penetration of country D's markets, different backward countries will have varying degrees of success . . . depending on the efficacy of trade preferences upon the process of natural selection among them.' But did the terms used convey the reality? The cessation of Cuban sugar exports to the United States, for example, had nothing to do with 'resource endowments' or 'natural selection'. Nor did such a substitution benefit other U's.

Further, there were a number of points within the limits of the model itself which concerned him. First, Dr. Arndt spoke of making changes in the productive structure, followed by whatever changes in the distributive system might be desirable, as if the two were independent. But suppose a given policy mix aimed at a certain resource allocation: in so far as the policy mix did not contain an incomes policy, there was nothing to ensure we would attain our target, for once such policies had affected the distribution of income among factors, we would be left with a different set of values for the variables of the model. Secondly, he queried the existence of such a thing as a 'community welfare function'. Thirdly, he was concerned about the specification of the production function. It would be better to use a model which permitted different production functions in U and D, and which could incorporate technical change and 'learning', factors which would certainly impinge on the pattern of dynamic comparative advantage.

Dr. Arndt, replying first to Dr. Bacha, said that of course any attempt to determine consistent and feasible world trade policies required that the goals of both developed and underdeveloped countries be considered. His diagrams had developed consequences for D alone simply in order to reduce the complexity of the geometry. The points raised by Dr. Bacha could be handled by the analysis: whether one opted for trade, aid, industrial development or some combination of these depended on the nature of the chosen targets. The policy mix selected for the pursuit of economic 'independence' would in all probability be different from the mix associated with the goal of maximising per capita income over a given period.

Replying to Professor Ranis, he said that one of the functions which a model ought to perform was to facilitate our understanding of the underlying structure of the system. There was little economic analysis deserving of the name which did not use a model, although the model might not always be spelled out. The present model presented a framework for analysing the policy-making process. As such it did not explicitly represent every conceivable policy situation. But it might be applied to a wide variety of cases, including any number of developed or underdeveloped countries each divided into as many sectors as required. This was a question to be disposed of in the context of the specific problem and set of countries to which the analysis was to be applied. Varying the number of countries and sectors complicated the decision problem, but did not alter the need for goals and targets to be specified and for targets and instruments to be consistent not only within countries but in the global context of the world policy system as well.

Further, the model was clearly not static. Every vector was a function, among other things, of time. Both its slope and dimension were determined by time. For policies whose effects on targets were not instantaneous, there existed a family of vectors which traced out a time path for the policy. Consequently any judgement as to the consistency of targets and instruments had to be made with reference to a time horizon, and it did not follow that two goals which were consistent for one time period would be consistent for any or all other periods.

Dr. Katz's point regarding the production function was well taken. The model's specification was deliberately general, first, because it was felt that this was not the place to deal with the many problems associated with the proper specification of production functions, and second, because it left open the possibility of specifying detailed and differing functions in an empirical test of the model. In another context, for example, labour was assumed to be available only as a result of investment in the production of skills. Questions concerning the embodiment of technological change might be analogously treated.

Dr. Katz was correct in arguing that goals concerning production levels and goals concerning income distribution were difficult to separate. In Figure 4.2, $\hat{T}$ represented output and absorption levels which were consistent with the collectivity of goals, each goal – whether it referred to distribution or to levels – being weighed according to its status in the hierarchy of goals, and being included in the loss function. Except where it was offset by a countervailing change elsewhere, any adjustment in a given goal, whether distributive or non-distributive, was likely to alter the location of $\hat{T}$. The location of $\hat{T}$ was, moreover, critically affected by the extent to which decision-making was decentralised.

As for Dr. Katz's concern about the presence in the model of a welfare function, it was worth remembering that this was a problem which vexed all discussions of economic policy. Rather than hiding these crucial ingredients of policy making, the present model required that targets and welfare criteria be made explicit. There was, of course, no easy way of specifying normative criteria; policy makers often did not understand why they pursued certain ends, and economists were not always clear about the reasons for proposing a given policy. The present paper brought these difficulties into the open.

Several speakers attempted some defence on behalf of the developed countries. *Mr. Schaeffer* commented on the two allegations which had been made concerning the E.E.C. The first allegation was that the Community had formally created a system of preferences for all, and that it had done nothing at the economic planning level to take account of the necessary structural changes within its own members' economies, which would have to follow from a new division of industrial activities which favoured the developing countries. In point of fact, although for obvious reasons the necessary studies had had to be undertaken with a measure of discretion, they had been initiated in a number of sectors. Furthermore, various means of action had existed since the creation of the E.E.C. in regard to facilitating the transformation of industrial structures, and these were still being improved: the European Investment Bank, for example, and the Social Fund which had recently been strengthened, among others.

The second claim was that the E.E.C. was following a commercial policy of regional preferences and forms of association which was bound to lead to a division of the world into closed zones of preference, each one polarised around a developed and dominant centre. This vision of the world in no way corresponded to the concepts of the Community; in fact, being the world's largest importer and exporter, with interests in every continent, the E.E.C. saw it as vital to its own interest that world trade should develop on the largest scale possible. Admittedly it was true that it had concluded trading agreements with a certain number of countries whose special historical situation or geographical position made their trade position particularly vulnerable to the consequences of European integration. But it was a question here of purely empirical measures, not a systematic policy aimed at polarisation. The more the E.E.C. moved to acquire a world role, the more firmly it evidently believed in a world context within which to develop its trade.

Mr. Macario's rejoinder to this defence was that his own interpretation was very different. Mr. Schaeffer did acknowledge that special relationships existed; the serious consequences followed whether the policy was deliberate or not.

Professor Reynolds asked to be allowed to speak on behalf of the Chairman, Professor Vernon, and inform Dr. Krieger that the problem of facilitating adjustments in the industrial structure of the United States was not one ignored by the present Administration. The Report of the President's Commission on Trade and Investment, of November 1971, called for a study of the restructuring problems that would follow from trade liberalisation, and a working committee was now preparing guidelines to be set up within a year to facilitate the adjustment process.

Further, *Dr. von Gleich* said that he felt that the views Mr. Macario had expressed were already widely accepted in the developed countries; certainly West Germany had already granted many preferences, in addition to the E.E.C. preferences for exports of manufactures from the developing countries.

Also, the argument was frequently made that international trade policies worked only to the benefit of the developed countries; he would like to point out that many of the problems mentioned were things that did affect the exports of many developed countries too. This confusion was part of a general tendency to use arguments drawn principally from experience in primary sectors to manufactured goods, whereas in fact there were significant differences.

He would also like to qualify two further points in Mr. Macario's paper: first, he had mentioned the necessity of higher prices and in the same paragraph the sluggish growth of world demand. This pointed to the need to assign production quotas, with all their consequent problems. Second, he had claimed that direct private investment abroad should not be considered aid: in fact few today so considered it, and the West German government had officially proposed to the O.E.C.D. that private investment figures should be removed from the list of D.A.C. credits. He also commented that if one's interest was solutions, then to talk of a 'world trade policy' represented far too high a level of aggregation, both of content and geographical coverage, to be useful.

There was discussion of both the exact form and the practical reality of the kind of changes in the structure of trade which were being proposed. *Dr. Ferrer* was seriously concerned that the proposal that U should concentrate on light industries and that D should abandon production in such lines would represent merely a return to the old problem of Centre–Periphery. With growth, demand shifted to the basic sectors, which were also those where technical progress was more rapid. Thus international policy should be dovetailed with the necessary internal structural transformation; Latin America had to find a place in world trade which allowed it to specialise in products which were experiencing both rapid growth and rapid technical change. The discussion of specialisation in terms of types of industry was in any case misdirected; specialisation occurred at the product level rather than the industry level.

A further element which should be central to the discussion was the question of integration; it might be that an important market for the kinds of goods he would like to see Latin America specialise in could lie within U itself.

Mrs. Warman supported Dr. Ferrer in his argument against specialisation in light industries for Latin America. The lack of dynamism which characterised Latin America's external sector had much to do with the nature of the product – typically primary products where there was extremely little scope for improvement in quality. To opt for light industry was to opt for a parallel situation, since this was the relatively slow growing section of industry with little prospect of technical progress. We would be excluding ourselves from the changes a dynamic highly developed technology generated. A highly selective policy was what was needed.

Mr. Macario likewise saw the preoccupation of ECLA with labour-intensive industry as very dangerous; the 'technology' gap was more significant than the trade gap, and to specialise in industries which were not experiencing dynamic technical change would only lead Latin America into another vicious circle.

Professor Eastman said that there had been instances where countries had achieved exports of manufactures based on a raw material without a change in international policies. Mr. Macario had pointed out the problem created by high effective protection against such exports. This seemed a clear case where we could move towards the optimum by prohibiting export of the raw material, or taxing at a rate which offset the tariff. Where the elasticity of demand was high, this would push down rent – but that was the situation implied anyway in saying export prices were too low. Where elasticity of demand was low, then the price would not fall, and if the country had a genuine comparative advantage, a shift of processing to the country in question would occur. The newsprint industry had been shifted to Canada by this means. *Mr. Macario* reminded him, however, that when precisely such a scheme was introduced for Brazilian coffee it had to be revoked because of pressure from the United States. He thought an important part of a new scheme should be that just as developed countries could subsidise their exports, so the developing countries should also be allowed to.

Dr. Katz queried the realism of suggesting that the United States should, for example, abandon the motor car industry, when 10–15 per cent of the American population were dependent on it – a concern shared by several other speakers – though *Dr. Ffrench-Davis* felt that Dr. Arndt was in fact too pessimistic in supposing that the granting of tariff preferences would generate significant unemployment in D_2. For Latin American manufacturing exports to double in three years, they would need to take up only 2 per cent of the increment in demand in D. Admittedly the impact would be concentrated in certain sectors. But the initial increment in supply from U would be limited by existing capacity. And in the medium term, both the possibility of reallocating funds coming from the depreciation allowances, and the fact that aggregate demand in D was growing, would provide flexibility.

Dr. Germidis was in agreement that a radical change was necessary in the industrial structures of the industrialised countries. But a new international division of labour would not come about unilaterally; it would also necessitate radical changes in structure in the developing countries. The kind of highly protected import substituting industrialisation which had occurred up to the present time had resulted internally in a worsening of the terms of trade between agriculture and industry, with consequences for migration, employment, etc.; externally, it had resulted in a serious handicap to industrial exporting and a worsening in the balance of payments, principally owing to imports of capital goods. A reorientation of industry to remove these structural biases was therefore essential if advantage was to be taken of any structural change the industrial countries might put into effect. He would like to mention that the Development Centre of the O.E.C.D. was beginning a new series of studies on the international division of labour and industrialisation policies in the developing countries.

Mr. Macario likewise did not agree that even a radical restructuring of trade was Utopian, though he thought an essential pre-condition was that the developing countries should really begin to negotiate jointly. As yet they had not; even C.E.C.L.A. produced little but joint declarations. Efforts at more serious co-operation had, incidentally, met with complaints about the infringing of national sovereignty. Integration had obvious potential as a means of presenting a joint negotiating front. He saw it as crucial to bring about greater awareness in the industrialised countries that the measures proposed were actually in their own interest, as indeed they were: witness the O.E.C.D. studies mentioned in his paper which showed that the cost of their agricultural policy to O.E.C.D. members was nearly $14 billion, and that the cost to the industrialised countries as a whole of protection in the engineering industry was $50,000 million. *Dr. Arndt* added that the time horizon was all-important; policies that appeared unrealistic for implementation tomorrow looked quite different when considered as a matter of long-term adjustment.

5 International Financial Institutions and Latin American Development

Wolfgang König

THE CATHOLIC UNIVERSITY OF AMERICA

Organisations of all kinds are now participating in the expanding system of international economic co-operation. The distinguishing feature of the financial institutions is that their output is more than verbal; for that reason they are often considered, and perhaps have become, the most effective mechanisms for multilateral collaboration. They are receiving and transmitting mechanisms, even though their members have conflicting interests, differing degrees of power, and substantial bilateral financial relations. As far as Latin American development is concerned, we might consider these international financial institutions to be not only independent variables, but also mechanisms shaped by the demands of that development.

This paper deals with the work of the International Monetary Fund (I.M.F.), the World Bank Group – i.e. the International Bank for Reconstruction and Development (I.B.R.D.), the International Finance Corporation (I.F.C.), and the International Development Association (I.D.A.) – and the Inter-American Development Bank (I.D.B.). The focus of analysis is on the conceptions that have shaped the posture of these institutions on development issues, the process of decision-making with respect to the provision of financial assistance to Latin America, and the power they acquire and use in the process. Let us first establish our terms of reference.

I. SOME FIRST PRINCIPLES

The case for multilateral monetary co-operation, including temporary balance of payments assistance mitigating the effects of short-run international instability, is not hard to make. Such co-operation may become necessary when, for example, shocks originating somewhere in the world economy are passed on through the international economy, when short-term variations in demand and supply occur, or volatile international movements of short-term capital ensue. The case becomes more complex, however, when we have to deal with long-run changes in the international economy and the specific issues of developing countries. Are these countries to bear the total responsibility for their development, i.e. an increase in productive

capacity and transformations in their social and economic structures? If we accept that, in an increasingly interdependent world,
regional disparities in the standard of living are to be substantially
reduced, the foundations for constructive partnership and co-
operation based on the interdependence of interest can be laid – the
more so if we also accept that the relatively open developing economies face external barriers to their growth. These may be the result
of long-run changes in international patterns of demand and supply
over which the developing countries have no control and which may
cause structural disequilibria limiting their import capacity and
capital formation. With this in mind, a coherent set of international
policy measures can be formulated.

Autonomous external development finance can play an important
supplementary role, quantitatively and qualitatively, in the national
development efforts of the recipient countries. Without it, inflationary
financing and current account deficits may occur and an induced
foreign capital inflow with intolerable consequences ensue. Permission to deviate from general international standards for the conduct
of foreign exchange policies must, in principle, be considered a
possible additional ingredient of a package of external assistance if it
leads to a more rational use of scarce resources. In this way, external
financial co-operation can help to overcome the rigidity of an
economic structure, lead to a more effective mobilisation and use of
financial resources, increase the rate of capital formation, accelerate
the process of industrialisation, and provide jobs for unemployed
manpower.

What are the potentially controversial aspects of such action?
The diagnosis of the causes of underdevelopment might result in a
decision to concentrate remedial measures on transforming social
structure rather than on accelerating the growth of the economy,
external financial assistance being considered unnecessary and/or
undesirable. In the case of Latin America such an approach might be
considered quite tempting for the following reasons: income per
capita is high in comparison with the rest of the developing world,
albeit very unevenly distributed; the savings effort is small; and
external financing accounts for barely 10 per cent of total investment.
In terms of economic efficiency the success of this approach to
development, i.e. without external co-operation, depends, among
other things, on the degree of substitutability between domestic and
foreign resources, or, expressed differently, on the relative importance of the foreign exchange gap and the savings gap. Politically, it
might require the introduction of forced methods of capital formation which are usually considered socialistic. One can, therefore,
conclude that, under certain circumstances and for the sake of

achieving high growth rates, external financial assistance makes it unnecessary for the state to take over the sources of income of the more affluent and obviates the need for social reorganisation. This explains why international financial co-operation is not necessarily based on humanitarian and economic considerations.

The question that remains to be answered is whether a choice between external financial co-operation or no external financial co-operation is necessarily present. The degree to which the conditions of this assistance are compatible with the given development options of the recipients may be decisive. In the end, both sides might consider that a price for financial co-operation is involved and that it is not necessarily economic; to the ultimate lenders of funds, the provision of financial assistance on bankable terms might be as secondary in importance for them as the achievement of high growth rates is for the recipients. The extreme cases are when the provision of assistance by a donor is an unnecessary sacrifice or, what is relatively more likely, when the receipt of external assistance is to the disadvantage of the recipient. With the prospect of long-term international stability, both sides would probably agree on a minimum condition for external assistance: that the self-help effort of recipients is not impaired.

In view of this, the case for multilateral international financial co-operation is easily made. Among its advantages are the following: allocation of assistance on the basis of development need and free of political pressure; decision-making, including the determination of performance standards and loan conditions, on the basis of multi-national expertise, represented by the specialised knowledge of the staff of multilateral agencies; and equitable sharing of the costs of development assistance, by all donors, and of its benefits, by all recipients. In reality, however, a multilateral financial system for development might have to forgo some of these advantages, and possibly gain a political dimension in order to mobilise financial resources.

It is generally held that external finance for development should be aimed at helping the recipients to achieve self-sustaining growth. This proposition involves complex and interdependent issues concerning the absorptive capacity of the recipients, the terms on which they receive financial assistance, and their capacity to repay. Their export performance has a bearing on the last mentioned issue in particular and, in turn, involves, besides domestic policies and other things, international co-operative programmes in foreign trade such as those designed to prevent the harmful effects of excessive fluctuations in their foreign exchange earnings including the elimination of restrictions on the part of creditor countries. The point to be made here is that, if financial multilateral action is to be effective, it might have to be part of a comprehensive and far-reaching international economic co-operation.

We will now examine the post-Second World War international system of public financial institutions.

II. INSTITUTION BUILDING, TASK EXPANSION AND RELATIONSHIPS WITH INTERNATIONAL PRIVATE CAPITAL

The guiding principles and operation of this system are largely determined by pre-Bretton Woods ideas and proposals, predominantly of United States origin. There was considerable discussion of a wide range of co-operation possibilities, but the proposition that the system to be established was to provide a suitable framework for the free operation of competitive market forces outside the government sphere was never questioned. Furthermore, White's 'Suggested Plan for a United and Associated Nations Stabilisation Fund and a Bank for Reconstruction and Development of the United and Associated Nations'[1] was gradually adjusted to what the U.S. Congress found acceptable and, to some extent, to the changes advocated by the British negotiators. The importance of international investment was recognised by Keynes, but initiative in that field was almost entirely left to the United States. In the end there were conflicting expectations: the British assumed that the Bank would primarily be concerned with guaranteeing private investments, whereas the Americans hoped, among other things, that it could help to make borrowers more responsible.[2]

But the principles and objectives of the Bretton Woods system, as embodied in the Articles of Agreement of the I.B.R.D. and the I.M.F., were clear: exchange rate stability, multilateralism, convertibility, access to a pool of international liquidity in the event of temporary balance of payments difficulties, and a high level of international investment with emphasis on the flow of private capital. The Bank as well as the Fund 'was bound to be politically controlled'[3] since in their work they would be dealing with politically vulnerable matters such as exchange rate policies and the generalisation of risks inherent

[1] Interestingly enough, White's Plan was an outgrowth of the Inter-American Bank proposal considered by the Committee of the United States Senate in April 1941. See Robert W. Oliver, *Early Plans for a World Bank*, Princeton Studies in International Finance, No. 29 (Princeton, September 1971), pp. 3–4.

[2] *Ibid.*, p. 49.

[3] J. Keith Horsefield, *The International Monetary Fund 1945–1965*, Vol. I, Chronicle (I.M.F., Washington, D.C., 1969), p. 130.

in foreign private investment. In fact, the Bretton Woods system's support of private enterprise gave it a political aspect and, therefore, made it, despite the membership explosion in the 1950s, less than truly representative of the world economy in the post-war period.

Nevertheless, under the circumstances, a major breakthrough in international co-operation had been achieved. By their functions, the two institutions were designed to effectively complement each other in restoring and maintaining international economic stability, but because the Bank did not have direct authority over international investment, its scope was relatively limited and its task was easier than that of the Fund which faced the challenge of assuming, through completely new approaches, a central position in the international monetary system.

Latin America, where since the early 1930s exchange controls and other devices had been used to support a new economic policy orientation quite out of line with the Bretton Woods spirit, had no influence on the course of events. It is worth recalling Raúl Prebisch's conversations in the Bank of Mexico with a group of economists who later became internationally known, as well as the contributions published by this group toward the end of the war and shortly thereafter.[1] With respect to monetary projects for the post-war period, Victor L. Urquidi held that the Keynes plan would run into difficulty in prac- tice, since the world was not yet ready for so ambitious a concept; Raúl Prebisch, while welcoming the establishment of an international credit system, doubted that international equilibrium would be ensured. The group took no definite position with regard to pro- tectionism and restrictive foreign policies, although Urquidi re- ferred to the need of deficit countries for long-term protection, and Prebisch favoured, under certain circumstances, a curtailment of imports through multiple exchange rates as well as the split of foreign exchange markets in order to separate financial from other

---

[1] Among others, the following took part in these conversations: Victor L. Urquidi, Javier Márquez, Rodrigo Gómez and Martínez Ostos. See Raúl Prebisch, *El control de cambios en la República Argentina*, conversaciones en el Banco de México, S.A. 24, 26 and 31 January, and 4 and 7 February 1944, Banco de México, S.A. (mimeo); *Lineamientos de una política monetaria nacional*, conversaciones en el Banco de México, S.A., 11, 14, 18 and 21 February 1944, Banco de México, S.A. (mimeo); and *El patrón oro y la vulnerabilidad económica de nuestros países*, El Colegio de México, Jornadas, 11 (probably 1944); Victor L. Urquidi, 'Los proyectos monetarios de la postguerra', *El Trimestre Económico* (México, 1943), pp. 539–71, and 'Elasticidad y rigidez de Bretton Woods', *El Trimestre Económico* (Mexico, 1945), pp. 595–616; V. L. Urquidi and Consuelo Meyer L'Epee, *Memorandum sobre las operaciones de México con el Fondo Monetario Internacional*, Banco de México, S.A., Departamento de Estudios Económicos (México, D.F., 20 March, 1946) (mimeo).

transactions.[1] Later, a feeling of uncertainty concerning the principles of the I.M.F. are expressed, Urquidi contending that the concept of the World Bank was more clearly formulated and welcomed in Latin America.

Although their delegations in Bretton Woods had voiced doubts about the outlook for future international co-operation, Latin American governments seemed more optimistic. For example, they appear to have overlooked the fact that, in the case of the Fund, overwhelming importance had been given to exchange rate stability and the creation of a multilateral payments system. In Mexico, which in July 1948 was to become temporarily ineligible to use the resources of the Fund because it let the peso float, the President of the country spelled out, as the first reason for adherence to the Fund, that international credits could be obtained without immediate sacrifice.[2] Carlos Lleras Restrepo, a member of Colombia's delegation to the Bretton Woods conference, stated that monetary stabilisation was not the main goal of the Fund and recommended the entry of his country to this institution because of the advantages to be derived from the possible access to international means of settlement administered by the Fund;[3] yet at the end of 1966, when he was President of his country and when the I.M.F., backed by the World Bank and the Agency for International Development (A.I.D.) made a standby credit of $60 million dependent on the devaluation of the Colombian Peso, he saw no other solution to the impasse but to publicly break off negotiations.[4]

Today, more than a quarter of a century after Bretton Woods, Prebisch has expressed what is probably a common feeling in Latin America, namely that international financial co-operation has not been sufficiently dynamic and that progress in international co-operation in general has been mainly limited to the intellectual field.[5]

[1] Prebisch also expressed satisfaction that in the statutes for a proposed central bank of Cuba drawn up by economists working for the U.S. government, including White, provisions had been made for the use of foreign exchange controls. The most conspicuous of all Prebisch's considerations was, however, that he already supplied the starting point for a theoretical justification of industrialisation in Latin America through import substitution. In so doing, he assigned certain functions to multiple exchange rates and other exchange controls.

[2] Victor L. Urquidi and Consuelo Meyer L'Epee, *op. cit.*, p. 3.

[3] Carlos Lleras Restrepo, *Fondo Monetario Internacional*, Banco de la República de Colombia (July 1945), pp. 3, 14, 31.

[4] See Richard L. Maullin, *The Colombia – IMF Disagreement of November–December 1966: An Interpretation of its Place in Colombian Politics*, the Rand Corporation, RM 5314-RC (June 1967), especially pp. VI–VII, 21, 27.

[5] Raúl Prebisch, *Change and Development, Latin America's Great Task*, Report submitted to the Inter-American Development Bank, Washington, D.C. (July 1970), pp. 8, 133.

What went wrong? Have the institutions come to play a role different from that originally intended? Three specific answers come to mind apart from general aspects inherent in post-war political and economic development. First, the failure to establish the International Trade Organisation (I.T.O.) was bound to reduce the effectiveness of multilateral financial action. Second, the Fund, which began its active phase late in the mid-1950s, was increasingly confronted with forces originating in the industrial countries that tended to displace it from its position as the centre of the international monetary system. Third, the relatively successful work of the international development finance institutions, i.e. the World Bank Group and the I.D.B., has been overshadowed by the significant revival of international private capital flows and a considerable growth of bilateral foreign aid that is co-ordinated and reviewed by another agency, the Development Assistance Committee (D.A.C.) of the O.E.C.D., established on the initiative of the United States. Furthermore, since the 1960s the atmosphere of disenchantment with the foreign aid component of development finance has made itself felt within the World Bank Group and the I.D.B.

The Bretton Woods organisations got off to a slow start. Their first years of operation were characterised by a high degree of inactivity; nevertheless, their interest in the stimulation of private capital flows in the development field was quite explicit. In fact, the Fund considered such action fully compatible with the achievement of the purposes of Article I[1] and the World Bank regarded the promotion of infrastructure projects as not only important for economic growth but also indispensable for the investment of foreign private capital.[2] Yet, this institution maintained that, because of a dearth of soundly conceived development projects ready for financing, the capacity of developing countries to absorb capital for productive purposes was limited.[3] Meanwhile, the dollar shortage in Europe and Marshall Plan aid led to the establishment of the Organisation of European Economic Corporation (O.E.E.C.) which took over some of the functions of international institutions in the financial field and was

---

[1] I.M.F., 'Statement on Financing Economic Development', United Nations, *Methods of Financing Economic Development in Underdeveloped Countries* (Department of Economic Affairs, Lake Success, New York, 1949), pp. 103–4.

[2] I.B.R.D., 'Memorandum on Financing Economic Development', United Nations, *Methods . . .*, *op. cit.*, pp. 98–9. Urquidi tells us of the first request from Latin America to the World Bank for substantial funds in 1947 which was favourably received because the applicant was a foreign enterprise with which the Bank negotiated even before it consulted the Brazilian host government which was to give a guarantee (Urquidi, as a World Bank official, took part in these negotiations). Victor L. Urquidi, *The Challenge of Development in Latin America* (Praeger, Third printing 1966), pp. 56–7.

[3] I.B.R.D., 'Memorandum . . .', *op. cit.*, p. 91.

subsequently transformed into the Organisation for Economic Co-operation and Development (O.E.C.D.). Latin American countries were extremely disappointed with the lack of activity of the World Bank,[1] and also felt let down at the end of the 1940s by the failure of the Fund to establish a mechanism for multilateral compensation within the region.[2] In fact, there was talk of the 'Bretton Woods illusion'.[3]

The 1950s saw the activation of multilateral financial policies, more institution building, and task expansion. Because the World Bank's own ability to directly promote private enterprise is limited for statutory reasons, the I.F.C. was established in 1956. It has been described as 'unique among inter-governmental organizations in that it is the only such institution operated for the sole purpose of assisting the international spread of private enterprise.'[4] Some years after its foundation the Corporation was authorised to invest in equities – a move at first opposed by the United States on the grounds that a multinational agency should not hold an equity interest in private business firms. Subsequently it was further authorised to borrow from the World Bank up to four times its own unimpaired subscribed capital and surplus. The I.D.B. was created in December 1959, after the considerable insistence of Latin Americans had overcome the negative attitude of the United States towards such a project and when the inter-American system was generally considered to be moving towards collapse. The foundation of this institution has been described as 'a political act through which the Latin American countries have affirmed their will to change the distribution of power within the inter-American system with the aim of democratising it'.[5] In view of the heavy debt service burden of many countries I.D.A. was established in 1960. It is held that its concessionary loans not only strengthen the borrower country's economy without adding to the short-term burden of foreign debt service, but also indirectly increase the safety of the conventional loans of foreign investors.[6]

How have these institutions fared up till now? The emergence of the U.S. dollar as a vehicle currency, and the international difficulties

[1] The Governor of Mexico on behalf of his Latin American colleagues, I.M.F., *Summary Proceedings* (1951), pp. 104–5.

[2] Victor L. Urquidi, *Trayectorio del mercado común latinoamericano* (Estudios, C.E.M.L.A., 1960), pp. 36–8.

[3] Ernesto Samhaber, 'Bretton Woods y América Latina', *Economía*, Nos. 32–3, (Chile, trimestre de 1949), p. 105.

[4] World Bank, I.D.A. and I.F.C., *Policies and Operations* (April 1968), p. 95.

[5] Gustavo Lagos, 'The Political Role of Regional Economic Organizations in Latin America', in Robert W. Cox (ed.), *International Organization: World Politics* (Macmillan, 1969), p. 62.

[6] I.B.R.D., *World Bank and IDA, Questions and Answers* (September 1971), p. 78.

arising from the persistent U.S. balance of payments deficits, were largely instrumental in concentrating rival power in the Group of Ten, thereby leading to the by-passing of the I.M.F. and a weakening of its position in important matters which as a result became the subject of negotiations between the United States and European countries. The I.M.F. granted the developing countries facilities for compensatory financing and for stabilising the prices of primary products – amounting in effect to some decontrol of its drawing policies. However, it has not yet seen fit to declare the post-war transitional period at an end. Nor has it amended or replaced Article XIV which still applies to a considerable number of countries; in addition the Article VIII status of another group of countries is impaired (see also Table 5.19). The extensive debate on the reform of the international monetary system in the 1960s finally led to a potentially important innovation, the Special Drawing Rights (S.D.R.s), which both made unconditional liquidity available to members for supplementing existing assets, and constituted the first planned international reserves. However, the allocation of the S.D.R.s in accordance with the members' quotas gave rise to considerable criticism by academic circles as well as, in the developing countries,[1] by those who had hoped to see a link with development finance established. As regards the latter, the I.M.F.'s arguments that the share of the developing countries in the total quotas of Fund members is in excess of their share in the total reserves of these members and that the S.D.R. liquidity can lead to an increase in development aid are hardly a consolation. A severe test for the Fund was the suspension of the convertibility of the dollar into gold and the introduction of an import surcharge by the United States within the context of the New Economic Policy announced on 15 August 1971. A month later, the Managing Director of the Fund considered it necessary to state publicly that since that date, his institution had not stopped operations, 'even as far as transactions go'.[2] Recently Latin American countries appeared to be divided in their views on whether or not the developing nations should take joint action to solve the current international monetary crisis outside the framework of the I.M.F.[3]

By contrast, the World Bank Group and the I.D.B. have

[1] 'Antisocial . . .', 'the L.D.C.s need development financing, not reserves': the Director of C.E.M.L.A., Javier Márquez, also stating that 'the points of injection, make very little sense'. Javier Márquez, 'Reserves, Liquidity, and the Developing Countries', I.M.F., *International Reserves* (I.M.F., Washington, D.C., 1970), pp. 98, 108–9.

[2] I.M.F., *Press Conference of Pierre-Paul Schweitzer*, Sheraton-Park Hotel, Washington, D.C. (25 September 1971), p. 1.

[3] *Latin America*, Vol. V, No. 44 (London, 29 October 1971), p. 1.

strengthened their position by expanding and diversifying the scope of their lending and other activities in line with their assessments of changing development priorities. The I.D.B. is now the largest single source of multilateral development finance for Latin America. For the World Bank Group, Africa and Asia come first in its lending activities. The five-year expansion plan of the Group, covering the fiscal period 1969 to 1973, during which lending is expected to double that of the previous five fiscal years, is on target. Like the I.D.B., the Group has shown a growing awareness of social problems in the developing world such as unemployment, income distribution, poverty, and inequality.[1]

Turning now to some specific aspects of the present relationships between the international financial institutions and private international investment, we find that with the exception of the I.D.B.,[2] these institutions have no reservations about private investment capital, although with the exception of the I.F.C.[3] they do not go out of their way to endorse it. That might perhaps be interpreted to signify that the institutions are more aware of their public character. However, even though they are intergovernmental organisations the World Bank and the I.D.B. remain highly dependent on private investors in mobilising resources for development. Furthermore their successful operations in capital markets largely depend on the granting of privileges by the countries concerned, since the scheduling and authorisation of bond issues are usually highly regulated. The I.D.B., which recently proposed a European Fund for Latin American Development, has not yet obtained the same degree of preferential treatment for its bonds in the capital markets of non-member countries as have the World Bank and the European Investment Bank. Other mobilisation techniques employed by the I.B.R.D. and I.D.B. (and of course by the I.F.C.), also involve close collaboration with private financial institutions in the developed countries, but there is no ready evidence to suggest that the ideas of the ultimate lenders of capital about suitable development options necessarily become binding for the ultimate borrowers. Nevertheless the World Bank and the I.D.B. are not only obliged to earn a solid financing

[1] See, for example, Robert S. McNamara, *Address to the Board of Governors*, Washington, D.C. (27 September 1971), pp. 21–2, 28.

[2] See for example Felipe Herrera, *The IDB and Extraregional Assistance for Latin America: New Prospects*, Speech delivered at the Round-Table Meeting on Foreign Private Investment in Latin America, Rome, 29 January 1971 (I.D.B., Washington, D.C., 1971), pp. 9–10.

[3] See for example, William S. Gaud (Executive Vice President of the I.F.C.), *Private Enterprise in Economic Development*, Speech to the Annual International Finance Conference of The American Management Association, New York, N.Y., 24 February 1971 (I.F.C., Washington, D.C.), pp. 1–5.

reputation; the I.D.B., for example, has been cautioned not to associate itself with Hirschman's divestment proposal if it wants to retain the trust and confidence it has gained among foreign investors.[1] In fact, the institutions are increasing their attractiveness to the private investor in various ways. The I.B.R.D., in addition to having a private enterprise arm, the I.F.C., directly encourages the flow of private capital by sponsoring the International Centre for the Settlement of Investment Disputes and advocates the establishment of an investment insurance organization.[2] The World Bank and I.D.A. may refuse to lend to members who fail to settle expropriation claims.[3] The I.D.B. is exploring the possibility of setting up a subsidiary along the lines of the International Finance Corporation.

Finally, the extent to which the international investor needs the international financial institutions must be examined. He has often felt that the absence of fully formulated projects ready for implementation or mechanisms for their identification and preparation is a major restraint on his activity. In developing countries, international business corporations need a number of complementary activities with which they are normally not concerned. Private international business considers itself an indirect beneficiary in that the infrastructure projects, for example, undertaken by the institutions improve the business climate. It benefits directly since the institutions are instrumental in opening up new export markets and give financial and technical assistance to the local development finance companies that are coming to be an increasingly important source of funds.[4]

III. POLICIES TOWARDS AND ACTIVITIES IN LATIN AMERICA

Like money in general, multilateral external finance implies command over resources and therefore power. The power international financial institutions acquire by their ability to provide financial assistance to Latin America and how they use that power is the subject of this section. But first we shall examine the magnitude of their financial assistance.

[1] Comments by Eckard von Heyden, Deputy Manager, Deutsche Bank, Frankfurt, I.D.B., *The IDB's First Decade and Perspectives for the Future*, Round Table, Punta del Este, Uruguay, (April 1970), p. 157.

[2] Most Latin American governments are opposed to such mechanisms.

[3] I.B.R.D., *World Bank and IDA.*, *op. cit.*, pp. 13, 88.

[4] 'International Bank for Reconstruction and Development, International Development Association', reprinted from *The United Nations and World Business*, (Business International Corporation, New York, October 1967), pp. 1–2.

(1) THE FINANCIAL RECORD

Over-view of gross inflows

Even if the flow of equity investment is left out of account, data for the second half of the 1960s suggest that the initiative in supplying external finance to Latin America is gradually shifting from the public to the private sector. Whereas, in the same period, multi-lateral loans and credits invariably accounted for about 12 per cent of the total of loans and grants to Latin American countries, the share of private loans and credits rose to as much as 50 per cent in 1969 (Table 5.1).

TABLE 5.1

DISTRIBUTION OF LOANS AND GRANTS TO LATIN AMERICAN COUNTRIES[a] BY SOURCE AND CATEGORY OF TRANSACTION (GROSS DISBURSEMENTS), 1965–69
(Percentages)

	1965	1967	1969
Private Loans and Credits			
Suppliers' Credits	15	18	18
Other Private[b]	32	31	32
Total	47	49	50
Official Grants	21	15	18
Official Bilateral Loans and Credits			
D.A.C. Countries	20	22	20
Other Countries	1	1	—
Total	21	23	20
Multilateral Loans and Credits	12	13	12

[a] Argentina, Bolivia, Brazil, Chile, Colombia, Costa Rica, Dominican Republic, Ecuador, El Salvador, Guatemala, Guyana, Honduras, Jamaica, Mexico, Nicaragua, Panama, Paraguay, Peru, Trinidad and Tobago, Uruguay, Venezuela.

[b] Mainly loans from private banks, bonds and other funded debt.

Source: World Bank, *Annual Report* (1971), p. 62.

Data on official external financing of Latin America published by the Inter-American Economic and Social Council suggest an accelerating multilateralisation of this assistance. Authorisations by the multilateral institutions under study accounted for less than 50 per cent of the accumulated total of nearly $22 billion in the ten-year period 1961 to 1970, but in 1970 the individual authorisations of the I.B.R.D. and the I.D.B. were roughly equal to U.S. bilateral assistance (Table 5.2). The annual totals during the period, however, did not show a trend in either direction.

TABLE 5.2

LATIN AMERICA: AUTHORISATION OF OFFICIAL EXTERNAL FINANCING FOR 1961-70

(Millions of dollars, authorisations of agencies, calendar years)

	1961	1962	1963	1964	1965	1966	1967	1968	1969	1970	Annual Average 1961-70
1. United States, Bilateral	1,403·1	838·8	897·0	1,450·5	950·5	1,072·3	1,140·8	1,114·6	676·6	625·9	1,017·0
A.I.D.	451·2	517·5	603·5	1,006·9	533·5	744·9	556·0	645·3	507·5	394·0	596·0
Loans[a]	270·8	305·6	326·3	616·9	343·7	509·9	394·9	328·5	282·1	155·8	353·5
Grants[b]	35·0	83·8	112·1	93·5	88·7	88·5	95·1	88·7	88·4	85·6	85·9
Food for Peace[c]	145·4	128·1	165·1	296·5	101·1	146·5	66·0	228·1	137·0	152·6	156·6
Eximbank[d]	803·0	186·1	214·3	314·4	313·5	277·0	478·6	433·3	143·1	203·5	336·7
Treasury[e]	147·0	125·0	60·0	96·3	69·8	12·5	75·0	4·8	0	0	59·0
Others[f]	1·9	10·2	19·2	52·9	33·7	37·9	31·2	31·2	26·0	28·4	25·3
2. International Financial Institutions	1,025·6	898·9	733·6	577·4	1,017·6	1,067·6	978·7	1,433·4	1,207·5	1,467·6	1,040·8
I.D.B.	292·9	328·8	260·1	299·3	375·6	394·0	495·8	430·9	637·1	629·2	413·7
Ordinary Capital	129·2	83·7	179·4	164·0	123·6	98·8	170·3	193·6	214·5	190·4	154·7
Fund for Special Operations	48·1	40·2	33·6	49·4	196·6	291·3	313·1	210·1	412·5	432·1	202·0
Social Progress Trust Fund[g]	115·6	204·9	47·1	85·9	51·2	0	0	0	0	0	50·5
Other Funds[h]	0	0	0	0	4·2	3·9	12·4	27·2	10·1	6·7	6·5
Other Financial Institutions	732·7	570·1	473·5	278·1	642·0	673·6	482·9	1,002·5	570·4	865·4	629·1
I.B.R.D.	206·8	328·0	303·7	103·3	371·1	322·6	156·8	551·4	339·3	603·9	329·4
I.P.C.	10·7	9·4	0	9·1	9·4	12·0	7·7	18·0	n.d.	n.d.	7·6
I.D.A.	59·0	11·4	3·6	23·0	3·5	7·5	2·0	9·1	11·7	21·0	15·2
I.M.F.	456·2	221·3	166·2	142·7	258·0	331·5	316·4	424·0	219·4	213·5	274·9
Subtotal (1+2)	2,428·7	1,737·7	1,630·6	2,027·9	1,968·1	2,139·9	2,119·5	2,548·0	1,876·2	2,124·9	2,057·8
3. Bilateral O.E.C.D.[i]	85·9	151·9	197·2	180·8	208·0	176·7	157·6	157·6	n.d.	n.d.	131·6

c Includes loans and grants. Data are for fiscal years. Also includes funds from other countries that are not members of the O.A.S., which amount to an estimated 2·5 per cent of the total. Source: *U.S. Overseas Loans and Grants as of 1970.* A.I.I.

d The principal function of Eximbank is to promote United States exports, but those loans also provide financing for development. Data include loans from Eximbank but not guaranteed investment funds. Source: *Eximbank, Statement of Loans and Authorized Credits 1961–70.*

e Short-term loans for stabilisation of balance of payments. Source: U.S. Treasury Department, *Treasury Bulletin 1961–70.*

f Includes Peace Corps and Pan American Highway. Data are for fiscal years. Source: Unpublished A.I.D. data.

g United States fund administered by the I.D.B.

h English, Swedish, Canadian, Argentine and Vatican funds administered by the I.D.B.

i Disbursements.

Sources: 1. United States: mentioned above. 2. International agencies: I.D.B., *Statement of Approved Loans 1961–70*; I.B.R.D., *Statement of Loans 1961–70*; I.M.F., *International Financial Statistics, 1962–70*; I.D.A., *Statement of Development Credits 1961–70*; I.F.C., *Statement of Operational Investments and Standby and Underwriting Commitments 1961–1969.* 3. U.N.–O.E.C.D., Geographical Distribution of Financial Flows to Less Developed Countries, 1960–64, 1965, 1966–67, 1968. O.E.C.D. Secretariat, Paris. Quoted in C.I.E.S. document 1636 rev. 1 (Analysis of the Economic and Social Evolution of Latin America since the Inception of the Alliance for Progress), 3 August 1971, pp. 115–16.

Gross disbursements of official loans and grants represented 73 per cent of the authorised total and amounted to $16 billion in the ten-year period 1961–70; of this amount, 49 per cent was provided by international financial institutions (Table 5.3). The I.D.B. and I.B.R.D. each accounted for 35 per cent of the latter share.

The World Bank Group

By June 30 1971 the loans, investments, commitments and credits of the World Bank Group amounted to nearly U.S. $20 billion, of which $5·4 billion or 27 per cent was for Latin American countries (Table 5.4). However, their share in the total of I.D.A. credits of $3·3 billion was only 5 per cent.

Of the $5·4 billion the World Bank Group lent to Latin America, 78 per cent was for infrastructure projects (electric power, transportation, water supply and sewerage, and telecommunications) and 19 per cent for industry (including development finance companies), agriculture, forestry and fishing. New sectors of lending activities include tourism, family planning and education. Over 50 per cent of the World Bank Group's financing in Latin America went to only three countries: Mexico, Brazil and Colombia (see also Table 5.5).

The Inter-American Development Bank

By the end of 1970 the I.D.B.'s cumulative loan total amounted to slightly over $4 billion; 37 per cent of this total was from its hard loan window, i.e. the ordinary capital resources, 50 per cent from its soft loan window, i.e. the Fund for Special Operations, and the remainder from the Social Progress Trust Fund and other resources (Table 5.6).

Of these I.D.B. loans of slightly over U.S. $4 billion, 41 per cent has been devoted to agriculture and industry; 31 per cent to transportation, communications, and electric power facilities; and 25 per cent to social infrastructure (water supply and sewerage systems, low-cost housing, and improvements of higher and technical education) (Table 5.7). Within its overall lending and technical assistance programmes, the I.D.B. allocated over $500 million to the financing of integration projects and other integration-oriented activities generally considered to be effective instruments for promoting industrialisation and diversifying exports. In recent years, the Bank has enlarged the scope of its operations in various areas of agricultural and rural development.

Over 50 per cent of the I.D.B.'s loans were made to Brazil, Argentina, Mexico and Colombia.

LATIN AMERICA: DISBURSEMENTS AGAINST LOANS AND DONATIONS AUTHORISED BY OFFICIAL AGENCIES IN 1961–70
(In millions of dollars, calendar years)

	1961	1962	1963	1964	1965	1966	1967	1968	1969	1970	Total 1961–70
1. United States, Bilateral	997·1	656·1	761·2	650·2	886·6	946·5	856·5	966·4	848·1	835·4	8,404·1
A.I.D. loans[a]	109·9	185·5	223·2	242·0	297·2	452·3	348·7	381·1	293·7	290·0	2,323·6
A.I.D. grants[b]	33·6	45·8	69·7	91·6	83·5	105·7	105·5	96·0	87·5	85·6*	309·5
Food for Peace[c]	107·4	68·5	126·2	151·4	251·2	152·2	141·8	159·6	148·4	152·6	1,459·3
Eximbank[d]	670·5	311·0	232·4	132·8	206·0	199·8	237·1	308·2	290·5	278·8	2,867·1
Treasury[e]	65·0	34·5	90·5	18·3	13·4	13·5	0	0	0	0	235·2
Others[f]	10·7	10·8	19·2	14·1	30·3	23·0	23·4	21·5	28·0	23·4*	209·4
2. International Lending Institutions	455·2	312·2	644·5	510·6	522·1	645·8	620·1	805·3	853·7	915·9	6,285·4
I.D.B.	6·6	58·8	141·0	198·0	181·9	213·4	241·1	292·1	393·6	427·6	2,154·1
Ordinary Capital	3·1	28·1	59·8	106·6	82·9	98·6	111·6	114·5	138·4	151·1	894·7
Fund for Special Operations	2·6	8·8	15·3	24·6	28·6	44·6	69·6	120·4	192·3	244·6	751·4
Social Progress Trust Fund[g]	0·9	21·9	65·9	66·8	70·4	70·2	59·9	55·1	58·5	23·2	492·8
Other Funds[h]	0	0	0	0	0	0	0	2·1	4·4	8·7	15·2
I.B.R.D.	96·0	138·7	261·0	232·7	162·9	228·2	223·7	219·1	265·9	359·7	2,187·9
I.D.A.	0	6·6	7·8	9·5	15·9	20·8	23·1	13·8	5·8	8·2	111·5
I.F.C.	5·1	12·4	3·2	7·9	14·2	9·4	9·5	6·8	11·2	n.a.	79·7
I.M.F.	347·5	95·7	231·5	62·5	147·2	174·0	122·7	273·5	177·2	120·4	1,752·2
Sub-total (1+2)	1,453·2	968·3	1,405·7	1,160·8	1,408·7	1,592·3	1,476·6	1,771·7	1,701·8	1,751·3	14,689·5
3. O.E.C.D.	85·9	151·9	197·2	180·8	208·0	176·7	157·6	157·6	n.a.	n.a.	1,315·7
Total	1,538·2	1,120·2	1,602·9	1,341·6	1,616·7	1,769·0	1,634·2	1,929·3	1,701·8	1,751·3	16,005·2
Accumulated Total		2,658·4	4,261·3	5,602·9	7,219·6	8,988·6	10,622·8	12,552·1	14,253·9	16,005·2	

*Authorisations.

Note: See footnotes and sources of Table 5.2.
Quoted in C.I.E.S. document 1636 rev. 1, *op. cit.*, p. 125.

TABLE 5.4

WORLD BANK GROUP FINANCING IN LATIN AMERICA
BANK LOANS, I.D.A. CREDITS AND I.F.C. INVESTMENTS BY PURPOSE
NET AS OF 30 JUNE 1971

(Millions of U.S. dollars)

	Total Bank, I.D.A. & I.F.C.	Bank Loans		I.D.A. Credits		I.F.C. Investments		Total Western Hemisphere
		Total	Western Hemisphere	Total	Western Hemisphere	Total	Western Hemisphere	
Grand Total	19,953·1	16,068·6	5,007·8	3,340·4	176·7	544·1	217·3	5,401·8
Electric power	5,284·0	5,010·6	2,462·9	273·4	37·5	—	—	2,500·4
Transportation	5,876·9	4,958·3	1,322·0	918·5	77·3	—	—	1,399·3
Telecommunications	575·2	348·6	151·1	226·6	—	—	—	151·1
Agriculture, forestry and fishing	2,370·8	1,497·4	528·3	850·2	46·9	23·2	8·7	583·9
Industry	3,017·4	2,413·2	267·3	104·0	—	500·2	202·2	469·5
General development and industrial imports	1,318·4	637·7	5·4	680·0	—	0·7	—	5·4
Education	424·4	212·7	84·3	211·7	12·0	—	—	96·3
Population	9·8	5·0	5·0	4·8	3·0	—	—	5·0
Water supply and sewerage	328·7	277·7	181·7	51·0	3·0	—	—	184·7
Tourism	30·0	10·0	—	—	—	20·0	6·4	6·4
Post-war reconstruction	496·8	496·8	—	—	—	—	—	—
Project preparation and technical assistance	21·1	0·9	—	20·2	—	—	—	—
Financing loan (I.F.C.)	200·0	200·0	—	—	—	—	—	—

Note: Multipurpose loans are distributed according to each purpose and not assigned to the major purpose. Due to rounding, details may not add to totals.

Source: Adapted from World Bank Group, *Profiles of Development* (September 1971), pp. 32–3.

TABLE 5.5

LENDING BY THE WORLD BANK AND I.D.A.
TO LATIN AMERICAN COUNTRIES AS OF
31 DECEMBER 1970
(Expressed in U.S. dollars)

	Bank Loans		I.D.A. Credits	
	Number	*Net Amount*[a]	*Number*	*Net Amount*[a]
Argentina	7	$357,602,049		
Bolivia	1	23,250,000	5	$25,800,000
Brazil	29	838,034,660		
Chile	18	232,537,762	1	18,997,755
Colombia	43	718,777,840	1	19,500,000
Costa Rica	11	84,876,251	1	4,550,243
Dominican Rep.	1	25,000,000		
Ecuador	9	63,300,000	4	24,600,000
El Salvador	9	57,918,024	1	7,999,331
Guatemala	4	46,500,000		
Guyana	3	8,819,017	2	5,100,000
Haiti	1	2,600,000	1	349,855
Honduras	9	52,317,613	5	24,027,974
Jamaica	7	46,459,421		
Mexico	24	978,705,679		
Nicaragua	15	59,858,828	1	2,994,834
Panama	6	60,047,426		
Paraguay	6	21,838,549	4	21,400,000
Peru	24	244,102,066		
Trinidad and Tobago	5	46,390,424		
Uruguay	8	126,461,803		
Venezuela	9	294,114,641		
Total	249	$4,389,512,053	26	$155,319,992

[a] Net of cancellations, refundings, and terminations.

Source: The World Bank Group, *Policies and Operations* (June 1971), p. 41.

The International Monetary Fund

As of 31 December 1970, gross borrowings by Latin American members amounted to $2·6 billion (Table 5.8) of which only $118 million was used for compensatory financing. Purchases from the Fund increased considerably after 1956, but, beginning in 1963, Latin American countries substantially reduced their financial operations with that institution (Table 5.9). Up to 1965 the Fund's holdings of some members' currencies had continuously exceeded 100 per cent of their corresponding quota; in the case of Argentina for 104 months, Brazil 98 months, Bolivia 93 months, Paraguay 69 months and Honduras 64 months.[1] In the second half of the 1960s, however, Latin

---

[1] J. Keith Horsefield, *op. cit.*, p. 447.

TABLE 5.6

THE I.D.B.s LENDING, 1961–70
(Thousands of U.S. dollars)

Country	Total		Detail by funds							
	Number of Loans	Amount	Number of Loans	Ordinary Capital Resources	Number of Loans	Fund for Special Operations	Number of Loans	Social Progress Trust Fund	Number of Loans	Other Resources
Argentina	61	$549,561	33	$282,604	23	$222,708	4	$43,500	1	$749
Bolivia	28	102,142			20	82,010	6	14,600	2	5,532
Brazil	77	875,594	36	395,477	28	403,541	10	61,510	3	15,066
Chile	57	297,900	17	102,273	23	151,635	14	34,579	3	9,413
Colombia	55	374,742	21	141,910	22	165,180	9	49,008	3	18,644
Costa Rica	23	61,509	6	15,271	11	34,539	6	11,699		
Dominican Republic	13	58,903	1	6,000	8	44,495	4	8,408		
Ecuador	28	109,675	4	13,836	13	64,362	9	27,449	2	4,028
El Salvador	18	49,581	4	6,958	6	15,483	6	21,952	2	5,188
Guatemala	19	79,416	5	11,292	10	53,804	4	14,320		
Haiti	4	12,250			4	12,250				
Honduras	17	55,005	2	460	10	46,942	5	7,603		
Jamaica	2	10,900			2	10,900				
Mexico	55	531,478	27	267,916	19	228,031	8	34,996	1	535
Nicaragua	21	75,410	7	19,525	10	42,850	4	13,035		
Panama	16	48,535	1	1,500	12	34,173	3	12,862		
Paraguay	23	98,205	4	6,050	15	83,563	3	7,800	1	792
Peru	37	224,259	13	43,674	12	134,055	10	45,136	2	1,394
Trinidad and Tobago	5	8,900			5	8,900				
Uruguay	24	99,835	10	47,888	11	40,247	2	10,500	1	1,200
Venezuela	29	269,000	12	104,939	9	91,200	8	72,861		
Regional	10	75,814	2	18,454	6	50,704	1	2,914	1	3,742
Total	522	$4,063,624	205	$1,486,027	279	$2,021,532	115	$494,732	22	$66,283

Source: I.D.B., *Eleventh Annual Report* (1970), p. 4.

TABLE 5.7

DISTRIBUTION OF I.D.B. LOANS
(Millions of U.S. dollars)

Sector	1970	1961–70	Percentage
Agriculture	236	1,067	26
Transportation and communications	162	685	17
Industry and mining	47	621	15
Electric power	103	577	14
Water supply and sewerage systems	29	486	12
Urban development and housing	29	351	9
Education	14	150	4
Pre-investment	12	79	2
Export financing	12	53	1
Total	644	4,069	100

Source: I.D.B., *Eleventh Annual Report* (1970), p. 7.

American countries became net contributors to the Fund's resources and, at the end of 1970, their total net borrowings amounted to only $335 million, an amount substantially less than the counterpart of their subscription in gold to the I.M.F.'s capital.

The Fund's Latin American members are all participants in the Special Drawing Account and on 1 January 1970 received an allocation of 330 million S.D.R.s, a 7·3 per cent increase over their end of 1969 reserves consisting of gold, reserve position in the Fund, and foreign exchange (Table 5.10). In 1970, they made a total net use of 58 million to obtain foreign exchange from other participants and to discharge repurchase and charges in the Fund's general account. On 1 January 1971 they received a further allocation of 276 million, a 4·9 per cent increase over their end of 1970 reserves (including the first S.D.R. allocation).

Net Flows, Debt, and Terms of Financial Assistance

The net flows of official financing received by Latin American countries from 1961 to 1970 represented some 60 per cent of official disbursements or $9·5 billion; of this amount, 36 per cent was provided by international financial institutions, the I.D.B.'s share in the latter being slightly over 50 per cent and that of the World Bank 44 per cent (Table 5.11).

Net flows are largely determined by the terms and conditions of development finance, and are therefore also related to levels of indebtedness. The World Bank, which has been concerned about the external debts of developing countries for many years, responded in 1970 to a request from the Inter-American Committee of the Alliance for Progress (C.I.A.P.) to assist in a special study of the indebtedness

TABLE 5.8

LATIN AMERICA AND I.M.F.: MEMBERSHIP QUOTAS AND TRANSACTIONS AS OF 31 DECEMBER 1970
(Millions of U.S. dollars)

Country	Year of I.M.F. Member- ship	Present Quota	Total Drawings	Re- purchases	Use of Member's Currency by Other Members	Total Net Drawings
Argentina	1956	440	425·0	349·1[a]	107·0	—
Barbados	1970	13	—	—		—
Bolivia	1945	37	45·4	30·4		15·0
Brazil	1946	440	578·4	553·6[a]	32·4	—
Chile	1945	158	348·0	307·0		41·0
Colombia	1945	157	374·9	280·8		94·1
Costa Rica	1946	32	42·6	40·5		2·0
Dominican Republic	1945	43	49·6	32·3		17·3
Ecuador	1945	33	68·2	46·2		22·0
El Salvador	1946	35	69·5	54·3		15·2
Guatemala	1945	36	36·0	27·0		9·0
Guyana	1966	20	—	—		—
Haiti	1953	19	29·1	23·1		6·0
Honduras	1945	25	38·7	32·5		6·2
Jamaica	1963	53	3·8	—		3·8
Mexico	1945	370	112·5	112·4[a]	117·5	—
Nicaragua	1946	27	80·5	65·7		14·8
Panama	1946	36	12·1	4·2		8·0
Paraguay	1945	19	8·1	8·1		—
Peru	1945	123	130·0	89·3		40·6
Trinidad and Tobago	1963	63	9·5	4·8		4·8
Uruguay	1946	69	91·7	56·2		35·5
Venezuela	1945	330	—	—	37·3	—
Total		2,578	2,626·1	2,189·7	294·2	335·2

[a] Member's repurchase obligation reduced through use of its currency by other members.

Source: I.M.F., *The International Monetary Fund and Latin America* (1971).

of Latin American countries. Some of the findings of the subsequent thorough research by the Bank on the subject have recently been published and provide much valuable information, although the Bank cautions that statistics are not completely reliable. At the end of 1969 the outstanding external public debt of Latin American countries amounted to $17·6 billion. Of this amount, 24 per cent was owed to multilateral institutions, the remainder being owed equally to bilateral official and private creditors (Table 5.12). Various aspects of

the development of Latin America's public external debt in the 1960s
are encouraging: the rate of growth of the outstanding debt averaged
11 per cent annually from 1960 to 1969 and was therefore not much
higher than the rate of growth of the gross national product at

TABLE 5.9

TRANSACTIONS OF LATIN AMERICAN MEMBERS
WITH I.M.F.
(Millions of U.S. dollars)

Year	Purchases	Repayments by Repurchase	Use of Latin American Currencies
1947	31·3	—	
1948	1·7	—	
1949	37·5	1·4	
1950	—	0·3	
1951	28·0	26·0	
1952	38·4	69·2	
1953	80·5	39·2	
1954	47·5	0·4	
1955	—	22·4	
1956	21·4	28·2	
1957	204·6	47·2	
1958	117·6	59·8	
1959	114·8	77·3	
1960	147·0	64·8	
1961	347·5	72·1	16·0
1962	95·7	164·1	
1963	231·5	118·0	
1964	62·5	148·2	
1965	147·2	172·4	9·5
1966	174·0	217·7	9·0
1967	122·7	148·5	54·0
1968	273·5	221·5	119·5
1969	177·2	190·4	49·0
1970	124·2	300·8	37·2
Total	2,626·1	2,189·7	294·2

Source: as Table 5.8, p. 30.

current prices; the annual rate of growth of service payments averaged only 6 per cent from 1960 to 1969; and, for most of the Latin
American countries, service payments on external public debts as a
percentage of the export of goods and services in 1969 were less than
in the previous year, although they were still substantial in the case
of Argentina, Mexico, Uruguay and Brazil (Tables 5.13 and 5.15; for
projected debt service, see Table 5.14).

The debt problem of Latin American countries is not one of size, but rather of the terms and conditions of financial assistance. Because of the hardening of loan terms and a significant decline in the volume of grants provided, the grant component of loans and grants to Latin America declined by about 25 per cent in the second half of the 1960s, from 39 per cent to 29 per cent (see Table 5.16).

TABLE 5.10

SPECIAL DRAWING ACCOUNT: ALLOCATIONS OF SPECIAL DRAWING RIGHTS TO LATIN AMERICAN PARTICIPANTS

Participant	January 1 1970	January 1 1971
Argentina	58,800,000	47,080,000
Barbados	—	1,391,000
Bolivia	4,872,000	3,959,000
Brazil	58,800,000	47,080,000
Chile	21,000,000	16,906,000
Colombia	21,000,000	16,799,000
Costa Rica	4,200,000	3,424,000
Dominican Republic	5,376,000	4,601,000
Ecuador	4,200,000	3,531,000
El Salvador	4,200,000	3,745,000
Guatemala	4,200,000	3,852,000
Guyana	2,520,000	2,140,000
Haiti	2,520,000	2,033,000
Honduras	3,192,000	2,675,000
Jamaica	6,364,000	5,671,000
Mexico	45,380,000	39,590,000
Nicaragua	3,192,000	2,889,000
Panama	4,704,000	3,852,000
Paraguay	2,520,000	2,033,000
Peru	14,280,000	13,161,000
Trinidad and Tobago	7,392,000	6,741,000
Uruguay	9,240,000	7,383,000
Venezuela	42,000,000	35,310,000
Totals	329,952,000	275,846,000

Source: as Table 5.8, p. 33.

As for the average terms for financial resources from official sources (Table 5.17) there was a general increase in the interest rates between 1961 and 1970, whereas there are no clear trends with respect to grace and amortisation periods. To obtain a clearer idea of the support received from official external financing, the Inter-American Economic and Social Council calculated the aid component of official non-compensatory financing, taking into account the interest rates and the grace and amortisation periods for each loan for the

TABLE 5.11

LATIN AMERICA: NET FLOWS OF OFFICIAL FINANCING RECEIVED IN 1961-70
(Millions of dollars, calendar years)

	1961	1962	1963	1964	1965	1966	1967	1968	1969	1970	Total 1951-70
1. United States, Bilateral	619.7	504.0	478.0	340.2	639.1	636.5	554.5	687.9	584.4	556.9	5,601.2
A.I.D. loans[a]	106.1	180.8	212.5	231.7	288.1	437.9	326.1	357.0	267.9	264.1	2,672.8
A.I.D. grants[b]	33.5	45.8	69.7	91.6	88.5	105.7	105.5	96.0	87.5	85.6	809.5
Food for Peace[c]	107.4	68.5	126.2	151.4	251.2	152.2	141.8	159.6	148.4	152.6	1,459.3
Eximbank[d]	343.9	170.7	24.7	-118.6	-1.2	-54.4	-35.5	59.0	52.6	25.6	466.8
Treasury[e]	18.0	27.4	25.7	-30.0	-17.8	-27.9	-6.8	-5.2	0	0	-16.6
Others[f]	10.7	10.8	19.2	14.1	30.3	23.0	23.4	21.5	28.0	28.4	209.4
2. International Lending Institutions	342.2	104.5	470.3	297.4	264.0	322.3	342.2	425.8	476.7	404.4	3,449.8
I.D.B.[g]	6.6	58.4	139.0	189.4	165.6	183.2	194.8	227.7	313.0	320.8	1,798.5
I.B.R.D.	55.1	96.7	208.9	179.5	97.0	154.7	144.0	127.7	162.3	235.8	1,481.7
I.D.A.	0	6.6	7.8	9.5	15.9	20.8	23.1	13.8	5.8	8.2	111.5
I.F.C.	5.1	11.2	1.1	4.7	10.7	7.3	6.1	4.6	8.8	n.a.	59.6
I.M.F.	275.4	-68.4	113.5	-85.7	-25.2	-43.7	-25.8	52.0	-13.2	-180.4	-1.5
Sub-total (1+2)	961.9	608.5	948.3	637.6	903.1	958.8	896.7	1,113.7	1,061.1	961.3	9,051.0
3. O.E.C.D.	22.8	97.2	122.5	50.6	45.3	20.9	31.8	9.0	n.a.	n.a.	400.1
Total	984.7	705.7	1,070.8	688.2	948.4	979.7	928.5	1,122.7	1,061.1	961.3	9,451.1
Accumulated Total		1,690.4	2,761.2	3,449.4	4,397.8	5,377.5	6,306.0	7,428.7	8,489.8	9,451.1	

Note: Footnotes *a* to *f*: see Table 5.2; *g* includes all I.D.B. funds.

Sources: See Table 5.2
CIES document 1636, rev. 1, *op. cit*, p. 127.

TABLE 5.12

EXTERNAL PUBLIC DEBT OUTSTANDING OF LATIN AMERICAN COUNTRIES
BY TYPE OF CREDITOR, 31 DECEMBER 1969
(Millions of U.S. dollars)

	Disbursed Only	Including Undisbursed			Private		
		Total	Bilateral Official	Multilateral	Suppliers	Private Banks	Other
Argentina	1,788·2	2,323·5	558·9	481·2	749·3	124·7	409·4
Bolivia	334·1	419·3	255·5	55·0	38·6	2·8	67·4
Brazil[a]	2,729·6	3,522·2	1,989·2	720·3	466·0	—	346·7
Chile	1,734·3	2,227·0	1,192·6	225·9	364·3	144·4	299·8
Colombia	1,079·0	1,515·9	659·7	634·4	141·3	b	b
Costa Rica	119·9	190·6	61·3	84·6	1·5	b	b
Dominican Republic	184·4	271·5	215·8	28·6	8·4	0·4	18·4
Ecuador	179·0	277·6	112·0	68·2	86·9	7·2	3·3
El Salvador	75·2	110·4	35·2	63·1	—	11·1	1·0
Guatemala	91·1	153·5	36·9	56·0	1·2	34·7	24·6
Guyana	65·8	113·9	94·8	10·8	0·2	0·6	7·4
Honduras	64·6	126·4	38·5	82·8	5·0	—	—
Jamaica	121·9	153·9	28·5	42·0	—	19·8	63·6
Mexico	2,963·5	3,511·3	716·2	889·4	491·0	711·9	702·9
Nicaragua	119·2	216·6	75·1	77·8	24·4	37·7	1·6
Panama	122·3	161·8	87·9	10·6	10·3	23·0	29·9
Paraguay	81·7	120·0	56·5	39·5	23·2	0·5	0·3
Peru	858·1	1,117·1	234·7	184·5	388·4	142·2	167·3
Trinidad and Tobago	75·8	101·4	26·5	42·4	4·7	13·1	14·6
Uruguay	264·9	320·1	110·7	84·2	25·2	80·5	19·6
Venezuela	514·3	664·3	135·5	344·6	20·5	122·9	40·7
Total	13,566·9	17,618·3	6,722·1	4,226·0	2,850·4	1,537·5	2,282·3

[a] Includes some non-guaranteed debt of the private sector to suppliers and excludes the undisbursed portion of suppliers' credits and of bilateral official loans except for those owed to the U.S. Government.

ten-year period 1961 to 1970.[1] It amounted to 45·7 per cent of the total of official non-compensatory financing, 33·8 per cent of I.D.B.'s lending, and 24·6 per cent of that of I.B.R.D. and I.D.A. combined.

(2) DECISION MAKING AND APPROACHES

It is very difficult for an outsider such as the author of this paper to gain an overall view of the decision-making process within and around

TABLE 5.13

SERVICE PAYMENTS ON EXTERNAL PUBLIC DEBT AS PERCENTAGE OF EXPORTS OF GOODS AND SERVICES, 1965–69

Country	1965	1966	1967	1968	1969
Argentina	20·1	25·3	26·8	27·2	23·9
Bolivia	4·7	4·7	5·8	5·5	5·6
Brazil[a]	n.a.	n.a.	n.a.	20·9	17·9
Chile	15·3	13·2	12·4	16·0	15·9
Colombia	14·4	16·5	14·0	12·8	11·2
Costa Rica	10·3	12·0	11·9	12·1	10·5
Dominican Republic	19·3	12·6	7·2	7·8	8·7
Ecuador	6·3	6·4	6·3	8·3	10·4
El Salvador	3·6	3·6	2·6	2·6	3·2
Guatemala	5·0	5·5	9·8	8·5	8·7
Guyana	4·1	3·9	4·3	3·5	3·5
Honduras	2·4	2·1	2·0	1·7	2·3
Jamaica	1·9	2·0	2·5	3·3	3·1
Mexico	24·7	21·2	21·5	25·1	22·4
Nicaragua	4·3	5·3	6·1	6·7	9·1
Panama	2·5	2·3	2·3	2·5	2·5
Paraguay	6·6	5·4	7·2	9·4	8·8
Peru	6·8	9·7	10·6	22·0	13·8
Trinidad and Tobago	1·9	2·0	1·9	1·5	2·1
Uruguay	6·7	12·3	20·3	19·2	18·8
Venezuela	1·6	2·7	2·0	2·0	2·0

[a] Includes debt service on some non-guaranteed private debt.

Source: World Bank, *Annual Report* (1971), p. 65.

the international financial institutions. It appears that more or less informal codes for the conduct of economic policies are assuming a greater importance in the channelling of financial assistance. On the one hand, this has on occasion caused considerable suspicion about the 'true' motives of the institutions. On the other hand, it seems natural that they should seek some assurance that their resources

[1] For methodology and details see Inter-American Economic and Social Council, *Analysis of the Economic and Social Evolution of Latin America since the Inception of the Alliance for Progress*, C.I.E.S./1636 rev. 1 (3 August, 1971), pp. 117–23.

TABLE 5.14

LATIN AMERICAN COUNTRIES: PROJECTED DEBT SERVICE ON EXTERNAL PUBLIC DEBT OUTSTANDING AS OF 31 DECEMBER 1969 BY TYPE OF CREDITOR

Type of Creditor	Debt outstanding (incl. undisbursed) 31 Dec. 1969	Projected										
		1970	1971	1972	1973	1974	1975	1976	1977	1978	1979	1980
Bilateral official	6,722·1	635·4	618·9	589·8	531·5	483·7	451·8	408·0	387·9	377·6	358·5	321·6
Multilateral	4,226·0	307·7	355·5	400·0	425·6	424·7	425·4	408·2	393·5	369·9	352·0	335·2
Private Suppliers	2,850·4	604·1	549·5	483·5	422·8	333·5	308·6	232·7	146·9	107·0	78·5	49·2
Private Banks	1,537·5	513·7	376·4	273·0	255·5	175·5	64·5	29·4	23·6	20·0	16·0	24·7
Other	2,282·3	249·9	260·4	305·7	348·9	292·7	228·5	164·4	152·3	142·7	132·8	96·1
Total	17,618·3	2,310·7	2,160·7	2,052·0	1,984·3	1,710·1	1,478·9	1,242·7	1,104·2	1,017·1	937·8	826·8

Note: Includes the same countries as Table 5.1. Projected service payments exclude loans for which repayment terms are not available. Items may not add to totals due to rounding.

Debt outstanding of Brazil includes some non-guaranteed debt of the private sector to suppliers and excludes the undisbursed portion of suppliers' credits and of bilateral official loans except for those owed to the U.S. Government.

Source: World Bank, *Annual Report* (1971), p. 67.

will be effectively used; the evaluation of the recipients' economic performance must, in fact, be considered important in making international financial co-operation for development effective.

Board – staff relations and related matters

Even though there are many similarities in the organisation of the development finance institutions and the I.M.F., important differences in their decision-making process exist because of the nature of their work. In the former, the decisions reached are based on the

TABLE 5.15

EXTERNAL PUBLIC DEBT OUTSTANDING
(INCLUDING UNDISBURSED) AND DEBT SERVICE
PAYMENTS OF LATIN AMERICAN COUNTRIES

Debt outstanding at 31 December 1969	$17,618,000
Debt service payments in 1969	$2,183,000
Average annual rate of growth 1960–9	
Debt outstanding	11%
Debt service payments	6%

Note: See Table 5.1 for list of countries included and qualifying notes.

Source: World Bank, *Annual Report* (1971), p. 51.

judgements not only of economists and lawyers, but also of accountants and engineers. Furthermore, in the development finance institutions there is a much higher degree of departmental interdependence and integration of activities. In the World Bank, two of the seven Area Departments are concerned with Latin America and collaborate closely with eight Projects Departments, and the Economics Department. The latter provides advisory and research support in many areas of importance for the success of the Bank's operations in Latin America such as methodological and policy problems related to industrialisation, population growth, unemployment, urbanisation, etc. By contrast, the Western Hemisphere Department, one of the five Area Departments of the I.M.F., appears to be relatively autonomous *vis-à-vis* other departments. Although this department grew out of the research department in the process of internal specialisation, many policy approaches, with complex theoretical implications and practical consequences for Latin America, were developed there quite independently.

The loan and policy proposals that come before the development finance institutions are usually initiated by their staffs and, by the time they reach the Board of Directors, they have been extensively discussed and probably brought into line with what the reaction of the directors is anticipated to be; in fact, in these Boards, consensus

TABLE 5.16

LATIN AMERICAN COUNTRIES: AVERAGE TERMS OF LOAN COMMITMENTS AND GRANT ELEMENT OF LOANS AND GRANTS, 1965–69[a]

Year	Loan Commitments					Grant[c] Amounts ($m.)	Grant Element of Loans and Grants[b] (%)	Amount of Loan Used for Terms Calculations[a]
	Amount ($m.)	Maturity (Years)	Grace (Years)	Interest (%)	Grant element[b] (%)			
1965	1,766·68	14·3	3·2	5·234	27	332·18	39	1,686·56
1966	2,016·30	16·5	3·6	5·499	27	317·04	37	1,975·56
1967	2,659·93	14·1	3·1	5·924	23	289·16	31	2,463·19
1968	3,048·20	14·5	3·4	6·126	22	334·29	30	2,938·60
1969	2,599·44	13·4	3·7	6·719	18	355·74	29	2,463·98

[a] Includes the same countries as Table 5.1 except for Brazil. Data on loans contracted in the earlier years may be incomplete.

[b] The grant element is the face value of loan commitments less the discounted present value of the future flow of repayments of principal and interest, using the customary rate of 10 per cent and expressed as a percentage of the face value.

[c] Data for grants are taken from O.E.C.D. (D.A.C.) and I.D.B. sources. Included are grant-like flows (loans repayable in local currencies), bilateral grants, and U.N. agency grants. Figures for grants are on a disbursement basis, while figures for loans are on a commitment basis. 1969 data for grants are partially estimates. The grant element of a grant is 100 per cent.

[d] This column shows the amount of loans for which repayment terms are known.

Source: World Bank and O.E.C.D., quoted in World Bank, *Annual Report* (1971), p. 69.

LATIN AMERICA: AVERAGE FINANCIAL TERMS OF DEVELOPMENT LOANS GRANTED TO LATIN AMERICA[a]

	1961 I (%)	1961 G (years)	1961 A (years)	1962 I (%)	1962 G (years)	1962 A (years)	1963 I (%)	1963 G (years)	1963 A (years)	1964 I (%)	1964 G (years)	1964 A (years)	1965 I (%)	1965 G (years)	1965 A (years)
I.D.B. I	5·8	3·6	10·8	5·9	3·1	12·0	5·8	3·1	13·1	6·0	3·6	12·0	6·3	3·4	11·5
I.D.B. II	4·4	3·7	12·8	4·0	4·1	16·1	4·0	5·8	16·2	3·9	4·9	16·6	3·6	4·0	17·3
I.D.B. III	2·3	1·1	21·4	2·5	1·2	24·5	2·3	1·4	25·8	2·5	1·3	22·3	2·5	1·6	23·4
I.B.R.D.	5·8	4·2	14·0	5·7	2·8	19·9	5·5	3·9	16·6	5·5	4·6	22·7	5·5	4·5	16·1
I.D.A.	0·75	10·0	40·0	0·75	10·0	40·0	0·75	10·0	40·0	0·75	10·0	40·0	0·75	10·0	40·0
A.I.D.	1·9	6·6	21·1	1·4	8·0	21·7	1·1	9·6	27·5	2·1	9·7	28·5	2·6	9·9	28·0
Eximbank	5·3	2·6	13·1	5·8	3·5	6·9	5·7	2·2	7·0	5·5	3·2	8·6	5·5	1·7	6·4
O.E.C.D.	n.a.	n.a.	n.a.	n.a.	n.a.	n.a.	n.a.	n.a.	n.a.	3·1	6·4	22·0	3·6	4·5	17·8

	1966 I (%)	1966 G (years)	1966 A (years)	1967 I (%)	1967 G (years)	1967 A (years)	1968 I (%)	1968 G (years)	1968 A (years)	1969 I (%)	1969 G (years)	1969 A (years)	1970 I (%)	1970 G (years)	1970 A (years)
I.D.B. I	6·3	3·2	12·3	6·8	3·7	12·4	7·9	4·3	14·7	8·2	3·7	15·5	8·2	3·8	15·3
I.D.B. II	3·4	3·6	19·4	3·4	3·8	19·7	3·7	3·9	18·5	3·8	3·5	18·6	3·5	4·1	18·1
I.D.B. III	—	—	—	—			—			—			—		
I.B.R.D.	6·0	5·2	17·4	6·0	4·9	16·5	6·2	4·5	16·6	6·7	4·0	15·5	7·0	5·1	19·0
I.D.A.	0·75	10·0	40·0	0·75	10·0	40·0	0·75	10·0	40·0	0·75	10·0	40·0	0·75	10·0	40·0
A.I.D.	2·5	9·2	29·2	2·5	9·9	29·9	2·5	9·8	29·9	2·9	9·6	29·1	3·1	9·3	28·6
Eximbank	5·3	1·1	8·1	6·0	3·1	9·7	6·0	1·8	9·7	6·0	3·2	5·4	6·0	4·6	4·5
O.E.C.D.	3·1	5·3	18·2	3·8	5·3	18·1	3·3	5·8	21·5	n.a.	n.a.	n.a.	n.a.	n.a.	n.a.

[a] *I*: Rate of interest. *G*: Grace period. *A*: Amortisation period. I.D.B. I: Ordinary Capital. I.D.B. II: Fund for Special Operations. I.D.B. III: Social Progress Trust Fund.

Source: Statement of the loans of the agencies for 1961–70. O.E.C.D.: Ninth Annual Report of the Social Progress Trust Fund, 1969. Inter-American Development Bank. Excluded are some loans for which information is not complete. C.I.E.S. document 1636, rev. 1, *op. cit.*, p. 118.

rather than voting appears to be the normal method of reaching agreement. A few large shareholders could, of course, defeat any proposal since a simple majority of votes is sufficient for a decision.

In the Fund, on the other hand, policy formulation is largely in the hands of the Board of Directors, which is responsible for the day-to-day operations of the institution and is in continuous session under the chairmanship of the Managing Director. The predominant role of the Board in policy formulation and decision-making as well as in the control of activities is quite contrary to earlier understandings that the directors were to be responsible to the countries they represented and the Managing Director and his staff, to the Fund as a whole.[1]

Although the Boards of the development finance institutions allow their staffs a higher degree of independence than in the Fund[2] the effectiveness of their co-operation with Latin American countries is challenged when technically approved loans are held up in the Board. The U.S. Director of the I.D.B. and the World Bank is reported to have provoked such a situation, for example, in connection with loans to Peru because of its purchase of military goods.[3] The U.S. Director abstained from voting on World Bank loans to Bolivia and Guyana which had nationalised foreign corporations.[4] It should be borne in mind that the increasing multilateralisation of U.S. official assistance is taking place at a time when in Latin American countries there is a growing demand for control over foreign enterprises, particularly in the extractive sectors.[5]

World Bank Group and I.D.B.: Country evaluation and programming

An essential condition for making development assistance effective is adequate information about the project to be financed and about the recipient's economy as a whole. Such information is not neces-

[1] J. Keith Horsefield, *op. cit.*, pp. 470–3.

[2] A Vice-President of the World Bank also observed that 'the Executive Directors have tended often to become as much the representatives of the Bank with their countries as they are representatives of their countries with the Bank'. Geoffrey M. Wilson, 'World Bank Operations', *Finance and Development*, Vol. I, No. 1 (June 1964), p. 17.

[3] Jerome Levinson and Juan de Onis, *The Alliance that Lost its Way* (Quadrangle Books, Chicago, 1970), p. 328.

[4] Stephen S. Rosenfeld, 'Is U.S. "Using" the World Bank?', *The Washington Post* (25 June 1971).

[5] John Hugh Grimmings, Acting Assistant Secretary of State, remarked that 'it is true that the United States sacrifices some of its sovereignty in an institution like the I.D.B.'. Hearing before the Committee on Foreign Relations, United States Senate, *Inter-American Development Bank Fund for Special Operations* (U.S. Government Printing Office, Washington, 1971), p. 43.

sarily contrary to the interest of the recipient but might, under certain conditions, result in a shift to outside the recipient country of the locus of decision-making concerning its development policies.

As a result of internal reorganisation in the I.B.R.D. at the beginning of the 1950s project considerations with respect to the availability of finance to members were divorced from country considerations.[1] This has meant that, over the years, the Bank has made lending dependent not only on the financial soundness and efficient management of the project in question but also and increasingly on its being satisfied that the recipient country is making what it believes to be a sufficient self-help effort in promoting its own development. For the latter purpose, I.B.R.D. economic missions periodically visit member countries and assess their performance, using as a yardstick such aspects as mobilisation and allocation of available domestic resources, foreign trade and investment policies, patterns of public expenditure, etc. Subsequently policy recommendations are made to the recipients.

During the last three years this approach has been increasingly systematised and is now deeply rooted in the programming system of the Bank Group.[2] In fact, there is now an Economic Programme Department whose purpose is to ensure consistency and rationality in the economic analysis of performance, creditworthiness, and lending policies in the countries. Consequently lending now bears a more direct relationship to the country reviews that are usually made on the basis of what are called Country Programme Papers at meetings of the President of the World Bank Group with the senior operational staff. These Papers are prepared by Area and Projects Departments for each potential borrower once a year and contain both macro-economic and sector analyses in the light of the countries' development needs and the Bank Group's proposed contribution.

In its approach to lending the I.D.B. mainly concentrates on projects and usually refrains from separate general evaluations of the economic and social policies of recipient countries. However, it does have access to material produced by other agencies and to the studies made within the framework of C.I.A.P.

What is the bearing of the approach of the international development finance institutions on the locus of decision making? If it were true that international institutions overrode the views of the recipient

[1] See Andrew M. Kamarck, 'Appraisal of Country Economic Performance', I.B.R.D., *Some Aspects of the Economic Philosophy of the World Bank*, Seminar for Brazilian professors of economics in Rio de Janeiro, 1967 (Washington, D.C., September 1968), p. 10.

[2] See John H. Adler, 'Programming in the World Bank Group', *Finance and Development*, No. 2 (1971), pp. 10–15.

countries, using the overwhelming multilateral expertise of their professional staffs for that purpose, then these institutions, and not the authorities in the recipient countries would become the judges of the latter's development objectives and priorities as well as of the tools to be employed in achieving these objectives. This would imply a diminution in the capacity of governments in recipient countries to implement decisions concerning what they consider to be in the best interests of their peoples and a lower degree of national independence might be seen as the price to be paid for obtaining foreign financial assistance. In actual fact, the present approaches of the international development finance institutions appear rather to make recipient governments more conscious of their development problems and of the need to take remedial action; in addition, their multilateral expertise is bound to be passed on to the recipient and lead, in principle, to an improvement in domestic economic development policy formulation. Conversely the staff of international institutions acquire a deeper understanding and appreciation of the recipient countries' economic and social problems which will in turn be reflected in an improvement of the development strategy recommended. It could be said that in submitting themselves to outside judgement, as for example in the Pearson and Prebisch reports, the institutions demonstrated their open-mindedness.

International Monetary Fund: stand-by arrangements and exchange policies

The risk of inflationary trends induced internally had seemingly appeared minor to the founders of the Fund. The maintenance of domestic monetary stability had been left in the hands of national authorities, and shortly after its establishment the I.M.F. stated that it was in no position to take vigorous measures against the internal causes of inflation.[1] Later, however, in the conduct of its growing financial operations, this institution recognised that stand-by arrangements offered a possibility of developing binding codes for the domestic policies of its members. These arrangements became, in fact, the most important single instrument of the Fund, although they are not even mentioned in the amendments to the Articles of Agreement that became effective in 1969.

The gradual shaping of stand-by arrangements by the Board of Directors is an interesting piece of decision making.[2] Originally, the arrangements were supposed to give the members the right to engage in transactions to the amount of the total credit granted, without

[1] I.M.F., *Report of the Executive Directors and Summary Proceedings* (1946), p. 25.
[2] J. Keith Horsefield, *op. cit.*, pp. 328–32; 373–6; 429–33; 488–91; 570–3.

further review by the Fund. But the continuously increasing inclusion of terms, the 'trigger' clauses, along with the gradually emerging technique of 'phasing' – meaning that the full extent of the stand-by could not be drawn in a lump sum but only in installments, the continuity of which was linked to fulfilment of the performance clauses – gave the Fund in effect the right to cancel these arrangements. The terms referred, among other things, to ceilings for credit expansion and government expenditure, and in a proposed arrangement for a stand-by with Chile in 1963, for example, provision was made for a further $10 million to be available in addition to the $2·5 million drawings a month, once import surcharges had been removed.[1]

Whereas beginning in the second half of the 1950s, stand-by arrangements were used by the Western Hemisphere Department for a shock therapy treatment of inflation in Latin America, in the 1960s this approach gave way to extensive quantitatively determined programmes which were designed to bind the countries more closely over time to gradual stabilisation. In fact, a 'model for financial programming' was developed by one of the department's deputy directors and described both as an important development in applied economics in the post-war period, and as an 'exercise dictated by the logic of the situation'.[2] It also claims a place in economic planning. The model consists simply of a projection of flows of funds through the banking system of a country based on estimates of various variables such as exports, foreign capital inflows, private savings and public expenditures. The aim is to adjust the demand for resources to their availability in such a way that inflationary tendencies and balance of payments deficits are avoided. The volume of bank credit and the exchange rate are adjustment instruments; controls in the external sector other than tariffs are rejected.[3]

In principle the model is directed against protectionist efforts to promote industrialisation, and implies that the full burden of adjustment of balance of payments disequilibria due to factors beyond the control of Latin American countries must be borne by them. Furthermore the ready application of exchange rate devaluation when credit brakes fail is bound to lead to a strengthening of the

[1] *Ibid.*, p. 571.

[2] Walter E. Robichek, *Financial Programing as Strategic Tool of Economic Planning*, Lecture given to visiting American professors in March 1965 (mimeo), pp. 1–2; – *Financial Programing Exercise of the International Monetary Fund in Latin America*, Address to a seminar of Brazilian professors of economics, Rio de Janeiro, Brazil, 20 September 1967 (mimeo).

[3] These controls are considered to have the inherent disadvantages 'of doing nothing by way of absorbing the purchasing power which they are instrumental in releasing', E. Robichek, *op. cit.*, p. 9.

traditional export-oriented sector. The model is probably effective if the goal is to strengthen as fast as possible the international reserve position of a country; this might, however, occur at the expense of some longer-term growth potential. Indeed, it appears that the Fund's policies in Latin America have rarely been consonant with a long-run development strategy. The model, which rests entirely upon demand restraints, is too formalistic to make allowance for a selective treatment of different investment needs or to even take into account inter-country differences in Latin America.

If their central aim was the stabilisation of the economies of the countries concerned, the confidential stand-by arrangements may be considered to have largely failed. Of a total of 271 stand-by arrangements concluded by the Fund with 58 members up to the end of 1969, 143 were made with 22 Latin American countries; half of that number accounted for as many as 107 agreements. Generally speaking, these arrangements have long been recognised as an exercise undertaken by Latin American countries to increase their prospects for external finance, since potential lenders of capital tend to consider their conclusion as an acceptable assurance of a proper conduct by the recipients. But what is 'proper' conduct? It is not necessarily complete stabilisation – rather, perhaps, the elimination of what are considered the worst types of exchange controls, and 'responsible' financial conduct in general. It would seem that the foreign investor is generally content to know that the I.M.F. has established, maintained, or enhanced its informal authority with the countries. This appears to be the intention of the Western Hemisphere Department and hence the conclusion of as many stand-by arrangements as possible. Interestingly enough, of the U.S. $4 billion of stand-by credits authorised up to the end of 1970 (Table 5.18), Latin American countries drew only some U.S. $2·5 billion (total gross drawings minus compensatory financing). Although 'stand-by arrangements can be employed only when a member is in balance of payments difficulty, or foresees it as a possibility and needs or may need to use the Fund's resources by purchasing the exchange from the Fund',[1] Brazil concluded its present arrangement of $50 million in February 1971 with foreign reserves at $1·2 billion, up from $200 million at the end of 1967.

In recent years the Fund appears to have lost some of the influence it had gained in Latin American affairs since the mid-1950s. In November 1967, this institution itself supplied the motives for a major revision of its stand-by arrangements in Latin America and other regions when it granted Great Britain a stand-by credit that

[1] Joseph Gold, *The Stand-By Arrangements of the International Monetary Fund* (I.M.F., Washington, D.C., 1970), p. 5.

reached the fourth credit tranche but was free of performance or phasing clauses.[1] Since then, the Board of Directors has agreed that the number of performance clauses should generally be reduced as much as possible, and the treatment of members has tended to be

TABLE 5.18

I.M.F.: STAND-BY ARRANGEMENTS WITH
LATIN AMERICAN MEMBERS UP TO
31 DECEMBER 1970
(Millions of U.S. dollars)

Country	Number	Cumulative Amount
Argentina	7	725·00
Bolivia	11	124·00
Brazil	8	665·00
Chile	11	390·10
Colombia	12	430·50
Costa Rica	5	62·10
Cuba[a]	1	12·50
Dominican Republic	2	36·25
Ecuador	8	99·00
El Salvador	10	114·75
Guatemala	7	94·40
Guyana	4	18·50
Haiti	10	45·20
Honduras	10	77·75
Jamaica	1	10·00
Mexico	3	230·00
Nicaragua	9	96·75
Panama	4	23·20
Paraguay	9	46·25
Peru	16	455·50
Uruguay	5	113·75
Venezuela	1	100·00
Totals	154	3,970·50

[a] Cuba withdrew from the I.M.F. on 2 April 1964.

Source: as Table 5.8, p. 32.

more uniform.[2] Also, Latin American representation on the Board of Directors has become much more effective since the second half of the 1960s when controversies arose among the industrial countries about international monetary reform. The emergence of stubborn

[1] See Joseph R. Slevin, 'Less Developed Nations Fret at I.M.F. Credit Given Britain', *The Washington Post* (2 January 1968).
[2] See Alexandre Kafka, 'Some Aspects of Latin America's Financial Relations with the International Monetary Fund', in Alberto Martinez Piedra (ed.), *Socio-Economic Change in Latin America* (Catholic University of America Press, Washington, D.C. (1970), pp. 96–7.

inflationary trends in the United States, the explanation of which is now partly sought in structuralist terms,[1] might also have contributed to a lessening of the influence of the Western Hemisphere Department in Latin America as did a clearer division of labour with the increasingly active international development finance institutions.

The Fund's standby arrangements with its Latin American members appear to have had a clearer purpose and more visible results in one of the various fields to which they referred, namely, exchange policies, in which this institution was given more direct authority. In reality, however, the picture here is complex and confusing and can only be touched upon in this paper. By the mid-1950s multiple exchange rates had increasingly become 'independent'[2] measures and key instruments in the ambitious efforts of the major Latin American countries to achieve a rapid industrialisation of their economies. Beginning in the second half of the 1950s, however, the Fund encouraged a move towards the simplification and elimination of these rates. Multiple exchange rate systems had in many cases been quite irrational but nevertheless they had performed important functions for the countries concerned. Therefore, early on, the Fund recognised the need to instal 'appropriate substitutes where necessary'[3] and later hinted that the simplification and elimination of the multiple exchange rates might 'include arrangements in other directions, especially the fiscal and trade fields'.[4]

For the Fund, the only acceptable solutions to the problem of introducing alternative measures were internal taxes and external tariffs, but since fiscal and tariff reforms are relatively time consuming, import surcharges, advance deposits on imports and export taxes were introduced and explicitly declared temporary.[5] For example, it was assumed that a period of from one to three years would be necessary to implement basic fiscal reforms.[6] Today however, the substitute measures are still in force and appear to have permanently taken over most of the former functions of multiple rates (Table 5.19). Indeed, import surcharges and export taxes 'may or may not technically constitute multiple currency practices in

[1] See *Economic Report of the President* (U.S. Government Printing Office, Washington, D.C. 1971), pp. 60–1.

[2] Eugene Richard Schlesinger, *Multiple Exchange Rates and Economic Development*, Princeton Studies in International Finance, No. 2 (Princeton 1952), p. 2.

[3] I.M.F., *Annual Report* (1948), p. 67.

[4] I.M.F., *Annual Report* (1957), p. 166.

[5] F. d'A. Collings, 'Recent Progress in Latin America Towards Eliminating Exchange Restrictions', I.M.F., *Staff Papers*, Vol. XII, No. 2 (July 1965), p. 279; G. A. Costanzo, *Programas de estabilización en América Latina* (Conferencias, C.E.M.L.A., Mexico, 1961), pp. 44–5.

[6] G. A. Costanzo, *op. cit.*, p. 45.

terms of the Fund agreement, depending upon whether they apply to exchange transactions or to the movement of goods'.[1] Advance deposits on imports are also very similar to multiple exchange rates in that the cost of financing them amounts to a penalty import rate. In the course of the 1960s various Latin American countries re-introduced multiple exchange rates and, in some of them, they now exist side by side with import surcharges, advance deposits on imports, and export retentions.

A relatively new technique is the application of the so-called crawling peg, first introduced by Chile at the end of 1962 (and terminated under the Allende administration) and also applied by Colombia since March 1967 and Brazil since August 1968. Although this innovation has caused a good deal of attention, two aspects are usually overlooked. First, this technique is not contrary to the intentions of the I.M.F. in Latin America and has, in fact, been actively supported by it. Its application is clearly implicit in the Western Hemisphere Department model if inflation cannot be brought to a halt. Furthermore on various occasions the I.M.F. has publicly urged a greater degree of exchange rate flexibility in developing countries in accordance with basic market trends and has pointed to 'the economic costs of an over-valued currency'.[2] So far Latin American experience also suggests that the technique can only be introduced and maintained by the simultaneous application of multiple exchange rates and/or non-tariff restrictions.

Among the many complex and interdependent questions posed in principle by Latin American and I.M.F. exchange and other non-tariff policies, we may single out the following three groups: (i) types of disequilibria, the degree of joint responsibility of surplus and deficit countries, and the relative advantage of adjusting as compared to financing imbalances; (ii) the relative effectiveness of the existing adjustment instruments, and their bearing on development policies, including the removal of structural imbalances and export diversification, and the possibilities of developing alternative devices; (iii) the process of social bargaining, the rate of inflation, capital flight, and the expectations of businessmen, particularly exporters and importers.

Although, in conducting their exchange policies, Latin American monetary authorities constantly face these questions of vital importance to the performance of their countries, they have not been thoroughly studied either by them or by the Western Hemisphere Department. The Fund has, of course, given various pointers to its

[1] F. d'A. Collings, *op. cit.*, p. 278.
[2] I.M.F., *Annual Report* (1967), pp. 39, 45. See also its *Annual Reports* (1958) p. 20; (1962), p. 66; (1966), p. 26.

TABLE 5.19

PRINCIPAL FEATURES OF LATIN AMERICAN COUNTRIES' RESTRICTIVE SYSTEMS

(as at date of country survey)

	Argentina	Barbados	Bolivia	Brazil	Chile	Colombia	Costa Rica	Dominican Rep.	Ecuador	El Salvador	Guatemala	Guyana	Haiti	Honduras	Jamaica	Mexico	Nicaragua	Panama	Paraguay	Peru	Tr'dad & T'go.	Uruguay	Venezuela
1. Article VIII status	×	—	×	—	—	—	×	×	×	×	×	×	×	×	×	×	×	×	—	×	—	—	—
2. Article XIV status	—	—	—	×	×	×	—	—	—	—	—	—	—	—	—	—	—	—	×	—	×	×	×
3. Agreed par value exists	×	—	×	×	×	×	×	×	×	×	×	×	×	×	×	×	×	×	×	×	×	×	×
4. Par value applied	—	—	—	—	—	—	×	×	×	×	×	×	×	×	×	×	×	×	—	—	×	—	—
5. Unitary effective rate not par value																							
(a) fixed rate	—	×	—	—	—	—	—	—	—	—	—	—	—	—	—	—	—	—	—	—	—	—	—
(b) freely fluctuating rate	—	—	—	—	—	—	—	—	—	—	—	—	—	—	—	—	—	—	—	—	—	—	—
(c) pegged rate	×	—	×	—	—	—	—	—	—	—	—	—	—	—	—	—	—	—	—	—	—	—	—
6. Special rate(s) for some or all capital transactions and/or some or all invisibles	—	—	—	×	×	×	—	—	—	—	—	—	—	—	—	—	—	—	—	×	—	—	×
7. Import rate(s) different from export rate(s)	—	—	—	×	—	×	—	—	—	—	—	—	—	—	—	—	×	—	×	×	—	×	×
8. More than one rate for imports	—	—	—	—	—	×	—	—	—	—	—	—	—	—	—	—	—	—	—	×	—	—	×
9. More than one rate for exports	—	—	—	×	—	×	—	—	—	—	—	—	—	—	—	—	—	—	—	—	—	×	×

	C1	C2	C3	C4	C5	C6	C7	C8	C9	C10	C11	C12	C13	C14	C15	C16	C17
10. Restrictions exist on payments in respect of current transactions[c]	–	×	–	×	×	–	–	–	–	–	×	×	×	×	–	×	–
11. Restrictions exist on payments in respect of capital transactions[c,d]	–	×	×	×	×	–	–	–	×	–	×	×	×	×	×	×	–
12. Prescription of currency	–	×	×	×	×	–	–	–	×	–	–	×	×	×	×	×	–
13. Bilateral payments arrangements with members	×	–	–	–	×	–	–	×	–	–	–	–	–	–	–	–	×
14. Bilateral payments arrangements with nonmembers	–	×	–	×	–	–	–	–	–	–	–	–	–	–	×	×	–
15. Import surcharges	–	×	–	×	×	×	×	–	–	×	×	×	×	×	×	×	×
16. Advance import deposits	–	×	–	×	×	–	–	–	–	–	–	–	×	×	×	×	–
17. Surrender of export proceeds required	×	×	×	×	×	–	–	–	×	–	–	×	×	×	×	×	×
18. Part of larger monetary area[e]	–	–	×	–	–	–	–	–	×	–	–	×	–	–	–	–	–
19. Participates in regional economic cooperation[f]	×	×	×	×	×	–	×	×	×	×	×	×	×	×	×	×	×

[a] × indicates that practice exists; – indicates that practice does not exist. Practices indicated as existing do not necessarily apply to all transactions.

[b] In most cases, 31 December 1970.

[c] Payments to member countries. Restrictions in the form of quantitative limits or undue delay other than restrictions imposed for security reasons.

[d] Resident-owned funds.

[e] Part of French Franc or Sterling Area.

[f] Membership in, or association with, Caribbean Free Trade Association, Central American Common Market, Latin American Free Trade Association.

Source: I.M.F., *Annual Report* on *Exchange Restrictions* (1971), pp. 491–95.

basic attitudes; for example, it has stated that, in comparison with multiple exchange rates and quantitative restrictions, it regarded fluctuating single exchange rates as a 'lesser evil';[1] it has referred to overvalued exchange rates as devices that lead to 'distortions in the allocation of resources';[2] it has pronounced itself sceptical of the devaluing countries' fear that their terms of trade might worsen in the process,[3] and it has flatly stated that the main cause of payments difficulties in primary producing countries is not the lack of export demand but internal inflation.[4] These statements, as well as the model and the policies of the Western Hemisphere Department for Latin America, make it clear that despite the absence of signs of success, the Fund is committed to a continuing attempt to eliminate the 'disequilibrium system'[5] of Latin American countries and that there is little disposition towards searching experimentation.

As we saw above the process of simplification and elimination of multiple exchange rates and of the introduction of substitute measures was in part a question of terminology. We shall now look at its practical consequences. The main advantage of introducing the substitute measures should have been a full liberalisation of the foreign exchange sector of the countries concerned. However, although payments transactions have become much simpler, there is still considerable control over current transactions, including surrender requirements for export proceeds. Nevertheless unlike multiple exchange rates, the new measures cannot be applied to financial transactions, with the result, of course, that the scope for external finance, including foreign private investment, has increased. This appears to be a major result of the I.M.F.'s activities in Latin America.

The I.M.F. induced exchange reforms have had further consequences. In many countries in which the administration of the multiple rates by the central banks had guaranteed a relatively rational and effective intervention, the substitute measures now enable other government mechanisms to intervene in the administration of the external sector. Second, exchange-rate flexibility with a unified foreign exchange market is more precarious and therefore limited; a devaluation of a single rate requires a complete reorganisation of the disequilibrium system because the import

[1] I.M.F., *Annual Report* (1958), p. 20.
[2] I.M.F., *Annual Report* (1967), p. 39.
[3] *Ibid.*, pp. 41, 45.
[4] I.M.F., 'Foreign Policies and Procedures in Relation to Compensatory Financing of Commodity Fluctuations', I.M.F., *Staff Papers*, Vol. III, No. 1 (1960), p. 24.
[5] Charles B. Kindleberger, *International Economics*, Third Edition (Richard D. Irwin, Inc., Homewood, Illinois, 1963), p. 289.

surcharges, usually calculated on the value of the imported goods expressed in national currency, magnify the effects of devaluation. Or expressed differently, other things being equal, the relatively frequent adjustment of exchange rates is easier with a simple multiple exchange rate system. Third, the I.M.F. recommended advance deposits on imports to Latin American countries as early as 1947,[1] and later described them as reliable means of domestic monetary policies and effective instruments for balance of payments adjustment.[2] After that, however, staff members admitted that these deposits were inferior to other kinds of import restrictions and to an effective monetary policy.[3] In fact, it was necessary for Latin American countries to learn by experience that once the deposits were established, they lost their effectiveness and became a burden for their monetary policies, in particular whenever the authorities wished to discontinue the deposit system. Finally, there is some indication that the abolition of multiple exchange rates and their replacement by advance deposits and surcharges have permitted the Fund to shift responsibility on to GATT, which does not contain provisions relating to such substitute measures, but which, since 1958, has increasingly dealt with these matters in consultations with its member countries (a number of Latin American countries do not belong to GATT).

'Aid Co-ordination'

Each of the international financial institutions can be regarded as a mechanism for co-ordinating external assistance for Latin American development. In the widest sense, however, external aid co-ordination involves informal agreements, as well as exchanges of opinion between donors, recipient countries, and mutilateral organisations. In principle, joint consideration of the development programmes and needs of Latin American countries should lead to an organised allocation of assistance, should increase the effectiveness of international action for development, and avert duplication. On the other hand, this approach might ultimately entail concurrence on the part of borrowers with the views of lenders, particularly in the process of rescheduling external debt.

[1] See for example Banco Central de Costa Rica, 'El problema de las divisas en Costa Rica y la intervención del Banco Central en la solución del mismo', *Memoria*, Tercera Reunión de Técnicos de los Bancos Centrales del Continente Americano, tomo 1 (Banco Nacional de Cuba, Habana, 1952), p. 343.

[2] Jorge Marshall, 'Advance Deposits on Imports', I.M.F., *Staff Papers*, Vol. VI, No. 2 (April 1958), pp. 240–1.

[3] A. Birnbaum and Moeen A. Oureshi, 'Advance Deposit Requirements for Imports', I.M.F., *Staff Papers*, Vol. VIII (November 1960), p. 125.

In co-ordinating aid for Latin America, the I.M.F. has long played an influential role, since from an early date foreign financial assistance from other sources was deemed necessary for the success of the stabilisation programmes it supervised. The Director of the Western Hemisphere Department explained that there had been collaboration with international private banks and that it was much easier for the Fund than for other institutions to serve as an intermediary between external finance and Latin American countries and that it did so on an independent, technical, and disinterested basis.[1] For example, at the end of 1958 Argentina, which shortly before had not had sufficient foreign exchange reserves for its most essential imports, received credits totalling $329 million from the I.M.F., the Export–Import Bank, the Treasury of the United States, the Development Loan Fund, and eleven private banks, when it embarked on a stabilisation programme. Also, from the late 1950s onwards, a number of Latin American members experienced increasing difficulties in servicing their external debt and had to negotiate with creditors a postponement of payments of interest and principal in which the I.M.F. played a significant role involving stand-by arrangements. In fact, many public and private institutions abroad would not enter into financial arrangements with Latin American countries unless the Fund had concluded a stand-by arrangement with them. For example, in the mid-1960s a refinancing commission established in Uruguay with a view to obtaining postponement of the public external debt falling due in 1966/7 and amounting to 40 per cent of the total external public debt of U.S. $400 million, had no success until Uruguay concluded stand-by arrangement for $15 million with the I.M.F.[2]

In their work in Latin America a source of potential conflict between the I.M.F., on the one hand, and the development finance institutions, on the other, is that the latter can contribute, in the eyes of the former, to inflationary tendencies by inducing recipients to contribute substantially to the local costs of projects via deficit spending. In fact, there was little co-operation and occasional conflict between the I.M.F. and the World Bank up to 1966 when an arrangement was made for liaison between these two institutions.[3] It was established that the Bank has primary responsibility for the design and appropriateness of development programmes and project

[1] Jorge del Canto, 'El papel del Fondo Monetario Internacional en los esfuerzos de los países latino americanos hacio la estabilización', *Revista del Banco de la República*, Vol. XXXII, No. 382 (August 1959), p. 934.

[2] Edgardo A. Noya, 'Antecedentes y medidas económicas de corto plazo del gobierno uruguayo', CEMLA, *Boletín Mensual*, Vol. XII, No. 7 (July 1966), pp. 323–4.

[3] J. Keith Horsefield, *op. cit.*, pp. 603–4.

evaluation as well as questions of development priority and that in these matters the Fund would adopt the views of the Bank.

On the initiative of the World Bank, a consulting group to co-ordinate long-term financing for Colombia was established as early as in 1962. Since then, the Bank has come to play more and more of a guiding role in the machinery for co-ordination of development assistance, and has taken the initiative in forming groups comprising capital exporting countries and international and regional financial institutions. A group for Peru has also been established. In the activities of these groups, the Bank serves as an intermediary seeking to harmonise the interests of the donors and the recipients, and provides information about, and assessments of, the economic performance of the recipients.

In 1963 the I.D.B. was designated by the Ecuadorian government as its financial agent for the creation of a consulting group. Recently this institution has entered into another area of co-ordination: it has made arrangements with the United Nations Industrial Development Organisation (UNIDO) to co-ordinate activities in identifying industrial projects in Latin America; in doing so, both agencies will give consideration to technological fields and the industrial aspects of economic integration.

As far as co-ordination is concerned, the hub of much activity of the international financial institutions under consideration is C.I.A.P. This organisation was created in 1963 by the O.A.S. Inter-American Economic and Social Council in order to promote and co-ordinate the joint economic development of O.A.S. countries. The principal operating procedure of C.I.A.P. are the country reviews in which the I.B.R.D., I.D.B., I.M.F. and A.I.D. always participate and for which they established an inter-agency advisory group in 1965.

The existence of C.I.A.P. makes possible an overall review of all the economic and social development problems of a given Latin American country. In this activity, C.I.A.P.'s role is viewed as that of an 'ombudsman'[1]. C.I.A.P. has strongly advocated the multi-lateralisation of U.S. development assistance to Latin America and recently expanded its tasks to include a country review of the United States, extension of technical assistance to Latin American countries, and increasingly closer collaboration with the above-mentioned agencies, particularly the I.D.B. and the I.B.R.D.

IV. CONCLUDING OBSERVATIONS

There is no agreed standpoint from which to view institution building and task expansion in the multilateral financing of Latin

[1] Inter-American Economic and Social Council, *op. cit.*, p. 185.

American development. In the final instance, the political dimension of the financial system may rule out a non-normative perspective.

In reviewing the effectiveness of the system, we might begin with the following questions: have appropriate institutional mechanisms been created at the multilateral level for dealing with the development needs of Latin America? If so, in which ways have these institutions actually responded to the opportunity to pursue development policies? Have they, in the process, achieved a legitimate authoritative position in the development field?

The questions themselves involve the problem of the degree of objectivity it is possible to achieve in identifying the causes of underdevelopment in Latin America and in prescribing remedial action. For practical purposes, we might use as a yardstick the extent to which the general evolution of ideas on development, as expressed for example by the United Nations Economic Commission for Latin America (ECLA) and the declarations of Latin American governments, is matched by the policies of the institutions. Since experience suggests that the institutions actually tend to follow the trend, both in time and in substance, we might simply ask how responsive the institutions are to changing development priorities. Admittedly, the institutions were not intended to be 'think tanks', although a considerable intellectual capacity whose full potential is usually not permitted to show in public is concentrated there.

The differing degrees of responsiveness of the Fund and of the development finance institutions is largely to be explained by the purposes for which they were established. The I.M.F. was not founded with the development problem in mind. Nevertheless, from the mid-1950s it seized opportunities for task expansion in Latin America by ways considered controversial in both form and substance and which led to an increase not in its repute but in its influence in Latin America. Political power is implicit in monetary arrangements, as for example, in the reform of the international monetary system. The significance attributed to the present type of S.D.R.s for Latin America again depends on one's view of its development problems. If Latin America's balance of payments disequilibria are due to structural and therefore rather persistent factors, an increase in financing made possible by the S.D.R.s is hardly significant, since the task is predominantly one of long term structural adjustment; if this is so, then apart from Latin America's general need for development finance, ways and means whereby the planned reserves can play a role in a much more broadly conceived adjustment process present a challenge.

By contrast, when viewed from the standpoint of efficiency and leaving wider implications aside, the development finance institutions have responded to the functional challenge of Latin American development. Admittedly with a time lag in their response, the institutions are constantly developing new techniques and increasingly financing projects that for long were thought unbankable. The World Bank has achieved a high level of proficiency in its professional work whereas the I.D.B., which is more familiar with the special problems of recipients in Latin America, is more innovative. However, the volume of financial resources Latin America has received from these institutions, though not negligible, is not yet a significant component of the total external finance available; and the continuous hardening of terms and conditions during the 1960s may be considered an unfavourable trend.

The respective contributions of these financial resources to the development process of Latin American countries depend, in large measure, on their development policies. Even where development doctrines and objectives have been fairly well defined, the choice of policy instruments and the implementation of policy in a consistent and planned fashion have left much to be desired. Indeed, Prebisch considered the shape of Latin American development policy important in explaining the failure of external finance to become more effective.[1] Another of Prebisch's findings is particularly alarming: not only have external financial resources not served to promote the mobilisation of Latin America's own resources, but the ratio of investment out of domestic resources has tended to decline.

The impact of external financial resources on Latin America's self-help effort is therefore a crucial question. Here we will deal with it in so far as it relates to multilateral financial co-operation, leaving aside the I.M.F., which we dealt with above, and the degree of substitutability of domestic and the respective foreign resources. Because a statistical basis is lacking it is not possible to prove or disprove the worst of all possible cases, namely that contrary to the usual assumption (that they significantly and effectively raise the rate of capital formation in Latin America), multilateral financial resources have in fact reduced domestic savings, largely supplemented consumption, and tended to lower the output capital ratio.[2] It would only be possible to substantiate this thesis if it could be shown, *inter alia*, that the resources had been devoted to low priority, marginal projects; that, despite the scarcity of resources, one project tended to lead to another in a given sector and/or country; that

---

[1] Raúl Prebisch, *Change . . ., op. cit.*, pp. 8–9, 59, 103.

[2] These and related aspects have been theoretically explored by Keith Griffin, 'Foreign Capital, Domestic Savings and Economic Development', *Bulletin*, Oxford University Institute of Economics and Statistics, Vol. 32, No. 2 (May 1970), pp. 99–112.

preference was given to the financing of large projects (possibly because the administrative costs and effort involved are smaller per dollar loaned); that publicly guaranteed resources were channelled into less directly productive activities (possibly because government ownership of directly productive activities is not promoted); and that the availability of the resources reduced the tax effort and geared public expenditure more to consumption. If this were so, a country might be well advised to do without the external financialre sources but then the maintenance of a given growth rate would require some restriction of current consumption, and probably some social reorganisation.

The possibility that external financial resources directly permit a higher level of current consumption in recipient countries, and their need to introduce changes in their socio-economic development policies, lead us to examine Latin America's membership in the multilateral financial system in relation to the degree to which development options are available to it. The increase in the lending activities of the international financial institutions in Latin America cannot be divorced from the fact that the ultimate lenders, in addition to recovering most of their funds, benefit from the resultant increase in exports and the reduction in the risk to their business investments. The development in the post-war period of closer economic and, therefore, by present standards, political ties of Latin America with the Western allied system, which are also in the foreign policy interest of the ultimate lenders, has not been predominantly the result of membership in the multilateral financial system. However, since the 1960s the increasing multilateralisation of assistance has been increasingly important for the maintenance of these ties, in that no Latin American country could afford to disregard the immediate and drastic economic consequences of withdrawal from that system. Decisions by recipients on development options always have a socio-political content, and are therefore of interest to the ultimate lenders, but not necessarily to the multilateral financial institutions as such. These institutions are expected to refrain from interference in the domestic politics of their members. However, their judgement on the economic performance of the recipients may take socio-political developments into account, and in turn the decision of the institutions may have an extra-economic influence in the recipient country.[1] On the other hand, experience has shown that socio-political transformations often lead to economic difficulties affecting the creditworthiness of the countries in question and may not be in the interest of the ultimate lenders who have significant voting power on the Boards of Directors.

[1] I.B.R.D., *World Bank and IDA . . ., op. cit.,* pp. 7, 13.

Future changes in the role of the multilateral financial system in Latin American development will ultimately be the result not only of changes in the priorities, and the degree of consensus, of the major powers, but also of the extent to which the institutions become more independent variables *vis-à-vis* these powers. In fact, the institutions have already become more independent in so far as internationalism has in general not kept pace with the growing economic and financial interdependence among nations. Their independence will be strengthened if there is a shift in the emphasis of the multilateral financial system from integration to co-operative relations – a prospect that would enhance the international character of the system itself and increase the development options of its members.

Discussion of the Paper by
Dr. König

Dr. Ferrer said that the paper produced a solid groundwork for the argument made by Professor Sunkel in his paper by showing us that all such international agencies in some degree respond to the interests of the industrialised countries. Examples of this could be found in the difficulties encountered by countries such as Chile and Peru in obtaining a continuing inflow of loans, difficulties no doubt related to the policies of those countries over copper and oil respectively. He also saw acceptance of developed countries' criteria, rather than the development needs of the less developed countries, in the use of tied loans, which hindered the development of the vital capital goods industry. Lending criteria were thus not only security but also the promotion of exports of goods and services from the lending countries.

The paper made clear a further important problem: that of actually determining the aid component of loan figures. The actual volume of aid, as Dr. König showed, was extremely small. It was interesting that the present crisis in aid policy had really sprung from the illusion tax-payers were under as to the actual size of the transfer.

He would, however, claim that this crisis in aid was in fact a positive thing. It would make Latin Americans more aware that development depended on their own efforts at mobilising resources. This awareness plus growing nationalism might lead to action.

He would emphasise Dr. König's argument that what was needed was real multinationalism in international financial agencies, through adequate participation in their boards of directors and administration of the views of developing countries. In this respect the I.D.B. provided a useful example.

Lastly, he would remind us of a neglected topic: disarmament. Success on this score could be the means of releasing a huge flow of funds which in principle could be directed towards the development needs of the underdeveloped countries.

Mr. Urquidi said that Dr. König had made an outstanding contribution in that he evaluated critically, but dispassionately, the role played by international financial institutions in Latin America. At the time of Bretton Woods, it was thought that the I.M.F. would be more flexible and understanding of Latin America's structural and monetary problems, and that the I.B.R.D. would be rigid, concerned mostly with European reconstruction. However, it turned out differently: the I.M.F. never concerned itself with the development aspects of monetary problems and behaved rigidly in terms of the orthodox principles it required Latin America to follow, whereas the Bank, although limited by its need to obtain capital from the private market, soon learned that its business was development, and it had consequently contributed much to infrastructure growth in Latin America. Even so, the total amounts involved had not been decisive, though they had increased. The I.M.F. reflected largely the interests of the 'great monetary powers' and was managed by them. The Bank, although largely run by its management, not by its Board, had opened up to a more positive role in many aspects of development. The I.D.B. had responded to Latin American interests, even if only on a project basis. Multilateral financing was necessary as an aid in Latin American development.

Dr. Mayobre spoke about the evolution of each of the three principal organisations under review – the I.M.F., the I.B.R.D., and the I.D.B. – in their relations with Latin America.

Up to the beginning of the 1960s, the I.M.F.'s policy was directed at achieving the convertibility of European currencies, in which it showed considerable flexibility and achieved success. By contrast, in its relations with Latin America, it was inspired by an exaggerated orthodoxy which neglected the true problems. This was the origin of conflicts which reached the level of politics. In recent years it had been possible to see two important tendencies in the Fund: on the one hand, it was showing a broader and better understanding in its relations with Latin America; on the other, the big powers, in the shape of the group of ten, had removed from the Fund's province the discussion of decisions on important monetary problems. This latter had been made very clear recently in discussions over the world monetary crisis. The Fund, he felt, must at least be given credit for trying to maintain monetary discipline in Latin America.

The philosophy of the I.B.R.D. was from its start one of supplementing private capital and not entering areas where private capital could fulfil its role. Hence for some years it concentrated on financing only infrastructure projects. For instance, State petroleum companies never had access to the Bank. This had begun to change and recently it had been possible to observe a more positive focus. He observed that in the Bank, as distinct from the Fund, the Director-General was the centre of decision making, and that because of the composition of its capital and its nationality, the institution followed more readily the policies of its chief shareholder.

Of the three organisations the I.D.B. had been the most positive force for Latin American development. This had been clear as much in its greater understanding of the Continent's problems as in its operations, and beyond a doubt the composition of its direction and personnel had been influential in this. Nevertheless there appeared to be strong pressure on the Bank to be less independent, and the tendency to deny the I.D.B. new resources was a cause for concern. These tendencies if they became more evident would be extremely harmful for Latin America.

Professor Hirschman would have liked to have seen some case studies of conflict in order to illuminate this problem of divergent interests (e.g. the I.M.F. and Colombia in 1966; the conflict with Kubitschek in Brazil). He saw as a prime danger the monopoly position such institutions held, leaving no possibility of 'shopping around'. He also saw a dangerous conviction among the typical professionals in such organisations that they possessed 'absolute truth', an attitude which by reducing the possibilities of experimentation could only handicap development, which was essentially an experimental process.

Further, he suggested that these agencies might actually have introduced a new source of instability. They had been established in the post-war period to substitute for deficient private capital flows. In fact, their willingness to lend funds had become instead a signal to private capital that the 'climate' was fine. A country considering structural change now ran the double risk of losing the support of both the international agencies and of private capital. It looked as though we now needed some new 'compensatory finance' for these situations.

Professor Reynolds appealed for realism in the discussion of the question of influence and pressure. It was an inescapable fact of life that primary net lenders were going to exert as much influence as possible over net borrowers; no institutional modification could ever alter that. The only way to change the nature of such pressures was to create constituencies within the net lending countries which favoured different policies. He did in fact think such changes were occurring, as evidenced in the new weight given to 'social responsibility' in investment policies. He felt a crucial field for action was in mobilising resources within Latin American countries themselves – hence his own proposal for an Inter-American Development bond.

Dr. von Gleich pointed out that the problems of aid lay also in local institutions. Did funds in fact reach the borrowing sector that needed them? How far were external funds simply substituted for internal? How important was government institutions' bias towards 'smooth' projects without problems? Who ultimately received the grant component of a loan? Did it remain with the agency and provide a profit? How far was it the case, as a recent report suggested, that funds typically went to large firms which could easily get them elsewhere?

Dr. Ffrench-Davis made three comments on the policies of the I.M.F. First, on exchange rates, there were really three options, not two: a fixed rate, a free rate, or a flexible but *programmed* rate, such as Chile had in 1965–70, adjustments in the rate being used to direct resource allocation in accordance with medium-term development strategy. Second, on the Fund's 'model for financial programming', which assumed that internal credit, defined in a somewhat strange fashion, was the determinant of aggregate demand: this was a very poor model since credit was only one component of aggregate demand and no account was taken of the inter-action of real and monetary variables. Third, an interesting point to consider following Dr. König's criticisms of the Fund was the proposal which had been made for a decentralised regional form of the I.M.F., with a regional common reserve pool. This could be of great interest, first in the context of attempts to reduce dependency, and second as a device to replace the highly unrealistic model of the I.M.F. by one suited to the needs and targets of Latin America.

Dr. König agreed with many of the observations made on his paper and said that Dr. Ferrer's remarks about the crisis in aid, Dr. von Gleich's worry about the final destination of funds obtained abroad, Professor Hirschman's pointing to the dangers of increasing multilateralisation and Professor Reynolds' stress on the more intensive mobilisation of resources within Latin America, all underlined the need for Latin American countries to develop new attitudes towards the role of external development finance and towards domestic financial management. This should be done in the context of development policies that were primarily geared to socio-economic change rather than growth goals. As far as the I.M.F. was concerned, he found Mr. Urquidi's recollection of the benefits expected from this institution very interesting; the inclusion in his own paper of Dr. Prebisch's discussions with Mr. Urquidi and others in the mid-1940s was intended to show early indigenous ideas about foreign exchange policies as an instrument of economic development policies, the methodical planned application of which had, however, hardly occurred. The recent improvement in Latin America's relation with the I.M.F., as pointed out by Dr. Mayobre, could be important for the introduction of adequate foreign exchange systems, but it remained to be seen to what extent the contribution of the I.M.F. to this improvement would be the result of substantive changes in the attitudes of its Western Hemisphere Department, or of the international monetary crises that had weakened the general position of the institution for the time being.

Responding to Professor Reynolds' remarks, Dr. König said that realism was indeed needed in assessing the multilateral financial system, but that this should not be used as an argument against attempts to unveil its development and functioning, including its political dimension; last but not least the paper was concerned with *public* institutions and there were many misconceptions about their work, including the aid component of financial resources they made available.

Dr. Ffrench-Davis's stress on the role of flexible but 'programmed' exchange rates was an important and timely observation in the light of the fact that Latin American countries had been urged to adjust their free and other rates according to so-called 'basic tendencies' of the market – in practice the application of the much criticised purchasing-power-parity doctrine. There were, of course, numerous pros and cons as far as an indiscriminate application of the crawling peg was concerned, but some arguments against it were particularly powerful in the case of Latin American countries: their exchange markets were usually unstable over a substantial range of possible exchange rates; the horizon for economic programming and planning would be reduced; since their price systems were relatively insensitive to small devaluations a reallocation of resources would be unlikely to take place and if it did it might be to the disadvantage of the non-traditional sector of the economy; financial co-operation for regional integration was then more difficult; and demand and supply elasticity conditions were more favourable to Latin America in larger and therefore less frequent devaluations because they would more easily bring about a desired reorganisation of existing foreign trade arrangements and new commercial channels. In fact, Latin American countries that had applied an I.M.F.-recommended crawling peg policy had had to back it up by a simultaneous application of multiple exchange rates and/or other non-tariff restrictions. This also pointed to the necessity of designing generally-acceptable principles and methods for external sector management in Latin America.

Finally, Dr. König made the point that in future there might be a conflict between international public institutions and multinational corporations if the latter challenged the former in the field of country evaluation and programming and pressed towards '. . . involving the private sector – international and local – in the development policy and planning process' (Charles Dennison, Vice President of International Minerals and Chemical Corporation). An association of about 200 U.S. corporations, the Council for Latin America, that claimed to represent 85 per cent of U.S. investments in Latin America, had, for example, established a technology task force in order to establish, among other things, continuing consultative relationships with Latin American policy makers; they were seeking 'initiatives that would build the triangle of government, science and industry which lies at the heart of much economic development' (Dennison).

6 Foreign Investment in Latin America: Recent Trends and Prospects

Ricardo Ffrench-Davis[1]

I. INTRODUCTION

In recent years there has been marked progress in the understanding of Latin American economic problems. However, the analysis of the role played by foreign investment has not advanced at the same pace. It is probably in this area of analysis that one finds the most sharply divergent points of view, reflecting partly the fact that foreign investment has profound political implications, but also partly the relative scarcity of both theoretical development and empirical research.[2]

Contemporary literature thus contains strong statements concerning the important contribution of foreign investment to economic development in Latin America, as well as others stating that its contribution has been null or negative. Likewise, policies proposed towards foreign investment extend from 'open arms' to 'closed doors'.

The purpose of this paper is limited. It cannot pretend to be either a synthesis of the literature or an exhaustive analysis. Rather, it will attempt a general retrospective view of foreign investment in Latin America in the past two decades (sections II and III), bearing in mind the limitations on any assertion referring to 'Latin America' as a whole. Then in section IV the actual and potential role of foreign investment in development will be briefly analysed, and in section V the implications of such an analysis for policy will be examined. Finally, we shall consider how far such policy requirements are met in the case of the Andean Pact's policy on foreign investment.

II. DATA ON FOREIGN INVESTMENT, 1950–69

It is not only the evaluation of costs and benefits from foreign investment which has been inadequate. The basic data on the flows

[1] Centro de Estudios de Planificación (CEPLAN), Universidad Católica de Chile. The author is indebted to the members of the CEPLAN seminar and to Mrs. Rosemary Thorp for their helpful comments.

[2] This does not mean that we ignore important contributions published in the last decades. Several of the most recent publications are mentioned in the bibliography at the end of the text.

of funds corresponding to foreign investment are also weak, since there has been scarce interest in arriving at quantitative data which are economically significant. Areas where the weakness is particularly notable include:[1]

(a) capital contributions in terms of 'technological knowledge';

(b) payments of patents, royalties and technical advice by subsidiaries to parent firms;[2]

(c) external loans obtained by foreign enterprises, which usually attain appreciable amounts, and which appear in the accounts as external debt of the recipient country, with no indication as to who retains control;[3]

(d) domestic indebtedness of foreign enterprises;[4]

(e) purchases by foreign investors of already operating domestic enterprises, which purchases are usually not reflected in the statistical data of the recipient countries;

(f) percentage of foreign ownership in individual enterprises and its behaviour over time.

Let us nevertheless examine what data we do have. In Table 6.1 we present figures concerning the evolution of the flows of foreign investment funds into Latin America since 1951. They are presented in the context of capital movements in the balance of payments, so that their importance relative to total capital flows may be appreciated.

In aggregate terms, it will be seen that foreign investment in Latin America is not important. From 1966 to 1969 it represented less than 5 per cent of gross domestic investment.[5] Moreover, as Table 6.2

[1] References to some of the shortcomings of the data on capital movements can be found in ECLA [47]; see especially page 157.

[2] In 1963, 'royalties or fees' received were as large as 14 per cent of the profits of U.S. enterprises abroad. See Wionczek in [52], footnote 21. Furthermore, the survey made in 1966 by the Department of Commerce of U.S.A. on direct foreign investment [51], shows for that year that 'royalties, fees, rentals and service charges' represented 16·3 per cent of the amount corresponding to profits; this figure climbs to 31·8 per cent in the manufacturing sector. The corresponding figure for Latin America is 24·5 per cent. These high percentages do contain an element of production cost, but they also include a share of disguised profit remittances. Their magnitude indicates that more attention should be given to them.

[3] This is a case in which a crucial difference between direct foreign investment and foreign borrowing disappears, since the foreign enterprise retains the decision power over both forms of capital inflows.

[4] According to figures prepared by ECLA, 31 per cent of gross U.S. investment in Latin America during the period 1963–5 was financed with local or third countries resources. This percentage has gradually risen from 17 per cent in 1957–9 (see [48], Table 11).

[5] Approximately two-thirds of gross domestic investment corresponds to the private sector, national or foreign.

TABLE 6.1

LATIN AMERICA: NET CAPITAL FLOW, 1951–69
(Annual averages, millions of U.S. dollars)[a]

Year	Direct investment and other private capital (1)	Net long-term loans (2)	Net movement of short-term loans (3)	Changes in foreign reserves (increase) (4)	Net movement of capital (1)+(2)+(3)+(4) (5)
1951–5	430	74	264	– 12	756
1956–60	1,057	81	342	– 25	1,455
1961–5	652	474	63	– 101	1,088
1966–9	1,084	995	118	– 411	1,786
1966	772	779	132	– 122	1,581
1967	819	945	196	– 338	1,622
1968	1,085	1,115	110	– 524	1,786
1969	1,658	1,120	35	– 658	2,155

Source: Pazos [35], Table 1, with slight changes. The grouping of years has been altered, and 'errors and omissions' excluded; consequently, column (5) has been recomputed.

[a] Cuba is excluded.

TABLE 6.2

LATIN AMERICA: RELATIVE EVOLUTION OF INTERNAL ACCOUNTS AND EXTERNAL TRANSACTIONS, 1951–69
(Annual averages, millions of U.S. dollars)

	1951–5	1956–60	1961–5	1966–9
G.D.P.	56,000	76,000	103,000	126,000
Gross domestic investment	10,100	13,700	16,300	22,700
Net flow of capital	756	1,455	1,088	1,786
Direct investment and other private capital	430	1,057	652	1,084
Exports	7,033	7,990	8,800	11,200
Net transfer of profits and interest	915	1,217	1,460	2,350
Rate of growth of G.D.P.	5·2	4·8	4·4	4·9
Net flow of capital as percentage of G.D.P.	1·4	1·9	1·1	1·4
Exports as percentage of G.D.P.	12·5	10·5	8·5	8·9
Profits and interest as percentage of G.D.P.	1·6	1·6	1·4	1·9
Profits and interest as percentage of exports	13·1	15·2	16·5	20·9
Net flow of capital as percentage of domestic investment	7·5	10·6	6·7	7·9
Direct investment as percentage of domestic investment	4·3	7·7	4·0	4·8

Source: Pazos [35], Table 4.

shows, net flows of all forms of foreign capital have fluctuated between 7 and 11 per cent of domestic investment in the period 1951–69.[1]

However, such aggregate data do not reveal the extent of the significance of foreign investment. To examine this further we must turn to data on (i) the sectoral composition of the flows and (ii) the average size of foreign firms relative to domestic.

Turning first to sectoral distribution, we find that foreign investment is not uniformly distributed, but is concentrated in certain areas and completely absent from others. Further, investment composition has changed over the last two decades, with significant consequences for its economic effects, as will be seen below. While foreign investment in the export sector has maintained its relative position (with a large increase in the share of petroleum during the 1950s), investment in the public utilities sector has diminished while that in manufacturing has risen rapidly, especially in the 'dynamic' industrial sectors. The net result has been foreign disinvestment in the second sector and an increasing share of foreign investment in the third. The available data concerning the main foreign investor in Latin America, the United States, show that the bulk of the new investment in the region has been concentrated in manufacturing, while the stock of foreign investment in transportation, communications and electricity has declined by about one-third in the period 1950–69.[2] The expansion in the manufacturing sector occurred principally in the second of the two decades, when 60 per cent of new U.S. investment in the region went to manufacturing.

In regard to the average size of the foreign firm, we find that 'small' foreign enterprises are practically non-existent, because of the technologies used and because of the fixed costs involved in an investment abroad. Data available for two countries support this statement. In Argentina, 'more than half of the sales of the 50 largest enterprises, mainly industrial ones, corresponded to enterprises controlled by foreign capital'.[3] In Chile, a sample that includes the 100 main industrial enterprises (measured by their assets) points out that in 61 per cent of the enterprises there is foreign participation and that in 28 per cent of the firms it exceeds the voting majority,[4] a percentage substantially greater than the foreign share in the total

[1] This figure reaches 15 per cent in developing countries as a whole. See Pearson [36], p. 14.

[2] See [50], several issues, and Tironi [42]. An analysis for the period 1956–66 can be found in a paper by Wionczek, included in [25].

[3] See Ferrer [14] p. 313. Furthermore, between 1961 and 1966 'U.S. owned industrial enterprises' increased their sales at a rate five times that of industrial output in Argentina.

[4] See Bitar [6]. This work also includes a breakdown by industrial grouping.

stock of capital of the industrial sector. Further, a deeper analysis reveals an even larger influence, since while foreign participation in each enterprise is concentrated in one or few shareholders, the national share is spread among many. As a result, foreign investors own 20 per cent of the capital of industrial corporations, but represent only one per cent of the shareholders.[1]

These characteristics of foreign investment – concentration in crucial sectors and in few decision centres – greatly reinforce the influence it has on the economic life of Latin America.

III. THE EXPLANATION OF RECENT TRENDS

The level of foreign investment in Latin America is the result of a number of economic and political forces. These include factors such as the levels of savings generated in industrialised countries and the opportunities for domestic investment in them, the net profits obtained in Latin America by foreign investors,[2] the tax treatment by the industrialised countries of their foreign investment, the 'recommendations' of governmental and international institutions that channel the allocation of 'foreign aid' to developing countries, the attitude and policies of Latin American countries towards foreign investment, their foreign trade policies and the level and rate of growth of domestic markets. In general terms, this set of forces influencing foreign investment in Latin America can be grouped under the two conventional economic categories of 'supply' and 'demand'. These two concepts allow a methodical arrangement of the effects that each one of the above-mentioned factors may have over the *volume* of foreign investment and over the *return* to the foreign capitalist.

On the supply side, a basic factor in the period under consideration has been that the investment opportunities for the principal foreign investor – the U.S.A. – have been particularly attractive in Canada and Western Europe.[3] Thus, in the period 1960–9 two-thirds of U.S. net direct investment has been directed to those areas. On the other hand, only little more than one-tenth has flowed into Latin America. As a consequence of the trends prevailing during the last

[1] See Pacheco [34]. Due to the larger dispersion of the national shareholders the author holds that '40 of the 100 principal industrial enterprises are controlled from abroad'.

[2] Reinvested earnings represented 45 per cent of U.S. net investment in Latin America in the period 1966–9. The percentage is larger when manufactures alone are considered. See [50], years 1967–70.

[3] U.S. direct investment represents about two-thirds of total foreign investment in Latin America. Figures for 1959 and 1967 can be found respectively in Urquidi [49] and in the essay by Mr. Schaeffer in this volume.

two decades, U.S. foreign investment in Latin America as a proportion of its total foreign investment decreased from 40 per cent in 1950 to 20 per cent in 1969.[1]

On the other hand, the official policies of industrialised countries, particularly those of the U.S. government, have affected to a certain extent both the level and geographical allocation of the flows.[2] In as much as policies consist in increasing the *supply* of funds (for example, through United States tax credits to American investors in the developing countries, or insurance systems against different risks, like that of O.P.I.C.) instead of affecting the *demand* for foreign investment (foreign loans tied to a freer policy of the developing countries towards foreign investment) Latin America's chances of obtaining a more favourable distribution of the costs and benefits of foreign investment are enhanced. In other words, a more abundant supply improves the bargaining position of the recipient country. Nevertheless, if the prevailing policy is that of unrestricted free entrance for foreign capital, the larger supply may only end in a stronger control over the economy of the recipient country, and an accumulation of a disproportionately large share of the benefits in the hands of foreign capital.[3]

On the demand side, one of the statements most frequently found in the literature, especially in the writings of U.S. authors, is that Latin American countries have pursued a markedly negative policy with respect to foreign investment.[4] However, when one considers both governmental attitudes[5] and the facts,[6] the data seem to indicate rather an excessive trust in such investment, based on the false assumption that foreign investment is intrinsically good.

There are several explanations for such an attitude. On the one

[1] See [50], several issues. Also see [48], Table 1, and Tironi [42]. This change in the direction of flows is also valid for the other rich countries: a large share of the world's foreign investment has been taking place among industrialised countries.

[2] See, for example, articles by Kaarsten and by Behrman in [11].

[3] One of the cases that leads to such a result appears in Hirschman [24], pp. 228–9.

[4] One of the exceptions to the rule is provided by Rosenstein-Rodan, who asserts that 'There was too much freedom for foreign investment and not enough freedom of import trade', in [4], p. 57.

[5] As Mayobre has stated, 'alongside an abstract nationalist feeling, in practice an attitude of open acceptance of foreign capital, without specific regulations, has prevailed'. See [30], p. 71.

[6] One of the few restrictions recommended in governmental and parliamentary circles is the reinvestment of a high proportion of profits. See for example, García Vásquez [52] and the parliamentary discussion of the 'copper agreements' during President Frei's administration in Chile, in 1965–6. At the level of industrialised countries, see Pearson, [36], p. 109, where it is recommended that developing countries should encourage the reinvestment of profits of foreign enterprises through tax incentives.

hand, there are 'ideological' reasons: promotion of 'private enterprise', national and foreign. On the other, balance of payments difficulties and the scarcity of domestic savings have induced a larger degree of openness towards foreign investment. This last argument, in addition to ideological reasons, led Chile to make continuous appeals to foreign capital, especially in the form of direct investment, in its two first programmes of price stabilisation in 1956–8 and 1959–61, while it was balance of payments difficulties which softened Mexican restrictions on foreign investment in the mid-fifties.[1]

In general it can be said that Latin American countries have not had a defined 'policy' towards foreign investment, that is, a consistent and stable body of proposals and actions in dealing with foreign capitalists. Such a policy was absent even in such a potentially important instrument as the Treaty of Montevideo, which contained only a brief general reference in one of its articles.[2] Nevertheless, there have been isolated actions. Thus, for example, the majority of the countries have closed certain specific sectors to foreign capital – e.g. petroleum, railroads, electric power. In the rest of their economies, some countries have kept free entrance and some have adopted in principle a policy of selective admission, although in practice little has usually been done. The Chilean case constitutes a good example: from 1953 there existed a Foreign Investor Statute which established a selective system of admittance; however, the purchase of already operating domestic enterprises remained free, and for new direct investment there was no move to establish either criteria or an administrative apparatus capable of evaluating the eventual contribution of each private capital inflow. Meanwhile, throughout Latin America there has been a tendency to grant tax and tariff exemptions, and bank credit incentives, frequently even to the detriment of national private capital.

Turning to the change in the composition of foreign investment in Latin America, this does in part reflect a conscious policy on the part of the Latin American countries, as revealed in expropriations or purchases of public utility services (for instance, electricity in Mexico in 1960). But it also reflects a trend in world trade towards the greater relative importance of manufactured goods and the rapid

[1] See Vernon, [52], p. 113.
[2] It must be mentioned that Mexico expressed, through Plácido García Reynoso, its Plenipotentiary Minister, its desire and recommendation for a common treatment of foreign capital; see [19]. A summary of the few efforts made by L.A.F.T.A. on the harmonisation of policies towards foreign investment can be found in Martínez, [28]. Also, during the last few years, there has been limited further progress. An analysis of the legal treatment and of the administrative regulations applied to foreign investment in Argentina, Brazil, Mexico, Paraguay, Uruguay and Venezuela can be found in Herrero, [23].

expansion of international enterprises in that area, and the policy of more intensive price controls exerted by the recipient countries in the public utility services sector, controls which have limited monopolistic profits in that sector. And further, probably a main cause of the recent trends shown by the investment flows has been Latin America's foreign trade and industrialisation policies together with the enlargement of its markets.

On the other hand, the geographical breakdown within Latin America seems to have depended more on the general characteristics of the recipient countries than on their policies towards foreign investment. While in the primary sector, investments appear linked to the relative abundance and quality of the natural resources, in the secondary sector they appear to be intimately related with the dimension of the domestic market,[1] and the external economies that it provides. Changes in the degree of confidence and safety that it inspires are probably the chief explanation of fluctuations in investment flows.

In brief, the sectoral and geographical allocation depends on a host of political and economic elements. Without going deeper into the subject, the available data do not support more accurate statements concerning the relative importance of each factor.

IV. THE ASSESSMENT OF THE ROLE OF FOREIGN INVESTMENT

As we have seen above, Latin America has lacked a defined coherent policy towards foreign investment; by contrast most countries have been characterised by an attitude of excessive openness, which has been very costly. The lack of a consistent policy has frequently resulted in an overpayment by Latin American countries for foreign capital contributions, be it because the return has been too high, or because, as will now be argued, its contribution to G.N.P. has been scanty, or no organised efforts have been made to reap the long-term

---

[1] The three countries with largest markets, that produced 68 per cent of the gross domestic product of Latin America in 1968, had at the end of that year 74 per cent of the U.S. investment in the manufacturing sector of the region. See [48], Table 5. A simple linear regression between investment stock and domestic product, where each country represents an observation, gives a coefficient of determination of 0·96 and a product-elasticity of 1·1. That is, the market dimension appears as determinant, the larger market exerting a proportionally greater attraction. Nonetheless, the elasticity appears 'very low'; among economists the opinion *a priori* is that it is notably larger than 1·1. Since the estimate made is obviously partial, it must be considered only as a gross first attempt without any further meaning.

benefits of the investment, in technology, training of personnel and conquest of foreign markets.

If we turn now to the analytic level, we find the same lack reflected here. ECLA, for example, an organisation that has exerted an important influence on the development of Latin American economic thought, concentrated its interest on other aspects, limiting itself to expressing its belief in the necessity to 'stimulate foreign capital investment in order to accelerate the rate of Latin American development',[1] and to collecting data on the direct impact of foreign capital on the balance of payments of Latin American countries.[2]

In general it is only in the last five years that economists have begun to be more intensively[3] concerned with what until then was mainly preoccupying sociologists and political scientists; subsequently governmental circles have followed suit. Recent academic interest with regard to the role played by foreign investment can be classified into two kinds: (a) aspects related to national sovereignty and foreign dependence and (b) economic costs and benefits of foreign investment.

Dependence reveals itself in many varied forms. One of them corresponds to the economic area. This may consist for example in the simple mental dependence of economic authorities with respect to models and authorities of extra-regional organisations: free submission to foreign recipes. But it may also consist in economic dependence of a coercive nature: i.e. when the nature of the economic relations with the outside world is such that the country is compelled to accept certain impositions or restrictions in its economic policy. Excessive dependence on foreign capital for the financing of development leads to obvious dangers in this sense. In this aspect each government faces a political choice among three alternatives: (a) stagnation (b) development on the basis of external savings and (c) development with a vigorous and sustained savings effort on the part of the present generation.

In our judgement, only alternative (c) offers a viable course. To raise the growth rate of the gross domestic product (G.D.P.) in Latin America by 1 percentage point, requires an additional annual injection of capital of approximately two and a half times the external financing of the region in the period 1966–9. If, hypothetically,

[1] ECLA, [44], p. 16. A brief reference to some of the negative aspects of foreign investment can be found in this publication. The analysis is developed in a framework characterised by the desire to 'increase the share of international public resources in the financing of investment in social capital, with the purpose of opening a broad road to both domestic and foreign private investment' (p. 16).

[2] See, for example, ECLA, [48].

[3] Once again we insist that this is a relative rather than an absolute statement. We do not forget that there were some valuable works published before this date.

the additional financing were obtained abroad, the annual rate of growth of foreign assets (direct investment plus indebtedness) in Latin America would leap sharply, from approximately 6 per cent to 20 per cent, while on certain assumptions the growth rate of G.D.P. would rise from about 5 per cent to 6 per cent.[1] Even if the more optimistic goals were to be attained, both in relation to the expansion of 'foreign aid' of the industrialised countries as well as its multilateralisation,[2] it seems hardly feasible to maintain both a reasonable degree of independence and access to that enlarged level of resources.

But this is not all. First, the above-mentioned figure refers to the growth of the *domestic* product. But the relevant variable is the *national* product. Increased financing based on foreign capital opens a widening gap between the two, as capital service payments increase.[3]

Second, we have so far assumed that the inflow of capital did contribute to an increase in G.D.P. If we consider the situation as it has actually developed in Latin America, particularly with regard to the increasing foreign investment in manufacturing, it is clear that this is to make a major assumption about changes in development policy. Foreign investment in the export sector, in economies with balance of payments difficulties and where it does not merely replace national investors, tends to generate a positive contribution to G.N.P., even though its remuneration may have been excessive.[4] The outcome, in the typical Latin American framework, is less evident in the manufacturing sector. When the project in question is that of a foreign firm producing only for the domestic market, enjoying a monopolistic position in a highly protected sector, it is quite possible for the earnings received by foreign capital to exceed its contribution to the domestic product. In other words, the national product, rather than increasing, might actually fall.[5]

Consider the case in which the alternative is domestic production by a foreign investor, or importation, with private costs being higher for the former. It might be that such an investment was still desirable,

[1] One numerical example, for 1967, is developed in Ffrench-Davis and Arancibia, [17].

[2] See Pearson, [36], pp. 150–52. For 1975 a target of 'net transfer of funds' equivalent to 1 per cent of G.D.P. of industrialised countries is proposed; it is recommended that one-seventh of that flow be channelled by multilateral institutions.

[3] See Ffrench-Davis and Arancibia [17], p. 6.

[4] Undoubtedly, if that investment enjoys tax incentives and preferential input prices, the conclusion with regard to its positive impact on G.N.P. may become altered.

[5] Obviously, the malallocation of resources also prevails if the investor is national. Notwithstanding, in this case, it is sufficient for the marginal productivity of capital to be positive, for G.N.P. to increase.

since private costs exceeded social costs, e.g. in the case of dynamic external economies.[1] On the other hand, it can be that both private and social production costs are higher than the opportunity cost (c.i.f. import price, *OC*), e.g. assembling industries, whose components are acquired abroad at surcharged prices, or situations in which the size of the domestic market does not allow economies of scale. It is this second case which provides the conditions that will most probably lead to a decrease of the national product. In fact, apart from the positive multiplier effects of the increase in investment, it is enough that the earnings of the foreign capital (*R*) – even if they are equal or below a normal level – exceed the excess of the import cost of the substituted good over the production cost *PC* (*net* of foreign capital earnings). That is, considering the present values, if $R > OC - PC$, the earnings of foreign capital will have been higher than its direct contribution to the domestic product.[2]

This analysis has been presented in an extremely simplified form in order to highlight the main conditions under which foreign investment will provide a negative contribution to the national product. The analysis can easily be extended to the case of infant industries, or other sources of differentials between social and market prices. Further, there is another aspect so far ignored, which is traditionally disregarded in social project evaluation but which is important in regard to foreign investment: the potentially large effect that foreign capital inflows can exert on the supply of domestic savings, thus providing another source of impact on the level of G.N.P.[3]

We can now see the significance of the change in the sectoral location of foreign investment which was discussed above. Such a shift may have an important effect not only from the point of view of dependence – i.e. the influence it exerts on the centres of economic decision. It may also significantly alter the relationship between the costs and benefits deriving from foreign investment in the aggregate. Thus the change in the composition of investment which has occurred over the last two decades has quite probably worsened the distribution of benefits between the parent countries and the host countries.

[1] See Ffrench-Davis and Griffin [18], chapters III and IX.
[2] *PC* includes all the costs represented by domestic and foreign intermediate inputs, the opportunity cost of domestic capital shares and depreciation allowances of domestic and foreign capital shares (*ND* and *FD*). The relation can also be written as $R + FD > OC - (PC - FD)$.
[3] For empirical research on the substitutability of domestic and foreign savings, see, for example, a paper by Weisskopf, [55]. Aggregate estimates of the incidence of both sources of impact on G.N.P. (productivity minus returns to foreign capital, and substitution between domestic and foreign factors) can be found in Griffin and Enos, [21], and in Kellman, [26].

Let us now consider the alternative development strategy based on a domestic savings effort. To reach the target of a percentage point increase in the national product, an increase of 3 to 4 percentage points in the rate of savings is required, that is, the growth of *per capita* product of approximately two years. Hence, postponing for two years any increase in *per capita* consumption, allows a 50 per cent increase in the growth rate of national product (to 3 per cent).[1] Thus, one possible alternative is to have permanently a 2 per cent annual growth rate in *per capita* consumption; or to reach a 3 per cent rate by the third year, whilst in the two first years consumption expands only at the growth rate of population. This sacrifice, which is then plentifully rewarded thereafter, is a necessary (but not sufficient) component of the effort required for independent development.[2]

The conclusion seems to be clear. Foreign capital cannot, has not and should not play a decisive role in Latin American development.[3]

However, we have emphasised only the financial aspect of the contribution of foreign capital: the contribution in the areas of technology, management capacity and access to foreign markets must now be considered, since these constitute, from our point of view, the only valid justifications for the acceptance of foreign investment.[4] If it is a question of 'pure' capital unaccompanied by such elements, it in any case is almost always less expensive for the recipient country to choose external loans rather than foreign investment.

[1] All the figures presented refer to orders of magnitude; the rates of change refer to *per capita* figures. The results vary according to the sources of information used. The sources used are described in [17].

[2] The political decision to choose the road of sovereign development requires the readaptation of foreign trade policies. For an analysis of the policy of greater aggregate incidence see Ffrench-Davis [16].

[3] This statement is compatible with the positive contribution foreign capital may make in easing balance of payments difficulties at a time of transition to a higher growth rate, when the high imported component of investment will tend to promote transitory difficulties in the balance of payments. The increase of the flow of resources towards developing countries, within the features proposed by UNCTAD 1968, would contribute to soften these difficulties.

[4] This may seem an unduly strong statement, after our emphasis above on the notorious lack of empirical research. But consider an example: one aspect where many questions remain unsettled is the degree of complementarity or substitutability between foreign investment and national factors of production. But although the historical experience is unknown in quantitative terms, it is still possible to determine which are the major negative features of foreign investment and to outline a policy on that data; therefore, the lack of empirical studies can block the design of an optimal policy, but not a *movement in that direction*, especially when actual policies are located at the wrong end of the range of possibilities.

However, quite often all three contributions can be obtained directly without resorting to foreign investors. That is, what has frequently appeared as a 'package' can be acquired by parts. In fact, capital can be obtained in financial markets, technology can be obtained through technical services and purchases of licences, and the markets through governmental agreements. Nevertheless, there are cases in which technology is not available in the market, or in which the markets are captive. The first is particularly true in the case of very 'dynamic' technologies, that experience permanent and significant changes. The second is especially relevant when product differentiation is important and when foreign markets are controlled by international enterprises. However, a general review of foreign investment in Latin America seems to indicate that in fact the foreign investor has frequently been paid for transferring what was actually directly accessible technology, and that instead of providing external markets he has himself entered in order to enjoy protected domestic markets.

V. THE IMPLICATIONS OF THE ANALYSIS FOR A FOREIGN INVESTMENT POLICY

The acceptance of the points made above fundamentally alters the framework of discussion on the role that foreign investment should be assigned. In general, past policies have emphasised what this analysis reveals as secondary, while neglecting the fundamental. Aspects concerning the contribution of capital and the reinvestment of profits have been emphasised, while the contribution of technology, management capacity and foreign markets has been left on one side.[1]

On the basis of the above analysis, the range of discussion on the role of foreign investment becomes drastically diminished. It reduces to two aspects, one technical, the other ideological. The first is a matter of the degree to which foreign markets and technology are accessible without foreign investment. The second is the political dilemma of whether to produce or not the type of good for which the

---

[1] Even the emphasis on the contribution of capital has not been consistent, as illustrated, for example, by the lack of concern for the absorption of domestic credit by foreign enterprises, often at subsidised rates. Only in recent years have some Latin American countries adopted regulations with respect to the domestic indebtedness of foreign enterprises. See for instance Ferrer [15], point 3. Further, the motivation for measures encouraging foreign investment has quite often been the foreign exchange rather than the savings gap. The policy of undervalued exchange rates has in this context implied a larger 'demand' for foreign investment.

market is captive and the technology monopolised by an international enterprise – i.e. the type of good to produce which at
reasonable cost the assistance of foreign capitalists is essential.
Possibly, and more appropriately, the decision would consist in the
definition of the aggregate incidence of such goods. Thus it is clear
that industrial development policy is inseparable from the question
of 'external independence'.

We have seen that an unrestricted policy of open arms towards
foreign investment offers the serious danger of a consolidation of
foreign dependence. Even relatively small amounts of capital may
control the vital economic centres of the domestic economy, with
the support of domestic and foreign loans and with the capitalisation
of monopolistic profits. Instead, a selective type policy, which
optimises the contribution of technology, managerial capacity and
markets, avoids those perils and may contribute to an important
degree (but complementarily) to the development of some dynamic
activities, especially in the industrial sector.

Such guidelines have strong implications for the design of a policy
towards foreign capital, implications that recommend a fundamental
change in actual policies. Some aspects of such a change will now be
briefly discussed.

(a) Reinvestment of profits. The policy of forcing the reinvestment
of a given percentage of profits has three important implications.
First, it means emphasis on balance of payments problems and
acceptance of the principle that foreign investment is good *per se*.[1]
Second, if there prevails a tax on profit remittances, it implies a cost
for the government which forgoes the tax on profit remittances:
the government finances a fraction of that reinvestment, without
directly reaping any benefit. Third, it implies an additional cost for
the country, because the foreign investor is not accustomed to give
anything away; one of the elements most appreciated by the foreign
investor seems to be his freedom to withdraw his earnings.

The first point holds for already established enterprises as well as
for new investments; the second one particularly applies in the case
of already established enterprises; the third one is more clearly
relevant when reinvestment regulations are part of the bargaining
process that precedes the investment. A strict and selective policy
anyway reduces 'structurally' the possibility of monopolistic profits.
Consequently, everything, except transitory balance of payments
problems, recommends that a *selective and strict* policy towards
foreign capital ought to include, notwithstanding, a liberal withdrawal of profits.[2]

[1] See Ffrench-Davis and Arancibia [17].
[2] The arguments also apply, though partially, to depreciation allowances.

(b) Investment incentives in poor areas of the recipient country. First, these imply that the foreign capitalist maximises his influence per dollar invested. Second, frequently the foreign investor is not likely to identify completely with the interests of his own country. He will be even less likely to do so in regard to the poor region; therefore his services must always be rewarded. Hence, the lower productivity of the region will require a form of subsidy to that investment. The appropriate recommendation seems to be not to rely on foreign investment for the solution of regional imbalances.

(c) It is essential to develop a state apparatus capable of evaluating the costs and benefits of each inflow of private foreign capital and the factors that accompany it. To advance towards a selective and effective policy it is necessary to be acquainted to some degree with the nature of the technologies involved in each possible inflow, and the possible foreign markets of the goods that are in question. Until now the bulk of foreign investment in the industrial sector has enjoyed the domestic market of each country, without contributing external markets. United States enterprises established in the Latin American manufacturing sector place 93 per cent of their sales in the market of the recipient country; only 7 per cent reaches foreign markets.[1] Undoubtedly, to an important degree, this outcome is the result of Latin American foreign trade policies adopted in the past, that have led to an inward-oriented development, characterised by a 'horizontal' instead of 'vertical' substitution of imports.[2] Nevertheless behavioural characteristics of foreign enterprises established in the region have also drastically influenced the outcome. In fact, the patents and royalties that accompany them frequently contain clauses that limit or forbid exports of their output.[3]

(d) Each country on its own is relatively weak if confronted with the gigantic multinational enterprises. Furthermore, the liberalisation of reciprocal trade, within a process of economic integration, without the harmonisation of industrial development and foreign investment policies, enhances such weakness; the gamut of choices for the foreign investor increases, since he can now count on the whole of the regional market while investing in only one of the

[1] See [48], Table 34.
[2] This is an important reason for the development of 'substitutive' rather than 'complementary' economies among Latin American countries.
[3] A report on research into the behaviour of foreign investment in the Chilean industrial sector can be found in Bitar, [6]; see especially p. 38. Provisional results of a survey for Latin America that covers 100 multinational enterprises appear in Lagos, [4]. In the analysis of the export behaviour of multinational enterprises, careful note should be taken of the fact that the proportion of such enterprises that export is diametrically different to the proportion of their output that they export; the available data show that the latter proportion is markedly smaller.

member countries. Hence, the more developed the liberalisation process, the higher the priority the harmonisation of policies towards extraregional investment acquires; the harmonisation must include a selective policy, a co-ordinated front replacing the present competition among member countries.

VI. THE PROSPECTS FOR FOREIGN INVESTMENT AND THE CASE OF THE ANDEAN PACT

It can be stated that the above-mentioned guidelines are gaining strength each day. The concern about the growing power acquired by foreign capitalists has reached broad professional, technical, academic and governmental circles. Simultaneously, an awareness has developed that technology and captive foreign markets are the main contribution foreign investment can make.

The best expression of support for this hypothesis, spectacular in its depth and significance, is the recent agreement among the Andean countries on the treatment to be given to foreign capital.[1] According to this agreement among five Andean countries, common legal provisions are adopted towards capital from outside the region. The agreement has collected the experience accumulated in the region with respect to the virtues and vices of foreign investment. Aware, in turn, of the intrinsic difficulties involved in arriving at an agreement on a subject such as foreign investment, different treatment is accorded to activities 'closely related' to the integration process as compared with the remainder of the economy. The former become subject to strict regulations, while for the latter these are less rigorous, each country being authorised to make exceptions to the rules.

Some of the basic aspects of the agreement are summarised in what follows. First, a selective policy is adopted; that is, every new investment will require the specific authorisation of a national agency (Art. 2); the same regulation applies to royalties and patents (Art. 18). Secondly, the use of domestic and foreign loans (Art. 17), and of contract clauses that limit the export of goods making use of royalties (Art. 20, clause 8 and Art. 25–a) or limit regional technical development (Art. 20–f), are regulated. Thirdly, liberal regulations on remittances of earnings are adopted (with a ceiling of 14 per cent

---

[1] Decision No. 24, *Tercer Período de Sesiones Extraordinarias, Comision del Acuerdo de Cartagena*, 14–31 December 1970. Some marginal adjustments have been made subsequently according to Decision 37. It should be mentioned that the Andean agreement has improved the bargaining position of the member countries in all those items covered by 'industrial programming' (Sectoral Programmes of Industrial Development), since the foreign investor cannot choose to invest in that country where he can benefit from a better treatment, but he can only choose that one that has been assigned the given industry.

per annum), and automatic reinvestment and purchases of shares of domestic enterprises are restricted (Art. 6). Fourth, it is recommended that new investment in strategic sectors such as the financial sector, advertising and communications media be forbidden (Art. 43), these being sectors in which each country can follow a more autonomous policy.

Finally, regulations are established for the gradual transference of existing and new foreign enterprises to domestic ownership. Three categories of enterprises are distinguished: domestic, mixed and foreign; domestic are those with a share of domestically-owned capital exceeding 80 per cent; mixed are those with a share between 51 and 80 per cent,[1] and foreign, the remainder. For those enterprises beginning operations after June 1971 capital shares belonging to residents of other member countries will be considered as domestic. The agreement states that foreign enterprises are to be gradually transformed into mixed enterprises within a period that varies between 15 and 22 years (Art. 28 and 29). Those foreign enterprises which do not fulfil these rules will not enjoy the benefits of the broadened market, that is, they will not benefit from the trade liberalisation. The sanction is fully effective, for the main danger of dependence, within the integration process, emerges in relation to investments of a regional scope.

The common regime, rather than a narrow, inflexible and unchangeable comprehensive set of rules, is a basic framework within which every country is to design the specific aspects of its own policy toward foreign investment, a policy which is to be improved as circumstances and experience recommend.

The adoption of a common set of rules for the treatment of foreign capital and regarding brands, patents, licences and royalties, is just beginning. Nevertheless, the most difficult task has been accomplished: a free agreement among five Latin American countries on a *selective* type of treatment towards foreign investment, and a definition of the basic framework for a policy. Now there remains its implementation.

The adoption of the agreement was the result of a long and conscious process. Undoubtedly, its implementation will face tough obstacles, and obviously there are to be difficulties in the interpretation of some of its clauses. It is the deeper understanding by each country of the phenomena under analysis that will best guarantee

---

[1] When the state holds a share of the capital and 'exerts a decisive role in the management of the enterprise' enterprises with a domestic share below 51 per cent can be considered as mixed (Art. 36, Decision 24). Subsequently, (Art. 1, Decision 47) the minimum state share of the capital to fulfil the requirements to be considered a mixed enterprise was fixed at 30 per cent.

the successful implementation of the agreement. It is foreseeable that each country will develop an effective bargaining and evaluative mechanism, an unavoidable requirement for a growing rationalisation of the inflow of foreign capital. The continuous exchange of experiences, established by the agreement, ought to contribute to an acceleration of that process of rationalisation. In other words, the agreement will eventually generate a healthy learning process, encouraging a restatement of attitudes and policies, and a redesign of priorities.

Among other consequences, the rationalisation of the treatment of foreign capital will undoubtedly mean that some investors will decide not to enter, while others will decide to leave. This will be especially so in the case of foreign enterprises that were entering Latin American countries to produce solely for each isolated domestic market, under complete protection. On the other hand, the process of rationalisation will also mean a better exploitation of the new world circumstances reflected by the appearance of multinational enterprises of diverse national origin, and diverse behaviour and leanings. This new circumstance grants a larger and more favourable bargaining margin to developing countries. Their bargaining capability will depend on the clearness of the objectives being sought, on the knowledge available on the behaviour of each foreign investor, and on the power exerted by recipient countries. The Andean agreement behaves well in all three cases. The outcome will depend, however, on the measures adopted by each country.

The degree of influence to be exerted on the rest of Latin America will depend on the concrete results obtained in the first years of implementation of the common set of rules. If the Cartagena Agreement follows the audacious, imaginative and dynamic course that it has followed until now, it is to be hoped that the example will spread, and will lead to a general restatement of the attitude towards foreign investment within the guidelines adopted by the Andean countries. This would mean a new important step towards the attainment, through integration, of the basic goal of serving Latin American people and the consolidation of their economic independence.

REFERENCES AND BIBLIOGRAPHY

[1] David A. Baldwin, *Foreign Aid and American Economic Policy, A Documentary Analysis* (New York: Frederick A. Praeger, 1966), (especially chapter IX).

[2] Jagdish Bhagwati, ed., *International Trade* (Great Britain: Penguin Books, 1969) (especially part five).

[3] Jagdish Bhagwati and Richard Eckaus, eds., *Readings: Foreign Aid* (Great Britain: Penguin Books, 1970).

[4] Inter American Development Bank, *Multinational Investment in the Economic Development and Integration of Latin America* (Bogotá: 1968).

[5] Sergio Bitar, 'La Inversión Privada Extranjera en la Industria Chilena', *Panorama Económico*, No. 257 (Santiago, Septiembre de 1970).

[6] Sergio Bitar, 'Políticas de Desarrollo Industrial', *Cuadernos de Economía*, No. 22 (Santiago, Diciembre de 1970).

[7] Sergio Bitar, 'Las Empresas Extranjeras en la Estrategia Industrial Chilena', Proyecto de investigación, CEPLAN-CEPLA (Santiago, 1972).

[8] Frank Brandenburg, *The Development of Latin American Private Enterprise* (Washington, D.C.: National Planning Association, 1964), Pamphlet 121.

[9] CECLA, *Consenso Latinoamericano de Viña del Mar* (Chile, Mayo de 1969).

[10] C.I.A.P., 'La Inversión Privada Extranjera en el Desarrollo Latino-americano', presentado en la VI Reunión Anual del CIES, Junio de 1969. Reprinted in *Comercio Exterior*, (Mexico, Agosto de 1969).

[11] Benjamin Cohen, ed., *American Foreign Economic Policy* (New York: Harper & Row, 1968).

[12] Sidney Dell, *Experiencias de la Integración Económica en América Latina* (Mexico, D.F.: CEMLA, 1966).

[13] Theotonio Dos Santos, *Dependencia y Cambio Social*, Cuaderno No. 11 (Santiago: CESO, 1970).

[14] Aldo Ferrer, 'El Capital Extranjero en la Economía Argentina', *Trimestre Económico*, No. 150 (Abril–Junio 1971).

[15] Aldo Ferrer, 'Empresa Extranjera: Observaciones sobre la Experiencia Argentina', Seminar on *Política de Inversiones Extranjeras y Transferencia de Tecnología en América Latina*, organised by ILDIS/FLACSO (Santiago, 1971).

[16] Ricardo Ffrench-Davis, 'Dependencia, Subdesarrollo y Política Cambiaria', *Trimestre Económico*, No. 146 (Abril–Junio 1970).

[17] Ricardo Ffrench-Davis y Samuel Arancibia, 'Notas sobre el Capital Extranjero y América Latina', Documento No. 1 (Santiago: CEPLAN, 1970). Also in *International Economics and Development*, essays in honour of Raúl Prebisch, ed. by Luis E. Di Marco (New York: Academic Press Inc., 1972).

[18] Ricardo Ffrench-Davis y Keith B. Griffin, *Comercio Internacional y Políticas de Desarrollo Económico* (Mexico: Fondo de Cultura Económica, 1967) (especially chapters III and IX).

[19] Placido García Reynoso, *Integración Económica Latinoamericana* (Mexico D.F., Publicaciones Especializadas, S.A. Coleccion ALALC (de SELA), 1965.

[20] Placido García Reynoso, *Economic Aid: A Brief Survey.* (London: Central Office of Information, 1968).

[21] Keith Griffin and John Enos, 'Foreign Assistance: Objectives and Consequences', *Economic Development and Cultural Change.* Vol. 18 (April 1970).

[22] Felipe Herrera, *El Desarrollo de América Latina y su Financiamiento* (Buenos Aires: Aguilar, 1967) (especially part 3, chapter 3).

[23] Felix Herrero, 'Tratamiento Legal Comparado de las Inversiones Extranjeras en los Países de ALALC (excepto de grupo Andino)', Seminar on *Política de Inversiones Extranjeras y Transferencia de Tecnología en América Latina*, organised by ILDIS/FLACSO, Santiago, 1971.

[24] Albert Hirschman, 'How to Divest in Latin America and Why', in *A Bias for*

Hope: Essays on Development and Latin America (New Haven: Yale University Press, 1971).

[25] Helio Jaguaribe *et al.*, *La Dependencia Político-Económica de América Latina* (México D.F.: Siglo Veintiuno, 1969).

[26] Mitchell Kellman, 'Foreign Assistance: Objectives and Consequences: Comments', *Economic Development and Cultural Change*, Vol. 20 (October 1971).

[27] Carlos Malpica, *El Mito de la Ayuda Exterior* (Lima: Francisco Mancloa Editores, S.A., 1967).

[28] Juan Pascual Martínez, 'La Política de la ALALC sobre la Inversión Extranjera', Seminar on *Política de Inversiones Extranjeras y Transferencia de Tecnología en América Latina*, organised by ILDIS/FLACSO, Santiago, 1971.

[29] Guillermo Martorell, *Las Inversiones Extranjeras en la Argentina* (Buenos Aires: Editorial Galerna, 1969).

[30] José Antonio Mayobre, *Las Inversiones Extranjeras en Venezuela* (Caracas: Monte Ávila Editores, C.A., 1970).

[31] José Antonio Mayobre *et al.*, *Hacia la Integración Acelerada de América Latina* (México: Fondo de Cultura Económica, 1965), especially chapter III).

[32] Raymond Mikesell, *U.S. Private and Government Investment Abroad* (Oregon: University of Oregon Books, 1962).

[33] Hlya Myint, 'International Trade and the Developing Countries', in *International Economic Relations*, ed. by Paul Samuelson (New York: St. Martin's Press, 1969).

[34] Luis Pacheco, 'La Inversión Extranjera y las Corporaciones Internacionales: el caso chileno', in *Proceso a la Industrialización Chilena*, ed. by Oscar Muñoz (Santiago: CEPLAN, 1972).

[35] Felipe Pazos, 'El Financiamiento Externo de la América Latina: Aumento Progresivo o Disminución Gradual?', *Trimestre Económico*, No. 150 (Abril–Junio 1971).

[36] Lester Pearson, *Partners in Development: report of the Commission on International Development* (New York: Frederick A. Praeger, 1969).

[37] Raúl Prebisch, *Towards a Dynamic Development Policy for Latin America* (New York: U.N., Economic Commission for Latin America, 1963).

[38] Raúl Prebisch, *Towards a Global Strategy of Development* (New York: UNCTAD, 1968).

[39] Carlos Quintana, 'Resultado de una Encuesta sobre Inversión Extranjera en México', *Comercio Exterior* (México: Agosto de 1969).

[40] Osvaldo Sunkel, 'Política Nacional de Desarrollo y Dependencia Externa', *Estudios Internacionales* (Santiago: Mayo de 1967).

[41] Osvaldo Sunkel, 'Capitalismo Transnacional y Desintegración Nacional en la América Latina', *Trimestre Económico*, No. 150 (Abril–Junio, 1971).

[42] Ernesto Tironi, 'Beneficios y Costos de la Inversión Extranjera en Chile', investigación en desarrollo, CEPLAN (Santiago: 1972).

[43] United Nations, *El Desarrollo de América Latina y sus Principales Problemas* (Santiago: CEPAL, 1949), (especially chapter V).

[44] United Nations, *The International Flow of Private Capital, 1956–58* (New York: U.N., 1959).

[45] United Nations, *La Cooperación Internacional en la Política de Desarrollo Latinoamericano* (CEPAL, 1954).

[46] United Nations, *The Status of Permanent Sovereignty over Natural Wealth and Resources* (New York: U.N., 1962).

[47] United Nations, *El Financiamiento Externo de América Latina* (New York: CEPAL, 1964).

[48] United Nations, *Estudio Económico de América Latina, 1970.* Vol. II, Capítulo I, 'La Expansión de las Empresas Internacionales y su Gravitación en el Desarrollo Latinoamericano' (Santiago: CEPAL, 1971).
[49] Víctor Urquidi, *Viabilidad Económica de América Latina* (México: Fondo de Cultura Económica, 1962). English translation: *The Challenge of Development in Latin America* (London: Pall Mall, 1964).
[50] U.S. Government, Department of Commerce, *Survey of Current Business* (Washington, D.C.: U.S. Government Printing Office).
[51] U.S. Government, Department of Commerce, *U.S. Direct Investments Abroad,* 1966, Part I, Balance of Payments Data (Washington, D.C.: U.S. Government Printing Office, 1970).
[52] Raymond Vernon, ed., *How Latin America Views the U.S. Investor* (New York: Frederick A. Praeger, 1966).
[53] Raymond Vernon, ed., 'The Multinational Enterprise: Power versus Sovereignty'. *Foreign Affairs* (July 1971).
[54] Raymond Vernon, ed., 'Progress Report: Multinational Enterprise Project, Calendar year 1970' (Cambridge Mass.: Harvard Business School, 1971).
[55] Thomas Weisskopf, 'The Impact of Foreign Capital Inflow on Domestic Savings in Underdeveloped Countries'. Economic Development Report, No. 156. Project for *Quantitative Research in Economic Development,* Center for International Affairs, Harvard University, July 1970.
[56] Miguel Wionczek, *El Nacionalismo Mexicano y la Inversión Extranjera* (México D.F.: Siglo Veintiuno, 1967).
[57] Miguel Wionczek, *Economic Cooperation in Latin America, Africa and Asia* (Cambridge, Mass.: M.I.T. Press, 1969).
[58] Miguel Wionczek, 'Hacia el Establecimiento de un Trato Común para la Inversión Extranjera en el Mercado Común Andino', *Trimestre Económico,* No. 150 (Abril–Junio, 1971).
[59] Miguel Wionczek, 'La Inversión Extranjera Privada: Problemas y Perspectivas', en *Crecimiento o Desarrollo Económico,* ed. M. Wionczek (México D.F.: SEP/SETENTAS, 1971).

Discussion of the Paper by Dr. Ffrench-Davis

Professor Hirschman opened the discussion by quoting the experience of a friend of his, who upon first trying to read Hegel's *Phenomenology of the Spirit* had exclaimed that he understood every word but not the *Zusammenhang* ('how it all hangs together'). His experience with Dr. Ffrench-Davis's stimulating paper was in many ways the opposite: he well understood the general meaning and the direction of the paper; he even largely agreed with them, but he found himself disagreeing with a fairly large number of the more detailed points. Obviously his comments should deal more with areas of disagreement than with those of agreement.

He would like to begin with Dr. Ffrench-Davis's statement that 'Latin American countries, except Mexico, have not had a defined policy toward foreign investment.' He demurred in part on grounds of factual inaccuracy, in part for more fundamental reasons. Some countries *had* adopted a comprehensive foreign investment statute; Colombia with Law 444 of 1967 was an example. In fact the *técnicos* who had worked out and applied this statute were so enamoured of its working that they were strongly opposed to the new provisions and guidelines of the Andean Pact, and made common cause with other interest groups who were against Decision No. 24 for quite different reasons.

More important, the fact of not having passed a law or made a comprehensive policy statement did not mean that one did not have a consistent policy. (This statement was just as true when reversed: if one had issued a comprehensive policy statement, a consistent policy was by no means assured; the case of Mexico was probably a case in point.) Brazil had not issued any statement as far as he knew, but it was fairly clear that since 1964 that country's government had followed a consistent policy of welcoming foreign investment and had only lately taken some indirect measures aimed at discouraging takeovers of domestic firms, through incentives toward mergers.

His next point related to the contrast Dr. Ffrench-Davis painted between an 'indiscriminate' policy of open arms toward foreign investment and a 'selective' policy which optimised the contribution in technology, management, and markets. If the alternative was presented in this form, who would not embrace its so much more attractive second term? Unfortunately decisions were not that easy in the real world. Restricting foreign investment inflow meant taking the hard decision to forego easy and, in the short run, welcome contributions not only of capital, but of technology, entrepreneurship, expertise and so forth, in the necessarily uncertain expectation that it would be possible to generate these various factors of production domestically once their steady inflow from abroad had been stopped. This was the reason for which such decisions were not easily taken in normal times when the conventional wisdom told us that a bird in the hand was better than two in the bush or '*mejor malo conocido que bueno por conocer.*'

The decision to forgo some foreign investment was even harder because of the multiplicity of its potential contributions. Dr. Ffrench-Davis stressed technology and market connections, rather than capital, but there were other valuable services the foreigner could be called upon to perform. In the Latin American environment of small oligopolistic markets with stagnant consumer goods industries, foreign enterprise had acted at times as the one who spoiled the cosy oligopoly-conspiracy of domestic entrepreneurs by competing aggressively, by reinvesting profits for growth, by extending credit to people who had long been considered unacceptable credit risks, and by improving quality – even by paying taxes. He submitted that this gadfly function of foreign enterprise was one of its most valuable attributes as it could help vitalise currently routine-and-decay-ridden branches of national industry. Moreover, in this function foreign enterprise would never attain the monopolistic position it was likely to acquire if it was brought in on account of its contribution of advanced technology. The establishment of a few such foreign-owned gadflies or *entreprise-témoins* – a term the French coined for a similar situation in which state-owned or state-approved enterprises would enter a sector dominated by privately owned firms – might well be a useful policy in a number of Latin American countries. Such a policy also had obvious dangers and limits unless it was combined with suitable divestment policies; for instead of stimulating the pace of the horse, this particular gadfly all too often ended up by devouring it.

This brought him to his last point. Dr. Ffrench-Davis celebrated the new foreign investment policy of the Andean Pact, and he himself would yield to no one in his admiration of what had been accomplished by the *Acuerdo de Cartagena* in evolving new bases for international economic co-operation in the foreign investment field. But there was a real intellectual and practical difficulty about advocating a *uniform* investment policy for Latin America or – why not? – for the Third World as a whole. While certain abuses of foreign investment should be curbed in all countries and while we needed a much wider array of institutional arrangements than was presently available, different policies were in his opinion desirable for countries at different stages in their development. As he had argued elsewhere, the search for a once-and-for-all optimal policy struck him as vain and optimality might well lie in judiciously alternating close contact and relative insulation.

This position, incidentally, permitted him to criticise Professor Vernon's earlier critique of Professor Sunkel's position on the consequences of withdrawal of contact. Once oscillation was agreed to be the correct policy, the poor performance of such countries as Indonesia and Guinea could be explained: they chose the wrong moment for withdrawal or, perhaps, they went too far. Moreover, nobody had argued that withdrawal was ever a sufficient, rather than merely a necessary condition. One further comment on this topic: the problems arising from close contact were, in his opinion, institutionally neutral: they were just as likely to arise between advanced and backward socialist countries as between advanced and backward market economies.

The appropriate moment at which openness to foreign capital should

---

[1] Eds.' note: this refers to the discussion reported on p. 423 of this volume.

give way to withdrawal from close contact and self-reliance would of course be different from one group of countries to another. For that reason, a common policy for all developing countries struck him not only as an impractical goal, but also as an undesirable one. Naturally, restrictive decisions were taken more easily if a number of similarly situated countries could agree to take them together. Moreover, in that case there was a real chance to achieve long-overdue *changes in the rules of the international investment game*. But he would like to suggest that the mobility of new investment capital and its search for the best possible investment climate were not always unmitigated evils for the countries of the Third World: it was likely that at the time when some countries should reduce contact, others should open up so that the foreign investor, in moving from the former to the latter, did not really 'play off one against the other' as he boasted and was accused of doing; rather, it was conceivable that in moving he behaved just as he should in the interest of both groups of countries. While he realised that there were other, much less happy situations, the thought just expressed struck so cheerful a note that it would be a pity not to end his comment on it.

Professor Felix said that the failure of foreign firms to be very visible in the older or more vegetative branches of industry, such as textiles, suggested a more restricted 'gadfly' function than that implied by Professor-Hirschman. Their orientation seemed to be mainly towards capitalising expected returns from new or differentiated products, which provided monopoly rents and for which the development costs had already largely been written off in their home market. In vegetative industries the payoff would come mainly from superior cost effectiveness in producing standardised products for the local market. Thus foreign industrial investment seemed to be mainly an extension of the product differentiation strategies of multi-national oligopoly firms.

A partial exception to this was the relocation of some phases of a manufacturing process to a low efficiency wage country for re-exporting. But in this case also, the relocation was usually of activities new to the host region. Thus Taiwan and South Korea, with little prior industrial experience, had drawn far more export-oriented foreign industrial investment than had Latin American countries.

This prompted him to raise a further problem. Conventional economic explanations did not seem to account for the paucity of export-oriented foreign investment in manufacturing in, say, Central America in the 1960s as compared to the two Asian countries in question. Central American countries were as avidly seeking it, had comparable wage rates, strong foreign exchanges, weak unions and very conservative governments. They were also much closer to the main export markets, and language was less of a barrier. He was not anxious to turn to more sociological or even Machiavellian arguments but perhaps that was the direction in which we had to look for a plausible explanation.

Dr. Ferrer said that he would like to take up another comment of Professor Hirschman's, that no coherent law did not mean no policy. The truth of this was well illustrated by his own recent experience as Minister of Economy in Argentina. First, though, he would like to point out the dangers in the common tendency to separate the foreign capital issue from general development policy; a foreign capital policy could only make sense as one element in a global policy of resource mobilisation.

Going back to his own attempt at policy making, during his time in office Argentina had had no legal code or administrative regulations, yet they had implemented a series of decisions amounting to a coherent policy. This policy centred on the basic industries, and was to operate by offering new opportunities preferentially to domestic enterprise, and by strengthening its bargaining power *vis-à-vis* foreign companies. One of the instruments of the new policy was the orientation of new credit extensions increasingly towards majority local-owned firms. The purchasing power of the public sector was also used to promote locally owned firms in the construction industry by giving them preference in public bidding.These examples showed that there was a policy even in the absence of a new legal code, which in due course would have become indispensable to consolidate the rules of the game. Interestingly enough, some local interests objected to such measures, on the grounds they they implied antagonism to private enterprise *per se*.

Dr. Katz said that this raised the whole issue of the alternative to foreign direct investment: once foreign firms had made contacts within a country, how far was it meaningful to speak of a 'national' *bourgeoisie*, a 'national' alternative, such as Dr. Ferrer was hypothesising?

Mr. Wionczek wished to second the author's comments on the limitations of the greater part of the research carried out to date on the problem of foreign capital. Analysis of balance of payments flows provided no answer. What were needed were cost–benefit studies looking at the effect of the package of capital, technology and management which comprised direct foreign investment. He had himself undertaken a study which included Colombia, Chile and Peru and had found that in fact the technological contribution had apparently been zero, in so far as the technology brought in had actually been freely available.

Dr. Katz agreed on the need for cost–benefit studies, but said he found the paper itself inadequate as an analytical base for such studies. One needed analysis of the economic effects of foreign investment on income distribution, employment, industrial structure – to mention only a few of the dimensions of the problem. He felt that in fact we were beginning to make progress in understanding the whole area of costs; on the benefit side, however, we were almost at the beginning. In particular there had been no attempt to handle the question of the learning process.

Finally, he disagreed with the author's association of the increased openness to foreign investment which developed in the 1950s with the lack of domestic savings. He would stress lack of technology as more often the crucial factor – as clearly seen for instance in the Argentinian petroleum industry.

Dr. Bazdresch said that the paper did not consider sufficiently the alternative ways of obtaining the benefits brought by direct foreign investment. He would stress two crucial factors in such an analysis: the first was the examination of the relation between human resources and the demand for foreign investment (it was Japan's human resources which had enabled her to buy, modify and generate technology largely independently of foreign investment), and the second, the inclusion of the cost of foreign investment as one form of society's expenditure to obtain technical and commercial information. He was of the opinion that an optimal resource allocation policy for obtaining information would generate a very substantially reduced demand for foreign investment, in comparison with current policies.

But he allowed that investment in human resources was a long-term policy; one needed also a short-term policy in regard to foreign capital, which was what the Agreement of Cartagena essentially was. What he disliked about this particular policy, however, was the role it gave to the joint venture, since it tended to eliminate competition between domestic and foreign firms, and would, he suspected, lead to a weakening of the State *vis-à-vis* the united group of domestic and foreign entrepreneurs.

Professor Vernon likewise was less confident than the author about the Andean Pact. He said he found in current thinking on foreign investment some degree of consensus. First, it was now widely accepted that the implicit savings model many people had been accustomed to use was wrong. Foreign investment could not be seen as a transfer of savings from the foreign to the local economy. Second, there was agreement that the process should be viewed as one whereby the 'package' already referred to, consisting largely of indigenous resources, was, once mobilised, attached to an international system, with certain private effects (e.g. reduced risk) and certain social effects, which might be negative or positive – i.e. the solution was indeterminate and might well be different at different times. But where the consensus broke down was when it came to a policy such as the Andean Pact's universal application of the fade-out principle. Were there not firms who might refuse to enter at all? If the technology was closely held this would constitute a loss to the country. Was the commitment of local capital and entrepreneurship in fact its optimum use? Was the fifteen-year provision the appropriate length of time to extract benefits? What was the cost benefit ratio of the alternative arrangements? In the case of a joint venture, the terms offered for auxiliary services were often relatively tough compared with those charged to a wholly owned subsidiary. And the latter was likely to get better access to markets. Would a joint venture in fact protect the social interest? He would argue for a flexible industry by industry approach. *Dr. Katz* suggested that ideally negotiations should actually be on a case by case basis.

Dr. König suggested that the lack of conclusive empirical studies was partly explained by the lack of data and by definitional and conceptual discrepancies among the sources that did exist. In some Latin American countries there was not even machinery for systematic gathering of information, or notable gaps occured where national authorities lacked knowledge of and control over the relevant transactions. In view of this lack of data he hoped it would be useful to present some figures from the most important source on U.S. business investments in Latin America: the U.S.

Department of Commerce. The latter took complete censuses of U.S. business investments abroad for 1950, 1957 and 1966 and operated an effective quarterly and annual reporting system. In the 1960s, 900 U.S. corporations (some 90 per cent of the total value of capital concerned) were required to report continuously. According to this source the book value of U.S. direct investment in Latin America[1] accounted for 47 per cent of total U.S. investment abroad and 91 per cent of that in developing countries; at the end of 1969 the figures were respectively 20 per cent and 69 per cent. From 1950 to 1969 the annual compound rate of growth of book value was 10 per cent for total U.S. investments abroad, 12 per cent for those in developed countries, 7 per cent for those in less developed countries and 6 per cent for those in Latin America. Latin America's share in the total book value of U.S. direct investments abroad was surpassed by Canada in 1954 and Europe in 1963, but profits in Latin America were higher throughout 1950–69, except in the case of Europe in the final year of the period. In the 1960s as a whole U.S. investment in manufacturing in Latin America began to grow more rapidly than that in any other sector, but its growth rate still fell short of that of total U.S. investments in manufacturing in developing countries as a whole. With the exception of Mexico, it was the less industrialised countries of Latin America which experienced the highest rates of growth of U.S. investment in their manufacturing sectors. In the second half of the 1960s manufacturing was replaced by 'other'[2] industries as the most dynamic element in U.S. direct investment in Latin America.

Turning to policy issues, he shared many of Professor Vernon's doubts on the joint venture. Foreign investors had recently been making it clear at various international meetings that they favoured *ad hoc* approaches and a wide distribution of ownership. Foreign investors were not likely to surrender financial and managerial control, particularly in export-oriented and science based industries. He considered Latin American governments were the only adequate partners in the bargaining process when issues such as the transfer of technology and the setting of investment priorities were involved.

Dr. Ffrench-Davis, in reply to Professor Hirschman, said that he agreed with the first of the points raised by him. In fact, he had himself pointed out in his paper that neither a law nor a comprehensive policy statement assured a defined policy. Furthermore, he had cited the case of Chile as a country which had had a law during most of the period under review, but in practice no policy at all until very recently. But he did think a law *per se* was of some significance, since it might create public awareness.

Turning to Professor Hirschman's next point, he agreed that in practice there was a field of hard decision. However, although a bird in the hand might be worth two in the bush, the relevant point was whether what was in the hand was a pigeon, a hawk, a snake or a spider. Each one had been alive in the field of foreign investment. Moreover, though in social life it

[1] Including other Western Hemisphere but excluding Canada.
[2] Other than mining and smelting, manufacturing and petroleum.

might be '*mejor malo conocido que bueno por conocer*', in economics it was not so if the '*malo*' represented a foreign investment with a negative contribution to national output.

He believed that Professor Hirschman overstressed the potential contribution of foreign capital. The discussion should not centre on an ideal type of foreign investment, but on what it had actually been. While it was true that foreign investment was potentially a gadfly, more often it appeared either to become one more member of the club, or to replace domestic enterprises within a highly protected internal market, as Professor Felix had pointed out. He thought that in any case the appropriate device to use when the spur of competition was needed was not foreign investment but potential import competition, which if suitably programmed could encourage improved productivity and avoid further segmentation of the small domestic market.

He was in full agreement with Dr. Ferrer that policy on foreign capital should be part of a broad and comprehensive development strategy. What this meant, however, was that foreign investment policy should be consistently co-ordinated with the other policy components. It did not mean that in the absence of a development strategy, or revolutionary policy, it made no sense to design a policy towards foreign investment. He felt that there was frequently much that could be done within a given system to improve that policy, even under a regime that was relatively committed to foreign investment.

In reply to Dr. Katz, he said he was puzzled that Dr. Katz had found the paper inadequate as an analytical base for cost–benefit analysis. He considered that the fundamental aspects of the cost–benefit relation were summarised in the text; beyond that point the problem became mainly one of social project evaluation. With respect to the somewhat peculiar side effects of foreign investment, on product quality, income distribution, factor intensity, 'learning' and so forth, he agreed that it would have been ideal to analyse them. But he had felt that that was too ambitious a task for a short paper.

In reply to Professor Vernon, he said that he considered it unfair to contrast reforms with the optimum, as Professor Vernon appeared to be doing, rather than with the existing situation. Decision 24 certainly had its problems: for example, it could not be asserted that 15 years was the unique optimal length of time. But the net effect of the host of regulations was clearly positive as compared to that generated by the *previously prevailing* regulations in the Andean countries. Furthermore, the increasingly more diversified forms of foreign investment and the flexibility contained in the Agreement reinforced the chance of a significant positive effect from the regulations. Finally, he would insist that he was optimistic about the results, while he fully recognised the internal and external obstacles the Agreement would face. The degree of success would mainly depend on the behaviour decided on by each member country.

7 Industrial Growth, Royalty Payments and Local Expenditure on Research and Development

Jorge M. Katz

INSTITUTO TORCUATO DI TELLA

I. INTRODUCTION

It is obvious that received theory is in a highly unsatisfactory state from the point of view of its usefulness in understanding the problems posed by the technological development of the so-called 'recently industrialised' nations.

The following 'ailments', as well as various others, figure prominently in the current experience of these nations: imports of technology are indiscriminate and cover the whole industrial spectrum; they are exploited monopolistically; local inventive activity is limited, has begun only recently and is concentrated in the local subsidiaries of large, multinational corporations, who appropriate the greater part of the benefits; and there is an almost total lack of communication between existing manufacturing activities and whatever output there is from the flow of research and development expenditure in the public sector. These are all problems which can hardly be adequately handled in terms of present theoretical tools.

In this paper we present part of the empirical evidence collected in the course of a broad investigation into the economics of technical change in a technology-importing country. The major aims of this investigation, carried out over the last three years, were as follows: (1) to construct a very simple framework with which to approach the problems posed by the technological development of technologically dependent nations, and (2) to study, in terms of this simple framework, the technological experience of the Argentinian manufacturing sector during the 1960s.

This paper represents only part of a more comprehensive, already completed monograph;[1] in order to avoid giving the reader a lopsided impression of the research, section II contains a summary of

---

[1] The present paper is based on statistics contained in chapter VI of a forthcoming publication by the author: J. Katz, *Importación de Tecnología, Actividad Inventiva Local e Industrialización Dependiente* (C.I.E., Instituto di Tella, Dec. 1971) (in press).

the whole inquiry. Also included in this section is a list of the various pieces of independent research that we considered necessary in order to cover the field adequately.

Section III summarises, in a rather aggregate fashion, the overall growth performance of the Argentinian manufacturing sector during the 1960s. This performance is then compared with that of the 200 largest industrial firms operating in the local environment; these firms were studied in great detail by means of a questionnaire specially designed to gather the information needed for this research.

Section IV presents the statistical results of an inter-industry correlation analysis whose purpose was to throw some light on the sources of technical progress in the manufacturing firms studied. The results from the Argentinian sample are then compared with available information for the U.S. manufacturing industry. In this connection we have drawn heavily on correlation data presented a few years ago by N. Terleckij[1] and on additional empirical evidence published by the National Science Foundation.[2]

Lastly, in an appendix to the paper, we discuss the definitions used here for the various relevant variables, as well as the major short-comings of the available data.

II. THE GENERAL FRAMEWORK OF THE ENQUIRY

Let us begin by considering two very general, and very simple-minded questions: first, how do we go about measuring the rate of technical progress of a given production unit, and second, in what way can we rationalise or 'explain' this progress? While the first question has been extensively discussed in recent literature, the second remains relatively unexplored.

We could answer the first question either directly or indirectly. We might, in the tradition of Schumpeter, identify the rate of technical progress with the rate at which new technology is created over a specified period, expressed in terms of the number of newly-granted patents and/or scientific papers, 'blue-prints', formulae, design and operating manuals, etc., which appear. J. Schmookler gives a clear presentation of this concept in the following paragraph:[3]

> We shall call the rate at which new technology is produced in any period the rate of technological progress. . . . Hence, as defined

[1] N. Terleckij. *Sources of productivity growth in the U.S. manufacturing sector* (Unpublished Ph.D. dissertation, Columbia, 1960).

[2] *Research and Development in Industry, 1966* (National Science Foundation, Washington), 1968.

[3] J. Schmookler, *Invention and Economic Growth* (Harvard University Press, 1966), p. 2.

here, an element of technology affects the rate of technological progress only once and only at one point on the globe.

Since a great deal has been written recently on the disadvantages of using 'proxy' variables (such as patents, blue-prints, and so on) as measures of technical progress, we shall not elaborate on this point here.[1] However, before we go on to discuss indirect measures of technological change, it is perhaps worth mentioning that some additional criticisms (apart from those which have already been suggested) have been levelled against the straightforward use of these proxy variables when dealing with technology-importing countries.

Consider, for example, the statistics on patents granted, which have been confidently used by various authors in the context of the U.S. economy as proxy variables for the rate of technical change.[2] In Argentina about 75 per cent of the total number of patents granted each year are in fact foreign patents taken out by the parent companies of large multinational groups, most of which have subsidiaries operating in the local market. Not more than, say, 5 per cent of these patents are ever used in production in Argentina; instead they serve as instruments for market control – i.e. they are simply another spanner in the toolbox of restrictive business practices characteristic of oligopolistic competition.

It is therefore obvious that, in Argentina, the significance of the flow of patents granted is very different from that attributed to it in the context of the U.S. economy.[3] These patents do not reflect local 'inventive activity' in the case of Argentina, nor are they related to the observed rate of technological progress.

In view of these objections, we now turn to indirect ways of measuring the rate of technological progress.

The most obvious indirect proxy, and the one that has traditionally been used, is the rate of growth of overall factor productivity. In the course of our research we estimated an index of overall factor productivity growth at the plant level, and this index was then used as the dependent variable which required explanation.[4]

---

[1] Two excellent surveys in this respect are: C. Freeman, *Measurement of Output of R and D, a Review Paper* (Mimeo, Unesco, Jan. 1969); and B. Sanders, 'Some difficulties in measuring inventive activity', in *The Rate and Direction of Inventive Activity*, (N.B.E.R., Princeton, 1962).

[2] An account of the most outstanding piece of research along this line is to be found in J. Schmookler, *op. cit.*

[3] For a discussion of this point, see D. Chudnovsky and J. Katz, 'Patentes e Importación de Tecnología', *Económica* (La Plata, Enero de 1970).

[4] It should be noted that the use of the growth rate of overall factor productivity as a proxy for the rate of technical progress is by no means the complete answer.

Let us now turn to the second of the two questions formulated above, concerning the origins of the technical change observed at plant level. It is obvious that both internal and external sources could presumably be traced for each of the coefficients of technical change. The internal source would be the flow of locally-generated 'inventive activity', while the external one would be the transfer of technology from outside, whether 'embodied' in the form of new capital equipment, spare parts, etc., or 'disembodied', in the form of operating manuals, formulae and so on.

When we consider the problem of local technology in this light, it becomes clear that there are two distinct though interrelated areas that have to be explored. On the one hand we need to study various aspects – such as the rate, nature and inter-industrial composition – of the flow of locally-generated inventive activity. On the other hand, a number of questions arise in connection with the international transfer of technology, especially in relation to factors determining the behaviour of sellers and buyers in the technology market.

Let us briefly consider both these areas, beginning with the local sources of 'inventive activity'.

What is it that generates a flow of inventive activity in the local environment?

We can identify at least three non-mutually exclusive sources, whose relationship to the observed rate of technological progress needs to be investigated: (1) private inventors, (2) the activity of departments in manufacturing firms (these departments may be called, for example, 'trouble-shooting', 'technical assistance to production',[1] 'process engineering', 'product engineering', etc.) and (3) the public sector, through universities, hospitals, the laboratories of the Atomic Energy Commission, and so on.

In the course of our research, all three sources of local inventive activity were studied by means of specially designed questionnaires, whose main – but by no means only – purpose was to collect information about R and D expenditure, expenditure on 'other associated

---

There are still numerous theoretical and practical difficulties to contend with; for example, we are faced with the old problem of isolating technical change from factor substitution. See for instance: C. Kennedy, 'Induced bias in innovation and the theory of distribution', *Economic Journal* (Sept. 1964). Regarding measurement problems the reader could see: E. Guftavson, 'R and D, new products and productivity change', *American Economic Review* (1962). Also: I. Adelman and Z. Griliches, 'On an index of quality change', *Journal of the American Statistical Association* (Sept. 1961).

[1] An excellent account of the role played by the 'technical assistance to production' group at Dupont de Nemeurs (U.S.) can be found in S. Hollander, *The Sources of Increased Efficiency* (M.I.T. University Press, 1966).

technical activities',[1] the employment of university graduates, technicians, etc., experimental equipment available, and so on.

In the remaining sections of this paper, the accumulated flow of R and D expenditure by each firm in the sample during the 1960s will be used as an indicator of the locally-generated flow of inventive activity. The impact of this expenditure on overall factor productivity growth at the plant level will be analysed in terms of a very simple statistical model.

Argentina is a technology-importing country; it is therefore important to investigate the conditions under which technology from abroad becomes available in the local environment. Apart from those cases where technology is imported by a wholly-owned subsidiary (when we cannot assume any market relationship between buyer and seller), it seems reasonable, *a priori*, to assume that the bargaining power of the two parties involved are distinctly unequal. Vaitsos has accurately described this situation:

From the seller's point of view the marginal cost of the technology is often virtually nil. Its marginal cost for the buyer, on the other hand, bearing in mind what he would have to spend in order to develop it independently, may amount to thousands, or even millions of dollars. The final figure agreed upon in the transaction might therefore range between zero and millions of dollars, depending on the relative bargaining powers of the two parties involved.[2]

It is not only in the actual price of the 'commodity' that differences in bargaining power would show up; they might also result in restrictive clauses in the contract of purchase, as for example: territorial limits on the buyer's export activities, 'tie-in' clauses relating to the source of intermediate inputs which the local manufacturer can use, clauses regulating a royalty-free return to the licensor of any additional technology generated locally in the process of adapting the product and/or process to the local environment, etc.

As part of our research, the conditions under which foreign

[1] Not necessarily classified as Research and Development according to conventional definitions; by 'conventional definitions' we mean those normally employed by the National Science Foundation in the U.S. and by O.E.C.D. in Europe. See: *Proposed Standard Practice for Surveys of R and D*, O.E.C.D., Paris, 1963. It seems to us that caution should be exercised by 'recently industrialised' nations in adopting these so-called 'conventional' definitions for the measurement of their internal technological progress.

[2] C. Vaitsos. *Transfer of resources and the preservation of monopoly rents* (Lima, April 1970) (mimeo).

technology is transferred for use in the local environment were investigated by dint of examining some seventy contracts between local entrepreneurs and their respective foreign licensors.

We felt it necessary to distinguish two separate, though inter-related, 'technological stages' in the process of technological change which takes place in any given industrial establishment. The first of these – which we call the 'Introduction Stage' of a new product and/or productive process – consists of the negotiations and bargaining that occur when an entrepreneur 'shops around' for technology. It is obvious that the great majority of new products and/or productive processes put into local operation are ultimately of foreign origin. The time-lag for their assimilation locally may be anything between five and fifteen years, depending on factors such as the size of the local market *vis-à-vis* the minimum size of a plant that can be operated economically, the existence, in certain markets, of barriers to the introduction of new products, the degree of oligopolistic control achieved by existing suppliers, and so on.

It is at the introductory stage that the local entrepreneur is most often subjected to monopolistic exploitation: the less information he possesses about alternative sources of technology and the greater the opportunity cost – in terms of time, risk and actual design cost – of developing the technology independently, the more inclined he will be to accept monopolistic price-fixing on the part of the licensor. The weaker his position, the more likely he is to be forced into agree-ing to collateral restrictive conditions such as territorial limitations, 'tie-in' clauses, etc.

The most important feature of the second 'technological stage' is the 'learning', which usually occurs as a side-effect of introducing a new product and/or productive process into the local environment. This 'learning' may conform to the traditional so-called 'learning-by-doing' models, in which learning takes place as a consequence of productive activities; or it may also result from a more explicit policy of 'investing in learning', involving expenditure on '"adap-tive" Research and Development', or 'other associated technical activities', such as quality control, 'trouble-shooting', 'debottle-necking' the processes of production, maintenance, and so on.

We have called this second 'technological stage' in the existence of a productive unit the 'learning stage'. One of the central objectives of this investigation was to collect information about how much was actually spent on this by the largest firms in the local economy, as well as about the impact of this expenditure upon the growth rate of overall factor productivity at the plant level.

We must now turn from this general survey of the research upon which the present paper is based to consider in more detail the aggregate results from our fieldwork on the two hundred or so largest firms in the Argentinian industrial sector.

III. THE OVERALL GROWTH PERFORMANCE OF THE ARGENTINE MANUFACTURING SECTOR DURING THE 1960s

According to the statistical series published by the Argentine Central Bank, G.D.P. rose by 34 per cent between 1960 and 1968, representing an annual cumulative rate of 3·3 per cent.[1]

During the same period cumulative growth in the manufacturing sector reached 47·5 per cent; this represents an annual rate of 4·4 per cent. Its share in G.D.P. rose from 31 per cent in 1960 to 34 per cent in 1968 as a result of its above-average rate of expansion.

For the purpose of this study we examined the growth performance of 200 major manufacturing plants distributed over nine branches of industry, considered at the two-digit level of aggregation according to the International Industrial Classification. Using the data from the 1964 census as our standard of reference, we found that these 200 plants were responsible in that year for 30 per cent of the total value of manufacturing output produced by these nine branches of industry.

These plants – the largest in the industries considered – had a rate of growth appreciably higher than that of the manufacturing sector as a whole during this period. Between 1960 and 1968 their cumulative expansion was 117 per cent, representing an annual growth rate of 9 per cent, which is practically double the annual growth rate of the industrial sector as a whole.

In the following pages several features of their growth performance will be analysed in detail. In particular, we shall investigate the source of this growth, as well as its relationship, on the one hand, to the flow of local 'inventive activity', and on the other to the acquisition of technological services from abroad.

Table 7.1 presents a summary of the main features of the recent growth performance of the 200 plants included in this study. Before we proceed, however, the following points should be noted: first, in the aggregation of the data collected at plant level each of the firms in the sample was weighted with its respective share of the total value of output produced in 1964 in each of the nine branches of industry concerned.[2] Secondly, the four variables are expressed as cumulative

[1] Banco Central de la Republica Argentina, *Origen del Producto y Distribución del Ingreso* (Buenos Aires, Enero de 1971).

[2] We are confronted here with a typical index number problem: the use of 1960 relative shares involves overweighting these plants within a given branch of

growth rates over the period 1960–8. Since the definition of each variable is dealt with below, in Appendix I, we shall not go into the conceptual problems at this stage.

Several points emerge from an examination of the figures in Table 7.1. First, as we stated above, the firms included in our sample show an appreciably higher rate of growth than that of the manufacturing sector as a whole. This superior performance, however, is not uniformly apparent in all the branches of industry from which the

TABLE 7.1

ARGENTINA: AGGREGATE INDICATORS OF INDUSTRIAL GROWTH
(Cumulative percentage growth, 1960–8)

Industrial Branch	Physical Volume of Output	Capital Stock	Employment	'Residual' or 'Technological Change'
1. Pharmaceutical industry	123·9	11·7	17·0	104·3
2. Electrical machinery and equipment	200·0	74·7	29·4	150·4
3. Vehicles and machinery	106·7	70·8	82·2	67·2
4. Metals	225·0	180·0	65·0	122·6
5. Chemical products	197·6	78·1	27·7	120·2
6. Oil refining	65·0	70·0	– 30·0	42·0
7. Textiles	40·0	30·7	– 8·0	30·1
8. Food	107·0	61·9	42·0	50·7
9. Non-electrical machinery and equipment	114·3	11·0	40·0	76·0
Total of the Sample	117·0	70·0	40·0	72·0

sample was drawn: for example, in the metallurgical, electrical and chemical industries, the rate of growth of output is significantly higher than in the oil-refining, foodstuffs and vehicle and transport equipment industries.

Secondly, the rate of capital accumulation is markedly higher than the rate of expansion of employment; this obviously means that the capital stock per worker has increased. As in the case of growth, however, this increase is not uniformly distributed among the various branches of industry: once again it is the metallurgical, electrical and chemical industries whose rates of increase in capital stock per worker are relatively high.

---

industry whose growth was relatively small. The use of 1968 relative shares, on the other hand, involves overweighting the less dynamic plants. It therefore seems reasonable to adopt the compromise of using 1964 weights – particularly as this has the further advantage that in 1964 there was a Census of Manufacturing Activities which provides otherwise unobtainable information at the five-digit level of disaggregation.

Thirdly, the rate of growth of overall factor productivity (or rate of technical progress) represents a significant fraction of the rate of growth of the physical volume of output. During the period 1960–8 the sample shows in aggregate an annual cumulative rate of technical progress of nearly 6 per cent. This means that the 'residual' must account for about 70 per cent of the observed growth in output. In this respect also, the metallurgical, electrical and chemical industries clearly fared better than the others, with rates of technological progress of 9·3 per cent, 10·6 per cent and 9·1 per cent respectively, as against 3 per cent, 4·1 per cent and 4·7 per cent in textiles, oil-refining and foodstuffs.

We shall now examine the origins of these observed differences in rates of technological progress. To this end, additional variables will obviously have to be introduced, notably the following: (1) local expenditure on Research and Development activities, (2) local expenditure on 'other associated technical activities', and (3) royalties paid abroad on account of patents, trade-marks, technical assistance, etc.

Using these variables in conjunction with the figures in Table 7.2, an inter-industry correlation analysis will be carried out with the aim of throwing light on the origin of the observed rates of technological progress.

IV. THE ORIGINS OF 'TECHNICAL PROGRESS'

Table 7.2 provides information relating to the additional variables mentioned above. Some points in connection with the variables in Table 7.2 require further explanation.

First, it can be seen from columns (ii) and (iii) that, in order to study the impact of local 'technological expenditure' on the growth rate of overall factor productivity, we have treated the variables cumulatively, as though they were actually stock variables.

Thus, in estimating the statistical incidence of the flow of local 'technological expenditure' upon the growth rate of productivity at the plant level, we shall consider accumulated expenditure over the period 1960–8.

Such a procedure implies additional assumptions which should be made explicit. On the one hand, it seems obvious that the impact of whatever technological expenditure there is at plant level does not depend exclusively upon the sums actually spent between 1960 and 1968. If the plant was operating before 1960, and if technological efforts of some kind were being made at that stage, then these should have been taken into account in 'explaining' productivity growth over the 1960s.

On the other hand, it also seems clear that we should have allowed for the fact that in 1960 the initial 'technological levels' of the various plants would presumably have been different.

We have not been able to do much to correct for these considerations. It should be recognised that, since we could not allow for differences in the initial 'technological levels' of the various industries, they are assumed for the purposes of this study to be identical.

TABLE 7.2

ARGENTINA: LOCAL EXPENDITURE ON RESEARCH AND DEVELOPMENT AND ROYALTY PAYMENTS IN MANUFACTURING, 1960–8[a]

Industrial Branch	(i) $\dfrac{RD+OT}{L}/\Delta t$ (Cumulative percentage)	(ii) $(\Sigma RD+OT)/L$ 1960–8 (Thousands of 1960 pesos)	(iii) $\Sigma RD/L$ 1960–8	(iv) Royalties Paid in 1968 (Millions of 1968 pesos)	(v) Royalties per Unit of Output (Percentage)
1. Pharmaceutical industry	142·4	214·0	106·7	2,024·5	5·3
2. Electrical machinery and equipment	72·8	271·0	112·0	750·9	1·6
3. Vehicles and machinery	270·9	190·0	40·1	5,475·0	2·5
4. Metals	246·0	180·6	44·6	602·0	0·6
5. Chemical products	173·0	233·9	106·4	1,017·0	1·1
6. Oil refining	103·0	302·2	85·0	1,500·0	0·7
7. Textiles	105·3	92·8	40·8	354·0	0·7
8. Food	226·0	95·0	33·6	10·0	—
9. Non-electric machinery and equipment	150·8	170·5	63·6	1,310·6	2·8

[a] 'RD' = Local expenditure on research and development. 'OT' = Expenditure on other associated activities. 'Royalties' include all payments abroad on account of patents, trade-marks, technical assistance in production, etc.

Similarly, it is assumed that the effect of any 'technological expenditure' previous to 1960 may be disregarded.

Secondly, it can be seen from column (v) in Table 7.2 that, for the regression and correlation analysis, we have attempted to use royalties per unit of output as a proxy variable for the flow of technological services received from abroad. This method is recommended by the O.E.C.D. in Frascati's well-known Manual, and has been employed repeatedly in recent years; nevertheless, it is, in our opinion, a highly dubious 'proxy' for what we really want to measure, namely: the physical flow (corrected for quality) of technical and scientific knowledge received from abroad.

We have shown elsewhere that in fact any given payment for technology arises from a bargaining situation between unequal partners. Consequently, the buyer has to pay, over and above the so-called 'competitive price' of the 'commodity' in question, a monopoly rent which will vary according to the degree of exploitation he is willing to accept in the given situation.[1] It was simply for lack of anything better that we used such a proxy in our analysis: this is obviously a point which calls for further refinement.

Having made these qualifications we can now proceed with the analysis. Table 7.3 shows various inter-industry correlation coefficients obtained from a cross-sectional study, ranging over nine different branches of industry at the two-digit level. Given the degrees of freedom with which the correlation coefficients have been calculated, values of $r \geq 0.61$ are significant at the 5 per cent level.

A number of interesting results emerge from Table 7.3 and will now be explored in greater detail. In the process we shall have occasion to refer to statistical data and comparative correlation results from the U.S. manufacturing sector. These will be found in Table 7.4.

GROWTH OF PRODUCTIVITY, GROWTH OF OUTPUT, AND LOCAL EXPENDITURE ON RESEARCH AND DEVELOPMENT

The data from both Argentina and the United States show a positive and statistically significant association between the rate of growth of overall factor productivity, the rate of growth of output, and accumulated expenditure on R and D over the period 1960–8. Figs. 7.1 and 7.2 describe these statistical associations for the Argentinian sample.

A literal interpretation of these results would indicate that a higher than average rate of technological progress was attained by those branches of industry, in the universe studied, which displayed the most rapid growth and which made larger than average investments in Research and Development. Conversely, a lower than average rate of expansion of production and expenditure on R and D tended to be associated with lower than average growth rates for overall factor productivity.

It is interesting to notice that this correlation exists both in the local economy and in the U.S. manufacturing sector. This is a fact

[1] See J. Katz, *op. cit.*, chapter II, 'The international transfer of technology and monopoly rents.'

TABLE 7.3

ARGENTINA: INTER-INDUSTRIAL CORRELATION COEFFICIENTS: NINE INDUSTRIAL BRANCHES OF THE MANUFACTURING SECTOR[a]

	Physical Volume of Output	Capital Stock	Employment	'Residual' or Technological Change	$\dfrac{\Delta RD+OT}{AT}$	$\dfrac{(\Sigma RD+OT)}{L}$	$\Sigma RD/L$	Royalties Paid Q
Value of output	—	0·637	0·510	0·927	0·220	0·319	0·367	−0·019
Capital stock	0·637	—	0·397	0·390	0·460	0·112	−0·221	−0·491
Employment	0·510	0·397	—	0·367	0·805	−0·263	−0·373	0·103
'Residual' or technological change	0·927	0·390	0·367	—	0·044	0·462	0·611	0·245
$(\Delta RD+OT)/AT$	0·220	0·460	0·805	0·044	—	−0·385	0·610	−0·088
$(\Sigma RD+OT)/L$	0·319	0·112	−0·263	0·462	−0·385	—	0·770	0·202
$\Sigma RD/L$	0·367	−0·221	−0·373	0·611	0·610	0·770	—	0·423
Royalties paid/Q	−0·019	−0·491	0·103	0·245	−0·088	0·202	0·423	—

[a] The values of $r \geqslant 0.61$ are statistically significant at the 5 per cent level and are given in italics.

TABLE 7.4

UNITED STATES: INTER-INDUSTRIAL CORRELATION COEFFICIENTS FOR MANUFACTURING SECTOR 1948–53[a]

	Physical Volume of Output	Capital/Labour Ratio	Engineers per 1,000 Workers	'Residual' or Rate of Technological Change	Expenditures on R and D	Degree of Concentration
1. Physical volume of output	—	0·18	0·78	0·65	0·84	0·51
2. Capital/labour ratio	0·18	—	0·42	0·21	0·05	0·50
3. Engineers per 1,000 workers	0·78	0·42	—	0·44	0·74	0·60
4. 'Residual' or rate of technological change	0·65	0·21	0·44	—	0·62	0·29
5. Expenditures on R and D	0·84	0·05	0·74	0·62	—	0·45
6. Degree of concentration	0·51	0·50	0·60	0·29	0·45	—

[a] 1. The underlined values of r are statistically significant at the 5 per cent level.

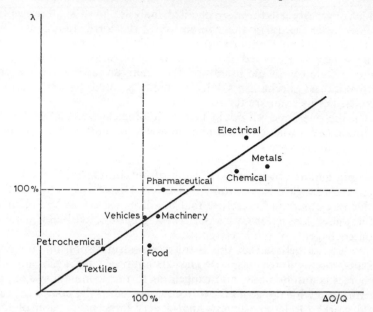

FIG. 7.1. Argentina: changes in productivity and rates of growth of product, manufacturing industry, 1960–8.

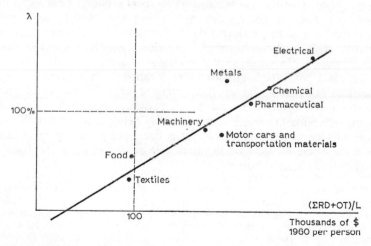

FIG. 7.2. Argentine: changes in productivity and cumulated expenditures in research and development and in 'other technical activities' for manufacturing industry, 1960–8.

which obviously calls for more detailed analysis and we shall return to it later, after discussing the significance of the correlation.

It is not a simple matter to deduce the direction of causality from the coefficients presented above. It is fairly obvious, and it has been noted previously in the literature, that there are at least two alternative causal mechanisms which might be used to explain our results. Let us compare them.[1]

On the one hand we could take technological progress to be an autonomous variable, exogenous to the economic system, whose effect is to increase overall factor productivity. Any such increase would lead to a fall in relative prices, followed by an increased demand and a subsequent expansion of output. On the assumption that 'technological expenditure' constitutes a fixed proportion of the value of output, and therefore that it will increase with the volume of business transactions, we would expect, *a priori*, to obtain correlation coefficients of the kind reported.

We do not believe that this is the mechanism responsible for our results, for two reasons: (i) The assumption that technological progress is autonomous, and exogenous to the economic system, is at variance with the general evidence collected in the course of our field work; the latter suggests that a very large proportion of the observed growth of overall factor productivity at the plant level results from solving problems and resolving bottlenecks in the production-line or product. Productivity rises *after* – but necessarily in association with – the realisation of local technological expenditure. (ii) Another reason for not taking the causal mechanism described above too seriously is that it requires an assumption of relative price flexibility between industries in order to reflect relative productivity differentials in the pricing system.

This is a point that calls for more detailed analysis; nevertheless, the little evidence so far available suggests that the industrial price mechanism is inflexible enough to reflect only a very small proportion of the differential changes in productivity between industries. Moreover this proportion seems to have been progressively dwindling with the observed increase in the degree of economic concentration in the local manufacturing sector.[2]

[1] The statistical relationship between the rate of growth of output and the rate of overall factor productivity growth, recently named the 'Verdoorn Effect', has been discussed extensively in the literature. See, for example, W. Beckerman, *The British Economy in 1975* (Cambridge University Press, 1966); R. C. O. Matthews and R. Hahn, 'The Theory of Economic Growth, A Survey', *Economic Journal* (December, 1964); J. Katz, 'Verdoorn Effects, Returns to Scale and the Elasticity of Factor Substitution', *Oxford Economic Papers* (July, 1968).

[2] Some evidence for this has been presented in J. Katz, *Production Functions, Foreign Investment and Growth* (North Holland Publishing Co., 1969). Chapter

In view of these considerations, it seems more reasonable to assume a different causal mechanism in which R and D expenditure and the rate of growth of output are independent variables 'explanatory' of the observed growth in overall factor productivity.

There is further evidence in support of this idea: a rather large number of the firms studied in the course of our research were established in recent years, notably during the period 1957–62, when the country had adopted an unduly benevolent attitude towards foreign capital and technology. It is reasonable to assume that, between 1960 and 1968, these firms were consolidating their experience and engineering know-how in the control and operation of their plants. We may therefore suppose that the rate of growth of the physical volume of output and local expenditure on 'adaptive' research and development acted as independent variables whose most immediate consequence was to expand local productivity.[1]

Assuming, then, that the direction of causality is from the growth of output and local expenditure on 'adaptive' R and D, to the growth of overall factor productivity – and remembering the relative independence of the first two variables, at least in the Argentinian context – we have adopted the following regression model for our investigation into the origins of technological change:

$$\lambda = \text{constant} + \alpha \, \Delta Q/Q + \beta \sum_{1960}^{1968} RD/L + \mu \qquad (1)$$

where:

λ: is the rate of technological change, or rate of growth of global productivity.

$\Delta Q/Q$: is the rate of growth of the physical volume of output.

$\sum_{1960}^{1968} RD/L$: is the accumulated expenditure on research and development per worker, at 1960 prices.

α and β: are the rate of change of λ – the rate of technological progress – following an infinitesimal change in $\Delta Q/Q$ and in $\sum_{1960}^{1968} RD/L$ respectively.

Estimating the above equation by least squares, we obtained the

---

VI shows that, in an inter-industrial comparison of the periods 1937–43 and 1954–61, the elasticity between relative prices and the rate of growth of overall factor productivity falls from 0·81 to 0·41.

[1] The rate of growth of output introduces a return-to-scale effect into the model and also a 'learning' effect in Arrow's sense, i.e. learning as a by-product of production. The accumulated R and D expenditure introduces yet another 'learning' effect, which we have here termed 'learning by spending'.

results shown in Table 7.5 and Appendix II. The standard error is specified under each estimator. For Table 7.5, which presents the results obtained for the sample as a whole, we ran the regression on inter-industry cross-sectional data; in Appendix II, on the other hand, the regression results were obtained by using the above model at the industry level, and are based on an inter-plant analysis.

A few very general points can be formulated on the basis of Table 7.5:

(i) The inter-industry variance in $\Delta Q/Q$ accounts for approximately 84 per cent of the inter-industry variance in our dependent variable (namely, the 'residual', or rate of technological progress in

TABLE 7.5

THE SOURCES OF TECHNOLOGICAL PROGRESS
IN THE ARGENTINE MANUFACTURING SECTOR
1960–8

	Constant	Growth Effect Q/Q	'Learning' Effect RD/L	R^2
Argentine manufacturing sample (1960–8)	– 10·54 (17·63)	0·567 (0·092)	0·188 (0·082)	0·90

a given industry). The statistical fit can be improved by using a more sophisticated model where R and D is treated as an additional independent variable, in which case 90 per cent of the inter-industry variance in the rate of technical progress can be accounted for.

(ii) The values of the 'Verdoorn Coefficient' are consistent with those previously quoted in the literature: 'Apparently there exists a stable and long-term relation between productivity and the level of output. This is confirmed by the fact that the coefficient between both variables is relatively stable, varying between industries and countries within the range 0·45–0·60.'[1]

(iii) Local expenditure on research and development has a significant effect at the margin upon the observed rate of technological change. However, it is interesting to note that this effect seems to be smaller than in the U.S. manufacturing sector. In order to examine this point in greater detail, we shall now introduce fresh comparative statistical elements taken from a study by N. Terleckij. Using cross-section data to estimate a statistical model similar to that embodied in equation (1) above, he obtained a value of $\beta = 0·34$ for the U.S. manufacturing sector. This figure is significantly higher than the estimate of β for the Argentinian industrial sector. On *a priori*

[1] J. Verdoorn, 'Fattori che regolano lo sviluppo della produttività del lavoro', *L'Industria* (Milan, 1949). Also: 'Complementarity and long-run projections', *Econometrica* (Oct. 1956).

TABLE 7.6

EXPENDITURES ON RESEARCH AND DEVELOPMENT IN ARGENTINA AND IN THE UNITED STATES AS PROPORTION OF THE VALUE OF OUTPUT

	United States[a]	Argentina			Proportion
		No. of Firms Within the Sample	(RD + OT)/Q	RD/Q	
	(a)	(b)	(c)	(d)	(d)/(a)
1. Pharmaceutical industry	6·3%	17	1·9%	0·8%	12%
2. Electrical machinery and equipment	12·6%	18	1·7%	0·7%	6%
3. Vehicles and machinery	3·6%	14	1·4%	0·3%	10%
4. Metals	0·8%	23	1·2%	0·4%	50%
5. Chemical products	5·4%	22	1·8%	0·7%	13%
6. Petrochemicals	1·1%	6	0·5%	0·3%	27%
7. Textiles	0·8%	21	1·7%	0·3%	37%
8. Food	0·6%	25	1·2%	0·2%	30%
9. Non-electrical machinery and equipment	7·3%	15	2·4%	0·7%	10%

[a] In all cases we are dealing with the proportion corresponding to the twenty main establishments in the branch, according to the data published by N.S.F. See *Research and Development in Industry, 1966* (National Science Foundation, June 1968), p. 78.

grounds one would have expected the reverse to be true, so this result seems to call for further explanation. To this end we present in Table 7.6 comparative figures on R and D expenditure in Argentina and the U.S. These figures, expressed as a proportion of the value of production, refer in both cases to the major firms in each branch of industry.

We saw above that R and D expenditure has a higher effect at the margin in the U.S. manufacturing sector than in that of Argentina. Table 7.6 now shows us that the various branches of industry in Argentina spend, on average, about 20 per cent of what is spent on R and D by U.S. firms.

It should be remembered that, in comparing the U.S. and Argentinian data, we have so far considered only the quantitative aspect. The reader might reasonably ask whether there are not also qualitative differences in the type of technical activities which U.S. and Argentine firms are willing to undertake.

This possibility cannot be entirely discounted. However, it seems to us that the reverse is also quite likely to be the case and that we might be in danger of falling victim to a myth. What we do know of the structure, goals and creative nature of private spending on R and D in the U.S. manufacturing sector tells a very different and much less spectacular story. In this connection, we are reminded of the following paragraphs by E. Mansfield:[1]

> Besides research projects related to defence and to the space race . . . the large majority of the research and development projects constitute very modest examples of design improvement, much the sort of thing that results in year by year changes in the design of automobiles, refrigerators, vacuum-cleaners, etc. Those interviews we had with business executives confirm our view that most corporations concentrate their efforts on very modest design improvements, as well as on very short pay-off periods for their R and D expenditure.
>
> Most of the projects do not involve very great technical risks. In about three-fourths of the cases the estimated probability of technical success exceeds 0·80.

This view is independently confirmed by various other authors[2] – which reinforces our feeling that a significant proportion of what we nowadays call the 'technological revolution' is simply a gigantic 'product-differentiation' game inherent in oligopolistic competition. This game does not rely to any great extent on new scientific discoveries, but rather upon the patient, cumulative work of engineering teams at the plant level, and there are strong grounds for believing that the nature of such activities does not differ very much in Argentina and the United States.

Admittedly this is a subject about which we still know very little, and a considerable amount of research needs to be done on it. Until further evidence is available, therefore, we shall have to ignore any qualitative differences there may be between U.S. and Argentine units of technological effort, and proceed with our analysis exclusively in terms of the observed quantitative differences.

Returning now to our (quantitative) comparison of the U.S. and Argentine figures for R and D expenditure and its impact on productivity growth at the plant level, we would like to make a few suggestions which may help towards explaining the results.

First, the difference between Argentinian and U.S. firms in terms of actual expenditure, and the marginal efficiency of this expenditure

---

[1] E. Mansfield, *Industrial Research and Technological Innovation* (Norton, New York, 1968).

[2] See, for example: S. Hollander, *op. cit.* (M.I.T. University Press, 1966); D. Hamberg, 'Invention in the industrial research laboratory', *Journal of Political Economy* (1963); R. Nelson *et al.*, *Technology, Economic Growth and Public Policy* (The Brookings Institution, 1967).

may be at least partially explained by the differences between the two countries in the product mix produced by each type of firm. The local product mix presumably contains a larger proportion of the so-called 'mature' goods, and it seems reasonable to suppose that these require less expenditure per unit of output, and also that this expenditure has a smaller than average impact upon productivity growth.

Second, these differences, and those concerned with the marginal efficiency of R and D expenditure, may also be related to the existing differences in plant size, as between Argentina and the United States. No matter which branch of industry we look at, we find that local plant sizes vary between 5 per cent and 15 per cent of those in the United States. Let us now assume – as contemporary analysis almost invariably does – that there are considerable economies of scale and 'technological' discontinuities in R and D activity. Taken in conjunction with the empirical evidence, this would indicate that most Argentinian plants still fall short of the minimum size necessary to reap the benefits of R and D expenditure on an acceptable scale.

Thirdly, another possible reason for the higher marginal efficiency of R and D expenditure in the United States is the fact that it benefits from considerable external economies generated by public expenditure on R and D. This effect is entirely absent in the Argentine case.

Let us now summarise the argument so far: (i) The marginal efficiency of expenditure on R and D, though significant, still falls far short of that in the U.S. manufacturing sector. (ii) These differences may be related to the product mix, the size of local firms, the externalities that private effort receives from public expenditure, and so on.

We here conclude our discussion of the relationship between the rate of growth of output, local expenditure on R and D activities and the rate of growth of overall factor productivity. We shall now go on to consider some other points that emerge from the correlation results in Table 7.3.

PRODUCTIVITY GROWTH, EXPENDITURE ON R AND D AND EXPENDITURE ON 'OTHER ASSOCIATED TECHNICAL ACTIVITIES'

It is worth noting that when we use overall technological expenditure at plant level as the independent variable in place of expenditure on R and D, the correlation coefficient falls from $r = 0.62$ to $r = 0.46$.

In general terms it can be said that R and D expenditure accounts for about 20–30 per cent of overall technical expenditure, the remainder covering items such as quality control and maintenance expenditure, which are classed as associated technical activities.

In view of the fact that about 70 per cent of the overall technical budget is spent on rather routine work, we have *a priori* grounds for expecting the observed fall in the statistical association between productivity growth and overall technical expenditure. It is not within the province of the production, maintenance or quality control departments to introduce modifications either in the product or in the productive process; these modifications, which are actually responsible for most of the observed growth in productivity, originate from the 'trouble-shooting', 'product-engineering' and/or 'process-engineering' departments.

It can hardly be surprising, therefore, to learn that our dependent variable (the rate of growth of overall factor productivity) has a significantly better correlation with a flow of expenditure more directly concerned with it – as the flow of R and D expenditure undoubtedly is.

ROYALTIES PER UNIT OF OUTPUT AND THE RATE OF TECHNICAL PROGRESS

We did not find any significant statistical association, within the framework of our research, between unit royalties transferred abroad on account of payments for patents, trade-marks, technical assistance to production, etc., and the observed rate of technical progress.

In order to interpret this result, let us begin by asking a very simple question: under what conditions would we expect, *a priori*, to find a positive degree of association between these two variables? Two conditions appear to be necessary:

(a) that the royalties per unit of output should be a reasonable approximation to the 'competitive price' of the technical and scientific knowledge transferred. If this had actually been the case, then a higher royalty per unit of output would have reflected a larger amount of technical assistance from abroad;

(b) that the licensing firm should continue to provide *additional* technical information, besides what was originally supplied. This information, used in production by the local firm, would have resulted in an increase in overall factor productivity.

While there is nothing to prevent the second of these conditions from occurring, it is obvious that the first does not. The market for technology is very far from being a perfect market where 'the' price reflects both the cost function of the seller and the preference function of the buyer.

Each royalty per unit of output reflects not only the competitive price of the commodity, but also an indeterminate degree of monopolistic exploitation accepted by the buyer in each particular situation. Furthermore, there is no reason to suppose that this 'coefficient of exploitation' is similar in different firms or industries. Taken in conjunction, these two facts suggest that the inter-firm, or inter-industry variance of unit royalties transferred abroad must make a very unsatisfactory 'proxy' variable for the inter-firm, or inter-industry variance of technological services received from abroad.

Apart from this unsuitability as a 'proxy' variable, there is a further reason why we should not expect to find a high degree of statistical association between unit royalties and the rate of technical progress obtaining *within the context of a given plant and product design*. To see why this is so we must first recall section I of this paper, where we argued that the overall process of technical change in a given industrial plant could be broken down into two separate though interrelated 'technological stages', namely:

(i) the 'introduction stage' of a new product and/or productive process; and

(ii) the 'learning stage' which takes place in connection with this product or process.

The above distinction – which can be seen very clearly in the present case, where the overwhelming majority of new products and/or productive processes come from external sources – is not entirely new to the literature. S. Hollander, after thoroughly investigating the growth performance of four rayon plants of Dupont's in the U.S., wrote:[1]

In the plants under investigation the most striking stream of minor technical changes were introduced during the first ten to fifteen years after the construction of a new-type plant. . . . There seems to exist what may be called a 'saturation effect' whereby without some preceding major change the potential stream of minor changes will be exhausted.

Consider now the following fact: the origin of quite a large number of the plants we investigated can be traced back to the late 1950s or early 1960s, when the country was explicitly following a policy of subsidising foreign capital and technology. In covering the local pharmaceutical industry, for example, our study included seventeen large industrial plants; of these, the plants set up in the late 1950s or early 1960s accounted for about 60 per cent of the total value of shipments by the industry in 1968. We discovered that the eight

---

[1] S. Hollander, *op. cit.*, p. 206 (M.I.T. University Press, 1966).

largest pharmaceutical plants were founded during the last ten to twelve years.

Similarly, in the Vehicles and Transport Equipment industry, almost the entire value of output is being produced by plants constructed in the late 1950s or early 1960s. Identical findings could be quoted for the electrical industry, the non-ferrous metallurgical industries, and so on.

In terms of our 'learning' hypothesis, the decade of the 1960s – which is the period covered by this study – has been a 'learning' decade for most of the firms included in our sample. Among other things, they had to learn how to play the oligopolistic game in a new environment, and to manipulate 'engineering expenditure' in the product differentiation game.

The empirical evidence presented in the previous section – indicative of a high degree of statistical association between local R and D expenditure and rates of technical change – reveals an interesting fact, namely that this 'learning' is primarily associated with local 'adaptive' research and development, rather than with a continuing and systematic flow of *additional* technical assistance from outside.[1]

To summarise the argument of the last few pages: the absence of any statistical association between royalties paid abroad and observed technological performance should not surprise us. For one thing, the independent variable is a very poor approximation to what we really want; for another, it seems probable that, once the 'introduction stage' is over, much of the 'learning' is actually based on domestic efforts, i.e. on local 'adaptive' research and development. The specificity of the local market, the much lower cost of local R and D inputs, the relatively small amount of new knowledge required in order to play the 'product-differentiation' game, all point to the convenience of such a policy.

V. ROYALTIES AND LOCAL EXPENDITURE – IN THE UNIVERSE AND IN THE SAMPLED FIRMS

Having discussed, in the previous section, the relationship between the observed rate of technical progress and its major 'explanatory' variables, we would like to close this paper with another look at the

[1] We believe that there are significant differences between Latin American countries in this respect. As far as it goes, our evidence indicates that the situation described here is fairly characteristic of both Argentina and Brazil, of Mexico and Chile to a lesser degree, and probably should not be considered valid for the rest of Latin America. Differences in the 'learning' experience of the Latin American countries would be accounted for by such factors as the degree of oligopolistic competition and the local availability of skilled university graduates (Argentina is relatively well-supplied in this respect).

available statistics on royalty payments on account of patents, trade-marks, technical assistance to production, etc., compared with those on R and D expenditure. How much money is actually transferred abroad on account of the former, and how much does the country spend on the latter?

Table 7.7 presents statistics for the 200 firms included in this enquiry; these may be compared with the scanty data available from the public sector, which are as follows:

	Values in Millions of 1968 pesos
1. Royalties, profits and dividends transferred abroad	53,145·0
2. Local expenditures on research and development, effected within the private sector of the economy	1,800·0

Sources:
    (1) Consejo Nacional de Desarrollo, *Plan Nacional 1970–1974*, Vol. 5, Sector Externo, p. 46.
    (2) Consejo Nacional de Ciencia y Técnica, *Potencial Científico y Técnico Nacional*, Vol. 1, 'Resultados e Informes', p. 103, Table 4.12.

Let us briefly examine the reliability of these figures. First of all, it is obvious that since the aggregate figure for transfers abroad includes profits and dividends, the amount effectively remitted (although not necessarily the amount earned) in payment for foreign technology would be much less. Taking only royalties into account, the figure for 1968 would be approximately 22,000 million pesos (or U.S. $64·0 million). By itself, however, this would constitute too low an estimate of the sum effectively transferred in payment for patents, trade-marks, manufacturing licenses, technical assistance to production and so on, since a number of firms remit technological royalties in the form of dividends or profits on capital.[1]

The second point is the difficulty of finding any explicit methodological reference explaining how the National Council for Science and Technology arrived at the above-quoted figure. Our own results

---

[1] A calculation of the proportion corresponding to technological royalties could be attempted by, first of all, isolating from the overall figure for dividends and profits that part which refers exclusively to the manufacturing sector. (It should be remembered that the part absorbed by banks and services is fairly large.) We would then have to introduce an assumption about 'normal' profits on capital and, using this assumption, split the remainder into two parts, representing payment for physical assets and payment for technology. This calculation would swell the figure for technological royalties in 1968 by something of the order of U.S. $100 million, or 35,000 million pesos. However, we decided not to develop this calculation in detail, because it would involve the 'correction', and modification through additional assumptions, of an already basically weak statistic – which could hardly be improved by such indirect methods.

TABLE 7.7

ARGENTINA: ROYALTIES AND LOCAL EXPENDITURES
ON RESEARCH AND DEVELOPMENT, 1968

Industrial Branch	RD+OT	RD	*Royalties*	RD+OT	RD	*Royalties*
	(Million pesos)			(Percentages of value of output)		
1. Pharmaceutical industry	715·9	301·5	2,024·5	1·9	0·8	5·3
2. Electrical machinery and equipment	790·1	360·2	750·9	1·7	0·7	1·6
3. Vehicles and transportation materials	2,827·9	703·8	5,475·0	1·4	0·3	2·5
4. Metals	1,460·2	480·0	602·0	1·2	0·4	0·6
5. Chemical products	1,743·8	751·5	1,017·0	1·8	0·7	1·1
6. Oil refining	1,040·0	394·0	1,500·0	0·5	0·3	0·7
7. Textiles	967·3	187·0	354·0	1·7	0·3	0·7
8. Food	1,061·5	152·6	10·0	1·0	0·1	—
9. Non-electrical machinery and equipment	1,049·4	356·6	1,310·6	2·4	0·7	2·8
Total of the Sample	11,656·1	3,687·2	13,044·0	1·2	0·35	1·3

provide strong grounds for believing that the C.O.N.A.C.Y.T. figures considerably underestimate present domestic expenditure on research and development.

Third, in view of these difficulties with the aggregate data from the public sector, it is hardly necessary to inform the reader that we are completely lacking in information at the industrial level.

Turning to the results from our own field-work on 200 large industrial plants in Argentina, as given in Table 7.7, we would make the following points:

(i) About 40 per cent of the total payments made by Argentina for patents, trade-marks, manufacturing licences, technical assistance to production, etc., was transferred abroad as technological royalties by these 200 firms. An obvious further question which urgently needs answering is: how much of this expenditure consists of payments for already worn-out patents, trade-marks and technical knowledge for which domestically generated technology could easily be substituted? At this stage we cannot provide an answer. Obviously, all types of external transfer cannot be given an equal status, in as much as many of them are clearly not justified by the flow of external resources which the country receives in exchange.

(ii) About 50 per cent of the total bill for technology transfers can be attributed to two industries: Vehicles and Transport Equipment and Pharmaceutical Products. It is worth noting that in both cases, for reasons we shall not go into here, negotiations could have drastically reduced the level of external transfers, if only the country had shown the political will to do so.

(iii) On average, no more than 0·03 per cent of current sales is spent on R and D, while as much as 1·5 per cent is transferred abroad in the form of royalties. To judge from our sample, the chemical and electrical industries seem to be making relatively greater technological efforts than the others.

V. CONCLUSIONS

Let us now briefly summarise the main conclusions of this paper. First, the chemical, electrical and metallurgical industries exhibited an above average all round performance during the 1960s. Second, larger firms in those industries grew significantly faster than average, thus resulting in a rapid increase in business concentration. Third, around 90 per cent of the inter-industry variance regarding overall factor productivity growth is statistically 'explained' by two variables, the rate of growth of output and accumulated R and D expenditure per person employed. Fourth, the sample of firms here investigated spends around 1·5 per cent of the value of shipments in payments for technology, patents, trademarks, and so forth. As little as 0·4 per cent of sales is being spent by these firms in research and development activities carried out locally. Fifth, the motor-car industry and pharmaceutical products account for nearly one half of the overall royalty remittances by the country in recent years. And sixth, most of what is presently going on in terms of local 'technological effort' takes the form of 'adaptive' R and D expenditure, whose major purpose is that of supporting a 'product differentiation' game typical of oligopolistic confrontations. The larger part of those efforts are carried out, and their benefits appropriated, by local subsidiaries of large multinational corporations.

APPENDIX 1

Definition and Measurement Problems

As was explained in section I above, most of the statistical data used here were specially collected by means of a questionnaire which was distributed to 250 large industrial firms in nine branches of the manufacturing sector.

The questionnaire contained a large number of questions concerning the growth performance of the plant over the period 1960–8. Because of its complicated nature the interviewing was done by a specially trained team of engineers and ex-engineering students, and the field-work was sponsored by the National Bureau of the Census.

The purpose of this Appendix is to discuss briefly the way the different variables were defined and handled in the course of the investigation.

(i) VOLUME OF OUTPUT

The index of volume was obtained by deflating output at current prices by a price index corresponding to the main product produced in each plant.

(ii) THE RATE OF CAPITAL ACCUMULATION

Measuring capital will always pose a problem, and the Cambridge school will always be there to remind us that such a thing cannot in fact be measured. For what it is worth, this is the procedure which was followed in this case: in 1959, Argentine manufacturing firms were allowed by law to adjust the book value of fixed capital stock to allow for inflation. We therefore asked each firm to indicate first what the adjusted figure was for 1960. We then asked what investment was carried out year by year 1960 to 1968, both in locally bought and in imported equipment. Finally, we asked each firm to give a figure for a 'normal' percentage for depreciation. Each figure was then corrected for underutilisation by using an index of the ratio between the actual physical volume of output and the maximum output obtainable from the existing equipment.

(iii) EMPLOYMENT

Data were collected on three categories: (a) technical personnel, (b) administrative personnel, (c) ordinary plant workers. No correction has so far been attempted for quality changes.

(iv) THE RATE OF TECHNICAL PROGRESS

As stated above, our 'proxy' variable for the rate of technical progress is the rate of growth of overall factor productivity. Three different possible measures were considered. Attempts were made with plant level data to estimate intertemporal Cobb–Douglas and C.E.S. production functions, for each firm in the sample, with various different specifications. Then a very simple, Kendrick-type measure of the growth rate of overall factor productivity was calculated using as weights – or factor-elasticities – the relative factor shares in value-added at the plant level.

After juggling for some time with these three estimates for the rate of technical change, we finally settled on the third because of the much larger number of observations that it allowed us to carry over to the second stage of the enquiry.

(V) RESEARCH AND DEVELOPMENT EXPENDITURE, AND EXPENDI-
TURE ON OTHER ASSOCIATED TECHNICAL ACTIVITIES

There are three points which have to be borne in mind in looking for a
definition of R and D expenditure.

(*a*) Research and Development is part of a much wider spectrum of
technical activities. We therefore have to make an *a priori* decision about
what to include and what to exclude in the R and D category. As always
in such cases, there is a middle ground where it is difficult to apply criteria
for inclusion and exclusion.

(*b*) Though a certain amount of international agreement exists with
regard to what should, or should not, be included in the concept of R and
D, it is far from unanimous, so that everyone is not measuring the same
thing. Naturally this casts some doubt on the currently fashionable international comparisons of R and D statistics.

(*c*) In our opinion there do not seem to be adequate grounds for using
precisely the same definitions in connection with both the 'recently
industrialised' nations and those which are relatively more developed. The
whole notion of what should, and what should not, be considered *routine*
in any given society seems to be closely related to the stage of development
which that society has reached. Yet it is precisely around the concept of
routine that the conventional definitions have been developed.

For the purposes of this study we have adopted the conventional definitions[1] of 'Basic Research', 'Applied Research' and 'Experimental Development'. However, we have also introduced two further categories, namely:
'Improvement and/or adaptation of the product and/or productive process', and 'Technical Assistance to production before the productive unit
has attained what might be considered its 'normal' operation'. In this
paper 'R and D activities' refers to the first group of technical activities,
whereas the much wider concept of 'R and D plus Other Technical
Activities' also includes the latter two forms of engineering activities,
which are carried out in the plant.

[1] On conventional definitions, see National Science Foundation, *Research and
Development in Industry* (U.S. Government Printing Office, Washington, D.C.,
1968). Also: O.E.C.D., *Proposed Standard Practice for Surveys of R and D*,
Directorate of Scientific Affairs, Paris, 1963).

APPENDIX II

'GROWTH' AND 'LEARNING' EFFECTS

Model: $\lambda = c_o + a\Delta \; Q/Q + \sum_{o}^{t} b \, (RD + OT)/L$

Industrial Branch	Number of Observations	Constant	Growth Effect a	'Learning' Effect b	R^2
1. Pharmaceutical industry	17	− 5·638 (27·520)	0·316 (0·143)	0·245 (0·121)	0·75
2. Metals	23	− 31,166 (19·067)	0·319 (0·040)	0·218 (0·112)	0·90
3. Food	25	− 24,016 (10·628)	0·315 (0·046)	0·313 (0·106)	0·89
4. Chemical products	22	− 66,271 (18·671)	0·469 (0·122)	0·250 (0·075)	0·87
5. Non-electrical machinery and equipment	15	− 40,306 (59·658)	0·260 (0·137)	0·558 (0·301)	0·62
6. Electrical machinery and equipment	18	− 34,584 (33·478)	0·501 (0·043)	0·207 (0·150)	0·92
7. Textiles	21	8·677	0·010	0·100 (0·025)	0·56
8. Vehicles and machinery	14	− 43,689 (27·836)	0·310 (0·207)	0·300 (0·191)	0·71
9. Petrochemicals	6	− 54,036 (30·035)	0·601 (0·171)	0·160 (0·069)	0·90

Discussion of the Paper by
Dr. Katz

Mr. Wionczek said that Dr. Katz had arrived at a number of important, if preliminary, conclusions, which could be of considerable assistance in designing a policy on technology for the larger Latin American countries. First, Dr. Katz had shown us that in a country like Argentina, in contrast to what happened in developed economies, there were reasons to believe that the direction of causality was from the growth in physical production and local expenditures on adaptive R and D, towards the growth in productivity; with the first two variables being relatively independent of each other. This enabled us to delineate the limits on the growth of productivity. Limitations would arise from (a) the size of the national market (b) the characteristics of the industrial structure (c) the weakness of local creative technological effort and (d) the indiscriminate import of technology into the manufacturing sector, subject to various forms of monopolistic exploitation on the part of the exporters of know-how – who were often in fact also the local importers, in the form of local subsidiaries.

Second, Dr. Katz had shown us that an extremely high proportion of the observed growth in productivity at plant level came from the resolution of problems or bottlenecks in the production line, and as such was necessarily associated with local technological expenditure. Expenditure on imported technology was much greater, and not significantly associated with increases in productivity, and it was not possible to know how far such payments in fact corresponded to the real flow of technical services. Since information available from other Latin American countries, though analysed in a less refined fashion, indicated a similarly high degree of dependence on foreign technology, it became clear that it was essential to consider how far one could really consider subsidiaries of multinational corporations vehicles of technical progress.

There were many difficulties in this, including as Dr. Katz had said the fact that royalties were 'a highly dubious proxy for what we really want to measure'; nevertheless he wondered if one might not draw out of the literature, especially from the work of Dr. Vaitsos, a way of quantifying the monopoly rents coming from the sale of technology as compared with the international price of the same technology. To use the phrase coined by Vaitsos, one might study 'the international market in technology'. It would be important not to forget that prices in such a market were determined among other factors not so much by forces of supply and demand as by the negotiating power of the participants. This power stemmed in turn from the degree of 'technological monopoly', real or supposed, of the supplier and from the amount of information the purchaser had as to the whole gamut of technological options open to him and as to the way the international system of patents operated. It had to be made clear that the acceptance of the concepts of 'technology', considered as a good, and of an 'international market in technology', did not eliminate the difficulties arising from the fact that while the terms could be used fairly straightforwardly in the case of processes, this was not true in the case of products, or where technology was incorporated in goods such as machinery or intermediate products. It was, he thought, likely that despite such difficulties we would one day be able to make case-by-case estimations of the competitive cost of imported innovations compared with the size of the monopoly rents received by the owners of technology in an imperfect market.

He was also optimistic that once the negotiating capacity of the purchasers had increased, at least in respect of processes, it would be possible to introduce into the policy the 'most favoured nation' clause, a practice applied with considerable success in Japan. It was essential to point out here that the efficient use of this procedure in this sphere would depend on the degree of co-operation it was possible to establish between the State and the firms seeking the technology, and on the State taking effective action to eliminate all such restrictive business practices as introduced an element of exclusiveness into the sale of technology. Here again Japanese practice came to mind: once the technology was purchased it was placed freely at the disposition of all interested firms, at the same cost for all, though the law did not oblige them to share with the others subsequent adaptations or their own innovations.

Japanese policies with regard to the purchase of technology were clearly not straightforwardly applicable to the Latin American situation. However, the situation was anyway changing rapidly. Ten years before, the whole question of trade in foreign technology had appeared a mystery; five years later, some countries were beginning to control purchases of technology for balance of payments reasons (a crude and often misguided policy in fact); by today we had in the Andean Group, in Argentina, in Brazil, attempts at far more refined selective control, which were trying, among other things, to eliminate the practice of transferring profit under the guise of royalty payments, and to put a brake on the negative social effects of certain kinds of so-called imports of technology, that is, the purchase of trade marks whose only function is frequently to create an artificial differentiation in consumer goods.

The important aspect of all such advances was that while their starting point was the growing recognition of the need to disaggregate the package of 'capital, technology and management' with the purpose of designing a policy on technology, their final aim was to design such a policy bearing in mind all its aspects – technological, economic and juridical, both national and international.

It appeared that 'learning by doing' was occurring not only at the plant level in Latin America, but also in respect of the elaboration of technology policies at the national or subregional level. It was evident that in the long run learning by doing could not totally substitute for learning by spending on technical research proper. It was to be hoped that within a reasonable period of time the region would move on to the stage of learning by spending, both in R and D itself and in the compilation of information on foreign technological development. At that point perhaps what would appear as of particular urgency would be to strengthen adaptive R and D and diversify the sources of technology.

Professor Vernon wished to underline the qualifications Dr. Katz himself had made on the figures for royalties paid. Such figures represented a major trap – especially in the case of a subsidy making what was simply an internal transfer payment to the parent company. First, the parent might not charge. It might wish to let profits develop and be ploughed back. Or a charge if made might take the form of adjusting transfer prices or interest payments. The result could be a profit figure distorted in *either* direction.

Moving to broader aspects of the need for technology, *Professor Felix* phrased the problem as (1) how to get technology that provided adequate employment and produced benefits for the mass of the population, and (2) how to hasten the time when Latin America could begin to adapt and even exchange its own technology. The solution as he saw it lay largely in Latin America – in identifying the key decision points and implementing changes in the parameters controlling these decisions. Unfortunately bargaining possibilities with respect to one's share of the rent on a given piece of imported technology were more limited in the area of industry than in natural resources. In the case of the latter, much of the economic rent was geographically immobile and the asset depreciated slowly, while in industry, a given technology was a rapidly depreciating asset, since the pay-off depended on a range of ancillary skills, trade secrets and so forth, which the foreign firm could readily withdraw. And being less tied to natural resources, the foreign firm could more easily play off one country against another.

In the present situation facing Latin America, the embodied technological choices were limited, and moreover the capital–labour ratio showed a rising trend over time. Such limits sprang from the nature of the decisions governing the choice of techniques in advanced countries. But this did not mean that without fundamental change there were no options; a major area of choice sprang from the fact that capital–labour ratios differed widely *between* different industries and different product lines. But controlling the output mix under import substituting industrialisation was a question of exploring and changing the parameters that governed domestic demand decisions, as well as enterprise decisions on investment and choice of technology. At present, with highly protected markets and pliable consumer preferences, the market bias operated powerfully in the direction of a rapid introduction of new goods – notably consumables – which in turn largely determined the direction of domestic industrial technology, with the consequence being low labour absorption and negligible material benefits for the masses. The same situation also tended to mean limited absorption of local engineers, chemists and other technical talent; thus despite a limited supply of such local talent the paradox of the brain drain occurred.

How much of the bias in consumer demand was due to local income, and how much to a powerful one-way cultural impact, was not clear; it seemed very probable that the latter carried fairly considerable weight.

But if such was the case, then demonstration effects were at least partially embodied in tangible transmission mechanisms, so could in principle be regulated, via, for example, regulation of the mass media and of goods promotion. Firms in Latin America, whether domestic or foreign, were differentiated oligopolies playing the product differentiation game in protected markets; this was leading to a rate of inflow of new goods beyond the optimum. The policy implications as he saw them, given that the market system was to be retained, included reduced protection and subsidies, increased pressures to reduce costs, heavy taxes to ensure that liberalisation did not lead to imports replacing home-grown luxuries, and direct government rationalisation efforts to raise productivity in the vegetative sectors. The adjustment problems would be serious, as would be the political obstacles in many countries; it might well be then that prior drastic political change was needed for Latin America to reach a position of reasonable material comfort and equality of power *vis-à-vis* the rest of the world.

Dr. von Gleich pointed out that the speakers had so far been concerned with large foreign firms. The small and medium firms, which were numerous, should not be overlooked. Such firms did not go abroad as part of a world-wide market strategy, in fact they usually did so because they were induced to do so by a major buyer in the home country. Capacity for research was of course positively related to size, but against this the desirable scaling down and development of labour-intensive technology was in fact more likely to be done by small firms. Yet it was precisely this kind of firm which was likely to be scared away by foreign capital legislation, lacking as it did both information and bargaining power. It was interesting that no legislation on foreign capital contained anti-oligopoly regulations. He would propose selection on the basis of size and relative market power, in addition to the more usual criteria.

Mr. Hosono agreed that too much emphasis was placed on large firms, especially since a country's technological progress consisted in the advance of the great mass of industries, whether large or small. In addition to the more usual fiscal and other measures discussed, he thought it was of particular importance to study the exchange of technical knowledge between firms, particularly between large and small. Equally, he would stress that standardisation was important: it not only contributed to improvement in quality but also permitted more specialisation, economies of scale, and technical progress in a broad sense, especially for medium and small enterprises.

Mr. Urquidi stressed that Latin America had to set about a far greater effort to expand her own capacity for both generating and adapting technology. To this end, many things would have to be given attention which were frequently neglected. Research and development expenditure was approximately 0·2 per cent of Latin American G.D.P. It was necessary to create almost from scratch the necessary educational and scientific infrastructure. Government support was necessary for university and other institutions, directly via subsidies and indirectly via fiscal and monetary incentives to domestic industrial enterprises. Finally, for small and medium firms, he would like to see 'extension services' created on the lines that they were used in agriculture.

Professor Hirschman described the basic problem as how to develop an independent Latin American technology: how could we learn to construct situations which induced thinking and tinkering? It seemed the most fruitful road would probably be detailed, in part psychoanalytic studies of special cases. Probably the most general truth was that one makes innovations when one must: hence the advantages of an 'arms length relationship' between the local engineer and the sources of foreign know-how. This could force a change of mentality and a corresponding reallocation of the engineer's time between consulting foreign sources and studying the local reality. He referred to a Harvard Ph.D. study of the pharmaceutical industry in Brazil which had found domestic firms less rigid than foreign in making adaptations; perhaps this was because they were further from the source.

Mr. Szekely said that the problems of technology transfer in relation to services also needed to be considered. It was an area where external economies from increased productivity could be very important. He thought that the communications media could be used to spread technological improvements in the service sector, and that increased tourism might also help through the demand for better services that accompanied it. *Dr. Ferrer* added that the problem of the transfer of technology in infrastructure was likewise important and typically overlooked.

Dr. Katz, replying, divided his comments into two groups, first those related to the 'explanatory' aspects of the ideas presented, and second, the normative, i.e. regarding what should be done about the vast technological and, more generally, industrial problems faced by Latin American countries.

Among the former, he took first the point made by Professor Vernon and by Mr. Wionczek, on the difficulties of using royalties as a proxy variable. He was of course fully in agreement with both, and had said so in his paper. He had in fact in the research he had been discussing gone a little way in attempting a better measure of external collaboration. Each one of the firms in the survey was asked to state in man years how much external collaboration they received at the stages of plant design, plant construction, operation and so on. A fairly stable pattern had emerged, showing a decreasing amount of external collaboration through the different stages. Considering the complexity of the information asked for, the rather systematic character of the data collected suggested that this was a line of enquiry well worth pursuing. He hoped to have further results in the near future.

Professor Vernon had explained that in a wholly owned subsidiary royalties were no more than accounting prices; his work on the electrical industry had in fact produced results which supported this thesis. Whereas he had found no trace of a statistical association between royalties and productivity growth among wholly owned subsidiaries, such an association was positive and significant in the remaining firms of the sample, all of them local firms operating under licensing agreements with U.S. firms.

Turning to Mr. Wionczek's idea of measuring monopoly rents, he thought it might be helpful to develop an example. Suppose one considered the case of a local firm willing to produce a final commodity for the domestic consumer goods market – say television sets. Such a firm would negotiate the purchase of the relevant technology from an external firm. If one looked at this very simple but common case, it became evident that the assumptions we were willing to make about the market structure on both sides strongly influenced the final outcome of the negotiation, and thereby the size of the monopoly rent absorbed by the seller of technology. The bargaining position of the purchasing firm would be highly dependent on how far he was a monopolist in the market for his product; it would also depend as Mr. Wionczek had said on the *ex ante* information he had about alternative technological sources, as well as on the opportunity cost – in terms of time, risk and engineering cost – of designing his own technology. The opportunity cost would also vary with his own 'learning' about the technology in question. On the side of the seller, his behaviour would be influenced by whether he considered himself a monopolist, for example because he held all the patents, or believed that a certain amount of free entry prevailed. It was interesting to note that he might well act as a monopolist if he believed that his buyer lacked information about alternative sources of technology. Then there were other aspects such as price elasticities in both markets, and the expectations and counter expectations typical of oligopolistic situations.

He turned next to the point made by Dr. von Gleich and by Mr. Hosono, concerning the viability of a technological strategy based on medium or small sized firms. He thought there was undoubtedly something in their argument, and his own study of private individual inventors confirmed it in a small but interesting number of cases. But caution was necessary: the mere fact that both Germany and Japan had specific entrepreneurial groups of great dynamism located in plants of medium or small size was not evidence that such groups existed at all in the sort of societies we were discussing. There was clearly very great disparity between different Latin American countries. Whereas the argument might make some sense in Argentina (and this only in specific manufacturing sectors where a significant amount of accumulated experience was to be found), it certainly could not be easily extended to most of Latin America. The social structure one was dealing with was characterised by discontinuities, and the kind of entrepreneurs they had in mind might simply be missing altogether. Given such considerations, it was once again the potential role of large public enterprises which emerged as significant. His own thinking pointed strongly this way rather than in the direction of stressing the role of a class which might not exist at all, or if it did, might not have much to gain in a process of independent development.

Finally, he would like to turn to more normative aspects of the problem by taking up the points Professor Hirschman and Mr. Urquidi had made about the need for looking in greater detail into the possibilities of independent technological development. He found himself very deeply concerned about what he saw as a serious lack of realism underlying their proposal. He did indeed wish it were possible to discuss seriously the features of an independent technological policy, especially for the larger Latin American countries. But he found himself here in a more sceptical position than most of the speakers, probably as a result of the political and institutional atmosphere of his own country, which had a record of continual failure in its attempts to build up a stable framework. To think about the elements of a scientific and technological policy in an environment in which other, much more elementary, aspects of life were not functioning well, appeared to him a luxury. Turning specifically to industry, did its structure in any way match with our *a priori* ideas of what it should accomplish in the future by way of endogenous technological development? His own answer was a negative one, and he would like to conclude by demonstrating why with some further examples from the electrical goods industry in Argentina. For this sector his research had covered the largest twenty or so plants, about 65 per cent of the value of production in that industry. Only four of the plants could be called entirely national, if by such was meant that the whole of its share capital was owned by Argentine nationals. Philips Gloeilampenfabrieken had a clear predominance, owning three of the four largest plants.

In broad terms, it was possible to identify four different groups within the industry. First, there was a small group of local subsidiaries of large multinational corporations in the communications business, long established in Argentina and until very recently carrying on little or nothing in the form of local R and D. Second, there were two fairly new firms producing active electrical components such as transistors, rectifiers, etc. A few fairly small local firms lived under the oligopolistic umbrella provided by the two foreign firms. The empirical evidence collected during the research indicated that Argentina normally started local production in active components with a significant time-lag. For a sample of sixteen electrical components he had estimated an average time-lag of the order of seven to nine years. Third, there was a fairly large group of local firms operating in the market for final durable consumer goods, such as radios, TV sets, etc. With one or two exceptions, these products were local versions of products already marketed in more developed countries, particularly the United States. All arrived in Argentina as the result of some form of negotiations with an external technological source, negotiations which achieved a certain transfer of knowledge but also involved the transfer of a trade mark whose major and probably sole purpose was to strengthen the oligopolistic position of a local producer. Only a very few of the firms in this group carried on significant technological effort, most of them being concerned with product design which would enable them to face oligopolistic competition in their respective markets. Fourth, there was a large number of family enterprises producing cheap transistorised radio sets for the lower end of the consumer market. These firms operated on the basis of using well-known electrical circuits obtained from any one of the large international firms and they actively participated in smuggling arrangements. It went without saying that they did no research.

Thus, the study had shown (1) a highly deformed output structure biased heavily in favour of consumer durables with the electrical capital goods industry almost absent from the local scene, (2) an almost complete dependence upon foreign designs, (3) a technology transfer mechanism heavily burdened by the role of trade marks brought in for the support of oligopolistic positions, (4) an almost entire control of the active components industry by a handful of foreign firms, making it impossible to reduce the time lag operating in this group, unless direct negotiation could be carried on with the two or three firms in question, (5) the transfer of a significant amount of royalties outside, mostly as a consequence of trade marks, and (6) a very limited 'technological effort', most of which went on adaptation or on product design for the product differentiation game. Such a situation was by no means the consequence of economic stagnation, as was frequently claimed. Rather, it was the consequence of a rapid, though uncontrolled, rate of expansion based on the inflow of foreign capital and technology.

It was obvious that the overall situation called for state intervention. It was also obvious, however, that such state intervention could not deal exclusively with problems of technology. The industry needed to be entirely reshaped. To call for 'technological development' in isolation from the dramatic collateral 'illnesses' here described, was pure fantasy.

Part II

Present and Prospective Trade and
Financial Relations with Major
Trading Areas

8 Relations with Latin America: an American View

Clark W. Reynolds

FOOD RESEARCH INSTITUTE, STANFORD UNIVERSITY

The purpose of this paper is to examine trade and financial relations between Latin America and the United States in a global setting. While this implies the sacrifice of detail, it is made essential by the fact that most U.S. policies affecting the hemisphere are reactions to problems elsewhere in the world. The Vietnam war, the growth of highly competitive economic blocs in Europe and the Orient, the reappraisal of international responsibility for defence support, and the U.S. anti-inflation recession have little or nothing to do with Latin America. Yet the apparent trend in American commercial policy from trade liberalisation to increasing protection follows from these problems and promises to have a severe impact on hemisphere trade and development. The impact can best be understood by examining the pattern of commodity trade growth between Latin America and the rest of the world, and by analysing the role of the United States in that process since the Second World War. This examination occupies the first section of the paper.

The second section examines recent trends in United States commercial policy, possible unilateral preferences on the part of the United States for developing countries in general or Latin America in particular, multilateral preferences among developed countries, and other measures, in terms of their potential impact on Latin American trade. It is suggested that increasing U.S. protectionism may contribute to a further division of the world market into economic blocs, furthered by European initiative and the remarkable success of Japan, which could have the effect of throwing Latin American countries back upon the Western Hemisphere.

The third section relates the pattern of real output growth and resulting changes in trade patterns to an intertemporal model of comparative advantage which links trade and capital movements. The model illustrates why those nations which have a 'comparative advantage in growth' tend to be net borrowers abroad, while those with a comparative advantage in present over future production will tend to be net lenders. As applied to the cases of Brazil, Mexico and Venezuela, the model helps to explain extreme examples of net borrowing and lending in Latin America in recent years. The position of the United States as financial intermediary among net borrowing and lending regions, as well as its role as direct investor in those Latin American markets with the most growth potential, is illuminated by this analysis. It is shown that offsetting balance of payments disequilibria on current and capital account may be expected wherever intertemporal comparative advantage differs among countries and regions, and that in the absence of political obstacles to the flow of international finance at least some regions in Latin America may well be net borrowers for decades to come. The efficient functioning of international financial flows is shown to be a necessary condition for the effective evolution of comparative advantage in commodity trade.

I. TRADE RELATIONS BETWEEN THE UNITED STATES AND LATIN AMERICA: PAST TRENDS AND FUTURE PROSPECTS

In this section of the paper we shall examine recent trends in the structure of commodity trade between the developing countries of the Americas and the rest of the world, with emphasis on the United States. The approach is to consider changes in trade structure as a reflection of an evolution in underlying economic comparative advantage and changes in commercial policy (including regional trading agreements), subject to political considerations, including United States foreign economic policy as conditioned by political changes in specific Latin American countries and by regional economic agreements. In view of the complex interaction of these factors over time it is not possible to separate out their impact on the pattern of trade with precision. However, historical examples abound in which individual elements have been particularly important, and these will be used to illustrate general trends.

The national origin of producers' goods and intermediate goods inputs imported by developing countries may well be influenced by the national source of long-term investment credits to the extent that imperfections exist in product and financial markets. But the underlying structure of trade may be said to depend more importantly on the stage of development of the economy concerned, its initial factor endowments, and its potential for growth as influenced by conditions of production, income distribution, tastes, and the efficiency of the resource allocation mechanism. This is to suggest, therefore, that beneath the web of special relationships which affect specific economic transactions lies a more fundamental set of natural conditions for trade and development which are based upon initial conditions of supply and demand and their dynamic potential for change. This phenomenon is discussed in considerably more detail in the section on capital movements, but the general principle is worth mentioning at this point in view of the implications it has for the treatment of U.S.–Latin American trade patterns.

In sectors or regions where the initial set of supply and demand conditions are relatively favourable to economic development (defined narrowly here as growth of output) one may expect an inflow of complementary factors of production, including those associated with foreign investment, whenever such factors are permitted to realise an expected stream of income flows, net of transfer costs, risk, and liquidity discounts, in excess of the expected rate of return in their place of origin. Such inflows will facilitate a shift in comparative advantage (and hence a shift in trade shares) towards those sectors and regions most favoured for growth, given the distribution of income, tastes, and technology in such economies at the outset. Some sectors, regions, and countries may have greater output growth potential than others to the extent that initial conditions of supply and demand differ, including international flows of factors of production such as labour, capital, and technology.

Even where development propensities are suboptimal, countries and regions may be selected by the governments of developed countries for special assistance for reasons of political expedience or social equity. Cases exist in which major world powers provide development assistance to those nations which will act as bastions on the frontiers of their spheres of influence (South Korea, North Korea, Taiwan, Czechoslovakia, Israel, Cuba and Indonesia). Such activities, which are frequently termed 'foreign aid', may well give rise to externalities reflected in rising rates of return to private investors, some of whom may be nationals of the aid-giving countries. There is a tendency for such nations to become vertically integrated into the markets of their respective developed country 'protectors', producing raw materials and processing progressively more stages prior to sale of the final product in the metropolitan market. That is because the initial trade and factor movements followed a pattern not of national economic comparative advantage but of politically induced comparative advantage. In cases such as these, capital, skilled labour, and technology tend to flow from the metropolis, under the protection of a foreign military presence, secured by extended balance of payment supports, and sustained by domestic political–military coalitions.

Developing nations not highly favoured by initial economic growth advantages or by political attributes which provide a non-economic justification for resource transfers from the metropolitan countries find themselves competing for scarce resources and even attempting to stem the outflow of capital. To an extent the success of one means the stagnation of another, since the international distributive mechanism is unable to provide resources to all countries on grounds of equity alone. For such nations a future source of support may be seen in those relatively advanced developing countries (such as Mexico and Brazil) which for economic as well as political reasons may eventually find it advantageous to share the proceeds of their disproportionate growth with less fortunate partners in the Third World, even whilst they are receiving a net inflow of skilled labour, capital, and technology from the developed countries.

LATIN AMERICAN TRADE IN THE PAST 25 YEARS

Since the Second World War Latin America's trade position with respect to the United States has progressively deteriorated, reflected in a loss of market shares for exports. Table 8.1 and Fig. 8.1 show that in 1946–8 goods and services from the Latin American Republics constituted one-third of United States imports of goods and services, owing partly, of course, to the disruptive effects of the war. By 1956–8 this figure had adjusted to 23 per cent, falling still further to 18 per cent by 1961–3. Between 1961–3 and 1967–9 the percentage of total U.S. imports of goods and services from the Latin American Republics plus other Western Hemisphere countries (not including Canada) fell from 21 per cent to 15 per cent. United States sales to Latin America, on the other hand, have tended to maintain their share of total exports, with the exception of a sharp upswing around 1950. Latin America's share of U.S. exports was 23 per cent in 1946–8, 26 per cent in 1950, returning to 22 per cent in 1956–8, and to 17 per cent in 1961–3. Exports by the United States to the Latin American Republics and other Western Hemisphere countries fell slightly from 19 per cent in 1961–3 to 17 per cent in 1967–9.

To the extent that such general trade patterns reflect the evolution of comparative advantage, these figures suggest that the competitive position of hemisphere goods and services in the United States' market has been seriously weakened. Conversely, U.S. goods and services have maintained a relatively strong position in Latin American markets, despite greatly increased competition from Western Europe, Japan and Latin America itself. To illustrate the initial point, if the Latin American share of U.S. imports in 1967–9 had remained at the 1961–3 ratio her exports would have been $9,893 million, or $2·8 billion higher than the actual average for 1967–9. This hypothetical 39 per cent gain in exports represents

TABLE 8.1

LATIN AMERICA'S SHARE OF UNITED STATES TRADE IN GOODS AND SERVICES, ANNUAL AVERAGES 1946–8, 1956–8, 1961, AND 1967–9[a]
(Millions of U.S. dollars, except as otherwise indicated)

	1946–8	1956–8	1961–3	1967–9
Total U.S. imports of goods and services	8,510	20,413	25,041	47,561
From Latin American Republics	2,723	4,655	4,370	
Per cent of total	32·0	22·8	17·5	
From Latin American Republics and other Western Hemisphere[b]			5,204	7,095
Per cent of total			20·8	14·9
Total U.S. exports of goods and services	17,362	26,971	32,148	51,602
To Latin American Republics	3,949	5,982	5,375	
Per cent of total	22·7	22·2	16·9	
To Latin American Republics and other Western Hemisphere[b]			6,009	8,804
Per cent of total			18·7	17·1
U.S. Gross National Product (Billion dollars)	232·5	435·9	557·0	862·4
Trade in goods and services as per cent of G.N.P.				
Exports	7·5	6·2	5·8	6·0
Imports	3·7	4·7	4·5	5·5

Source: U.S. Department of Commerce, Office of Business Economics, *Balance of Payments Statistical Supplement: Revised Edition (1963)*, and *Survey of Current Business*, June 1968, March 1971; for G.N.P., Ditto, July 1971.

[a] Data for the Latin American Republics without 'Other Western Hemisphere' are not published for 1964 and later years. Exports of goods and services are as reported in U.S. balance of payments statistics.
[b] Other Western Hemisphere, excluding Canada.

1·6 times the deficit of the balance of payments on current account of the 11 largest countries in Latin America in 1967–9 ($1·7 billion). Declining trade shares for Latin America run counter to the trend in the share of total U.S. imports in G.N.P. which has risen from 3·7 per cent in 1946–8 to 5·5 per cent in 1967–9, suggesting that the U.S. demand for Latin American products is declining relative to that for products from the rest of the world (Table 8.1).

Changes in the configuration of productive capacity around the world, and in particular the post-war recovery and growth of the industrial centres of Europe and Asia, appear to have altered the comparative advantage of the United States in such a way that its initially strong competitive trade position at the end of the Second World War has been considerably weakened in the markets of

Europe and Japan, though less so in the Western Hemisphere. Immediately after the war American suppliers were able to sell almost any merchandise in excess of internal demand in foreign markets with little fear of competition from the other industrial centres, the latter facing shortages in most branches of industry. Such trade was facilitated by public and private capital transfers to foreign markets serving to finance a substantial U.S. export surplus.

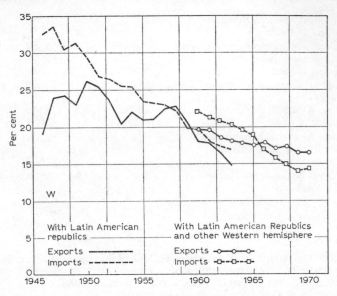

FIG. 8.1. United States trade in goods and services with Latin American republics 1946–63, and with Latin American republics plus other Western Hemisphere countries, 1960–70. Source: Computed from data in sources cited for Table 8.1.

Full employment policy in the United States was consistent with such transfers in the immediate post-war period, as external credits helped to sustain the market for American industry and agriculture once the temporary stimulus of war-time and immediate post-war demand had ended.

However, as the economic capacity of Europe and Japan recovered and grew these nations were progressively able to satisfy internal demand and export an increasing surplus to the United States. By the 1960s excess demand characterised important sectors of U.S. manufacturing. This demand was met increasingly by imports. To some extent the initial outflow of machinery and equipment from the United States helped to tool up industries in Europe and Japan which, in combination with their lower labour costs (at existing exchange rates), began to compete effectively within the American market in such important lines as textiles, motor vehicles, and electrical goods. By the same token technical assistance in foreign agriculture, provided in part by the U.S. government and U.S. foundations, helped to develop new varieties of seed and methods of cultivation which began to reduce the demand for certain temperate zone agricultural products such as wheat, which owing to price supports in the United States still retain a potentially large exportable surplus.

The Latin American countries played only a marginal role in these developments in view of their relatively small share of United States trade, itself only a fraction of U.S. G.N.P. While Europe and Japan attempted to recover their initial trade advantages, upset by the war, and to progress from that point, most Latin American countries pursued policies designed to shift their comparative advantage away from exportables towards home goods. That alteration was not sufficient to reverse the comparative advantage of the region so as to favour manufactured exports over raw materials and primary products. For comparative advantage to change, the price of initial exportables must rise relative to initial importables, or both, so as to reverse the order of relative rates of return on new investment in these activities, bringing about a relative expansion of capacity in initially import competing activities such that the price of these products will fall relative to traditional exportables. The resulting shift in relative prices will in time elicit a favourable response in the world market, provided that exchange rates are allowed to adjust. However, the transition may well be a slow one.[1] Latin American attempts at import-substituting industrialisation at the cost of traditional exports weakened their initial trade position with the United States, and because of the lag in transition from one structure of production to another, few countries have reached the next stage of producing manufactured goods capable of competing in the markets of the industrial countries. This is revealed in the following section.

[1] No matter how exchange rates adjust, comparative advantage refers to *relative* prices of importables and exportables rather than absolute prices. This lesson has not always been learned, since policy makers behave as though they wished to retain their traditional comparative advantage in raw materials and primary products while gaining an advantage in new lines as well. Except in cases where the conditions of supply in traditional activities are totally unresponsive to changes in relative internal prices and costs, one cannot expect to have one's cake and eat it.

THE UNITED STATES' SHARE OF LATIN AMERICAN
COMMODITY TRADE

In the previous section it was shown that the Latin American share
of U.S. imports fell sharply in the post-war period. In order to view
this decline in perspective one must examine the pattern of Latin
American trade with the rest of the world, including the United
States, by major commodity groups. Total Latin American commodity exports increased by 48 per cent between 1956–8 and
1967–9 (Table 8.2). Of the $4,047 million net increase, purchases

TABLE 8.2

TOTAL VALUE OF LATIN AMERICAN TRADE BY
REGIONS, 1956–8 and 1967–9
(Millions of U.S. dollars)

	Total	United States	Canada	Japan	Western Europe	All others
Latin American Exports						
1956–8 average	8,500	3,800	138	248	2,607	1,708
1967–9 average	12,547	3,980	403	663	4,117	3,383
Increase	4,047	180	265	415	1,510	1,675
Per cent	47·6	4·7	192·0	167·3	57·9	98·1
Latin American Imports						
1956–8 average	8,060	4,097	200	170	2,360	1,233
1967–9 average	12,017	4,517	365	633	3,680	2,822
Increase	3,957	420	165	463	1,320	1,589
Per cent	49·1	10·2	82·5	272·3	55·9	128·9
Sum 1965–9						
Exports	60,350	19,360	1,820	3,000	19,840	16,330
Imports	55,780	21,440	1,735	2,775	16,800	13,030
Balance	4,570	– 2,080	85	225	3,040	3,300

Source: Appendix Tables I and II.

by the United States accounted for only $180 million, Canada for
$265 million, Japan almost as much as the two together ($415
million) and Western Europe $1,510 million, the remainder being
divided among Latin American countries and the rest of the world
($1,675 million). Thus the importance of the United States market
to the net growth of Latin American exports in recent years has been
only 4 per cent compared to 7 per cent for Canada, 10 per cent for
Japan, 37 per cent for Western Europe, and 41 per cent for Latin
America and the Third World. On the import side, the United
States' share of Latin America's import growth was a much higher
11 per cent, that of Canada 4 per cent, Japan 12 per cent, Western
Europe 33 per cent, and Latin America and the rest of the world
40 per cent.

Latin America's resulting balance of trade deficit with the United States was compensated for, in part, by a significant commodity trade surplus with Western Europe and the rest of the world. For example, Table 8.2 shows that for the period 1965-9 Latin American commodity imports from the United States exceeded exports to that country by an accumulated total of $2,080 million. By contrast the export surplus with all countries except the United States amounted to $6,650 million in the five-year period, Western Europe accounting for 46 per cent, Japan 3 per cent, Canada 1 per cent, and the rest of the world the remaining 50 per cent. Of this amount some $2 billion served to offset the commodity trade deficit with the United States, while the remainder may be regarded as helping to offset Latin America's large deficit on invisibles account, particularly in the form of interest and principal payments on foreign investment, much of which also accrued to the United States. During the same five-year interval 1965-9 the United States showed a cumulative net credit balance with Latin America in the form of income on U.S. investments abroad minus income on foreign investments in the United States (direct investments and other private assets) of $6,486 million.[1]

[1] This represents the cumulated sum of lines 11 and 12 in the U.S. balance of payments (Income on U.S. investments abroad: direct investments, other private assets) minus line 21 (Income on foreign investments in the United States: private payments) from the U.S. Department of Commerce, *Survey of Current Business*, June 1968, June 1970, March 1971. The figures refer to 'Latin American Republics and other Western Hemisphere' and are therefore more inclusive than the merchandise figures in this paper, which present exports to and from 'Latin American Republics', as reported in the United Nations' *Monthly Bulletin of Statistics*, March of selected years. The main difference is that 'Other Caribbean' is included in the available Department of Commerce figures for Latin America. Since 1964 the Department of Commerce has been presenting U.S. balance of payments statistics with respect to 'Latin American Republics and Other Western Hemisphere' (Canada excluded) whereas through 1963 'Other Caribbean' countries were separated out. On the average in 1961-63, years in which overlapping statistics under the two classifications exist (see Table 8.9), the United States showed a large balance of trade deficit on its merchandise account with 'Other Caribbean' countries while it showed a merchandise account surplus with other 'Latin American Republics'. An additional complication arises from the fact that U.N. statistics are reported only in terms of *exports* from country of origin to country of destination. Thus, a comparison of U.N. figures with U.S. balance of payments statistics on merchandise trade is likely to reveal inconsistencies, particularly on the import side. In fact, U.N. statistics on Latin American exports to the United States for 1961-63 are some 3·1 per cent below the U.S. balance of payments statistics for merchandise imports from Latin America. On the other hand, U.N. statistics on U.S. exports to Latin America are only 0·6 per cent below the U.S. balance of payments figure. It is reasonable to assume a slight upward bias in the cumulative deficit on merchandise account for Latin America as reported in the text (based on U.N. data) in comparison with figures for the United States balance of payments. Thus the two figures are not entirely

CHANGING COMPOSITION OF LATIN AMERICAN COMMODITY TRADE

Latin American commodity trade has shifted on the export side away from food products and fuels towards machinery and transport equipment and other manufactures (see Table 8.3). The percentage of machinery and other manufactures in Latin American exports has increased from 7 to 14 per cent between 1956–8 and 1967–9, while the share of food products and fuels has fallen from 73 per cent to 66 per cent. This is a reflection of a change in the production base of the economy away from raw materials and primary products towards manufactured goods and services and a comparable shift in domestic demand towards minerals, fuels, agricultural products, and other raw materials and locally produced intermediate goods to serve the home market and provide inputs for future exports. On the import side the share of primary product imports (S.I.T.C. 0 to 4) has fallen from 26 per cent to 23 per cent between 1956–9 and 1967–9, while imports of chemicals, machinery and transport equipment (S.I.T.C. 5 and 7) have risen from 45 to 52 per cent of all imports. It is notable that import substitution has been most effective in light manufactures (S.I.T.C. 6 and 8 – 'other manufactures') which have decreased their share of Latin American imports from 27 to 23 per cent.

The United States market has responded less positively than those of Europe and Japan to changes in hemisphere comparative advantage as reflected in the pattern of commodity trade (Table 8.4).[2] Latin American exports of manufactures (S.I.T.C. 6 to 8) increased

---

comparable even after adjustment for the inclusion of 'Other Caribbean' in the U.S. balance of payments total. Taking these factors into consideration, the United States balance of trade with 'Latin America and other Western Hemisphere' for the years 1965 to 1969 inclusive showed a (U.S.) credit item of $403 million, while the Latin American Republics (not including 'Other Caribbean') showed a cumulative deficit of $2,080 million with the U.S. on merchandise account. This indicated a large U.S. deficit on merchandise account with 'Other Caribbean' countries in that period. For comparison cumulative U.S. Census Bureau figures show the United States with net exports of $661 million to the larger area, net exports of $1,713 to Latin American Republics alone, and net imports of $1,052 million from 'Other Western Hemisphere'.

[2] These shares differ markedly from those in Alfred Maizels' paper in this volume, primarily because Maizels discusses trade with specified industrialised countries only, whereas we include trade with the rest of the world as well. This trade accounted for a large part of the increase in exports shown in Table 8.4. Maizels' definition of manufactures differs from ours by the inclusion of chemicals and the exclusion of non-ferrous metals, which accounts for most of the rest of the differences. Some further non-comparability arises from the use of slightly different time periods. Both papers have depended on the U.N., *Monthly Bulletin of Statistics* for data on exports by commodity groups.

TABLE 8.3

COMMODITY COMPOSITION OF LATIN AMERICAN EXPORTS AND IMPORTS, 1956–8 AND 1967–9

(Per cent of total)

Commodity group	S.I.T.C. section	Exports			Imports		
		1956–8	1967–9	Increase	1956–8	1967–9	Increase
Food, beverages, and tobacco	0, 1	46·6	41·9	31·9	11·5	10·8	9·5
Crude materials[a] and oils and fats	2, 4	18·0	18·2	18·5	5·8	5·9	6·1
Mineral fuels and related materials	3	26·5	23·8	18·0	9·1	6·2	0·2
Chemicals	5	1·0	1·9	4·0	9·1	12·0	18·0
Machinery and transportation equipment	7	0·2	1·3	3·7	36·1	40·4	49·2
Other manufactured goods	6, 8	7·2	12·8	24·5	27·3	22·9	13·8
Total[b]		100·0	100·0	100·0	100·0	100·0	100·0

Source: Appendix Tables I and II.

[a] Excluding fuels.

[b] Including commodities not classified according to kind, S.I.T.C. section 9.

TABLE 8.4

LATIN AMERICAN EXPORTS AND IMPORTS BY COMMODITY GROUPS, 1956–8 AND 1967–9 WITH PERCENTAGE INCREASES BY GEOGRAPHICAL AREAS

S.I.T.C. Sections

	0–9 Total	0 and 1 Foods	2 and 4 Crude materials	3 Fuels	5 Chemicals	7 Machinery	6 and 8 Other manufactures	6–8 Total manufactures
Exports (million dollars)								
World								
1956–8	8,500	3,963	1,530	2,253	82	17	613	630
1967–9	12,547	5,253	2,280	2,980	243	167	1,607	1,774
Increase	4,047	1,290	750	727	161	150	994	1,144
Per cent of increase								
World	100	100	100	100	100	100	100	100
United States	11	−10	−7	16	19	29	18	19
Canada	7	−2	1	39	—	—	—	—
Western Europe	37	47	42	14	12	7	46	41
Japan	10	5	33	4	2	—	8	7
All others	41	60	31	28	68	63	28	33
Imports (million dollars)								
World								
1956–8	8,060	923	470	733	730	2,910	2,200	5,110
1967–9	12,017	1,297	710	740	1,443	4,857	2,747	7,604
Increase	3,957	374	240	7	713	1,947	547	2,494
Per cent of increase								
World	100	100	100	100	100	100	100	100
United States	11	−9	28	−329	23	16	−19	8
Canada	4	4	10	—	−1	5	6	5
Western Europe	33	18	−4	114	53	46	−1	36
Japan	12	—	4	—	4	12	34	17
All others	40	87	62	314	21	21	80	34

Source: Appendix Tables I and II.

by $1,144 million between 1956–8 and 1967–9. Of this increase the United States consumed only 19 per cent, while Japan accounted for 7 per cent, Western Europe 41 per cent, and Latin America and the rest of the world 33 per cent. Thus the European market was the largest single consuming region for those new lines of standardised manufactured exports in which Latin America has an increasingly competitive position. Had the United States retained its initial share of the market for these commodities (53 per cent in 1956–8), its consumption of manufactured imports from Latin America would have increased to $940 million by 1967–9 rather than the actual $555 million. (There is, of course, no reason to assume that the North American share of the market for Latin America's manufactured goods would have remained constant over time, since the expansion of marketing facilities and diversification of trade ties towards non-Western Hemisphere countries would almost certainly have caused a disproportionate growth in new markets.)

As far as imports are concerned chemicals, machinery and transport equipment (S.I.T.C. categories 5 and 7) have shown the greatest increase at the expense of raw materials, primary products, and light manufactures. Chemical imports in 1967–9 were $713 million above the 1956–8 figure, with Western Europe accounting for 53 per cent of this increase, the U.S. 23 per cent, Japan 4 per cent, and Latin America and the rest of the world 21 per cent. Machinery and transport equipment imports increased by $1,947 million, with Western Europe accounting for 46 per cent of the total growth, the United States 16 per cent, Canada 5 per cent, Japan 12 per cent, and Latin America and the rest of the world 21 per cent. It is apparent from these figures that Western Europe and Japan together have increased their share of the Latin American market in the areas of most rapid import growth by a disproportionately large amount, jointly accounting for 53 per cent of total import growth in the two categories. Thus the changing commodity composition of Latin American trade, reflecting as it does an interaction of changing underlying conditions of supply and demand plus respective commercial and financial policies, has shifted the market towards Europe and Japan for both exports and imports.

The implications of this shift for the United States' share of Latin American trade are revealed in Tables 8.5 and 8.6. Latin American exports to the United States as a share of the total fell from 45 per cent in 1956–8 to 32 per cent in 1967–9. The sharpest declines in relative shares were for machinery and transport equipment (category 7) and other manufactures (categories 6 and 8), each of which fell 22 percentage points, from 53 to 31 per cent of total exports. The smallest decline was for mineral fuels and related materials

TABLE 8.5

EXPORTS TO THE UNITED STATES FROM LATIN AMERICA AS A WHOLE
AND FROM SPECIFIED INDIVIDUAL COUNTRIES, BY COMMODITY GROUPS,
ANNUAL AVERAGES, SPECIFIED YEARS, 1956–69

(Per cent of exports to the world)

Exporter and period	*0–9 Total*	*0 and 1 Foods*	*2 and 4 Crude material*	*3 Fuels*	*5 Chemicals*	*7 Machinery*	*6 and 8 Other manufactures*
				S.I.T.C. Sections			
Latin America							
1956–8	44·7	50·3	35·8	39·0	40·3	52·9	52·9
1967–9	31·7	35·4	21·8	33·3	25·9	31·1	31·3
Colombia							
1962–4	53·7	60·1	18·8	34·6	—	—	54·5
1967–8	42·7	44·0	9·7	58·7	7·1	12·5	35·0
Brazil							
1962–4	36·8	44·5	18·4	66·7	41·2	2·4	22·7
1967–9	30·5	38·8	13·0	—	33·3	10·4	28·2
Chile							
1962–3	35·4	18·8	27·3	—	33·3	—	39·2
1967–8	20·6	33·3	15·0	—	28·6	25·0	21·0
Argentina							
1962–3	9·5	6·7	11·6	4·2	33·3	6·2	24·0
1967–8	10·1	8·0	8·9	50·0	23·4	15·6	29·7
Mexico							
1962–4	68·9	85·3	51·3	96·4	45·9	36·4	66·7
1967–8	63·2	75·6	49·2	98·6	45·6	56·7	53·7

Source: For Latin America, Appendix Table I; for individual countries, U.N., Commodity Trade Statistics (Statistical Papers, Series D), various issues.

TABLE 8.6

IMPORTS FROM THE UNITED STATES BY LATIN AMERICA AS A WHOLE AND BY SPECIFIED INDIVIDUAL COUNTRIES, BY COMMODITY GROUPS, ANNUAL AVERAGES, SPECIFIED YEARS 1956–69

(Per cent of imports from the world)

Importer and period	0–9 Total	0 and 1 Foods	2 and 4 Crude material	3 Fuels	5 Chemicals	7 Machinery	6 and 8 Other manufactures
					S.I.T.C. Sections		
Latin America							
1956–8	50·8	49·1	34·7	23·2	57·9	62·6	44·7
1967–9	37·6	32·2	32·4	19·9	40·7	43·9	31·9
Colombia							
1962–4	49·3	63·0	36·0	57·1	47·2	55·1	37·8
1967–8	47·7	38·5	33·3	50·0	49·0	53·5	35·1
Brazil							
1962–4	32·0	47·4	27·5	13·6	35·6	40·0	19·7
1967–9	32·0	30·9	38·6	17·3	35·6	41·3	24·2
Chile							
1962–3	36·7	25·5	23·6	26·6	37·1	47·7	35·3
1967–8	37·1	15·8	13·3	14·8	38·5	52·4	37·3
Argentina							
1962–3	27·5	6·5	11·7	16·7	34·2	36·8	14·5
1967–8	22·6	3·7	8·4	16·2	29·8	37·6	15·8
Mexico							
1962–4	67·8	80·3	66·0	96·8	63·2	69·2	60·4
1967–8	63·1	55·7	63·8	95·6	62·3	62·4	60·8

Source: As Table 8.5.

(category 3), reflecting in particular the growth of petroleum exports from Venezuela. The U.S. share of the market for Latin American exports in category 3 declined from 39 per cent to 33 per cent during this period.

Of the five countries for which figures were available by commodity group, Chile showed the sharpest decline in *relative* sales to the U.S., falling from 35 per cent in 1962–3 to 21 per cent in 1967–8, or by 14 percentage points. Next in order was Colombia with a decline of 11 percentage points, followed by Brazil and Mexico. Argentina showed a slight gain in United States market shares of plus 0·6 percentage points (Table 8.5).

The United States also experienced a decline in its share of world exports to Latin America, from 51 per cent in 1956–8 to 38 per cent in 1967–9 (Table 8.6). The greatest relative decline was 19 percentage points in machinery and transport equipment, from 63 per cent to 44 per cent. Next were chemicals and the food group, which both declined by 17 per cent. There was a decline of only 2 percentage points in the U.S. share of exports of crude materials, animal and vegetable oils and fats. The U.S. relative share declined most sharply in the case of Mexico, falling from 68 to 63 per cent between 1962–4 and 1967–8. Here the major reductions were in food, beverages and tobacco, and machinery and transport equipment as Mexico replaced imports by domestic output and diversified its purchases towards the rest of the world. Argentina also showed a decline in its relative demand for imports from the U.S. of 4·9 percentage points. There was practically no change in the U.S. share of imports for Colombia, Brazil, and Chile (Table 8.6).

There have been changes in those areas of commodity exports for which Latin America has the clearest comparative advantage with North America relative to the rest of the world, as evidenced by relative trade shares. We shall suppose that those categories of goods which show a share of total Latin American exports exceeding the average U.S. share reveal a comparative advantage in the United States market (Table 8.5). In 1956–8 those categories with a U.S. share greater than the average 45 per cent were S.I.T.C. sections 0–1 and 6–8 (animal and other food products, and manufactures). By 1967–9 the average United States share in total Latin American exports had fallen to 32 per cent, and only the large food group remained clearly above average. The significant share of the United States in the machinery and transport equipment market in the earlier period (1956–8) may be partly explained by the low absolute volume of these exports in those years and the relatively favourable commercial and credit ties with the United States in that period. Machinery and transport equipment exports increased tenfold by 1967–69 but still represented only 1 per cent of Latin American exports, most of the growth being within the region itself, due principally to development of the Latin American Free Trade Area. The United States share in Latin American exports of each commodity group declined from the late 1950s to the late 1960s.

In summary, Latin American commodity trade with the United States has not kept pace with U.S. import growth and has shown a widening gap on merchandise account. In those new areas of comparative advantage for standardised manufactured goods exports, the United States has increased its purchases from Latin America but not in proportion to Latin American sales to Europe, Japan, and other regions. Moreover, the areas of most rapid export growth are now facing increased American threats of protection in the form of higher tariffs, quotas, and even embargoes.[1] It seems unlikely that recent trade trends will lead to a return to liberal trade policies in the United States, a question with which we shall deal in the following section.

II. COMMERCIAL POLICY

Commercial policy barriers clearly stand in the way of the most effective evolution of international comparative advantage and the gains to be derived from a more efficient division of labour. While the focus of this paper is upon trade relations between the United States and Latin America, U.S. commercial policy has in practice reflected measures designed to bring its balance of payments as a whole into equilibrium as well as to achieve full employment in politically sensitive industries, occupations, and regions threatened by increased international competition. Since most U.S. trade is

[1] See A.F.L.–C.I.O., *A Trade Policy for America*, testimony by George Meany before the Subcommittee on International Trade of the Senate Finance Committee, 18 May 1971. This pamphlet attacks both U.S. imports and U.S. foreign investment, which is alleged to have shifted production from the American market to low-wage regions abroad thereby reducing the domestic level of employment. 'The U.S. Department of Labor estimates that there was a loss of about 700,000 job opportunities in the 1966–9 period because of imports.' The argument fails to estimate jobs gained because of new exports induced by greater efficiency of resource allocation, but implies that the balance is strongly negative. It calls for the U.S. government to 'regulate, supervise, and curb the export of American technology', to 'press . . . for the establishment of international fair labor standards in world trade', and 'to regulate the flow of imports into the U.S. of those goods and product lines in which sharply rising imports are displacing significant percentages of U.S. production and employment'. While such anti-free-trade arguments are not untypical of organised labour in any period of American history, they take on increasing weight in periods of recession, high unemployment, and balance of payments deficit such as characterise the early 1970s.

with developed countries, principally Europe, the United Kingdom and Japan, and since the dominant component of changes in comparative advantage arises from the growth of these major nations relative to the United States rather than that of the developing world, the latter tended to receive residual treatment both in the earlier Kennedy Round negotiations which dismantled trade barriers and in the more recent 'Nixon Round' which has re-erected them. Recent United States efforts to effectively devalue the dollar, which included a temporary 10 per cent import surcharge, voluntary export quotas, and negotiated revaluation of foreign currencies, focussed on Europe, Japan, and selected Asian developing countries and tended to neglect implications for the developing countries as a whole.

The United States had earlier pressed for the adoption of multilateral tariff preferences for developing countries on the part of the United States, the E.E.C., Japan and the United Kingdom. Both the Rockefeller and Peterson Commission Reports proposed that if such an agreement on multilateral preferences could not be reached, owing to the special relationships of the United Kingdom and Europe with specific developing countries, then the United States should unilaterally provide preferences to developing countries not so favoured. As cited in the Rockefeller Report:[1]

> The United States should make vigorous efforts to secure agreement on the part of other industrial nations to extend generalised preferences to all developing nations. Until such agreement is reached, the United States would extend preferences only to nations which are not receiving special treatment from other industrial countries.

(In return for these tariff preferences the report proposed that favoured developing countries should progressively lower their barriers against imports from industrial countries.) The argument for special preferences to all developing countries not now enjoying special preferences was echoed in the Peterson Commission report.[2]

Agreement was reached in principle within the O.E.C.D. last year to extend temporary generalised tariff preferences to the developing countries, but the U.S. Congress has provided no enabling legislation. Since then tariff quotas on a more restrictive basis than that proposed by the United States have begun to be implemented by the E.E.C. and Japan on their own. What factors account for the ap-

[1] *The Rockefeller Report on the Americas* (New York Times edition, Quadrangle Books, Chicago, 1969), p. 75.
[2] *U.S. Foreign Assistance in the 1970s: A New Approach*, Report to the President from the Task Force on International Development, Washington, D.C., 4 March 1970, p. 19.

parent reversal in American trade policy from progressive liberalisation under the Kennedy Round to a new aggressive posture involving a surcharge, quotas, and threats of additional restraints on the most competitive lines of imports, plus policies designed to reduce domestic borrowing for overseas investment? Those seeking an explanation must determine the extent to which the new protectionism is a short-term phenomenon as distinct from a re-evaluation of the political economy of trade liberalisation.

There is considerable evidence that the Republican administration favours a relatively free trade and investment policy over the long run. But there is also growing evidence that the administration is prepared to use commercial and financial policy as strong bargaining tools in negotiations for improved U.S. access to foreign markets, more favourable treatment of U.S. investment abroad, and a greater degree of international political co-operation. The recent report of the President's Commission on Trade and Investment takes a moderately liberal position calling for policies to facilitate changes in the structure of American trade, production, and employment to better reflect underlying trends in comparative advantage. According to the report these policies should provide for increased adjustment assistance to labour including 'more generous' benefits for the retraining, upgrading, and relocation of workers displaced by a liberalised trade programme. Moreover, assistance would be requested for firms which find themselves incapable of competing with imports so as to rationalise, modernise, diversify, or convert their capacity to new product lines.[1] Similar measures had been proposed earlier in the Rockefeller Report with respect to liberalisation of trade in the Western Hemisphere. Clearly before such a programme could be adopted, the case would have to be made that the initial cost of adjustment measures in economic terms would be outweighed by the economic benefits to the United States from increased trade liberalisation and greater long-run efficiency. It must also be shown that the political effects of such a liberalisation programme would not be seriously adverse to the administration seeking to implement it. This would almost certainly call for compensation mechanisms of significant proportions financed by the proceeds from expanded trade. While the President's Commission touches on the need for such a mechanism its machinery must be planned in much greater detail in co-operation with the representatives of organised labour, management, and political representatives of those industries and regions most likely to be affected.

[1] *United States International Economic Policy in an Interdependent World*, Report to the President submitted by the Commission on International Trade and Investment Policy, Washington, D.C., July 1971.

At least one earlier attempt to measure the potential economic benefits to developed countries from multilateral liberalisation of trade in manufactured goods predicted only modest gains for the United States. Professor Balassa in his comprehensive study, *Trade Liberalization Among Industrial Countries*,[1] estimated 'revealed comparative advantage' in trade among developed countries during the post-war period in order to project potential gains from trade in industrial materials and manufactured goods (foodstuffs and fuels are excluded) for the United States, the E.E.C., Canada, Japan and the United Kingdom. These gains were calculated in terms of four alternative commercial policy strategies: (a) a free trade area among the industrial countries (Atlantic Free Trade Area), (b) multilateral tariff reductions through the most favoured nation clause with 50 per cent across the board cuts extended unilaterally to non-industrial countries, (c) similar trade concessions among Atlantic industrial countries but excluding the European Common Market, and (d) economic integration of Western Europe.

Balassa's results indicate that with approach (b) substantial gains as measured by the trade share of G.N.P. and in terms of allocative efficiency would be achieved by Canada, Japan and the United Kingdom, while much smaller benefits would accrue to the European Common Market and the United States (op. cit., p. 148 ff.). All other strategies were rejected by the author for their discriminatory bias, but nevertheless none showed significant gains for the U.S. Static export expansion under plan (b) as a share of Gross Domestic Product would amount to 0·5 per cent for the United States, 0·8 per cent for Canada, 1·0 per cent for the European Common Market and the United Kingdom, 2·2 for the continental EFTA, and 2·5 per cent for Japan (*op. cit.*, p. 83). The total trade effect would be most conspicuously favourable to Japan, exports rising by 15 to 16 per cent, and imports rising by 7 to 8 per cent. (For the United States exports would rise by 10 per cent and imports by 11 to 13 per cent.)

Moreover the study indicated that the United States would receive only a small percentage of the dynamic gains from multilateral tariff reductions, as measured by cost reductions through economies of scale and improved production methods resulting from increased international competition. The smaller industrial nations with the highest tariffs had the most to gain from growth of manufacturing beyond the confines of their limited domestic markets. Balassa found it not surprising that the Scandinavian countries, Switzerland and Austria were, in fact, among the strongest advocates of trade liberalisation (*op. cit.*, p. 149). Canada too would gain considerably

[1] Bela Balassa, *Trade Liberalization Among Industrial Countries* (Atlantic Policy Studies Series, McGraw-Hill, New York, 1967).

through greater efficiency since he estimated the present cost of protection in that country to be as high as 3·5 to 4·5 per cent of gross private expenditure (*op. cit.*, p. 159).

With respect to developing countries, Balassa saw two alternative possibilities resulting from trade liberalisation among industrial countries. The establishment of an Atlantic Free Trade Area in which the developed countries would mutually lower internal tariff barriers at the expense of the rest of the world (including the developing countries) would certainly discriminate against the latter (*op. cit.*, p. 167 ff.).

The establishment of an Atlantic Free Trade Area would, then, run counter to the objective of raising living standards and encouraging economic growth in less developed areas. And, aside from its economic effects, such an arrangement would not fail to have unfavorable political repercussions since it would be regarded as a 'rich man's club' in the developing countries. The adverse political effects may, in fact, overshadow the immediate economic consequences.

But could special concessions be offered to the developing nations to offset the losses due to tariff discrimination? I have doubts about the political feasibility of such a scheme. Experience indicates that the national legislatures of the industrial countries tend to regard compensatory measures as a form of foreign aid and are reluctant to increase commitments. Thus, while they may be prepared to accept the 'side effects' of multilateral tariff reductions that automatically benefit third countries, it appears questionable that they would be willing to undertake unilateral obligations – even though these would serve the purpose of compensating for the discriminatory effects of an AFTA.

On the other hand a gradual process of multilateral trade liberalisation among all Western industrial countries on a most favoured nation basis would, in his opinion, have a significantly favourable impact on the growth of developing countries. The impact would be felt first in terms of an initial increase in the market for their exports, and secondly in the derived demand for their trade from increases in G.N.P. of the developed countries through improved allocative efficiency. Frictional problems notwithstanding, he estimated that export earnings of the developing countries might be increased by $7·5 to $9 billion if industrial nations were to apply a mere 1 per cent of the increase of their Gross National Product between 1960 and 1975 to imports from the Third World. 'While an expansion of trade of this magnitude could create few problems in the manufacturing sector of the industrial economies, it would help to deal with the projected $11·3 to $13·7 billion deficit of the developing countries and would contribute importantly to their economic transformation.'[1]

If these calculations are to be believed they indicate that whatever the outcome of international trade liberalisation negotiations, the results are likely to be relatively more important to Latin American trade than to the industrial countries, and more important to EFTA countries and Japan than to the United States. Christopher Clague has estimated that tariff preferences under consideration by the United States, the E.E.C., Japan and the United Kingdom would add a modest $303 million dollars to exports of O.A.S. member countries as of 1975, compared with projected total exports of manufactures in that year of $1,934 million in the absence of preferences.[2]

The impact on Latin American trade of the present U.S. recession is far greater than that of the surcharge. Robert Mundell's application of 'Okun's law' relating potential output to the unemployment rate in the United States suggests that the economic cost of present administration policies to reduce inflation through recession amounted to approximately $64 billion in 1970 and $32 billion in 1971, or a total of $96 billion. Mundell points out that 'this bloodletting is probably the minimum bill for getting inflation to 2 per cent a year by the method adopted and yet it probably understates the actual bill the economy is likely to pay. Spread over two years, $96 billion is greater than the annual G.N.P. of most countries in the world.'[3] Taking $96 billion as a rough rule of thumb of growth foregone in the American economy over the past three years, and applying to it the average coefficient of U.S. merchandise imports from Latin America to G.N.P. of 0·0059 (0·0056 in 1969, 0·0061 in

[1] Balassa, p. 170, citing from his earlier work, *Trade Policies for Developing Countries* (Irwin, Illinois, 1964), pp. 35–6, 104.

[2] Christopher Clague, 'Tariff Preferences and Manufactured Exports of OAS Countries' (unpublished manuscript, July 1971). Clague estimated that total exports by Latin America to the United States, the E.E.C., Japan, and the United Kingdom of 'other manufactures' (excepting shoes, textiles, and clothing exports to the United States, which he assumed did not receive preferential treatment) were $615 million in 1969. That figure was projected to rise on the basis of past trends to $1,934 million in 1975 in the absence of preferences. He concludes that 'Preferences would add another $303 million to O.A.S. exports, most of which ($210 million) would be in the U.S. market' (p. 6). The net growth in exports of 'other manufactures' would be increased by approximately 23 per cent by 1975 owing to a multilateral preference scheme favouring developing countries. The U.S. share of this gain would be 70 per cent. If shoes, clothing, and textiles were included in the preference scheme, the percentage gain in exports of 'other manufactures' to the U.S. due to preferences would be 20 per cent, E.E.C. 11 per cent, Japan 12 per cent, and the United Kingdom 18 per cent.

[3] Robert A. Mundell, *The Dollar and the Policy Mix: 1971*, Essays in International Finance No. 85, International Finance Section, Princeton University, Princeton, New Jersey, May 1971, pp. 16ff.

1970) the shortfall in Latin American exports due to U.S. recession was approximately $560 million. Potential Latin American exports foregone by the slowdown of the American economy between 1969 and 1970 amount to two and one-half times the hypothetical gain in manufactured exports to the United States by 1975 resulting from multilateral trade preferences to developing countries, and almost 50 per cent more than the total gain in exports to all four developed regions by 1975 resulting from such preferences ($380 million).

A number of conclusions follow from the foregoing. First there has been at least a temporary halt in U.S. trade liberalisation policy with respect to the developed countries, tending to postpone the possibility of potential gains which might have accrued to Latin America from multilateral tariff reductions among developed countries applied on a most favoured nation basis. If the present posture of commercial policy confrontation between the U.S. and Europe is associated with the growth of a stronger and more economically independent European Economic Community, this may eventually cause the United States to reconsider Western Hemisphere relations and to re-examine the possibilities of special preferences for its neighbours. Working against such a rapprochement is the increasingly evident desire on the part of Canada, Latin America, and Caribbean countries for greater autonomy in economic and political development. This desire may serve to frustrate whatever efforts may be made by the United States in the future to develop a *de facto* Western Hemisphere trade bloc. Additional opposition to such an eventuality may be expected to arise from Europe, Japan, the Socialist bloc, and other countries in the third world who will increasingly seek to benefit from the expanding Latin American market.

In the possible but improbable event that the U.S. will ultimately extend special preferences to Western Hemisphere developing countries, the greatest gains will be achieved for exports of standardised manufactures and processed raw materials. Comparative advantage in these sectors at present tends to favour only a few Latin American countries, most conspicuously Mexico, Brazil and Colombia, as shown in the previous section. Moreover the overall gains from special preferences would be only a fraction of those which may be expected from increased growth of the American economy, assuming no additional tariffs, quotas, and other restrictions. The recent 10 per cent surcharge had the heaviest negative impact precisely on the most rapid growth areas of Latin American exports. Future unilateral preferences by the United States would in the best of circumstances tend merely to offset the disadvantages of the existing tariff schedule, which taxes disproportionately the more advanced stages of processing raw materials and manufacturing. If Latin American commodity trade with the United States is to continue to expand in such areas, this may well have to be at the expense of Europe and Japan, unless the United States can adopt compensatory measures to offset the loss of jobs to American workers in industries which are losing their comparative advantage.

For political as well as economic reasons, Latin America may be expected to gain a growing marginal share of trade in manufactures and processed raw materials at the expense of Europe and Japan. But this will only come about through negotiations on the basis of bargaining among equals, and such bargaining is only likely to occur between the larger countries of Latin America and the United States, or between institutions representing groups of countries such as the Special Committee for Latin American Co-ordination (CECLA) and the United States. For such bargaining to be effective, Latin American countries must be capable of negotiating from strength. While the larger Latin American countries are demonstrating an increasing ability to engage in such negotiations, the smaller states must rely either upon the use of these countries as spokesmen, or upon a greater degree of regional co-operation. Such co-operation would, presumably, require a greater degree of complementarity in comparative advantage and political economic development objectives than is presently the case for Latin America as a whole, though perhaps not for subregions such as are defined by the Central American, Caribbean, or Andean trading areas. It would also require that Latin American exporters join forces with interest groups in the United States which would benefit from freer trade, including consumer protection groups, importing firms, and marketing outlets (including retail chain stores), as well as industries which import semi-processed intermediate goods. The loss in relative shares of Latin American exports to the U.S. market, described in the preceding section, reflects in part the fact that the natural evolution in comparative advantage of the region has not been accompanied by comparable political, commercial and financial efforts essential to an efficient restructuring of trade.

III. FINANCIAL RELATIONS BETWEEN THE UNITED STATES AND LATIN AMERICA: PAST TRENDS AND FUTURE PROSPECTS

The preceding sections analyse the statistical evidence for changes in the pattern of Latin American comparative advantage as reflected in commodity trade between the region and the rest of the world. The data suggests that those nations which experienced most changes in the structure of commodity trade tended also to be those enjoying relatively rapid rates of growth. This may be explained in part as a cause and in part an effect of the interaction between trade and growth. For economies heavily dependent upon trade and faced with exogenous changes in external demand, the ability to transform the structure of the economy is essential for growth. For economies faced with the possibility of expanding rapidly in some sectors relative to others, and for which internal demand grows in a more balanced fashion, the opportunity to trade will permit growth to take place more rapidly than under autarchy. In this section we shall show how the relationship between trade and growth may be more fully understood in terms of the relationship between growth and international finance.

A simple model is developed to illustrate how regional development potentials, and regional preferences for development, may differ. It will be shown that in autarchy (the absence of interregional capital movements) such conditions will lead to different equilibrium rates of return on capital in the different regions (or countries). But once the possibility of interregional and international financial exchange is introduced, overall output growth possibilities will be increased and both regions will be able to achieve a higher rate of income growth than before trade. Thus, growth may be said to depend upon both optimal trade flows (in response to shifts in the pattern of comparative advantage at any point in time) and optimal international financial flows (in response to intertemporal comparative advantage) and the two may be regarded as interdependent.

The approach taken is to apply the concept of comparative advantage, as developed for the analysis of international trade in goods and services at one point in time, to the exchange of goods and services between two or more periods of time. This permits the formulation of a theoretical model which relates initial factor endowments to production functions and intertemporal preferences. The model then shows the rate of growth that may be expected in equilibrium in the absence of financial flows between the economy and the rest of the world. It also shows the gains in output and/or income growth associated with interregional (and international) financial flows in cases where growth possibilities differ sharply from region to region (or among countries). The model illustrates that apparent 'disequilibria' in the balance of trade (an excess of imports or exports of goods and services) may well reflect the equilibrium of demand and supply for present and future goods and services under conditions of unequal intertemporal comparative advantage.[1] In cases where

---

[1] A similar though independent analysis was developed by Professor Norman C. Miller, 'A General Equilibrium Theory of International Capital Flows', *The*

trade and growth are closely associated, changes in the structure of trade may well be related to disequilibria in the balance of trade through the additional relationship between growth and international finance.

A SIMPLE MODEL OF INTERTEMPORAL COMPARATIVE ADVANTAGE

It is assumed that homogeneous goods are being produced by potential trading nations and that the production possibilities in each country may be expressed in terms of identical units of present goods and future consumer goods. It will be supposed that existing factors of production may be utilised to produce a given consumable directly in the present or indirectly in the future by using some present resources for producers' goods production. Future goods are said to be produced for simplicity at a single point in time in the manner of the traditional Irving Fisher diagram illustrating the determination of the rate of interest.[1] Thus, present versus future production possibilities are illustrated by an intertemporal produc-

---

Economic Journal, June 1968, pp. 312–20. His model illustrates international capital flows in terms of offer curves of countries with differing intertemporal comparative advantage. While not applied to the development context this analysis is extremely suggestive.

[1] Irving Fisher, *The Theory of Interest* (1930), reprinted: Augustus Kelly, 1970, New York, Part III. The derivation of the intertemporal production frontier in Figs. 8.2 to 8.6 is taken from W. Leontief, 'Theoretical Note on Time-Preference, Productivity of Capital, Stagnation, and Economic Growth', *American Economic Review* (March 1958), as elaborated by Robert Baldwin, 'The Role of Capital Goods Trade in the Theory of International Trade', *American Economic Review* (September 1966). The formal analytical steps missing in these diagrams represent (1) the use of present resources to produce present consumer or capital goods, (2) the relationship between present capital goods production and future consumer goods production (marginal productivity of capital), and (3) the resulting trade-off between present and additional future consumer goods production as illustrated by the horizontal and vertical axes in the diagrams. The vertical axis measures *additional* consumer goods from point 0 assuming that productive capacity will be at least maintained such that at point 0 output would be equal to the maximum possible production of consumer goods in the initial period. In cases where the marginal productivity of capital is lower, or where the possibility of transforming production from consumer to capital goods is less and/or where the possibilities of present exchange of consumer for capital goods through trade are impeded, that economy's intertemporal production frontier will be less steep (case *B*) as opposed to more favoured economies (case *A*). The analysis is developed more fully in Reynolds, 'Intertemporal Comparative Advantage: A Basis for Integrating Real and Financial Flows' (draft). See also B. Ohlin, *Interregional and International Trade*, revised edition (Harvard, 1967), and R. Eckhaus and L. Lefeber, 'Capital Formation: A Theoretical and Empirical Analysis', *Review of Economics and Statistics* (May 1962).

tion frontier such as $T_aT_{a'}$ in Fig. 8.2 for economy A. This economy is drawn as having a strong growth potential, that is as having resource endowments relatively well equipped to produce future rather than present consumer goods, subject to a diminishing marginal rate of transformation. It is assumed that the preferences of consumers in economy A may be expressed by community indifference curves of the form $U_aU_{a'}$, though we recognise the conceptual problems which such a convention entails. The pattern of consumer preferences between present and future goods is assumed to be influenced by the age composition of the population, the level and variance of expected future earnings, relative income, present levels of income and wealth, and intertemporal tastes.

Economy A may be said to characterise a less developed country, such as Brazil, with strong growth potential but moderately low levels of *per capita* income, close to a subsistence minimum and thus with a low capacity for savings. Intertemporal consumer indifference curves are accordingly drawn to bias demand in favour of present over future goods, while transformation possibilities are drawn to favour the production of future over present goods. At the point of

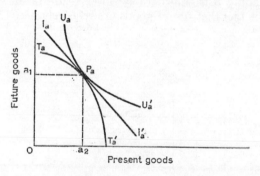

FIG. 8.2. Economy A: Strong growth potential (before trade).

tangency between the production frontier and the highest possible indifference curve (P_a) marginal rates of transformation and substitution between future and present goods may be shown to be equal, represented by the slope of $i_a\,i_{a'}$ which, as in the Fisher analysis, represents the pure domestic rate of interest. Thus P_a is the point of intertemporal equilibrium for economy A in perfect competition in the absence of trade (exchange of present and future goods with other economies) or capital market policies which would alter domestic relative prices. This equilibrium could be affected, for example by interest rate ceilings in economy A below the rate of $i_a\,i_{a'}$ raising the relative price of future over present goods to lenders and lowering the price to borrowers. This would shift production in the direction of present goods causing excess demand for loans by those wishing to produce future goods. The resulting movement along the frontier $T_a \, T_{a'}$ downward and to the right would reduce welfare by forcing consumption to shift to a lower indifference curve.

Economy B in Fig. 8.3 characterises a country with moderate growth potential, such as Venezuela, the shape of production frontier $T_b \, T_{b'}$ favouring the production of present over future goods relative to that of Economy A. Such conditions might well reflect a higher level of economic development, and/or an economy whose development depends on a non-renewable resource. The marginal productivity of capital may be assumed to be subject to strongly diminishing returns as the economy grows. On the other hand, with higher *per capita* incomes consumer preferences may be biased more in favour of future over present consumption as compared with economy A. Indifference curves are drawn accordingly to show a bias in favour of future over present goods compared with economy A. The community indifference curve $U_b \, U_{b'}$ is tangential to production frontier $T_b \, T_{b'}$ at point P_b, at equilibrium rate of interest $i_b \, i_{b'}$. The interest rate in economy B is considerably lower than that of economy A, reflecting the fact that future goods are relatively more expensive in

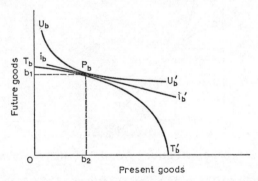

FIG. 8.3. Economy B: Moderate growth potential (before trade).

terms of present goods than in economy A due to the bias of production possibilities and consumer preferences. Despite the high price of future goods, the consumption bias causes the economy to produce O_{b_1} of future goods relative to O_{b_2} of present goods in the absence of trade.

Economy C (Fig. 8.4) is drawn to represent less fortunate developing countries or regions which have relatively little capacity to channel present resources into the production of future goods while at the same time they face a relatively strong demand for present

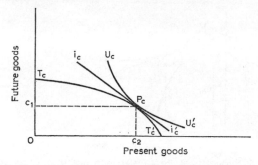

FIG. 8.4. Economy C: Weak growth potential (before trade).

over future consumption because of low initial *per capita* income. Here the production of future goods is O_{c_1} and of present goods O_{c_2} in the absence of trade, with the internal interest rate i_c $i_{c'}$ somewhere between those of economies A and B. While this case may more closely reflect the condition of many developing countries than one would like to believe, it is not focussed upon in this paper since the production and consumption effects of the convergence of international interest rates through trade will almost certainly be less extreme, with ambiguous implications for comparative advantage in present versus future production and for gains from international financial flows.

We see then that in the absence of intertemporal exchange the relative price of present to future goods (equal to the real rate of return on capital) may well differ among economies, enabling the realisation of potential gains from interregional or international financial flows. Those exchanging present for future goods will acquire promises to pay in the form of financial assets,[1] to be exchanged at a later date for 'future goods'. The barriers to intertemporal exchange are similar to those affecting the contemporaneous exchange of goods and services, such as tariffs, quotas, licenses, transport costs, information costs, and quality differentials. The difference is that since intertemporal transactions customarily involve the exchange of goods for financial assets, barriers may well be raised against the latter. The influence of such barriers to intertemporal exchange can be analysed as in conventional trade theory by showing a divergence between domestic and international real rates of interest.

Suppose that economies A and B are no longer encumbered by barriers to international exchange of future for present goods. The

[1] Present claims on future goods or promises to pay in the form of future goods, normally expressed in terms of nominal units of a national currency.

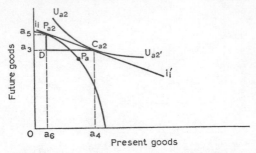

FIG. 8.5. Economy A: Strong growth potential (after trade).

effect of intertemporal exchange on the respective economies is revealed in Figs. 8.5 and 8.6. In the case of Economy A with strong growth potential and with weak future preferences, buyers and sellers are faced with a lower international price ratio of present to future goods than the domestic interest rate i_a $i_{a'}$. With trade the international interest rate becomes the domestic rate and producers shift to production point P_{a_2} where the marginal rate of transformation equals the new interest rate. Consumers shift to point C_{a_2} from P_a, improving welfare, since C_{a_2} is on the higher indifference curve U_{a_2} $U_{a_2'}$. In the first period economy A imports present goods $a_6 - a_4$ in exchange for claims on future goods $a_3 - a_5$. Production is now O_{a_6} of present goods and O_{a_5} of future goods. Society finds itself at a higher level of utility than before trade, but the balance of trade in the initial period becomes negative due to the net import of present goods $a_6 - a_4$. This is just offset by claims on future goods. In the future period the balance of trade will be positive by an amount of future goods $a_3 - a_5$. Measured at the international interest rate of i_i $i_{i'}$ the present value of the future balance of trade surplus exactly equals that of the initial deficit. The reflection of the balance of trade deficit (debit balance) in the initial period will be a capital account surplus (credit) in the same amount. The reverse will hold in the future period as the trade balance will show a credit and the capital account a debit of equal amount.

In the case of economy B with only moderate growth potential and strong future preferences, openness to intertemporal exchange brings about a lower relative price of future goods as indicated by the international interest rate i_i $i_{i'}$. In the absence of transport costs, direct and indirect controls, and other barriers to intertemporal exchange, interest rates in economies A and B will equalise for identical transactions as shown in the similar slopes of the i_i $i_{i'}$ curves in Figs. 8.5 and 8.6. However, the impact on resource allocation in the two economies will differ. Production in economy A will shift from

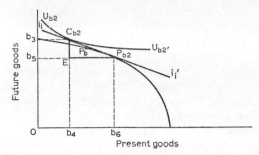

FIG. 8.6. Economy B: Moderate growth potential (after trade).

present to future goods moving from P_a to P_{a_2}. Income effects will dominate substitution effects increasing consumption of both present and future goods despite the relatively higher price of the latter with trade. Production in economy B will shift towards present from future goods moving from P_b to P_{b_2}. Because of the consumption bias favouring future over present goods, however, income and substitution effects combine to cause an increase in future over present goods consumption as indicated in the movement from consumption point P_b to C_{b_2}.

Assume that economy A and economy B are exclusive trading partners. Then economy A's equilibrium commodity trade deficit $a_6 - a_4$ in the form of present goods imports will be exactly offset by economy B's trade surplus in the initial period $b_4 - b_6$. In the future period, however, economy A will have a net surplus of future goods on commodity account $a_3 - a_5$ which will be exactly offset by economy B's deficit $b_5 - b_3$. Pareto optimality in intertemporal international exchange gives rise to net debtor–net creditor relationships which reflect underlying differences in intertemporal production possibilities and consumer preferences among regions, nations, and even sectors of a given economy.[1]

---

[1] This discussion deals with the relationship between trade and investment among countries which arises from portfolio decisions reflecting international differences in growth potential. Note that in the ideal frictionless case interest rates tend to equalise through the process of exchange. This is most relevant for indirect capital movements. Direct investments are more likely to reflect decisions to capitalise on opportunities to earn a return not only on capital goods but on other scarce factors such as entrepreneurship and technology which may well earn rents well in excess of a 'normal return on capital'. Such transactions are distinct from international capital movements in which the 'interest rate' or relative price of present and future goods as reflected in the internal capital market plays an important role. Direct investment decisions tend to be far more specific, focusing on individual sectors and activities, and enterprises are more sensitive to international disequilibria in relative prices of other factors such as entrepreneurship, technology, and the opportunity cost of monopoly or monopsony

IMPLICATIONS OF THE MODEL OF INTERTEMPORAL
COMPARATIVE ADVANTAGE FOR U.S. – LATIN AMERICAN
FINANCIAL FLOWS

One main implication of the foregoing analysis for U.S.–Latin American trade and financial relations is that in equilibrium one would expect to find differences in production potential or consumer demand reflected not in differential rates of interest among countries but in the balance of trade. One would expect interest rates to be relatively the same among countries in Latin America while their balance of trade position with the U.S. would be highly dissimilar. Those regions with a strong growth potential should be running a balance of trade deficit on current account offsetting a surplus on capital account. In addition, one would expect the capital account to reflect a relatively large proportion of long-term credits (or shorter term 'roll over' credits which tend to be substituted for long-term lending by international creditors who are averse to taking risks and prefer to maximise liquidity.[1]

---

in goods and factor markets than to international interest rate differentials. In practice the balance of payments of an economy open to international lending and borrowing is influenced by transactions over many periods past, present, and future. The overall balance of payments position is a reflection of the weighted average of these multiperiod transactions expressed in terms of commodity and financial asset flows in the present period. Since growth potential is likely to reflect the stage of a country's development, with diminishing returns to future over present goods production setting in over time, one may expect the economy to gradually evolve from stage *A* to stage *B* and its balance of payments on current account to shift from deficit to surplus as the capital account shifts from net debtor to net creditor. This 'age cycle' of the balance of payments is discussed in C. P. Kindleberger, *Foreign Trade in the National Economy* (Yale University Press, 1964), chapter 11.

[1] Observed differentials in nominal rates of interest in Latin America are misleading to the extent that discounts for risk, liquidity, and inflation should be taken into consideration before a comparison is made. Moreover, controls on financial transactions tend to cause lenders and borrowers to circumvent the institutional financial market in many countries such that the 'interest rate' is not reflected in reported transactions. Here the institutional credit markets are likely to be in disequilibrium (excess demand for loanable funds) while net lenders place their funds in the informal credit markets ('*mercado extra bancario*' or '*mercado informal*') and abroad. In such cases the 'interest rates' of primary relevance to this analysis would be those for financial assets and liabilities most likely to be influenced by conditions in the international capital market. Portfolios of such assets must be assumed to adjust freely so that interest rates in the 'internal capital market' subject to the least disequilibrium (quite possibly the informal credit market) will faithfully reflect the international 'price' of future over present goods. To this observer of Latin American capital markets, the real rates of return on financial assets of given term and risk in the informal credit market tend to be comparable for the major countries, and to be highly sensitive to changes in

The above analysis shows that regardless of the preference of policy makers in a developing country for growth, market-induced net resource transfers from the more developed countries are not likely to occur unless the desire to grow is matched by a comparative advantage favouring growth. Furthermore, consumption preferences favouring future over present goods by no means indicate that the structure of production of an open economy will shift towards future over present goods production unless the underlying transformation possibilities favour future goods. Otherwise its citizens are likely to send their savings (present goods consumption foregone) abroad in exchange for future goods imports. In an economy with a comparative advantage favouring present over future production, attempts to alter tastes, thereby shifting indifference curves upward and to the left, corresponding to those of economy *B*, will cause domestic interest rates to *fall* relative to international interest rates, forcing capital to seek outlets abroad, an outflow the counterpart of which will be an export surplus in exchange for future imports. By such behaviour individuals seeking to maximise present plus future consumption will work directly against policy objectives, since investments placed abroad at a significantly higher rate of return than the repressed domestic interest rates offered will give greater long-term utility than those placed at home at a lower rate of return. Alternatively policymakers may try to cheapen credit domestically by placing a ceiling on lending and/or borrowing rates below the potential equilibrium rates of interest. Our model illustrates that this will serve to increase the gap between domestic and foreign rates of return and thus to increase the potential outflow of savings and reduce the availability of credit to domestic borrowers.

One would expect balance of trade deficits and surpluses to arise among countries in response to desired patterns of intertemporal exchange, such that regions with a strong growth potential would be likely to be in deficit to regions with moderate or weak growth potential. Growth potential is likely to be influenced by initial endowments of natural resources, physical and human capital (including the possibility of developing resource-based 'vent for surplus' commodities for export), political stability, absolute population size, and integration of the economy through transport and communications networks. The absence of any of these conditions may make of a potentially strong growth region one of

---

prime international rates of interest. If all internal credit markets are in initial disequilibrium, and if some markets remain in severe disequilibrium after the adjustment to 'free trade' in financial assets, the result will be a second-best solution which does not necessarily assure an optimal intertemporal allocation of resources. The writer is indebted to Sven Arndt for this point.

moderate or weak growth potential. For example, extreme political instability through either internal or external causes will substantially increase the discount for risk attached to expected future income and product, thereby raising the effective price of future over present goods with a resultant flight of savings to more stable regions. Limited or unbalanced resource endowments may also prevent a region from exhibiting significant growth potential, such as export monocultures based upon exhaustible resources in which opportunities for diversification of the structure of production are limited.

Success does not always breed success and previous growth may actually bring about destabilising political and social conditions, such as in the case where growth results in a greater inequality in the distribution of income and wealth which may hamper future growth. The stage of a country's development may influence its growth potential, to the extent that diminishing returns set in to the expansion of basic sectors of the economy. For all of these reasons one would expect Latin American countries to exhibit dissimilar comparative advantages in terms of present versus future goods pro-

TABLE 8.7

ELEVEN LATIN AMERICAN COUNTRIES:
MERCHANDISE EXPORTS AND IMPORTS,
ANNUAL AVERAGES 1956–8, 1967–9, AND 1970
(Millions of U.S. dollars)

Country	1956–8		1967–9		1970	
	Exports	Imports	Exports	Imports	Exports	Imports
Argentina	971	1,224	1,481	1,280	1,770	1,680
Bolivia	71	80	162	162	—	—
Brazil	1,373	1,170	1,949	1,763	2,739	2,450
Chile	419	423	897[a]	790[a]	—	—
Colombia	603	478	613	576	796	821
Ecuador	131	99	200	203	—	—
Mexico	777	1,127	1,280	1,933	1,399	2,478
Paraguay	36	41	52	74	—	—
Peru	315	356	827	711	1,032	695
Uruguay	159	206	180	167	—	—
Venezuela	2,498	1,484	2,531	1,526	—	—
Total						
Gross	7,353	6,688	10,172	9,185	—	—
Net	665		987			
Total excluding Venezuela						
Gross	4,855	5,204	7,641	7,659	—	—
Net		349		18		

Source: International Monetary Fund, *Balance of Payments Yearbook*, various issues.

[a] 1967–8 average.

duction, different intertemporal preference patterns, and therefore different balance of payments relationships with the rest of the world, even in the absence of disturbing political conditions. One would expect to see these factors reflected in the pattern of capital movements between such countries and the United States. It is also to be expected that regional averages would cancel out these differences and obscure the nature of the development process through trade. This is indeed the case as we shall see.

Net capital flows are measured by the opposite sign of the net balance of trade, while the balance of payments on current account also includes invisibles, which reflect servicing of previous investment. For the eleven major Latin American countries for which we have detailed statistics in comparable values, their summed balances of payments on current account with the rest of the world have been in deficit since the mid 1950s: – $1,135 million on the average in 1956–8 and – $1,745 million in 1967–9 (Tables 8.7 and 8.8). None of these countries ran an annual average credit balance of payments on current account in 1956–8 or in 1967–9. In 1956–8 the Mexican share of the overall deficit for the ten countries excluding Venezuela

TABLE 8.8

ELEVEN LATIN AMERICAN COUNTRIES: NET DEFICIT ON MERCHANDISE TRADE AND ON CURRENT ACCOUNT (NET TRADE IN GOODS AND SERVICES), ANNUAL AVERAGES 1956–8, 1967–9, AND 1970[a]
(Millions of U.S. dollars)

Country	1956–8		1967–9		1970	
	Merchand-ise	Current account	Merchand-ise	Current account	Merchand-ise	Current account
Argentina	253	229	+201	17	+90	134
Bolivia	9	30	0	50	—	—
Brazil	+203	176	+186	423	+289	502
Chile	4	82	+107[b]	131[b]	—	—
Colombia	+125	50	+37	166	25	293
Ecuador	+32	14	3	76	—	—
Mexico	350	156	653	709	1,079	1,057
Paraguay	5	10	22	35	—	—
Peru	41	126	+116	106	+337	110
Uruguay	47	44	+13	+2	—	—
Venezuela	+1,014	218	+1,005	32	—	—
Total	+665	1,135	+987	1,745	—	—
Total excluding Venezuela	349	917	18	1,713	—	—

Source: As Table 8.7.

[a] Debit balance, except as marked + for credit balance.
[b] 1967–8 average.

was 17 per cent, that of Brazil 19 per cent, and that of Argentina 25 per cent ($156 million, $176 million, and $229 million, respectively). In 1967–9 the Mexican share of the deficit was 41 per cent of the ten-country deficit ($709 million) and that of Brazil 25 per cent ($423 million).

Brazil and Mexico have dominated the current account deficit of the eleven Latin American countries during the 1960s, the relative importance of Mexico increasing by the end of the period. Both countries had economies with significant growth potential. Mexico throughout the period and Brazil in the second half were characterised by relatively stable political administrations. The rate of growth and rate of return on capital was greater in each country than in the United States. It is not surprising that such economies reflect a net inflow of U.S. investment in their balance of trade, to the point that both have accumulated substantial gold and foreign exchange reserves.

From the previous model we see that growth in productive capacity will result from international capital movements only under circumstances in which the capital importing country has a comparative advantage in growth. Otherwise foreign capital inflows will tend to displace domestic savings which go abroad seeking higher rates of return. It is clear that Latin America is pushing to develop within severe resource, political, and social constraints. Most governments pursue a goal of development through growth rather than through redistribution of present income and therefore attempt to maximise the production of future over present goods. The opportunity to run an import surplus (through foreign borrowing) may permit an expansion of the domestic resource base (at some cost to future national income) *if* pre-trade marginal rates of transformation of present to future goods exceed the level of international interest rates. Otherwise attempts to borrow abroad will be self-defeating (such an economy may be said to have no savings constraint and in our model no savings constraint means no import constraint).

In the case of Venezuela international interest rates have tended to exceed the expected domestic rate of return on investments of comparable risk so that in each of the years 1960–67 that country had a significant credit balance on current account, and for the years 1950 to 1969 a surplus on merchandise account. (Owing to the periods chosen in Table 8.8 the balance on current account appears slightly negative in both intervals.) Economies like Venezuela based on extractive industries are frequently net lenders abroad since the domestic marginal return on capital is not attractive to recipients of rent on scarce resources. If Brazil and Mexico are described by case *A* in Fig. 8.2, and Venezuela case *B*, most Latin American countries

LATIN AMERICA'S BALANCE OF PAYMENTS WITH THE UNITED STATES IN GOODS AND SERVICES, IN MERCHANDISE TRADE AND IN INVESTMENT INCOMES, ANNUAL AVERAGES 1946-8, 1956-8, 1961-3, AND 1967-9[a]

(Millions of U.S. dollars)

Item	Latin American Republics			Other W. Hemisphere	Latin American Republics and other W. Hemisphere		Line no.[b]
	1946-8	1956-8	1961-3	1961-3	1961-3	1967-9[a]	
Goods and services							
Imports	3,949	5,982	5,375	634	6,009	8,804	1
Exports	2,723	4,655	4,370	834	5,204	7,095	14
Balance	-1,226	-1,327	-1,005	200	-805	-1,709	23
Merchandise[c]							
Imports	3,056	4,211	3,358	331	3,689	5,158	3
Exports	2,267	3,820	3,423	497	3,920	5,002	15
Balance	-789	-391	+65	+166	+231	-156	—
Income paid on U.S. private investment in Latin America							
Rent	394	774	764	126	890	1,228	11
Other assets	17	57	164	4	168	408	12
Total	411	831	928	130	1,058	1,636	21
Income received from private investments in the U.S.	10	21	46	7	53	272	—
Net paid in investments	-401	-810	-882	-123	-1,005	-1,364	—

Source: U.S. balance of payments tables with reversed directions – i.e. showing U.S. exports to Latin America as Latin America's imports from U.S., etc. Data are as reported in U.S. Department of Commerce, Office of Business Economics, *Balance of Payments Statistical Supplement*, revised edition (1963), and *Survey of Current Business* (June 1968 and March 1971).

[a] Starting with data for 1964 the Office of Business Economics no longer publishes data for the Latin American Republics separately from 'Other Western Hemisphere'.

[b] Line numbers in *Survey of Current Business* (June 1965 and March 1971).

[c] Excluding military.

are somewhere in between, as we shall see below, having neither a strong comparative advantage nor disadvantage in growth and hence reflecting neither a strong deficit nor surplus in the balance of trade. The net direction of international capital flows for such countries is difficult if not impossible to predict and the gains from intertemporal trade are likely to be modest to the extent that internal rates of interest before trade are probably less divergent from international lending and borrowing rates than those of economies of type A or B.

The principal contribution to Latin America's deteriorating balance of payments on current account with the United States in the past decade has come from invisibles (Table 8.9). For the wider area including 'Other Western Hemisphere'[1] the current account deficit was − \$805 million in 1961–3 and − \$1,709 million in 1967–9. Of the latter amount − \$1,364 million represents the net income on U.S. investments abroad, a figure which has risen from approximately − \$400 million in 1946–8. Invisible items in the balance of payments, and particularly income on U.S. investments abroad, represent the major destabilising factors. Latin American countries appear to be eliciting new investments from the United States in order to service previous American investments without having to run an increasing commodity trade surplus. To the extent that the U.S. government provides net credit flows to Latin American governments, and net payment of interest and principal flow back to private individuals in the United States, this represents a transfer of funds in the developed countries from the taxpayers in general to those who previously elected to invest in Latin America. It is not surprising, therefore, that strong second thoughts are being raised in Congress about the wisdom of continuing a 'foreign assistance' programme which in effect represents a subsidy from U.S. taxpayers to U.S. investors who set up shop in the Third World. To the extent that such public credit flows at subsidised rates, this allows such investors to re-finance abroad at below equilibrium rates of interest or receive rates of return at above equilibrium yields since the funds being used to service these payments are being obtained at below their private opportunity cost in the developing countries.)[2]

[1] See footnote 1, pp. 243–4 for a discussion of the data problems.

[2] The argument may be raised that such indirect subsidies of American direct investments abroad are, on the margin, favourable to the interests of the American public to the extent that they increase the demand for American exports of capital goods, provide cheaper imports to U.S. consumers, and increase the general purchasing power of Latin American countries for American goods and services. It is not likely that the continuing demand for U.S. replacement parts and intermediate goods by American firms located in Latin America would be sufficient

U.S. PRIVATE INVESTMENT IN LATIN AMERICA

What is the pattern of U.S. private investment in the Western Hemisphere? Should one expect the future U.S. portfolio of real and financial assets to shift towards Latin America? The model would suggest that this would depend largely on Latin American comparative advantage for growth compared to that of the United States. It does not, however, deal with cases in which private investment seeks to take advantage of market imperfections (e.g. import restrictions) in another region, or where externalities of the nationals of the investing country arise from political, military or other ties. Annual net U.S. capital outflows have increased from $1,675 million in 1960

TABLE 8.10

U.S. DIRECT INVESTMENT ABROAD WITH COMPARISONS, 1960 TO 1970

Item	1960	1965	1970	*Sums* 1960–5	1966–70
U.S. direct investment abroad					
Total (*million dollars*)	− 1,674	− 3,468	− 3,967	− 12,698	− 17,044
Latin America*a*					
Million dollars	− 149	− 272	− 555	− 1,017	− 2,180
Per cent of total	8·9	7·8	14·0	8·0	12·8
U.S. Gross National Product (G.N.P.)					
Billion dollars	503·7	684·9	974·1	3,491·9	4,311·2
U.S. gross private domestic investment					
Billion dollars	74·8	108·1	135·3	518·8	637·1
Per cent of G.N.P.	14·9	15·8	13·9	14·9	14·8
Per cent of gross private domestic investment					
Total U.S. direct investment abroad	2·2	3·2	2·9	2·4	2·7
U.S. direct investment to Latin America	0·2	0·3	0·4	0·2	0·3

Source: U.S. 'net direct private investment' (net private capital flows) abroad from balance of payments data in U.S. Department of Commerce, Office of Business Economics, *Survey of Current Business* (June 1968, June 1970 and March 1971) (line 33). U.S. Gross National Product and gross private domestic investment from *ibid.* (July 1971), p. 46.

a Latin American Republics and other Western Hemisphere.

---

to offset the loss of demand for finished goods through import substitution. On the other hand, if such investments abroad produced goods which competed effectively with American manufactures, the U.S. economy would have to adjust its structure to permit continued full employment unless, of course, a growing amount of potential available labour time were shifted to leisure pursuits by those clipping coupons on investments in the Third World.

to $3,468 million in 1965, and $3,967 million in 1970.[1] The share of net U.S. capital outflows to Latin America has risen from 8·9 per cent in 1960 to 14·0 per cent in 1970, the average rising from 8·0 per cent for the period 1960–5 to 12·8 per cent for 1966–70.

This is a noteworthy development in that despite political disturbances in the Western Hemisphere and increasing opposition to foreign direct investment in many quarters, the proportion of U.S. private investments placed in Latin America has increased conspicuously. Nevertheless, the total amounted to only $149 million in 1960, $272 million in 1965, and $555 million in 1970. The cumulative total of U.S. net capital outflows to Latin America between 1966 and

TABLE 8.11

U.S. NET PRIVATE CAPITAL FLOWS TO LATIN AMERICA
AND OTHER WESTERN HEMISPHERE: TOTAL,
AND FOR SELECTED COUNTRIES, 1960 TO 1969[a]
(Millions of U.S. dollars)

				Sums	
Country	1960	1965	1970[b]	1960–5	1966–70
Total	149	271	559	1,170	2,214
Latin American Republics	95	176	307	624	1,457
Mexico	56	99	87	344	267
Panama	30	20	103	94	291
Other Central America[c]	+17	26	22	77	191
Argentina	70	16	46	322	192
Brazil	83	+6	103	54	376
Chile	2	23	+56	60	+94
Colombia	15	11	+5	67	113
Peru	7	55	+40	95	97
Venezuela	+150	+93	+9	+530	+153
Other[d]	+1	24	56	39	178
Other Western Hemisphere[e]	54	95	252	547	752

Source: As for Table 8.10, various issues.

[a] Figures are net outflow from U.S. except as marked + for inflow. Small differences between the totals shown here and in Table 8.9 are due to later revisions for the totals not published for individual countries.

[b] Revised.

[c] Includes Costa Rica, El Salvador, Guatemala, Honduras and Nicaragua.

[d] Includes Bolivia, Dominican Republic, Ecuador, Haiti, Paraguay and Uruguay.

[e] Includes all Western Hemisphere except Canada and the 19 Latin American Republics listed in *c* and *d*.

[1] Row 33 ('direct investments') which in fact represents total net capital outflows as reported in the United States balance of payments, *Survey of Current Business* (June 1970 and March 1971). The concept is explained in U.S. Department of Commerce, *U.S. Direct Investments Abroad, 1966, Part I: Balance of Payments Data* (1970), p. 15f.

1970 was $2,180, or less than three-tenths of 1 per cent of U.S. gross investment in the same five-year interval. Total U.S. private investment abroad as reported in the balance of payments amounts to only 3 per cent of gross private domestic investment, which from 1966 to 1970 averaged 14·8 per cent of G.N.P.

Although only a minimal share of new savings being generated in the United States is being invested in Latin America, this does not assure that the funds will have a minimal impact on economic decision making in the region. Latin American gross domestic product in 1970 was less than 20 per cent of the U.S. figure, or approximately $142 billion (in 1960 prices).[1] Assuming a capital/output ratio of 2·5, the value of Latin America's G.D.P. in 1970 reflecting changing U.S. private investment during the 1960s would have amounted to only $1·3 billion or less than 3 per cent of the estimated growth of Latin American output from 1960 to 1970 ($57 billion).[2] With the same capital output ratio the increased capital stock required to produce this additional flow of output would have been approximately $143 billion as compared with the net change in capital stock due to U.S. net investment in the sixties of $3·2 billion. Even if U.S. private investment abroad had involved an indirect control over Latin American assets amounting to twice its nominal value, or $6·4 billion, this would still have represented only 4·5 per cent of the total increase in capital stock required for growth in the sixties.

Cumulative United States net private investment in Latin American Republics and 'Other Western Hemisphere' between 1960 and 1965 was $1,170 million, of which 29 per cent was in Mexico ($344 million) and 28 per cent in Argentina ($322 million). Net disinvestment in Venezuela was – $530 million, presumably reflecting the depletion of U.S. owned petroleum reserves. From 1966 to 1970 U.S. net private investment in the region rose to a total of $2,214 million, of which Latin American Republics accounted for $1,457 million and 'Other Western Hemisphere' (principally the Caribbean) $752 million. Mexico's share of the total was only 12 per cent ($267 million), while that of Brazil increased to 17 per cent ($376 million). In both periods Panama and other Central American countries accounted for a significant share of the total, 15 per cent in 1960–5 and 22 per cent in 1966–70.

[1] *United Nations Economic Survey of Latin America 1969* (New York, 1970), p. 44. Based upon the application of an assumed 6·4 per cent rate of growth to the 1969 figure of 133,142 million 1960 dollars (U.S. G.N.P. for 1970, in 1958 prices, was approximately $724 billion).

[2] Taking the U.N. figures for Latin American gross domestic product in 1960 of $84,688 million (1960 U.S. dollars), 1969, $133,142 million, and our estimate for 1970 of $141,663 million, giving a net growth between 1960 and 1970 of $56,975 million.

One of the hypotheses proposed in the earlier part of this section was that economies with a comparative advantage in growth would be likely to be net attractors of foreign investment, relative to those with less growth potential. We have seen that the performance of the overall balance of payments on current account of specific Latin American countries tends to support this hypothesis during the post-war period. It is reasonable to expect that the case of foreign direct investment will be considerably more complex, since direct investment decisions are less sensitive to international interest rate differentials than to relative opportunities to earn a return on other scarce factors such as technology, entrepreneurship, and marketing techniques. Yet a look at those Latin American countries receiving the most U.S. direct investment in the 1960s is quite revealing in terms of our theory.

TABLE 8.12

RANK ORDER OF NINE LATIN AMERICAN COUNTRIES ACCORDING TO GROWTH RATE OF GROSS DOMESTIC PRODUCT (G.D.P.) AND LEVEL OF U.S. NET CAPITAL OUTFLOWS (U.S.N.C.O.), 1960–5

	1960–5			*1966–9*	
Rank	*G.D.P.*	*U.S.N.C.O.*	*Rank*	*G.D.P.*	*U.S.N.C.O.*
1	Panama	Mexico	1	Panama	Brazil
2	Mexico	Argentina	2	Brazil	Panama
3	Peru	Peru	3	Mexico	Mexico
4	Other Central America	Panama	4	Other Central America	Other Central America
5½	Chile	Other Central America	5	Colombia	Argentina
5½	Venezuela	Colombia	6	Venezuela	Peru
7	Colombia	Chile	7	Chile	Colombia
8	Brazil	Brazil	8	Peru	Chile
9	Argentina	Venezuela	9	Argentina	Venezuela

Source: Ranks for growth of G.D.P. based on U.N., Economic Commission for Latin America, *Economic Survey of Latin America* (1969), p. 45; ranks for U.S. net capital outflows based on Table 8.11.

In Table 8.12 nine of the principal Latin American countries are ranked by descending order of growth rate of gross domestic product. Ranking is also made in descending order of U.S. net capital outflows to that country during the same period. We see that for the period 1960–5 the four economies showing the highest rate of growth in output, Panama, Mexico, Peru and Central America, were among the top five recipients of U.S. direct investment. The only country significantly out of line in the ranking is Argentina, which showed the slowest rate of growth but the second highest level of net U.S. investment in the early 1960s. Venezuela, characterised earlier as a country with relatively low growth potential, ranked sixth in output growth and last in U.S. direct investment flows, as might be expected from our earlier model. For the period 1966-9 the results are even more favourable to this hypothesis, since the top four growth economies in this period also occupy the top four positions in U.S. direct investment: Panama, Brazil, Mexico and Central America. Again Venezuela is sixth in growth and last in U.S. direct investment. Also Argentina is again placed last in growth but fifth in the level of U.S. private investment. There is some indication that net capital flows to Argentina may have been less responsive to growth potential than to the opportunity to participate in oligopolistic profits of a highly protected (if stagnant) internal market.

The earlier hypothesis that capital tends to flow to regions of relatively rapid growth (in the absence of political risk), is borne out by the Latin American experience in the 1960s and particularly in the last five years. Mexico and Brazil have participated in the lion's share of both direct investment and overall capital flows from the United States. Both are nations with significant rates of growth in recent years and a high degree of internal political stability. They are 'good risks' in the minds of the international investment community and have tended to receive an even greater inflow of capital than the balance of payments on current account would require, permitting a significant accumulation of foreign exchange reserves.

Our analysis suggests that underlying conditions of intertemporal comparative advantage, the emergence of a new pattern of regional trading blocs, and shifting conditions of supply and demand in international markets will tend to increase pressures for capital outflows from the United States to the countries with the largest growth potential in the Western Hemisphere. If these flows are to be accommodated, in view of rising political obstacles to traditional forms of international investment, it will be necessary to devise new institutional channels to minimise the political and economic problems associated with an excessive foreign control over domestic resources. Experts have discussed at length the need for 'Latin Americanization' of direct foreign investments, including the establishment of Latin American–U.S. and public and mixed enterprises in which the countries of the Western Hemisphere will be assured an adequate degree of control over their internal operations.[1]

[1] A detailed examination of these problems is provided by Carlos F. Diaz Alejandro, 'Direct Foreign Investment in Latin America', in Charles P. Kindleberger, ed., *The International Corporation*, (M.I.T., 1970); also by Diaz Alejandro, 'The Future of Direct Foreign Investment in Latin America', Yale Economic Growth Center Discussion Paper No. 131 (December 1971); and Albert

By the same token differentials in growth potential among Latin American countries will give rise to increasing intraregional capital flows, including significant foreign direct investment by Latin American enterprises in the area. One may expect the same kinds of objections to be raised against these flows as are presently directed to multinational enterprises with bases in the United States, Europe, and Japan. Much creative thought must be given to the development of institutions, including those of the regional capital markets, which will facilitate these transfers with a minimum of social cost and a maximum of benefit.[1]

IV. CONCLUSIONS

The preceding has been a rough sketch of the evolution of Latin American comparative advantage, as it affects trade with the United States. The pressures on future trade that this evolution may be expected to create will require increasing flexibility in U.S. commercial policy to admit the host of new products expected to compete with American manufactures and agricultural commodities. That such flexibility will be achieved is uncertain and will remain so at least until the temporary disequilibrium in the U.S. balance of payments caused by the Vietnam war and the unemployment caused by the present recession are ended. Once the U.S. economy recovers its momentum, and if market access is retained, the gains to Latin American trade from that growth alone will tend to exceed the potential benefits of special tariff preferences to developing countries. Furthermore, the resistance to structural changes in the domestic market occasioned by increased international competition may be expected to weaken as the American economy becomes more dynamic, and with it pressures for more 'orderly marketing arrangements' in the form of voluntary export quotas to the U.S. Changes in a context of growth are considerably less painful than those during the times of recession and widespread unemployment.

The paper also shows that Latin American trade with Europe and Japan in the 1960s underwent both more growth and more structural

---

O. Hirschman, 'How to Divest in Latin America, and Why', in *Princeton Essays in International Finance*, No. 76 (November 1969), reprinted in the author's *A Bias for Hope, Essays on Development in Latin America* (New Haven, 1971).

[1] For a proposal by the author to establish a Latin American Development Board sponsored by major Latin American countries to facilitate the development of intraregional financial flows, see C. W. Reynolds, 'Some brief comments related to the use of capital markets to effect a more efficient and equitable mobilization of resources in Latin America' (Rio de Janeiro, January 1971), (mimeographed).

change than with the U.S. It is possible that Europe will place even greater emphasis in the 1970s on developing its own continental trading area, incorporating the U.K. and the EFTA countries into the European Common Market, the implications of which for Latin American trade with the U.S. are uncertain. From the standpoint of the United States, this may result in a new look at the feasibility of furthering special trade relationships in the Western Hemisphere, including those with Canada, the Caribbean, and Latin American countries in a system of special trade preferences and additional investment incentives. Clearly this policy would be resisted by economic nationalists in all three areas, as well as by internationalists, and the outcome of such a hypothetical set of pressures and counter-pressures cannot be predicted. Europe may be expected to offer inducements to favour the continued relative growth of Latin American trade outside of the Western Hemisphere, as most certainly will Japan, although the position of the U.K. as reflected in Professor Nove's revealing paper promises to be ambiguous at best.[1]

Finally the paper justifies the existence of large and sustained disequilibria in the balance of trade for certain regions by use of a model of intertemporal comparative advantage. An examination of balance of payments statistics for the U.S. and Latin America provides evidence to support the argument that intertemporal comparative advantage differs significantly among countries. The relationship between international finance and growth through trade is examined within the framework of the concept of intertemporal comparative advantage. The analysis reveals that regions having a comparative advantage in growth will be seriously limited by the scarcity of international finance, while those without such an advantage will find that efforts to provide savings from abroad are abortive. The model illustrates that in cases where output growth or income savings propensities differ among regions (or countries) maximisation of the growth of income and welfare may well depend upon the efficient functioning of interregional (or international) finance. In Latin America some countries may be expected to be secular net lenders and others secular net borrowers, while the area as a whole may be expected to be a net borrower with respect to the United States for decades to come.

[1] 'Great Britain and Latin American Economic Development', Part I, pp. 331-348 of this volume.

APPENDIX TABLE I

LATIN AMERICAN EXPORTS BY COMMODITY GROUPS
AND DESTINATION, ANNUAL AVERAGES 1956–8 AND 1967–9
(Millions of U.S. dollars, f.o.b., except as otherwise indicated)

S.I.T.C. Sections[a]

Destination	0–9 Total[b]	0 and 1 Foods	2 and 4 Crude material	3 Fuels	5 Chemicals	7 Machinery	6 and 8 Other manufactures
1956–8							
World	8,500	3,963	1,530	2,253	82	17	613
United States	3,800	1,994	547	878	33	9	324
Canada	138	73	6	52	2	—	4
Western Europe	2,607	1,390	600	357	25	2	222
Japan	248	79	160	—	2	—	5
All others	1,708	428	217	966	19	6	58
1967–9							
World	12,547	5,253	2,280	2,980	243	167	1,607
United States	3,980	1,860	497	993	63	52	503
Canada	403	48	15	332	2	—	6
Western Europe	4,117	2,000	917	460	44	13	677
Japan	663	145	405	28	5	—	80
All others	3,383	1,199	446	1,166	129	101	341
Increase							
World	4,047	1,290	750	727	161	150	994
United States	180	− 134	− 50	115	30	43	179
Canada	265	− 25	9	280	—	—	2
Western Europe	1,510	610	317	103	19	11	455
Japan	415	66	245	28	3	—	75
All others	1,675	771	229	200	110	95	283

Source: U.N., *Monthly Bulletin of Statistics*, March issues. For the United States and Canada separately for 1956–8: UNCTAD, *Handbook of International Trade and Development Statistics, 1969* (U.N. T.D./Stat 2).

[a] S.I.T.C. sections somewhat more fully described are as follows: 0 food and live animals; 1 beverages and tobacco; 2 crude materials, inedible, except fuels; 3 mineral fuels, lubricants and related materials; 4 animal and vegetable oils and fats; 5 chemicals; 6 and 8 manufactured goods; 7 machinery and transportation equipment.

APPENDIX TABLE II

LATIN AMERICAN IMPORTS BY COMMODITY GROUPS AND ORIGINS, ANNUAL AVERAGES 1956–8 AND 1967–8[a]

(Millions of U.S. dollars, f.o.b., except as otherwise indicated)

S.I.T.C. Sections

Origin	0–9 Total	0 and 1 Foods	2 and 4 Crude material	3 Fuels	5 Chemicals	7 Machinery	6 and 8 Other manufactures
1956–8							
World	8,060	923	470	733	730	2,910	2,200
United States	4,097	453	163	170	423	1,823	983
Canada	200	50	12	—	18	50	73
Western Europe	2,360	122	85	8	262	940	893
Japan	170	2	1	1	6	60	100
All others	1,233	297	209	554	21	36	150
1967–9							
World	12,017	1,297	710	740	1,443	4,857	2,747
United States	4,517	418	230	147	587	2,133	877
Canada	365	64	35	—	14	143	108
Western Europe	3,680	188	75	16	638	1,837	890
Japan	633	2	11	1	32	300	285
All others	2,822	624	358	576	172	443	587
Increase							
World	3,957	374	240	7	713	1,947	547
United States	420	– 35	67	– 23	164	310	– 106
Canada	165	14	23	—	– 4	93	35
Western Europe	1,320	66	– 10	8	376	897	– 3
Japan	463	—	10	—	26	240	185
All others	1,589	327	149	22	151	407	437

Source: As for Appendix Table I.

[a] Imports of Latin America represented by exports to Latin America from the areas indicated.

APPENDIX TABLE III

LATIN AMERICA: DESTINATIONS AS PER CENT OF TOTAL EXPORTS, AND ORIGINS AS PER CENT OF TOTAL IMPORTS, 1956–8 AND 1967–9

	World	United States	Canada	Western Europe	Japan	All others
Exports						
1956–8	100	44·7	1·6	30·7	2·9	20·1
1967–9	100	31·7	3·2	32·8	5·3	27·0
Imports						
1956–8	100	50·8	2·5	29·3	2·1	15·3
1967–9	100	37·6	3·0	30·6	5·3	23·5

Source: Calculated from Appendix Tables I and II.

9 Relations with the United States: a Latin American View

Rodrigo Botero

FUNDACÍON PARA LA EDUCACIÓN SUPERIOR
Y EL DESARROLLO, BOGOTA

Economic relations between Latin America and the United States became a matter of particular importance during the 1960–70 decade, when the Inter-American System assigned special priority to economic and social affairs in the Western Hemisphere. Within the general framework of the Alliance for Progress, the Latin American countries undertook to carry out reforms with the purpose of achieving certain objectives of economic growth, social welfare, regional integration and administrative modernisation. At the same time, the United States undertook to provide a certain volume of resources supplementary to the Latin American effort, a part of which would take the form of bilateral and multilateral aid. An essential part of this joint effort was the strengthening of regional financial agencies such as the Inter-American Development Bank and the Central American Economic Integration Bank, and certain multilateral mechanisms were institutionalised for the joint formulation of policies and recommendations and for periodic evaluation of progress achieved: the Inter-American Economic and Social Council (C.I.E.S.) and the Inter-American Committee for the Alliance for Progress (C.I.A.P.).

Now that ten years have passed since the launching of the Alliance for Progress, the inter-American community has had an opportunity to evaluate the degree of success achieved in fulfilling the objectives of the Punta del Este Charter adopted in 1961 and its various complementary documents.[1] The purpose of this paper is to summarise

[1] For detailed information on economic growth in Latin America in the preceding decade and the share of the United States in Western Hemisphere financing, see among others the following documents:

Analysis of the Economic and Social Evolution of Latin America from the Beginning of the Alliance for Progress. O.A.S. Secretariat, Document C.I.E.S./1636, August 1971.

Principal Aspects of Social Development in the 1970's. O.A.S. Secretariat, Document C.I.E.S./1384, May 1969.

Transformation and Development – The Great Task before Latin America. Report presented to the I.D.B. by Raúl Prebisch, Washington, May 1970.

The First Decade of the IDB: Future Prospects. Round Table, I.D.B., Punta del Este, April, 1970.

External Financing for the Development of Latin America, O.A.S. Secretariat, Document C.I.E.S./1382, 1969.

the achievements of the previous decade in growth, foreign trade and external financing and to draw attention to the new international conditions affecting Latin America's development effort. Suggestions are also made on possible inter-American co-operation in the 1970–1980 decade.

The Punta del Este Charter adopted as a growth target for Latin America a minimum of 2·5 per cent annually in *per capita* income during the decade. As may be seen in Table 9.1, this target was practically achieved: growth averaged 2·4 per cent *per capita* in comparison with 2·1 per cent during the 1950–60 decade. Seven countries in the region (Bolivia, Brazil, Costa Rica, El Salvador, Mexico, Nicaragua and Panama) exceeded the adopted growth target.

The growth achieved differed by country and by sector. The average annual increase in product in the agricultural sector was only

TABLE 8.1

LATIN AMERICA – AVERAGE ANNUAL RATE
OF GROWTH OF GROSS DOMESTIC PRODUCT
PER CAPITA, AT FACTOR COST, 1951–60, 1961–70

Growth above regional average in 1961–70	1951–60	1961–70
Bolivia	– 1·7	3·2
Brazil	3·7	2·9
Costa Rica	3·3	2·6
El Salvador	1·8	2·6
Mexico	2·7	3·6
Nicaragua	2·2	3·9
Panama	1·9	4·6
Growth below regional average in 1961–70		
Argentina	1·0	2·1
Colombia	1·4	1·7
Chile	1·1	1·9
Dominican Republic	2·6	0·3
Ecuador	1·8	1·7
Guatemala	0·8	2·3
Haiti	– 0·1	0·7
Honduras	0·4	1·7
Paraguay	– 0·2	1·0
Peru	2·9	2·1
Uruguay	0·6	– 0·1
Venezuela	3·6	1·3
Total for Latin America	2·1	2·4

Source: O.A.S. Secretariat, based on data prepared by ECLA and on country national accounts.

2·6 per cent, which was less than the growth of population and less than the increase in the same sector during 1950–60.

In the industrial sector, annual growth was 6·2 per cent, which was slightly above the rate of 6 per cent in the previous decade. Available indicators on the distribution of wealth and income do not show any appreciable improvement during the 1960s. According to ECLA estimates, in 1965 50 per cent of the region's population earned 13·4 per cent of the income, while 5 per cent of the population (the

TABLE 9.2

LATIN AMERICA. GROWTH OF INCOME *PER CAPITA*,
1960–70 BY GROUPS OF COUNTRIES
(G.D.P. in millions of U.S. dollars at 1960 prices)

	1960			1970		
	G.D.P.	Population (mil.)	G.D.P. per capita	G.D.P.	Population (mil.)	G.D.P. per capita
Argentina	15,810	20·9	758	22,718	24·4	934
Chile	3,769	7·7	491	5,770	9·8	590
Mexico	15,774	36·0	438	31,559	50·7	622
Uruguay	1,736	2·5	683	1,954	2·9	677
Venezuela	4,557	7·7	589	7,163	10·8	666
Group subtotal	41,646	74·9	556	69,164	98·5	702
Brazil	18,468	70·3	263	32,646	93·2	350
Colombia	4,731	15·9	298	7,861	22·2	355
Costa Rica	448	1·2	364	843	1·8	469
Ecuador	1,043	4·3	241	1,713	6·0	284
El Salvador	578	2·5	230	1,026	3·4	298
Guatemala	956	4·0	241	1,597	5·3	302
Nicaragua	304	1·5	202	600	2·0	297
Panama	381	1·1	359	829	1·5	566
Paraguay	411	1·7	237	638	2·4	264
Peru	2,919	10·0	291	4,897	13·6	360
Group subtotal	30,239	112·6	269	52,650	151·4	348
Bolivia	526	3·7	142	915	4·7	196
Dominican Republic	571	3·1	183	815	4·3	187
Haiti	352	4·1	85	415	5·2	79
Honduras	320	1·8	173	528	2·6	204
Group subtotal	1,769	12·8	138	2,673	16·8	159
Total for Latin America	73,654	200·2	368	124,487	266·8	467

Source: O.A.S. Secretariat, ECLA and Latin American Demographic Center (CELADE).

upper income groups) received 33·4 per cent of the income (see Statistical Appendix, Table I).

Table 9.2 shows the changes in income *per capita* in the Latin American countries between 1960 and 1970. The five countries with the highest level of income (Argentina, Chile, Mexico, Uruguay and Venezuela), with 37 per cent of Latin America's total population, achieved in 1970 an average income *per capita* of U.S. $702. This figure is slightly less than that of Italy in 1965 (U.S. $771) and higher than that for Japan in the same year (U.S. $653) (see Appendix Table II).

The *per capita income* of Latin America in 1970, which was U.S. $467, is an average of countries with considerable differences in economic achievement. Table 9.2 shows three groups of selected countries by level of *per capita* income: the highest has an average of U.S. $702, whereas the lowest averaged U.S. $159 and the intermediate group U.S. $348. While bearing in mind all the difficulties involved in the comparison of incomes between groups of countries and regions, it is important to underline the quantitative and qualitative differences implicit in the U.S. $467 average for Latin America, as compared with the majority of the less developed countries of Asia and Africa where the average is of the order of U.S. $150. These differences involve different development strategies and also indicate a limitation to the possibility of joint action among the countries of Latin America and those in other less developed areas in the matter of trade and financial relations with the more developed countries.

In contrast to the previous decade, Latin America's foreign trade increased considerably during the 1960s. Latin American exports of goods increased at an annual average rate of 5·7 per cent between 1961 and 1970 (as compared with 1·4 per cent during 1951–60); in the last three years of the decade, the increase was as high as 9 per cent annually (see Appendix Table III).

Table 9.3 shows the growth of merchandise exports of the Latin American countries between 1960 and 1969. The region's total exports increased from U.S. $7,000 million in 1951 to U.S. $7,952 million in 1960, an overall rise of only 13·7 per cent. In 1969 the total value of Latin American exports was U.S. $12,507 million, with a growth during the decade of 57·3 per cent.

Not only was the rate of growth high but Latin American exports were considerably diversified during the decade both with regard to destination and to product composition. In 1960, the United States purchased 41 per cent of Latin American exports and Europe (including Eastern Europe) 35 per cent. In 1968, while Europe's share did not change, that of the United States declined to 34 per

TABLE 9.3

LATIN AMERICA. MERCHANDISE EXPORTS, 1960–9
(Millions of U.S. dollars)

	1960	1969	Average annual rate of growth, 1961–9
Argentina	1,079	1,612	4·6
Bolivia	51	169	14·2
Brazil	1,269	2,297	6·8
Chile	488	1,145	9·9
Colombia	466	658	3·9
Costa Rica	86	192	9·3
Dominican Republic	174	184	0·6
Ecuador	144	188	1·4
El Salvador	117	202	5·6
Guatemala	117	261	9·3
Haiti	33	37	1·3
Honduras	63	172	11·8
Mexico	764	1,430	7·2
Nicaragua	56	158	12·2
Panama	27	136	19·7
Paraguay	27	55	8·2
Peru	430	888	8·4
Uruguay	129	200	5·0
Venezuela	2,432	2,523	0·2
Latin America	7,952	12,507	5·2

Source: I.M.F., *International Financial Statistics.*

cent at the same time as the share of Japan, Canada and Latin America itself increased; in the latter case it was a result of intensification of intraregional trade. It is likely that the 11·9 per cent of intraregional trade in 1968 underestimates the real volume of transactions in view of the unregistered border traffic of various Latin American countries. However, as an order of magnitude it is also an expression of the moderation in the advance of Latin American integration during the decade. It also shows that there is still an opportunity to further diversify the geographic distribution of exports in the present decade. A share of 15 to 20 per cent for intra-Latin American trade by 1980 does not appear to be an exaggerated projection.

Given the figures in Tables 9.3 and 9.4, it is clear that for Latin America it is essential that the world economy maintains a satisfactory rate of growth, with its consequences for the rate of increase of international trade. The figures also underline the importance to Latin America of obtaining preferential tariff treatment for

TABLE 9.4

LATIN AMERICA: DESTINATION OF EXPORTS BY GEOGRAPHIC AREAS
(Percentages)

Destination	1960	1965	1968
Western Hemisphere	51·1	47·5	49·9
United States	41·1	34·0	34·3
Canada	1·7	3·0	3·6
Latin America	8·3	10·4	11·9
Western Europe	33·1	34·0	33·1
E.E.C.	19·3	21·1	20·2
EFTA	12·2	10·0	9·6
Other countries*a*	1·7	2·9	3·3
Rest of World	15·8	18·6	17·0
Japan	2·8	4·4	5·5
Eastern Europe*b*	1·9	3·0	2·2
Other countries	11·0	11·2	9·3
Total	100·0	100·0	100·0

a Excludes centrally-planned economies except Yugoslavia.
b Except Yugoslavia.

Source: United Nations, *Monthly Statistical Bulletin.*

exports of manufactures and semi-manufactures to all industrialised countries.

The change in the product composition of Latin American exports in the preceding decade is also significant. While the share of foodstuffs and fuels declined, that of industrial products (machinery, chemical products and other manufactures), which had been only 10 per cent in 1960, increased to 17 per cent of the total in 1968 (see Table 9.5). This was the result of industrial growth over the decade and of the effort of several Latin American countries to increase the percentage of value added in their exports and to reduce dependence on the external sector for raw materials exports. Exports of manufactures, though still small, are increasing rapidly, but these have been dealt a serious blow by the import surcharge established by the U.S. Government in August 1971. With the exception of Mexico (see Appendix Table IV), the proportion of Latin America's exports affected by the 10 per cent charge is not very significant. The damage suffered – which is more psychological than real – lies more in the fact that the products affected are those with the greatest growth potential in the 1970s and those which are best adapted to priority objectives in employment and growth in the Latin American countries.

TABLE 9.5

LATIN AMERICA, COMPOSITION OF EXPORTS,
1960, 1965, 1968
(Percentages)

Classification	1960	1965	1968
Foodstuffs	40·5	40·8	39·3
Raw materials	19·9	20·5	19·8
Fuels	29·5	26·4	24·3
Chemicals	1·4	1·5	2·0
Machinery	0·2	0·6	1·4
Other manufactures	8·5	10·2	14·2
Total	100·0	100·0	100·0

Source: United Nations, *Monthly Statistical Bulletin.*

Table 9.6 shows the amount of external official financing received by Latin America during 1961–70, by source. Of the total of U.S. $21,894 million, more than half was bilateral in nature (U.S. $11,486 million) and the rest was derived from international financial agencies. The gross amount disbursed during the period was U.S. $16,005, which was slightly less than 80 per cent of authorised loans and grants. Latin America repaid an amount of U.S. $6,554 million, so that the net amount of official financing received was U.S. $9,451 million, 43 per cent of the amount authorised.

Official external finance helped to offset in part the sizeable current account balance-of-payment deficit of the region. The largest item

TABLE 9.6

LATIN AMERICA: OFFICIAL FINANCING RECEIVED,
1961–70
(Millions of U.S. dollars)

Source	Authorisations	Disbursements on loans and grants	Net flow
Bilateral	11,486	9,720	6,001
United States	10,170	8,404	5,601
O.E.C.D.	1,316	1,316	400
Multilateral	10,408	6,285	3,450
I.D.B.	4,137	2,154	1,799
I.B.R.D.	3,294	2,188	1,482
I.M.F.	2,749	1,752	− 1
Other	288	191	170
Total	21,894	16,005	9,451

Source: O.A.S. Secretariat, based on data from the U.S. Government, international financial agencies and the O.E.C.D.

in this deficit is the payment of foreign financial services which amounted to U.S. $19,943 million over the decade. The rate of growth of this item is of some concern. Whereas in 1961 net payments abroad for financial services were U.S. $1,414 million, by 1970 they had increased to U.S. $2,551 million. The average rate of growth over the decade was 6·8 per cent annually, which is higher than that of Latin American exports of merchandise during the period (5·7 per cent). As a result of this divergence, the ratio of financial services (ratio of net financial payments to the value of exports) increased from 13·9 per cent during 1961–3 to 16·6 per cent during 1967–9.

TABLE 9.7

UNITED STATES: BILATERAL LOANS AND GRANTS,
AND CONTRIBUTIONS TO MULTILATERAL FINANCIAL
AGENCIES, 1961, 1970 AND AVERAGE FOR THE DECADE
(Millions of U.S. dollars)

	1961	1970	Average for 1961–70
Bilateral grants and loans	1,403·1	625·9	1,017·0
1. A.I.D. loans	270·8	155·8	353·5
2. A.I.D. grants[a]	35·0	85·6	85·9
3. Eximbank	803·1	203·5	336·7
4. Food for peace	145·4	152·6	156·6
5. Treasury Department	147·0	—	73·8
6. Other[b]	1·9	28·4	25·3
Multilateral loans	584·0	—	346·8
1. Contributions to I.D.B.[c]	190·0	—	281·2
2. Social Progress Fund	394·0	—	262·5
Total	1,987·1	625·9	1,264·5
Total less Eximbank	1,184·0	422·4	925·5

[a] Fiscal years. Basically, technical assistance.
[b] Peace Corps, Pan American highway and others.
[c] Contributions to ordinary capital and Special Operations Fund.

Source: O.A.S. Secretariat, based on reports from U.S. Government and international agencies.

As may be seen in Table 9.7, the annual average authorisations of bilateral loans and contributions to multilateral agencies by the United States with respect to Latin America amounted to U.S. $1,264·5 million. There was a considerable decline in authorisations in 1969 and 1970. The total, excluding Eximbank, was U.S. $1,184 million in 1961 but it fell to U.S. $810 million in 1969 and only U.S. $422 in 1970. If this trend continues in the coming years and the amount of service payments abroad increases, there will be a considerable decline in external aid support for Latin America unless new sources of concessional aid are opened up.

PROSPECTS FOR THE 1970s

At the beginning of the decade, both Latin America and the United States find themselves in a substantially different situation from that prevailing at the start of the Alliance for Progress. This change will certainly affect inter-American relations in the coming years and will be reflected in economic relations between the two areas.

On the one hand, the political premises of the Alliance for Progress have changed radically. The United States is preoccupied by domestic problems and as a result of the conflict in Indo-China is less than ever disposed to develop a 'special relationship' with Latin America, particularly if this implies economic sacrifice. At the same time the Latin American countries are less willing than ever to accept North American leadership or to limit their freedom of political and economic action in favour of the United States. This helps to explain the atmosphere of confrontation that has been perceptible in recent inter-American meetings.

Economic conditions have also changed. For the United States, its own balance of payments problems have become paramount. For Latin America the critical problem for the 1960s is unemployment. According to estimates of the Latin American Economic and Social Planning Institute, open unemployment in the region increased from 5·6 per cent in 1950 to 11·1 per cent in 1965. In the case of Colombia, if account is taken of disguised unemployment and underemployment, about one-quarter to one-third of the labour force in urban areas is lacking in employment opportunities.[1]

At the same time that Latin America is trying to increase its exports even more rapidly, the United States is adopting a restrictive trade policy, stimulating protectionist attitudes and deliberately running the risk of precipitating a contraction in international trade.

The recent decision by the United States Senate to suspend external aid in 1972 coincides with a rather negative attitude both in Europe and in Japan to any new proposals in the trade and financial field in favour of development, as a result of the monetary crisis.

The way in which the United States Senate took this decision and the reasons invoked for suspending foreign aid, do not allow any

---

[1] *Towards Full Employment. A Programme for Colombia*, prepared by an international mission organised by the I.L.O., Geneva, 1970. On the problem of employment at the regional level, see also *Employment and Growth in Latin America's Development Strategy: Implications for the 1970s*. Report to the C.I.E.S. by the O.A.S. Secretariat, September 1971.

optimism with regard to the future of U.S. bilateral aid. During the debates on the Foreign Aid Bill a senator who is known for his liberal attitude and is a member of the Foreign Affairs Committee of the Senate made the following statement (which could be adopted as an epitaph for the U.S. programme of aid for development):

> United States foreign aid was not able to obtain support for us on the occasion of the two recent votes in the United Nations related to the admission of the People's Republic of China. . . . The Bill proposes total authorizations for approximately U.S. $2,400 millions for 55 member countries which voted against our position or which abstained on the second proposal which resulted in the admission of the People's Republic of China into the United Nations and the expulsion of Nationalist China.[1]

The frustration arising out of the fact that bilateral aid is not an efficient instrument of political persuasion should serve as an argument for not diverting development aid to other objectives, rather than as an argument against aid itself. A clear differentiation between the international transfer of resources for development and the political objectives of the donor countries is of special importance to Latin America and the rest of the less developed countries. Such a separation could be achieved by channelling an increasing volume of resources through the multilateral financial agencies. The United States could avoid the undesirable aspects of its bilateral aid programme without reducing the total volume of financing for development by increasing its contributions to the World Bank and the Inter-American Development Bank, and by stimulating the strengthening of sub-regional agencies such as the Caribbean Development Bank, the Central American Economic Integration Bank and the Andean Development Corporation.

The necessary reorganisation of the international monetary system is an opportunity to channel additional resources towards Latin America and other developing countries through the issue of Special Drawing Rights. In view of the increasing difficulty in obtaining from the United States Congress approval for appropriations for international aid, the recently created capacity to issue drawing rights on an international scale for the financing of development should be taken advantage of.[2]

[1] 'Farewell to Foreign Aid: a Liberal Takes Leave'. An address in opposition to the F.Y.1972 Foreign Assistance Act, by Senator Frank Church. Washington, 29 October 1971.

[2] For an account of this alternative see *A Proposal to Link Reserve Creation and Development Assistance*. Report of the Sub-Committee on International Exchange and Payments, Joint Economic Committee of the United States Congress. Washington, 1969.

FOREIGN PRIVATE INVESTMENT

It is unlikely that during the coming decade foreign private investment will constitute an important share of net resources flowing
towards Latin America. Economic evolution during the 1960s and
the political changes in the Western Hemisphere are resulting in an
even more intense economic nationalism. Even taking account of the
different politico-economic models coexisting in the region, there is
an increasing consensus on the need to keep under national control
certain economic sectors considered of vital importance. Among
them are energy, minerals, communications and basic products
which are predominant in the export sectors. This position has been
expressed recently by the former President of Chile, Eduardo Frei, in
the following form:

> The degree of awareness and development reached by these
> nations has led them to feel that it is against their interests and
> their very identity to allow natural resources, which are essential
> to them either as raw materials for their industry or as prime
> export items in their economies, to remain in foreign hands. Thus,
> the nationalization of these resources will be unavoidable.[1]

Moreover, this attitude is not peculiar to Latin America but
represents the desire of the Third World as a whole for a more
equitable distribution of political and economic power on a world
scale. Thus the Government of Iran has announced its intention not
to renew petroleum-company concessions when they expire in 1979,
in spite of the existing option to extend them for another fifteen
years. According to the Shah of Iran, Mohamed Reza Pahlevi, 'it is
ridiculous for a country such as ours, in the midst of intense indus-
trialization, that foreign countries should come to carry petroleum
from the well to the tanker. We can do this by ourselves.'[2] According
to *Fortune* magazine, in a recent analysis of petroleum negotiations
carried out in Teheran and Tripoli at the beginning of 1971, the rate
and opportunity for nationalisation of petroleum in the Middle East
will depend more on the speed at which the producing countries
learn to manage large-scale petroleum enterprises than on political
and ideological factors.[3]

It is thus not surprising that as technical and administrative levels
rise in the Latin American countries, the conditions under which

---

[1] See 'The Second Latin American Revolution', *Foreign Affairs* (October, 1971).
[2] Cited in *Fortune* (August 1971), in an article by Gurney Breckenfeld entitled
'How the Arabs Changed the Oil Business' in which the implications of recent
petroleum negotiations in the Middle East are analysed.
[3] *Fortune* (August 1971), *loc. cit.*

foreign investors may be allowed to participate in their economies should change. It is to be expected furthermore that Latin American negotiators will pay more attention to the international political and economic situation in order to obtain advantage for their own country from any particular change in the ratio of forces in the international field. As a distinguished Latin American economist expressed it:

> The Latin American countries presumably will utilize any change in their bargaining power to push a little further in the direction of (greater national control). For example, Venezuela, which fourteen years ago was wide open to foreign private investment, has intelligently taken advantage of circumstances in the Middle East to obtain a larger participation in revenues from petroleum and gas as well as a larger degree of control over the industry. The history of Chilean copper is another, although more complex, example of these trends.[1]

It is thus not logical to expect that Latin America will receive a vastly increased volume of foreign private investment in basic sectors in the production of commodities for the market of the industrialised countries. On the contrary, it is more likely that in those sectors there will be disinvestment in the near future, with various levels of political friction between the governments and the countries involved, depending on the maturity and responsibility of each of the parties. On the other hand, it can be assumed that in the manufacturing sector there will be further opportunities for foreign private investment, especially when such investment is indissolubly linked to scarce technologies or when it may contribute new management techniques and distribution networks in the world market. But even in the manufacturing sector, the Latin American countries are likely during the present decade to put pressure on foreign investors in order to obtain a larger local participation in the capital of the enterprises. It is also likely that Latin America will try, as soon as possible, to break down the investment/technology/management 'package' and to control more carefully the cost of the transfer of technology whether it comes together with capital or independently.[2]

It is not the purpose of this paper to consider the desirability of

---

[1] Carlos F. Díaz Alejandro, 'The Evolution of Latin American policies Toward Direct Foreign Investment and United States Perceptions of Those Policies'. Paper submitted to the Conference on Trade and Investment Policies in the Americas. Southern Methodist University, Dallas, Texas, 8 October 1971.

[2] This trend can be perceived in the Andean Group's Code on Foreign Investments adopted by Bolivia, Colombia, Chile, Ecuador and Peru.

the economic nationalism prevailing in Latin America at the beginning of the 1970s. It is a fact to be taken into account in considering the various forms of transfer of resources to the region. Also the tension between certain governments in the area and foreign investors with regard to natural resources should not be taken as a permanent feature for each and every Latin American country. However, the shock created by nationalisation of mining and petroleum enterprises, even if only temporary and limited to a small number of countries, will affect for quite some time the investment climate in Latin America. It is not unlikely that after certain events a new *modus vivendi* will be established with foreign investors, with a new set of rules of the game, as is happening in Eastern Europe. But even under optimal conditions, it would appear unrealistic to expect that the net flow of foreign private capital to Latin America between now and 1980 will be very large.

A NOTE ON PROSPECTIVE TRENDS IN THE UNITED STATES ECONOMY

Probable future trends in the United States economy have considerable significance for world trade. Looking at employment data and its distribution by sectors, it can be seen that the United States, as a mature industrial society, has already entered the stage of post-industrial development to become a services economy. Table 9.8

TABLE 9.8

UNITED STATES: NON-AGRICULTURAL
EMPLOYMENT, BY ACTIVITY, 1947–69
(Thousands)

	1947	1969	Percentage Variation
Output of goods	18,482	24,158	30·7
Mining	955	628	– 34·2
Construction	1,982	3,410	72·0
Manufacturing	15,545	20,120	29·4
Durable goods	8,385	11,898	41·9
Non-durable goods	7,159	8,255	15·3
Output of services	25,399	45,979	81·0
Transport and utilities	4,166	4,449	6·8
Trade	8,955	14,643	63·5
Finance, insurance, real estate	1,754	3,558	102·9
Education, health and others	5,050	11,102	119·8
Governments (Federal, State, Local)	5,474	12,227	123·4
Total	43,881	70,138	59·8

Source: U.S. Department of Labor, Bureau of Labor Statistics.

shows the distribution of the gainfully employed in sectors other than agriculture in the United States between 1947 and 1969. While total employment increased by almost 60 per cent during that period, employment in the production of goods rose only by 31 per cent whereas employment in the production of services increased by 81 per cent. The expansion in employment in the manufacturing sector, 29 per cent, was only half the total increase in employment. In one particular sector, mining, there was a 34 per cent decline in employment during the period. Within the service sector there were extraordinary increases: government, 123 per cent; education, health and others, 120 per cent; and finance, insurance and real estate, 103 per cent.

A projection of the U.S. economy to 1980 made by the U.S. Department of Labor[1] foresees a continuation of these trends, as may be seen in Fig. 9.1. Whereas in 1947 more than half the labour force was employed in the production of goods, by 1980 this sector will employ less than a third of the labour force.

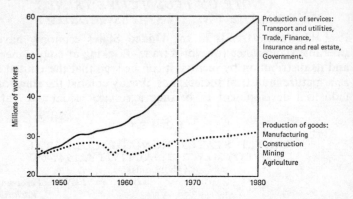

FIG. 9.1. U.S. employment trends in the production of goods and services. 1947–68: actual. 1968–80: projected for a service economy with 3 per cent unemployment. The figures relate to wage-earners only, except in agriculture which includes self-employed and non-remunerated household workers. (—) Production of services; transport and utilities; trade; finance, insurance and real estate; government. (.....) Production of goods; manufacturing; construction, mining; agriculture. Source: U.S. Department of Labor.

This change in the structure of employment in the United States reflects the changes in aggregate demand in that country as income rises. As is evident, the dynamic growth sector is that of govern-

[1] *The United States Economy 1980*, United States Department of Labor, Bureau of Labor Statistics, Bulletin No. 1673, August, 1970.

ment, education, health and financial services. Therefore, it can be foreseen that merchandise exports will be even less important than hitherto for the North American producers. On the other hand, the more dynamic sectors of the United States' economy will open up new opportunities in international markets:

> Therefore, the United States may well specialize in the export of services possibly with concentration in management services that are combined with education and capital inputs, both of which factors are relatively abundant in the United States. . . . Other enduring comparative advantages for the United States will be found in industries with a high science-content, where rapid changes in technology will give certain American products a technological advantage over competitors.'[1]

As the production of goods declines in relative terms in the American economy, it can also be foreseen that imports will satisfy a larger share of the total consumption of goods in the United States. This prospective trend, accompanied by a relative decline in exports of merchandise, suggests that the United States trade deficit will increase considerably over the decade. According to an analysis made by the American economist Lawrence Krause, such a deterioration may occur although there may not be any overall balance of payment disequilibrium.

TABLE 9.9

UNITED STATES BALANCE OF PAYMENTS:
ACTUAL FOR 1969 AND HYPOTHETICAL FOR 1980
(Billions of U.S. dollars)

Net balances	1969	1980
Trade	0·7	– 5·0
Payments and income on investments	5·8	16·0
Other services	– 4·4	– 3·0
Goods and services	2·1	8·0
U.S. private capital	– 5·0	– 10·0
Foreign private capital	9·9	7·0
Net private capital	4·9	– 3·0
U.S. government grants, loans and private transfers (net of repayments)	– 4·2	– 5·0
Overall balance	2·8	0·0

Source: Lawrence Krause, 'Trade Policy in the Atlantic World'. Paper presented to the Atlantic Conference, Dorado Beach, Puerto Rico, 12–15 November 1970.

---

[1] Lawrence Krause, 'Trade Policy in the Atlantic World', Paper presented at the Atlantic Conference, Dorado Beach, Puerto Rico, 12–15 November 1970.

Table 9.9 shows the actual balance of payments of the United States in 1969 and hypothetical figures for 1980, in which year it is assumed that a large trade deficit will occur (U.S. $5,000 million). This deficit will be more than offset by a surplus of U.S. $16,000 million in respect of payments and income received on foreign investment, which is a reasonable assumption if present trends in profits from foreign investments and new foreign investments are taken into account. There will thus be a surplus of U.S. $8,000 million for goods and services. (A deficit of U.S. $3,000 million is assumed on account of other services, mainly tourism and military expenditure.) Such a surplus could be divided between foreign investment in an amount, say, of U.S. $3,000 million per annum, and foreign aid at an annual rate of U.S. $5,000 million.

The conclusion to be drawn from this exercise is highly relevant to the present discussion on trade policy precipitated by the Nixon administration measures taken in August 1971:

> Actually, it would not be difficult to visualize a situation of external equilibrium for the United States even with a large trade deficit in world terms. Over many years North Americans have been investing considerable sums abroad mainly as direct investment. These investments are already yielding to their head offices large amounts in respect of dividends and interests and they will tend to grow during the 1970s. In effect the question to be asked is: *How will other countries balance their international accounts if the United States does not show a substantial trade deficit?*[1]

The above suggests how the Western Hemisphere might adopt an international division of labour that takes account of present trends in the U.S. economy and of Latin America's need to increase employment and exports. Thus, Latin America should deliberately try to achieve a surplus in its trade balance with the United States by establishing in the region labour intensive manufacturing industries which could supply the United States market (and any other markets that may be available). At the same time, the share of value added in present Latin American exports to the United States should be increased (foodstuffs, lumber, raw materials), by reversing the present structure under which tariff rates increase with the degree of elaboration of the products. The increase in merchandise exports to the United States would give Latin America additional resources to enable it, among other things, to increase its purchases of services, technology and complex-technology equipment in which the United States maintained a comparative advantage. A trend in this direction would be advantageous to the United States. It coincides with

[1] Lawrence Krause, *op. cit.* My italics.

present trends in its economy and would also raise the level of welfare of its consumers through price effects.

FINAL COMMENTS

The context of inter-American relations has changed fundamentally between the past decade and the present one. Therefore it can be expected that economic relations between the United States and Latin America will change considerably.

It may be expected that the total amount of United States bilateral aid will decline substantially during the present decade. Private foreign investment will continue to play an important role in Latin America's economic development, particularly as a source of new technology and modern management systems, and also as a means of access to international markets. For some countries such investment may be an important source of external resources, but for the region as a whole, a large net inflow is not very likely. Latin America's interest lies in a multilateral world economy with vigorous foreign trade and a minimum of restrictions. In order to achieve an increase in Latin American exports and greater diversification of such exports, it will be important to assure access to the markets of the industrialised countries. There is an opportunity for an international division of labour between the United States and Latin America which will be advantageous for both parties. Such a division of labour would tie in with the probable evolution of the United States economy in the present decade towards a service economy and also agrees with the priority objectives of Latin America with regard to employment growth and exports.

A bold policy of trade liberalisation on the part of the United States in favour of Latin America would offset the expected reduction in bilateral aid during the decade. However, if the reduction in aid should be compounded by a restrictive attitude on the part of the United States in trade matters, the task of development in Latin America during the decade will become much more difficult.

STATISTICAL APPENDIX

TABLE I

LATIN AMERICA: PERCENTAGE DISTRIBUTION OF INCOME IN 1965

	Lower 20%	Lower Middle 30%	Upper Middle 30%	15% below upper 5%	Upper 5%
Argentina	5·2	15·3	25·4	22·9	31·2
Brazil	3·5	11·5	23·6	22·0	39·4
Colombia	5·9	14·3	23·1	26·3	30·4
Costa Rica	6·0	12·2	21·8	25·0	35·0
El Salvador	5·5	10·5	22·6	28·4	33·0
Mexico	3·6	11·8	26·1	29·5	29·0
Panama	4·9	15·6	22·9	22·1	34·5
Venezuela	3·0	11·3	27·7	31·5	26·5
Latin America (average of 8 countries)	3·1	10·3	24·1	29·2	33·4
United States	4·6	18·7	31·2	25·5	20·0

Source: estimated by ECLA, *Economic Survey of Latin America 1969* (March 1970).

TABLE II

GROSS DOMESTIC PRODUCT *PER CAPITA* IN LATIN AMERICA AND SELECTED INDUSTRIALISED COUNTRIES
(U.S. dollars at 1960 prices)

	1960	1965	1970[a]	Average annual rate of growth 1961–70
Latin America	368	408	467	2·4
Untted States	2,567	3,013	3,353	2·7
Canada	1,812	2,160	2,481	3·2
France	1,127	1,400	1,773	4·6
Italy	626	771	996	4·8
Japan	425	653	1,094	9·9
E.E.C.	966	1,184	1,466	4·3

[a] Preliminary.

Source: O.A.S. Secretariat, United Nations, ECLA, O.E.C.D.

TABLE III

LATIN AMERICA: GROWTH OF REAL PRODUCT, EXPORT PROCEEDS, AND GROSS FIXED INVESTMENT
(Average annual rates of growth)

	1951–60	1961–70
Group I[a]		
Population	3·0	3·1
Gross domestic product	6·2	6·5
Merchandise exports	– 1·5	8·0
Gross fixed investment	7·3	6·6[c]
Group II[b]		
Population	2·6	2·7
Gross domestic product	4·0	4·2
Merchandise exports	3·0	4·6
Gross fixed investment	5·5	4·0[c]
Total Latin America		
Population	2·8	2·9
Gross domestic product	5·0	5·4
Merchandise exports	1·4	5·7
Gross fixed investment	6·4	5·3[c]

[a] Bolivia, Brazil, Costa Rica, El Salvador, Mexico, Nicaragua and Panama.
[b] Other Latin American countries.
[c] Average annual rate for 1961–9.

Source: O.A.S. Secretariat.

TABLE IV

LATIN AMERICA: IMPACT OF THE 10 PER CENT U.S. SURCHARGE
(Millions of U.S. dollars)

Country	Total Exports	Exports to U.S.	Dutiable Exports to U.S.	Percent C/B
Argentina	1,775	171·8	147·1	85·2
Barbados	40	8·8	4·9	55·7
Bolivia	182	24·7	1·6	6·5
Brazil	2,739	669·4	123·8	18·5
Colombia	608	268·9	26·4	9·8
Costa Rica	229	116·4	7·3	6·3
Chile	1,069	154·0	128·5	83·4
Dominican Republic	214	183·8	13·7	7·5
Ecuador	218	108·7	11·1	10·2
El Salvador	229	48·3	2·1	4·3
Guatemala	298	87·1	6·1	7·0
Haiti	37	31·9	13·8	43·2
Honduras	167	102·4	10·4	10·2
Jamaica	299	185·7	19·6	10·6
Mexico	1,402	1,222·4	679·4	55·6
Nicaragua	155	61·3	10·3	16·8

Table IV (*continued*)

Country	Total Exports	Exports to U.S.	Dutiable Exports to U.S.	Percent C/B
Panama	114	75·5	6·0	7·4
Paraguay	64	10·6	8·7	82·1
Peru	1,044	340·5	174·1	51·1
Trinidad and Tobago	482	235·6	10·1	4·3
Uruguay	233	19·2	18·8	97·9
Venezuela	2,638	1,082·1	21·1	1·9

Source: O.A.S. Secretariat, based on data in I.M.F., *International Financial Statistics*, for 1969 and 1970.

TABLE V

LATIN AMERICA: SUMMARY OF EXTERNAL TRANSACTIONS, 1961–70
(Millions of U.S. dollars at current prices)

1. Transfer of real resources (surplus on goods and non-financial services)	6,061
2. Payment on financial services and private donations (net)	– 20,152
3. Net external financing (current account balance of payments deficit: 1 + 2)	– 14,091
4. Increase (–) in reserves	– 3,553
5. Total capital inflow, net (3 + 4 = 6 + 7 + 8 + 9)	17,644
6. Net official financing from U.S. to other O.E.C.D. countries and international financial agencies	9,399
7. Direct investment, net	5,129
8. Other net capital flows	3,408
9. Errors and omissions	– 289

Source: O.A.S. Secretariat, based on I.M.F. data and annual reviews by C.I.A.P.

TABLE VI

LATIN AMERICA: SOURCES AND USES OF EXTERNAL FINANCE RECEIVED, 1961–70
(Millions of U.S. dollars)

Item		Percentage
Uses	17,644	100·0
Offset to current account balance	14,091	79·9
Increase in monetary assets	3,553	21·1
Sources	17,644	100·0
Non-compensatory official capital	9,402	53·3
Direct investment	5,129	29·1
Compensatory official capital	6	—
Other flows	3,408	19·3
Errors and omissions	289	1·7

Source: O.A.S. Secretariat, based on I.M.F. data and annual reviews by C.I.A.P.

TABLE VII

UNITED STATES: BALANCE OF PAYMENTS WITH LATIN AMERICA, 1970
(Millions of U.S. dollars)

	1970
Merchandise exports	5,651
Merchandise imports	4,861
Trade balance	790
Travel and transport balance	34
Other services (mainly financial)	1,602
Surplus on services, net	1,636
Net surplus on goods and services	2,348
Unilateral transfers, net	– 441
Private U.S. capital	– 976
Official U.S. capital	– 509
Foreign capital	– 7
Recorded transactions, net	415
Adjusted recorded transactions, net	215
Errors, omissions and intra-area transfers	– 203
Surplus or deficit (–) in U.S. liquid assets[a]	12

[a] Includes net flow of U.S. securities (except treasury securities), long term liabilities, deposits and money market flows.

Source: O.A.S. Secretariat, based on U.S. Treasury and Commerce Department data.

Discussion of the Papers by
Professor Reynolds and Dr. Botero

Mr. Szekely's first point concerned the trade section of Professor Reynolds' paper, in which he gave more or less equal weight to the protectionist policies of both the United States and Latin America as being responsible for the relative decline in Latin American exports to the United States. Mr. Szekely said that in the first place he would stress more heavily than Professor Reynolds the extent to which U.S. policy was responsible for the decline, not only through tariff barriers but also through non-tariff barriers, which the paper ignored. Second, he thought import substitution might not have been quite as deleterious to Latin American exports as Professor Reynolds assumed. He would like to prove this by referring to some figures of his own, given in Tables A and B.

Table A 'explained' the difference between the growth rates of world imports into industrial countries and regions, on the one hand, and the growth rates of Latin American exports to those same regions. In the case of the United States commodity imports from all over the world grew by 49 per cent, while imports from Latin America grew only by 13 per cent. The 36 per cent difference between the two rates was to be explained as follows: one-third of the difference, or 11 per cent, was due to the fall in Latin America's share of U.S. imports of *individual commodities*, while the remaining two-thirds of the difference, or 25 per cent, was due to the concentration of the vast majority of Latin American exports on those items of U.S. import demand which experienced relatively slow growth. (It might be noted in passing that the difference between the growth rate of total import demand and that of Latin American sales was greatest in the case of the United States, in comparison with all other regions, and that the relative effect of the change in demand structure was a great deal more severe with respect to the market of the United States.)

In Table B, Latin America's share of U.S. imports of the total of all categories could be seen to have fallen during the period under examination. Examining each category, it could be seen that for those cases where the majority of Latin American exports were concentrated, a fall in the share of individual commodities was responsible for most of the overall fall in the region's share of each category.[1]

Thus, at most one-third of the fall in Latin America's share of the U.S. market was actually explained by a weakened competitive position in the market for traditional products. It was as well to inquire, therefore, whether the failure to take advantage of the growth of the remaining non-traditional markets was due, as Professor Reynolds suggested, to damage inflicted by Latin American import substitution policies upon the

[1] Some of the remaining categories showed an improvement in Latin America's share, due to relatively high rates of growth of the region's exports of individual commodities. He noted that this did not contradict the overall results for the entire United States market as shown in Table A. It merely provided some disaggregation which, as usual, qualified somewhat the initial findings.

LATIN AMERICAN EXPORTS TO INDUSTRIAL COUNTRIES.
RATES OF GROWTH AND THEIR EXPLANATION IN TERMS OF CHANGES IN
COMPETITIVE POSITION AND IN DEMAND STRUCTURE, 1961–2 TO 1965–6
(Percentages)

Industrial Countries	Growth Rates of Latin American Exports		Actual Growth Rate of Commodity Imports into Industrial Countries	Difference Between Growth Rates	Difference Due To:	
	Actual	Hypothetical			Change in Demand Structure	Change in Competitive Position
	(A)	(H)[a]	(I)	(A–I)	(H–I)	(A–H)
U.S.A.	12·73	24·13	49·01	–36·28	–24·88	–11·40
Canada	37·88	31·98	54·54	–16·76	–22·56	5·80
E.E.C.	30·87	42·60	52·90	–22·03	–10·30	–11·73
U.K.	1·16	21·17	36·14	–24·98	–4·97	–20·01
Other Western Europe	35·13	34·75	42·41	–7·28	–7·66	0·38
Japan	54·65	59·95	63·52	–8·87	–3·57	–5·30
Total	20·36	35·01	47·63	–27·27	–12·62	–14·65

[a] The hypothetical rate of growth of Latin American exports, i.e. that which would have occurred with an unchanged market share in each commodity group, was measured as follows:

$$H = \frac{\sum\limits_{c}\sum\limits_{i} X_{iI}^{c}\{(M_{iII}^{c}/M_{iI}^{c}) - 1\}}{X_{I}}$$

Where:

X = Total Latin American exports to industrial countries.

M = Total imports into industrial countries.

i = Subscripts denoting the ith country or region: (1) U.S.; (2) Canada; (3) E.E.C.; (4) U.K.; (5) Other Western Europe; (6) Japan

I, II = Subscripts denoting period I (1961–2) and period II (1965–6)

c = Subscript denoting the following commodity groups of the S.I.T.C.: (0 and 1) food, beverage and tobacco; (2 and 4) raw materials except fuel, oils and greases; (3) mineral fuels; (5) chemical products; (6 and 8) other manufactures; (7) machinery and transport equipment.

Source: *Increasing Latin America's Share in the U.S.*, C.I.E.S./1376, May 1969, Table I–4, based on data from U.N. *Monthly Bulletin of Statistics.*

TABLE B

LATIN AMERICAN EXPORTS TO THE UNITED STATES BY COMMODITY GROUPS: RATES OF GROWTH AND THEIR EXPLANATION IN TERMS OF CHANGES IN COMPETITIVE POSITION AND IN DEMAND STRUCTURE, 1961–2 TO 1966–7

(Percentages)

Commodity Groups	Actual Growth Rates of Imports of each Commodity into the U.S. (I)	Latin American Exports to U.S.			Difference due to Change in	
		Actual (A)	Hypothetical (H)	Difference (A–I)	Demand Structure (H–I)	Competitive Position (A–H)
Food	22·93	13·05	19·15	–9·88	–3·78	–6·10
Agricultural Commodities	–0·54	–3·47	–0·54	–2·94	0	–2·94
Fuel	18·47	–4·57	13·89	–23·04	–4·58	–18·46
Metals and Minerals	43·03	10·48	49·24	–32·55	+6·21	–38·76
Processed Foods	57·39	51·07	64·04	–6·32	+6·65	–12·97
Raw Materials	29·77	9·45	20·51	–20·32	–9·26	–11·06
Oil and Derivatives	37·19	32·16	37·19	–5·03	0	–5·03
Light Manufactures	79·96	113·34	62·65	33·38	–17·30	50·68
Final Consumption Manuf.	81·74	173·05	48·14	91·31	–33·38	124·91
Intermediate Goods:						
Chemical	25·81	34·45	70·70	8·64	–44·89	–36·25
Basic Metals	120·66	61·38	114·46	–59·28	–6·20	–53·08
Non-metallic Minerals	29·44	–1·60	35·81	–31·04	6·37	–37·41
Machinery and Equipment	254·93	935·35	237·61	680·42	–17·32	697·74

Source: *Increasing Latin America's Share in the U.S. Market*, CIES/1376 (May 1969), Table II–3, based on data from U.N. *Monthly Bulletin of Statistics*.

region's competitive position for *new*, as well as traditional, exports. The fast rates of growth shown by exports in some of the last few lines of Table B suggested the opposite. Their effect was minimal on overall results, but this was because of the almost negligible share of the region in the respective markets at the outset. Moreover Professor Reynolds' own analysis suggested that the region was capable of expanding those same types of exports at a faster rate than accessibility to the U.S. market allowed, since exports of manufactures to Western Europe and Japan grew so much more rapidly. If, as was said earlier in the meeting, most of the growth in these exports to Western Europe and Japan came from Latin American countries other than Mexico and Brazil, his point was then more likely to be a valid one. For apparently it was for most of the remaining countries that greater doubts existed with respect to their ability to become exporters of manufactures.

It would therefore seem to be important to disaggregate the figures for exports of manufactures to Europe and Japan in order to ascertain whether restrictions on the imports of the corresponding products were in operation in the market of the United States.

Some of those restrictions might turn out to be non-tariff. It was somewhat surprising, in view of Professor Reynolds' acknowledgement of the importance of tariff restrictions, as well as of the relatively modest impact that the tariff preferences would have, (*vide* his reference to Clague) that he did not choose to expand on the possibilities of improvement for Latin America's exports to the United States through removing quantitive and other non-tariff restrictions.

Turning now to his second point, which concerned the financial flows aspect of the paper, he would argue here too that it underplayed the role of U.S. policy. To use Professor Reynolds' own tools of analysis, he seemed to have overlooked the existence of two types of loans available in any financial market, i.e. consumers' loans and producers' loans. A producer's loan would enable a capital importing country to slide along the market line, starting from the point of tangency between this line and the transformation curve, towards a point north-east in the quadrant, where a steeper transformation curve could be 'purchased'. It was in fact precisely this type of 'producer's loan' that was made available by the United States to Western Europe, through both the massive inflow of direct investments and the Marshall Plan, and to Japan, through post-war private and official finance. Professor Reynolds in his paper had recognised that it was American capital and technology that nurtured industry in both regions.

This was not to suggest that Latin America should therefore try to attract a massive inflow of direct investment from the United States and rely upon that as a means of becoming a large exporter. As Professor Reynolds had pointed out, technology and private capital alone were not sufficient to achieve structural transformation in the case of Europe. Massive amounts of official capital in the form of long-term balance of payment supports were also necessary.

It would hardly be appropriate in the present world context to argue for a resuscitation of the Marshall Plan idea. Both the United States and Latin America were now convinced that massive, bilateral balance of payments financing would be neither desirable nor practical. However, if we wanted structural change to take place in a gradual fashion, we had to continue seeking a method to mobilise massive financial resources to Latin America, resources not tied to direct investments nor to any individual projects. At least two important kinds of structural change, which everybody agreed were indispensable, could not be made gradually without having recourse to such financing. First, everybody agreed that Latin American countries should reorient their economies towards the export market, and he did not see how the initial stage of import liberalisation could be withstood if the balance of payments was left to its own devices. Second, a reallocation of physical capital in industry, away from activities catering for the upper income groups and towards activities supplying popular consumption goods, was indispensable if a process of improvement of human capital available to the low income groups was to be seriously launched. This was because the required expansion in training activities, which should not be effected at the expense of other investments, would pump in a strong injection of autonomous demand which would swell the relative size of the consumption of low income groups. Such a redistribution of physical capital could be achieved either by dismantling existing capital stocks, or by working on the margin, by allowing laggard industries to grow to the required size, while holding the line on the growth of industries which had grown excessively. The former method would entail grave disruption of economic processes and, more than likely, the discarding of the market system for a long while. The latter could be achieved with the help of the market, by relying to a certain extent on the manipulation of certain key prices. In the process, a good deal of heat was liable to be generated, and he could not see how that could be withstood without a large inflow of long-term balance-of-payments-type financing. He would like to repeat, with Professor Reynolds, that 'changes in the context of growth are considerably less painful than those during the times of recession and widespread unemployment'; and for the case of Latin America it might be the whole feasibility of the changes that was at stake.

Again, the present moment might not be right for optimism about the kind of financial programmes that he was talking about. Yet, we could not simply wait until the storm blew over the U.S. balance of payments picture, and expect that then suitable types of financial programmes would be organised spontaneously. The time for drawing lessons from the relevant experience of the last few years was now. 'A good deal of creative thought should be devoted' to shaping the future participation of the United States in multilateral sources that might nurture those programmes. And constructive schemes giving access to Latin America into the United States capital market, such as the Horowitz proposal presented to UNCTAD I, should be given more serious consideration.

Professor Vernon, however, proposed a rather different interpretation of the data presented by Mr. Szekely. Where positive signs appeared in Table B in the final column, the categories concerned were in each case manufactures. This, he suggested, reflected an association between these successes and increased multinational enterprise activities and stronger ties between U.S. buyers and Latin American sellers. This represented 'success' for Latin American policy, contributing to the diversification of Latin American economies. Where negative signs appeared, they were predominantly in raw materials, where Latin America had deliberately cut supplies for foreign markets and reduced the role of multinational enterprises (e.g. sulphur, copper, oil). This therefore also represented 'success'. In view of the much greater weight of raw materials in exports, it was inevitable that such a shift should worsen the balance of payments position with the United States. In others words, what was depicted here was simply the trade-off between conflicting objectives on the part of Latin American policy makers, and it should realistically be seen as such.

Professor Ranis wished to add two small qualifications to the first half of Professor Reynolds' paper. First, he found the emphasis on union pressure in explaining the rise in U.S. protectionism misplaced. Especially under a Republican Administration the pressure from business was now far more telling. And secondly, it was not correct that the U.S. policy of adopting a *de facto* devaluation (to force a *de jure* devaluation on its main trading partners) was only half carried out; the U.S. had also proposed DISC, which was an export subsidy scheme.

Turning to the second half of the paper he said that it introduced a very interesting concept, in 'comparative advantage in growth'. But how was it defined dynamically? Surely the difference between countries A, B and C must be due to more than differences in resource endowments. It must include the ability to organise factors of production, to be efficient and flexible over time – i.e. the heart of the growth problem. Moreover these capacities would change over time, so that a country which had a 'comparative advantage in growth' today, e.g. Brazil or Mexico, might not have it in the next period, and vice versa. The analysis of such changes brought us back to the core issue of growth – thus it was not clear how the new concept helped.

In the same context it was not clear why countries with the largest growth potential should always attract more private foreign capital. The inflow of such capital – even if we could ignore differences in political stability – surely depended also on the extent of protection and the size of the domestic market, the extent of oligopoly power, the existence of investment guarantees, etc. Table 8.12 needed adjusting for size of country.

Finally, a small point: he did not agree that resistance to aid in the United States was related to its use to secure repayment of private debt; this was rather a main reason why aid was difficult to eliminate outright as far as U.S. business interests were concerned.

Dr. Arndt raised two further problems concerning Professor Reynolds' model. First, Professor Reynolds had assumed the absence of distortions not only in contemporary goods and factor markets, but in intertemporal exchange as well. As he mentioned in another connection, the economies of developing countries were characterised by a variety of distortions caused by externalities, monopoly elements, factor market rigidities, etc. The existence of such domestic distortions prevented the achievement of Pareto optimality; rather than tangency conditions, the result was to move the consumption and/or production points to the interior of the production block prior to the opening of trade. When trade was introduced, achievement of the tangency positions shown in Professor Reynolds' diagrams required domestic policies – taxation or subsidisation, for example – designed to remove the distortions in domestic production and consumption. That such distortions would exist, particularly in the context of intertemporal production and exchange, was quite likely.

Secondly, Professor Reynolds' diagrams were conceived in real terms. Specifically, the rate of interest was a real rate. However, many policy decisions were conducted in terms of nominal rates, which might or might not reflect accurately the underlying real rates, depending upon such factors as the differential rate of inflation in two countries. Consequently, the optimal conditions which determined a country's net lender or borrower position were intimately related to monetary and exchange policies in that country and in the rest of the world.

Dr. König referred to Professor Reynolds' statement[1] that net capital outflows from the U.S. as given in Department of Commerce data, included funds raised abroad. This was misleading: only those funds channelled to the subsidiary *via* the parent company were included. Funds raised by U.S. affiliates in Latin America were not included. But it was certainly true that a 'net capital outflow' might not involve any dollars leaving the United States; rather it might well represent branch (not corporation) earnings left abroad and intra-company book transactions relating for example to the shipment of goods by the parent company to its foreign affiliate for credit. He proposed as a tool to evaluate some of the balance of payments effects of U.S. direct investment the calculation of the ratio of profits to change in book value. A value of more (less) than one would indicate that the foreign investor had directly drawn upon (added to) the host country's resources. For the period 1951 to 1969, this ratio was 1·3 for all U.S. direct investments abroad; by area the values for U.S. investment were, among others, 0·9 in Canada, 0·8 in Europe, 0·8 in Japan, 1·0 in Australia, New Zealand and South Africa, 1·3 in other African countries and 2·3 in Latin America.

Professor Sunkel drew attention to the data which Dr. Botero's paper contained on income distribution but which he had not used or elaborated. If one combined his Appendix Tables I and II, one saw that in the mid-1960s half the population had an annual income of less than $125 *per annum* while 20 per cent had $1,500 or more. Viewing these figures historically, there could have been very little growth in the incomes of the poorer half. Extrapolating forward and assuming that the kind of development Dr. Botero was discussing, based on subsidised manufactured exports, required continuing low relative wages, the picture was one of growing inequality. He doubted that such a growth process was politically possible, let alone desirable, since it would inevitably involve worsening discrepancies in income levels in Latin America.

[1] In his oral introduction: Eds.

Professor Hirschman suggested that while we were speculating on the future, perhaps we should incorporate also the 'no growth' proposals currently being put forward in the United States. Conventional wisdom would suggest that such a policy would have disastrous repercussions on the growth of developing countries' exports, but Dr. Maizels' paper had shown us we had possibly been exaggerating that argument. And 'no growth' would presumably mean no technical progress, which he had shown to be a significant negative factor via synthetics, and also a reduction in the distortions in consumption patterns in developing countries, which were said to be caused by the continual introduction of new goods on the international scene.

Dr. Ferrer took up Dr. Botero's argument that as the U.S. economy shifted increasingly to services it would accordingly import a higher proportion of its manufactured goods and increasingly export services, especially technical and managerial services. Dr. Botero presented this as an opportunity for Latin America to expand labour-intensive production of manufactures and so solve its growing unemployment problem. But the key problem in his view was not only employment but the shift in demand with rising income to advanced technology goods and the need to integrate the productive structure. The relationship between the expansion of capital intensive lines and employment should, thus, be looked at within the framework of the transformation of the productive structure and the overall rate of growth. He saw the projected U.S. move into the export of services as merely a further extension of the Centre–Periphery relationship, whereby Latin America would be left specialising in the technologically stagnant lines – *unless* she made a determined effort to move now into production in sectors of the most advanced and dynamic technology.

A further criticism of Dr. Botero's paper was that the future of U.S.–Latin American economic relations should surely be analysed within its international context.

Professor Reynolds stressed his strong agreement with Professor Sunkel that the continuation of present trends in income distribution was inconsistent with long-term political stability. In so far as he was optimistic as to the possibilities of an improved bargaining position for Latin America *vis-à-vis* the United States, it was entirely based on the substantial income redistribution which as he saw it had to come about in the next ten to twenty years in Latin America. It was the change in income distribution which would fundamentally modify the composition of production and thereby, for example, reduce the region's reliance on U.S. technology.

In response to Professor Ranis, he emphasised that his model was taxonomic in nature, not predictive. He saw intertemporal comparative advantage as a function principally of market size, income distribution, the configuration of labour skills, size of capital stock, the availability of technology and the ability to assimilate it, and natural resource endowments.

Replying to Dr. Arndt, he argued that his model *could* use the geometry to handle distortions due to internal intervention in the capital market, just as distortions due to commercial policy could be handled in international trade theory. But he agreed that it could not handle departures from the frontier – i.e. inefficiencies in the capital market for example.

He agreed with Dr. König that subsidiaries' borrowing in the host country was not included in net capital outflow figures. But over the last two years, if one excluded reinvested earnings from the net capital outflow figures, then between 40 and 50 per cent of the remainder represented U.S. parent companies' borrowing abroad.

On the use of the ratio of the change in profits to the change in book values, he would argue that so long as the investment generated value added greater than its net worth, there would be a net contribution even with a ratio less than one.

Dr. Botero, in reply, stressed his strong agreement with Professor Vernon that access to markets was perhaps the most important asset multinational corporations brought with them. He had implied in his paper that the factor of nationalism meant foreign investment could not play a large role; this was not to say it would play no role, since it did indeed hold the key to success in manufacturing exports; thus some kind of negotiated agreement with the multinational corporations was essential.

Dr. Ferrer had argued that such exports should not be labour-intensive but rather products of 'advanced technology'. He did not see the two as mutually exclusive. There were capital goods which could be labour-intensive and still benefit from rapid growth in demand and dynamic technical change. Textile machinery he thought had proved to be an example and there would be more. Labour-intensive specialisation did not have to mean shoes and textiles.

On Professor Hirschman's suggestion, he believed that a 'zero population growth' policy in the United States would lend itself to increased opportunities for labour intensive exports from Latin America to the United States.

Finally, in response to Professor Sunkel, he commented that this was not the most appropriate forum to discuss income distribution. In his opinion the unequal distribution of income in Latin America was fundamentally related to internal national causes rather than to the relations between Latin America and the industrialised countries. Experience seemed to suggest that whenever the political will to do so existed, redistribution of income had taken place without significant interference from the outside world. He would underline that a better income distribution would never be achieved with 20 or 25 per cent unemployment; this was why he was so concerned about the employment aspect of industrial strategy.

10 The European Economic Community and Latin American Development

Maurice Schaeffer

EUROPEAN ECONOMIC COMMUNITY, BRUSSELS

With its position in the forefront of international trade, its growing influence in the world as a major economic unit which is approaching completion and is seeking political unity, and its willingness to help the developing countries towards take-off, the Community exerts a very real pull on all the countries of the Third World – a pull which is bound to increase in the years ahead. The progress it expects to make towards economic and monetary union and hopes to make on the political front, and the openings for enlargement now afforded, will certainly give the Community additional weight and greater responsibilities *vis-à-vis* the rest of the world, and hence encourage the developing countries to turn to it still more.

This will undoubtedly be the case with the Latin American countries, since their close ties with Europe are the result of an historical process going back some five hundred years. This is an established political fact which to a great extent explains why so many of these countries are tending economically to turn again more markedly towards Europe. For their part, visiting heads of State and Ministers from most of the E.E.C. Member States have declared that their countries will see to it that Latin American interests are looked after in the framing of a Community policy on relations with this part of the world.

Moreover as has been frequently pointed out in this connection, the economies concerned – those of the Community on the one hand and those of Latin America on the other – are by and large complementary, by reason not only of climatic and geographical differences, but also of different degrees of development. Thus, both regions could benefit from a balanced mutual promotion of their economic relations, in regard to both traditional trade and technical and financial co-operation.

Then again, although Latin America is a mosaic of sovereign States varying in potential, size and development, a certain trend towards integration is already in evidence there, more especially in Central America and the Andean countries. The Community's practical experience of economic integration, and also of development aid – even though its development aid has so far been confined to the associated countries and territories – could well prove helpful to Latin America.

Admittedly, the whole human and economic problem of Latin America is on an infinitely vaster scale than that of the A.A.S.M. (Associated African States and Madagascar) and the Mediterranean countries, and this makes sharply apparent the lack of all proportion between the need and the Community's means of meeting it, and the consequent necessity of operating selectively.

However, the Community as such has repeatedly shown itself concerned with expanding trade relations with the Latin American countries, as witness the various decisions taken at, for instance, the tariff talks in Geneva and recently in UNCTAD regarding the introduction of generalised preferences. Meanwhile over the years the Member States individually have gone ahead with schemes of their own for, in particular, technical and financial co-operation with Latin America.

But it is more especially in the last two years that the Community's Latin American policy has been assuming a new dimension, with the Commission's memorandum to the Council on the subject in July 1969 and the Buenos Aires Declaration of July 1970, by the member countries of C.E.C.L.A. These two documents, which provide a comprehensive picture of the issues involved and the wide variety of possible arrangements for dealing with them, form a suitable basis for *further* Community study of the matter. More work was in fact under way in 1970 and 1971, partly in preparation for the scheduled Community/Latin American conference in Brussels on 18 June 1971.

What the Community is seeking is to strike a balance between the more or less specific, but geographically restricted, policy it has adopted in regard to the associated countries, and the arrangements which its increasingly important role in world trade compels it to offer to the other developing countries.

With this in view it has been taking more and more account of other Third World interests over and above those of the associated countries, engaging in dialogue with other parts of the world such as Latin America, and playing its part in world-level action such as that which is the primary concern of UNCTAD. This policy is designed not to supersede but to complement association.

The policy is, however, at present somewhat constricted by the very special situation and incomplete degree of integration of the Community: to form a realistic appraisal of potential economic and financial relations with Latin America we have to bear in mind the evolving and expanding nature of the Community's scope for action in the field of international co-operation.

I. PRESENT CHARACTERISTICS AND LIMITATIONS OF COMMUNITY ACTION

The experience of the last ten years has shown that the external factors influencing the economic growth of developing countries are many and varied, stemming not only from financial and technical co-operation, but as much or even more from the state of international demand, given the influence of exports on growth. So what is needed, along with better co-ordinated technical and financial co-operation, is that conditions be established for the stronger expansion and speedier diversification of the developing countries' exports, both in their trade with one another and in their trade with the industrialised countries in general and the Community in particular.

A Community policy towards Latin America ought to be as far as possible an *integrated* policy: integrated in the first place within the Community itself and integrated also as among the different facets of that policy, namely the commercial, the technical and the financial. This is vital to a more rational and effective policy *vis-à-vis* Latin America. However, the present position is that on the trade side the Community possesses in its common commercial policy a weapon favouring international co-operation, whereas in respect of technical and financial co-operation the bulk of the powers remain in the hands of the Member States individually.

So far as trade policy is concerned the Community has been equipped, since the Common Market entered its definitive period, with a major instrument of co-operation *vis-à-vis* the developing countries generally – which even covers credit insurance and export credits, inasmuch as a systematic push to harmonise and co-ordinate national policies in these respects at Community level was made even before the end of the transitional period.

By virtue of this, the Community as such is represented at international deliberations, having full charge where the business being dealt with is wholly within its province, and acting as part of a joint Community/Member States delegation where the business covers both Community and national matters (such as the negotiation of the international sugar agreement, the international grains agreements and so on).

On the other hand each Member State independently determines the overall amount of public funds it allots to technical and financial co-operation, the breakdown and geographical distribution of that amount, the aims and principles to be followed in laying out the funds, and the proportion to be channelled through multilateral systems. Also, despite the efforts at harmonisation just referred to, the individual Member States still act, on the whole, independently as regards incentives to the private sector to help promote the economic progress of the developing countries, such as tax, credit and investment guarantee arrangements. The Community's own scope for financial action is limited: so far it has only been able to act on any significant scale in the case of Turkey, Greece and the A.A.S.M. and the associated countries and territories, within the limits of the amount available from the European Development Fund (E.D.F.) and the European Investment Bank (E.I.B.).

This, it must again be noted, is largely the result of special historical circumstances. When the Treaty was drawn up, France possessed a great many territories, mostly in Africa, with which she was closely interwoven economically, and she pointed out to the other five countries the problems that would be created in this connection by her own integration into a European common market. This situation, the political aspects of which were no less important than the economic, could have been disposed of radically in two ways, either by straight integration of the territories concerned into the Community or, at the other extreme, by their total exclusion from it. For obvious political and economic reasons both courses were impracticable. Consequently the middle course of 'association' was adopted for these French territories, and was extended to include the overseas countries and territories having special links with Belgium, Italy and the Netherlands. Similarly, in view of a number of other *de facto* situations existing when the Treaty was concluded, the contracting parties appended to the Final Act a series of declarations of intent with respect to certain developing countries.

Since that time three further reasons have emerged which have led the Community to pay attention to the developing countries:

(1) the political and constitutional picture in practically all of these countries has completely altered, posing for them and the Community problems as to their relation to one another which would not have arisen otherwise;

(2) as the Community itself has developed it has worked out, with developing countries not initially associated with it or entitled to establish a privileged relationship under the declarations of intent, ways and means for dealing with problems encountered by them in their relations with it;

(3) economic underdevelopment has become a basic issue of world policy following the developing countries' attainment of political independence: their leaders having given top priority to economic problems and urged these on the attention of the world organisations, the Community of course could not

possibly hold aloof from the efforts made thereafter from such quarters.

Hence, as a result of the original circumstances and these various subsequent developments, the Community has itself constructed, and joined with others in constructing, an intricate fabric of different types of relationship, broadly classifiable into 'bilateral', 'regional-level', and 'world-level'.

For all that, the Community is in some ways ill-provided in the matter of its relations with the developing countries: the E.E.C. Treaty only explicitly affords it the means for technical and financial co-operation in respect of certain associated countries, and since the Community has not furnished itself with any other means of action, all it has had to fall back on in response to pleas from other developing countries – apart from food aid and certain special agreements – has been tariff and quota concessions, for which there will be less and less scope in the future. For it does not look as though there is really much more the Community can do in that direction if it is to retain its substance and preserve the existing association agreements, and at the same time avoid creating serious internal difficulties and exacerbating the conflicts already brewing with certain non-member countries, both industrialised and developing.

The enlargement of the Community, which will extend its international reach and could mean an increase in the number of associated countries, will make it all the more necessary that it should have an economic, financial and technical armoury more in proportion to its stature and to the responsibilities attaching to its steadily growing individual identity. But in the final analysis it must be accepted that there can be no genuine Community policy on development co-operation until substantial further progress has been made towards economic and political union. In the meantime we can only think in terms of step-by-step advances in the operations undertaken and the means provided. However, the Community has never regarded the limited facilities available to it as a reason for limiting its efforts to expand, pragmatically but perseveringly, its economic and financial relations with Latin America.

II. E.E.C.'s TRADE RELATIONS WITH LATIN AMERICA

Tables 10.1 and 10.2 show us the development of trade between the Community and the developing countries. Table 10.1 reveals very clearly that since the Community's inception the developing countries have built up a substantial surplus *vis-à-vis* the Community, whereas as we know their trade balance *vis-à-vis* the rest of the world is for the

TABLE 10.1

TREND IN E.E.C. TRADE WITH THE LESS DEVELOPED COUNTRIES

(millions of U.S. dollars; imports c.i.f., exports f.o.b.)

	1958	1960	1962	1964	1966	1967	1968	1969	1970	Percentage 1958–70
E.E.C. trade with:										
I. Class 2 Countries (except Overseas Associates)[a]										
1. Imports	5,278	5,822	6,318	7,784	9,043	9,314	10,015	10,994	12,589	239
2. Exports	4,265	4,856	4,764	5,239	6,250	6,510	7,248	7,470	8,293	194
3. Trade Balance	−1,013	−966	−1,554	−2,545	−2,793	−2,804	−2,767	−3,524	−4,296	
II. Latin American Countries										
(a) The 20 Latin American Countries										
1. Imports	1,569	1,810	2,122	2,429	2,689	2,702	2,630	3,110	3,528	225
2. Exports	1,450	1,534	1,645	1,604	1,827	1,968	2,225	2,436	2,807	194
3. Trade Balance	−119	−276	−477	−825	−862	−734	−405	−674	−721	
(b) Countries and Territories of Statistical Office Classification[b]										
1. Imports	1,647	1,873	2,223	2,465	2,731	2,808	2,680	3,166	3,591	218
2. Exports	1,604	1,693	1,784	1,676	1,906	2,054	2,326	2,578	2,945	184
3. Trade Balance	−43	−180	−439	−789	−825	−754	−354	−588	−646	
III. Associated African States and Madagascar										
1. Imports	914	952	930	1,150	1,319	1,308	1,466	1,718	1,862	204
2. Exports	712	603	666	821	847	926	1,019	1,117	1,265	178
3. Trade Balance	−202	−349	−264	−329	−472	−382	−447	−601	−597	

[a] 'Class 2' countries: the developing countries. 'Overseas associates': the Associated African States and Madagascar, Overseas Departments, Overseas Territories, Algeria (including Surinam and Netherlands West Indies from 1 January 1963; excluding West New Guinea from 1 January 1963)

TABLE 10.2

PRINCIPAL E.E.C. IMPORTS FROM LATIN AMERICA AND FROM THE A.A.S.M.[a]

(comparative trends; thousands of U.S. dollars, c.i.f.)

Product	1958 L.A.	1958 A.A.S.M.	1966 L.A.	1966 A.A.S.M.	1968 L.A.	1968 A.A.S.M.	1969 L.A.	1969 A.A.S.M.
Coffee	299,2-6	161,236	407,120	152,525	440,084	169,248	477,850	163,716
Cocoa	32,0-7	75,638	11,998	70,150	18,253	114,302	22,121	170,614
Bananas	66,871	48,507	126,824	56,205	126,042	48,671	133,073	46,031
Beef and veal	38,725	1,005	118,130	1,620	69,720	1,086	106,418	1,249
Wheat	30,958	—	45,610	—	39,863	—	41,702	—
Maize	66,936	1,142	235,280	—	167,993	—	179,496	—
Powdered meat and fish	16,3-5	33	96,693	223	88,153	50	115,659	190
Oil	178,309	10,352	143,283	16,003	175,142	10,034	181,243	19,054
Cotton	132,204	53,033	217,391	33,310	168,014	52,906	243,318	56,419
Silver	18,998	—	39,658	—	46,156	2	37,073	—
Copper for refining	—	—	74,851	242,314	93,933	257,140	79,420	158,101
Copper, smelted	80,050	119,447	169,298	31,627	214,298	85,819	335,489	294,910
Iron ore	181,277	287	109,523	57,110	123,918	49,532	151,469	55,300
Tobacco, unmanufactured	18,850	9,820	33,651	7,166	23,435	3,489	35,424	5,006
Wool	28,799	134	51,756	93	35,083	23	30,523	65
Total	1,189,585	480,633	1,881,066	708,346	1,830,089	792,481	2,170,278	971,155

[a] L.A. = Latin America (20 countries); A.A.S.M. = Associated African States and Madagascar.

most part in deficit. Consequently, their surplus with the E.E.C. has enabled them to finance a good deal of their own buying from other industrialised countries and in part to close their own overall trade gap. Thus, the developing countries would appear, taken as a whole, to have been the beneficiaries of the economic growth of Europe, whose progressive integration has done much to expand its import capacity.

As regards Latin America specifically, the trend is very much in line with the wider pattern (again see Table 10.1): the Latin American countries' exports to the Community rose from 1958 to 1970 by 125 per cent and their imports from it by only 94 per cent, with the result that their net credit balance mounted from $119 million in 1958 to $721 million in 1970. Incidentally, the Community's share of Latin American exports increased over the same period from 16 per cent to more than 21 per cent.

This favourable trend has undoubtedly been fostered by the Community's various trade policy moves during these years – in particular, its highly constructive co-operation in the Kennedy Round, its unilateral tariff concessions on Third World commodities, its active contribution to the policy of world agreements, and its preparation of a system of generalised preferences for finished and semi-finished products, due to come into effect in 1971.

Take the Kennedy Round, for instance: if we look at 160 headings for which the aggregate value of E.E.C.'s imports from Latin America in 1963 was $1,124 million, we find that

    (i) on 53 products representing an import volume of $187·7 million the duties were cut by 50 per cent or more;

    (ii) on 30 products representing an import volume of $341·3 million the duties were cut by between 21 and 45 per cent;

    (iii) on 30 products representing an import volume of $67·7 million the duties were cut by between 4 and 20 per cent.

Further, notwithstanding some criticism levelled against certain aspects of the common agricultural policy and association policy, a similar drive has been going on to liberalise and promote E.E.C.–Latin American trade, in both commodities and manufactures.

The main tropical products the Community imports from Latin America (to a value in 1967 of $739 million, 27 per cent of total imports from the region) are coffee, cocoa and bananas. So here the aim has been to find ways to ensure not only that the traditional volume is maintained, both tonnage- and value-wise, but that the share too is maintained as the market grows.

Accordingly, in the 1969 negotiations for the renewal of the E.E.C.–A.A.S.M. convention fresh tariff adjustments were agreed in respect of certain tropical products of importance to many developing countries, including those of Latin America, the duty on coffee being further temporarily reduced from 9·6 to 7 per cent (as against 16 per cent in 1958), and on cocoa from 5·4 to 4 per cent (as against 9 per cent in 1958). These cuts apply to E.E.C. imports from Latin America representing a value of some $500 million. Temporary reductions were also introduced for a number of minor products likewise of importance to Latin America.

As concerns market organisation, of which the Latin American countries have high hopes, the fact that the International Coffee Agreement is working so well will certainly be taken by the Community as a reason for seeking to strengthen it, more especially in the matter of securing a long-term balance between production and rising consumption.

As to cocoa, the Community is continuing to back the efforts for a long-term agreement stabilising prices and thereby, as consumption increases, making for a steady rise in the export earnings of the producer countries, including those in Latin America.

And lastly as regards bananas, it is recognised that whatever arrangement the Community adopts must take account of Latin American interests and allow Latin America a fair share in the growth of the market.

Of the temperate agricultural products imported by the Community from Latin America, far and away the most important are of course grain, sugar, beef and veal. In the case of grain and sugar, the overcoming of Latin American problems depends to some extent on the existing world agreements and possible improvements in their terms. In the case of beef and veal, having regard to the claims of the countries concerned – notably Argentina and Uruguay – ways and means are being considered for arriving at understandings on these products, within the framework of broader economic agreements. A trade agreement between the E.E.C. and the Argentine, instituting co-operation in the agricultural sector generally and on beef and veal in particular, is to be initialled in the near future.

One of the most important issues which has had to be tackled in the last few years, however, has been the question of Latin American exports of manufactures and semi-finished products. It is hardly necessary to recall what a vital part the Community played in the framing of the system of generalised preferences, from the time when the idea was originally mooted in Geneva by the Ministers of the E.E.C. to the time when, ahead of all others, the Community put the system into effect on 1 July 1971.

Leaving aside processed agricultural products (these are covered under partial preferences with margins varying according to product), the E.E.C.'s offer on semi-finished goods and manufactures proper comprises three elements in basic balance with one another – duty-free entry, non-exclusion, and partial imposition of ceilings.

Preferential free entry into the Community had to be made subject to quantitative limits if the Community industries were to be able to accept the idea of generalised preferences at all. But, given that this was necessary, it did not seem beyond the wit of man to devise an arrangement that would be acceptable both to the developing and to the leading preference-giving countries. Thus the system of quantitative ceilings is to be regarded not as a restricting but as a balancing factor, since it is in some measure offset by the preferential exemption from duty and the fact that no semi-finished products or manufactures are excluded.

The ceilings are moreover determined uniformly for all products, and determined very liberally. In the first place the beneficiaries are assured of preferential exemption in respect of their present exports to the E.E.C., defined as the level obtaining in 1968, and in the second place they are likewise to have preferential exemption for an additional volume equal to 5 per cent of the growing imports from the non-beneficiaries – that is, in the main, the industrialised countries. This extra amount thus affords the developing countries the assurance that they will enjoy a share in the expansion of the E.E.C.'s trade with the rest of the industrialised world.

With like intent, in order to safeguard the interests of the non-competitive beneficiary countries, and more particularly the least developed among them, a so-called 'buffer' or 'longstop' clause has been included whereby as a general rule no beneficiary country may exceed 50 per cent of the ceiling for any given product. This does of course limit the extent to which the most competitive developing countries stand to benefit, but since it helps to make the system more evenly balanced it served to get the whole arrangement accepted more readily by the countries likely to benefit the least.

Since its development is considerably further advanced than that of much of the Third World, Latin America will probably be one of the foremost beneficiaries of the generalised preferences, though the benefit will be unevenly distributed owing to the differences in levels of development among the individual Latin American countries. It should be specially noted, by the way, that the Community's offer specifically includes textiles, a sector to which several of the Latin American countries attach great importance.

For the Community, in contrast, the introduction of the generalised preferences involves sacrifices: it will mean an appreciable drop in customs revenue, and could in addition give rise in a number of industries to serious production and labour troubles.

Clearly, following such a substantial lowering of the E.E.C.'s tariff protection, the other instruments of trade co-operation and economic policy generally will from now on assume correspondingly greater importance for its international relations. Such instruments include the various arrangements for the promotion of demand, financing of infrastructure and provision of technical assistance and training – in short, what is known as technical and financial co-operation.

III. SCOPE FOR FINANCIAL AND TECHNICAL CO-OPERATION BETWEEN THE E.E.C. AND LATIN AMERICA

Addressing a seminar on Latin America and the European Economic Community held in 1968 by the Italo-Latin American Institute, the President of the Inter-American Development Bank said:[1]

The flow of funds made available by Western Europe to Latin America has been comparatively meagre and has shown a tendency to fall off in the last few years. This is due in part to the scale of the overall resources the Western European countries are able to devote to foreign aid, but also to the way in which that aid is geographically distributed. The bulk of the foreign aid from European countries – particularly public-sector bilateral aid – has gone to areas and countries with which there have been closer historical and political ties than with Latin America.

Examination of the pattern of the flows of funds furnished by Europe to Latin America suggests two conclusions. Firstly, the greater part of these funds is of private origin, consisting mainly in supplier credits. These are less useful than public-sector funds for area development purposes, as the terms are less attractive and the redemption periods shorter. Secondly, the very fact that private funds account for the greater part of the total flow is indicative of the opportunities and advantages offered by economic relations between the two areas, which gives reason to suppose that if the official assistance by European Governments to development schemes in Latin America were stepped up this source of mutual benefit could become a much richer one.

This picture no doubt calls for some qualification, but it does by and large represent a fairly widely-held view. Although it is very hard to determine what the amount of financial aid to Latin America ought to be given its state of development relative to other parts of the world, the general feeling is that capital flows between Western

[1] Speech delivered in Rome, June 1968.

Europe and Latin America in recent years have not occurred on the scale that might have been expected given the European countries' soaring growth rates: Latin America's share in the overall volume of such flows has been a comparatively small one.

It should be pointed out, however, that bilateral public aid from the six E.E.C. countries to Latin America rose from $70 million in 1960 to $175 million in 1966 and $202 million in 1968 (see Table 10.3), while the proportion of total aid to the Third World going to

TABLE 10.3

TREND IN PUBLIC AND PRIVATE SECTOR FUNDS
FURNISHED TO CENTRAL AND SOUTH AMERICA
BY THE E.E.C. COUNTRIES
(net disbursements in millions of U.S. dollars)

Country	Gifts	Loans	Total Public Aid	Private Flows	Grand Total
1960					
Germany	0·25	23·00	23·25	124·00	147·25
Belgium	—	—	—	1·19	1·19
France	38·60	6·00	44·60	62·20	106·80
Italy	0·19	− 1·39	− 1·20	67·62	66·42
Netherlands	3·70	0·20	3·90	60·00	63·90
Total, E.E.C.	42·74	27·81	70·55	315·01	385·56
1966					
Germany	21·43	23·97	45·40	64·80	110·20
Belgium	1·54	—	7·54	—	1·54
France	119·50	30·60	150·10	80·00	230·90
Italy	0·93	− 36·15	− 35·20	247·95	212·75
Netherlands	5·70	8·06	13·76	4·00	17·76
Total, E.E.C.	149·10	26·50	175·60	396·75	573·15
1968					
Germany	27·53	0·41	27·12	353·00	380·72
Belgium	2·11	—	2·11	16·51	18·62
France	130·70	18·00	148·71	230·00	378·70
Italy	1·23	− 8·81	− 7·58	98·20	90·62
Netherlands	18·26	14·38	32·64	83·50	116·15
Total, E.E.C.	179·83	23·16	202·99	781·21	984·20

Latin America rose from less than 10 per cent in 1960 to 12·5 per cent in 1968, having reached 14·9 per cent in 1967. These figures include technical assistance, which accounted for $94 million in 1966 and $104 million in 1967, i.e. 16·7 per cent and 17·8 per cent of the world total respectively.

Taking the overall volume of net money flows from the Six to

Latin America over these same years – that is, including private flows – we find that funds furnished by the E.E.C. for the development of the Latin American economies increased from $385 million in 1960 to close on $1,000 million in 1968 as shown in Table 10.3. (Table 10.4 gives a detailed breakdown of private investment for the latter year.) Although these flows fluctuated somewhat from year to year, and were very much smaller than those from North America, they nevertheless represent a by no means inconsiderable contribution to the financing of Latin American development.

TABLE 10.4

D.A.C. COUNTRIES: DIRECT PRIVATE SECTOR
INVESTMENT IN CENTRAL AND SOUTH AMERICA[a]
as of 1 January 1968
(millions of U.S. dollars)

Country of Origin	Central America	South America	America, Total	Total, Developing Countries
Belgium	—	112·7	112·7	692·1
France	62·5	405·6	468·1	2,924·0
Germany	102·4	686·3	788·7	1,198·3
Italy	22·0	370·4	392·4	878·0
Netherlands	185·3	754·7	940·0	1,789·3
Total, E.E.C.	372·2	2,329·7	2,701·9	7,481·7
United Kingdom	777·0	869·6	1,646·6	6,740·2
United States	4,396·6	7,384·0	11,780·6	17,448·3
Others	267·7	1,472·7	1,740·4	2,676·2
Total, D.A.C. countries	5,813·5	12,056·0	17,869·5	34,346·4

[a] Very rough approximations, taken from a study now in hand and not yet issued.

The figures just quoted are admittedly those for the division 'Central and South America' in the D.A.C. statistical breakdown, and so include aid from member countries (more particularly France and the Netherlands) to the Caribbean area: if we take only the twenty countries rated by some calculations as constituting Latin America proper, the figures are of course considerably lower (see Table 10.5).

It should be added that the concept of technical and financial co-operation covers a varied and complex assortment of transfers, valued in different ways and practically impossible to aggregate. Besides, as we have seen, the allocation of powers by the Treaty of Rome does not, for the present at all events, afford the E.E.C. institutions much scope in this regard. Clearly, however, in a dialogue between the Community and Latin America there can be

TABLE 10.5

TWO METHODS OF ASSESSING
EUROPEAN AID TO LATIN AMERICA[a]

I. *European aid to Central and South America in 1967 according to D.A.C. yearly statistics*

Country	Public Aid	Private Flows	Total
Germany	56·92	192·60	249·52
Belgium	1·88	32·42	34·30
France	146·40	89·50	215·90
Italy	3·76	– 0·94	2·82
Netherlands	14.04	—	14·04
Total	223·00	295·46	516·58

II. *European aid to Latin America (20 countries) in 1967 according to a special O.E.C.D. study in 1968–9*

Country	Public Aid	Export Credits	Direct Investment and Loans	Total
Germany	57·80	86·40	88·80	233·00
Belgium	2·19	32·41	—	54·60
France	11·90	9·30	59·20	68·50
Italy	6·80	– 12·40	(15·00)	(20·00)
Netherlands	(13·00)	—	—	(13·00)
Total	91·69	115·71	163·00	389·10

[a] The main difference in the overall amounts is due to the fact that the second set of figures (relating to twenty countries of Latin America only) does not include the substantial French public aid to the Caribbean.

Figures in parentheses are rough approximations.

no question of simply ignoring this whole set of problems, which we know to be of such concern to Latin American leaders and of such importance to the development of their countries.

The suggestions made to the E.E.C. by the President of the Inter-American Development Bank on his visits in the last few years may be summed up as follows:

(a) the establishment of a European Investment Fund for Latin America, to be managed by the I.D.B.;

(b) technical and financial participation by Europe in the process of Latin American economic integration, by contributing to and supporting the Pre-Investment Fund for Latin American Integration;

(c) access to the capital markets of the E.E.C. countries, by the abolition of restrictions on loan issues by the Bank and the securing of immunities and privileges enabling such issues to be placed at less expense;

(d) more extensive use of the machinery of parallel financing agreements.

These various proposals have been subjected to study by the Community institutions, and in particular by the Commission. In such a complex matter, it must necessarily take some considerable time for any new decision or move to mature, especially as with some of the suggestions Community unification would need to have progressed further before a start could be made on putting them into effect: thus for instance it is too soon to envisage a Community policy on third-country loan issues which favoured Latin America at the expense of other non-E.E.C. issuers, since most of the Member States have not yet agreed to do away with all exchange and administrative obstacles to loan issues even where the issuer is resident in the Community (see draft of third directive based on Article 37), and would probably therefore be still more disinclined to accept this with respect to third countries.

As concerns private flows, however, the Commission's officials have roughed out a number of guidelines for ensuring better returns and greater ease of investment through financial co-operation between the Community and Latin America.

The Community's role in the former regard can be no more than a marginal one; however, it could see what might be done to adjust the terms of loans (interest rates, redemption periods), and proceed further with the harmonisation already in progress, notably in the O.E.C.D. Another matter arising in this connection is that of tax reliefs.

A further problem that arises constantly is the question of tied loans, borrower countries complaining that these increase the cost of the goods they import. It might be possible to contain such increases to some extent by Community adjustments to the strings. The matter of loan and investment guarantees could also be subjected to special study with respect to Latin America.

In the field of credit insurance the Community is seeking to deal with the intricate problems that bear so closely on exports of capital goods to the developing countries; since exports to Latin America are consisting increasingly of capital goods, it would seem desirable to devote consideration to harmonising the rules governing investment by E.E.C. countries in Latin America.

As to the second aspect, that of ease of investment and lending, this necessitates fuller knowledge of the practical conditions – economic, commercial, financial, legal and political – under which investment and lending activity is to be conducted.

There is still a great deal to be done to make Latin America known to prospective investors in Europe, and conversely to familiarise Latin Americans with conditions in the European money market. This is of course really the sphere of the credit institutions themselves, and more particularly of the regional and sub-regional ones in Latin America and Europe; nevertheless there could well be some Community co-ordination and Community incentives.

It is necessary that the Community should step up its efforts in these various connections. Moreover, this is a sector in which some of the Community countries possess exceptionally valuable experience, of which the rest could take advantage, to the benefit of all concerned, both European and Latin American.

The European Investment Bank should likewise be to the fore in these different fields.

As concerns additional public funds that the Community and the Community countries could allocate to Latin America, obviously as things now stand the funds available are limited, so that it would be necessary to proceed selectively. However, different forms of action, going with different scales of funds, could be considered. For instance, there might be Community participation, in an appropriate form, in the I.D.B.'s Pre-Investment Fund. Or again, the Community might provide the I.D.B. with funds in trust to be loaned out, with the terms and purpose embodied in a suitably flexible procedure agreed to by the donors and the Bank. A third possibility would be for the Community to consider the I.D.B.'s suggestion of setting up a European Investment Fund for Latin America, with operating rules and a legal status to be settled later.

In any event, in working out the practical arrangements to be adopted, it is obviously essential to bear in mind the following two points:

(i) Community activity must be organised as a progression, starting on a comparatively small scale and increasing thereafter as more experience is gained, more accurate intelligence and analysis become possible and the procedures and means of action employed are tested;

(ii) Community activity proper must be carefully co-ordinated with the activities of the Member States conducted bilaterally.

In point of fact, it seems clear that the field in which Community activity proper will expand most rapidly in relation to Latin America is that of technical assistance.

Generally speaking, there could in the first place be co-ordination of Member States' intended bilateral activities for the benefit of Latin American countries through the E.E.C.'s Technical Assistance Group. Then again, the E.E.C. could offer these countries cadre traineeships in the offices of the Brussels institutions and university or postgraduate study scholarships, financed out of the Community budget. In addition, it could supply on request a number of specialists in regional integration.

On the trade side the E.E.C. could do much to help secure improved sales prospects for Latin American export products by a variety of means already tried out, including in particular the establishment of Community or national bodies to arrange for these countries to be represented at fairs and exhibitions in the Member States, as has been done in some of them.

CONCLUSION

Given the European Economic Community's and the Latin American countries' will to work together, what is needed from now on is to display imagination – to seek where possible new and original modes of co-operation, and thereby impart fresh momentum to the efforts the Community and its members are already making, so that the outcome for Latin America may be the most beneficial possible. This can only be achieved, though, by judicious choice of the sectors where the Community's activity can be deployed to best effect and of the measures seen to be the most appropriate.

This approach, as we have seen, underlies the Declaration and Resolution of 29 July 1970, by the Ministerial meeting of CECLA in Buenos Aires, calling for regular co-operation between the two groups of countries to enable them to work out together arrangements satisfactory to both for dealing with problems arising in their economic and trade relations.

With the same end in view, at the suggestion of the E.E.C. Council of Ministers, a Conference between the European Communities and the Latin American countries belonging to the Special Commission for Latin American Co-ordination met in Brussels on Friday, 18 June 1971. Both sides emphasised that they were most anxious to develop their relations with one another and firmly resolved to do so. The Conference, convened to pinpoint the aims and procedures for constructive co-operation between the Latin American countries and the Communities, adopted a joint Declaration which included provision for the establishment of a 'machinery for dialogue' to serve as the means for instituting, and progressively refining and improving on a pragmatic basis, arrangements for co-operation between them. Through this machinery, the CECLA and Community countries will together be able:

(i) to consider ways and means of dealing with the problems arising in their economic and trade relations;

   (ii) to endeavour to work out non-preferential arrangements designed to expand and diversify their trade, without prejudice to the concessions to be granted by the Community under the generalised preferences;

  (iii) to consider matters in connection with the upholding of their interests, without prejudice to their respective policies;

  (iv) to have a framework of reference facilitating the development of relations between the Latin American countries and the Community: the dialogue will thus supplement but not encroach on bilateral relations between one or more Latin American countries on the one hand and one or more Community countries, or the Community itself, on the other;

   (v) to consider, by agreement, certain matters handled by the international organisations, with due regard for each party's specific responsibilities at the international level, so as to make a constructive contribution to the work of these organisations without interfering with their activities.

The basic framework is thus now in place and the dialogue instituted for more active and effective co-operation between the European Economic Community and Latin America.

The E.E.C.'s own experience has already taught it, time and again, that dialogue on these lines is the most workable procedure for joint efforts to devise the practical arrangements needed in its relations with countries of the Third World. We may therefore rest assured that those in charge of affairs will bring to bear the practical sense that is required to obtain ever more fruitful results as time goes on.

11   Great Britain and Latin American Economic Development

Alec Nove
UNIVERSITY OF GLASGOW

If this were a historical survey, then of course I would have much to say about the vital role of British investment, managerial skills and capital goods, in many Latin American countries. Indeed one encounters to this day legends concerning British responsibility for the underdevelopment of some countries. Thus I once met an economist who had written a dissertation designed to prove that British-financed railway building in Argentina was not deliberately designed to weaken economic development.

However, Great Britain's role was declining already before the last war. The financial necessities of the war years, and of their immediate aftermath, led to the sale of many British-owned capital assets. War-time and post-war shortages of goods inhibited exports, financial stringencies inevitably led to a virtual ban on overseas investment. At the same time the war gave a powerful impetus to Latin American industrial development, under the shelter of high tariff walls and import restrictions. Traditional patterns of trade and investment were disrupted, and so were old associations with Latin American affairs. A new generation of business men grew up who knew little or nothing about Latin America. For a few years special bilateral links survived with some countries, for instance Argentina: meat was bartered for scarce industrial materials. But with the coming of multilateralism and currency convertibility, Britain and other European countries had to try to regain their former share of the Latin American market in competition with the United States, which had become by far the largest supplier of goods and capital alike.

This paper will explore Great Britain's trading and financial relationship with Latin American countries in recent years, with the aim of identifying those factors most likely to influence developments in the future. These include possible membership of the European Economic Community.

I. TRADE WITH LATIN AMERICA

We must begin by looking at the pattern of trade and its evolution. The figures show clearly that Latin America is not a major factor in

British foreign trade. Roughly 3·5 per cent of British exports go to all Latin American countries, or the same value as to the Netherlands alone. It may seem that this low percentage figure is evidence of a marked decline in British–Latin American economic relations. However, this is not so. These percentages were very similar before the war. Thus in 1938 it was about 3·5 per cent also. Since the volume of British exports is now nearly 2½ times greater than in 1938, it follows that British exports with Latin America are also that much higher. However, before the war a mere 3·5 per cent of British exports represented a higher proportion of Latin American imports than it does today. In the post-war years the trade of Latin American countries has grown very rapidly, and so Britain's *share* has fallen, even while the absolute volume has risen.

Imports have also risen, but the trend in the most recent years has been a fall in the relative share of Latin American countries, due largely to stagnation or reduction in imports from Argentina and Venezuela. The basic statistics are set out in Table 11.1. (The reader

TABLE 11.1

U.K. IMPORTS FROM LATIN AMERICA
(£ millions)

	1966	1967	1968	1969	1970
Argentina	70·5	72·1	51·7	78·7	65·6
Bolivia	22·3	23·8	26·3	34·2	28·5
Brazil	31·5	26·5	37·8	50·7	62·8
Chile	44·2	46·5	56·5	72·1	64·9
Colombia	10·1	9·8	9·0	7·5	8·9
Costa Rica	0·4	0·4	0·4	0·4	0·4
Cuba	4·6	4·7	6·9	5·4	5·7
Dominican Republic	0·07	0·8	0·05	0·7	1·1
Ecuador	0·2	0·2	0·4	0·4	0·6
El Salvador	0·1	0·2	0·2	0·2	0·3
Guatemala	0·6	0·7	1·0	0·8	0·9
Haiti	0·3	0·1	0·2	0·2	0·1
Honduras	0·3	0·2	0·3	0·3	0·3
Mexico	12·3	11·5	18·0	14·5	6·3
Nicaragua	0·6	0·7	1·2	1·0	0·8
Panama and Canal Zone	1·8	2·0	2·5	2·7	1·8
Paraguay	1·6	2·3	2·7	2·1	2·3
Peru	9·8	7·7	11·6	13·9	15·2
Uruguay	12·7	13·7	17·5	13·1	8·6
Venezuela	58·1	68·3	73·1	56·6	50·8
Total	282·3	292·3	317·5	355·7	325·9
Per cent of all British imports	4·7	4·5	4·0	4·3	3·6

Source: Board of Trade, *Overseas Trade Statistics of the United Kingdom.*

will doubtless bear in mind the price increases which have occurred, and the devaluation of sterling in 1967.)

Venezuelan oil is a special case, reflecting the supply policies of international companies. But even so the trend is not a particularly favourable one. When, as is likely at the time of writing, Britain joins the European Economic Community, matters will not improve, as will become apparent from the commodity analysis which will follow. Or, to put it more precisely, the exporters of minerals (Chile, Bolivia, to a lesser extent Venezuela and Mexico) will benefit from British industrial growth, if it is stimulated by entry into the E.E.C., while exporters of foodstuffs will probably lose on balance.

An analysis of all Latin American sales to Britain for the year 1970, by divisions of the international trade classification, will be found in Appendix A.

With British membership of the E.E.C. in mind, let us now look at the performance and prospects of sales of principal commodities in the U.K. market.

BRITISH IMPORTS OF TEMPERATE FOODSTUFFS

The pattern of the more recent years is given in Table 11.2. These are all items in which Argentina used to dominate the British market. In 1937 she exported to Britain 14·7 million cwt of beef. In 1970 it was barely a seventh of this. In 1937 Britain bought 15·5 million cwt of Argentinian wheat, a sixth of all her imports; in 1970 this trade was quite negligible. Maize in 1937 came almost all from Argentina, 62 out of the total of 71 million cwt. Now Britain's principal suppliers are the United States and France, with Argentina occupying a place below not only South Africa but (astonishingly) the Netherlands.

The reasons for this trend are well known, and are essentially Argentinian: the export surplus has fallen. Canned meat has held up better, but even there Argentina has fallen to third place behind Denmark and the Netherlands in the British market. More of Argentina's limited export surplus has gone to Western Europe (see Appendix D), one reason being British sanitary restrictions imposed on certain kinds of beef from Argentina.

E.E.C. membership will have obvious adverse effects on 'outsiders' through the common agricultural policy. This is designed to ensure an adequate income for the peasants of France and Germany, and prices are therefore fixed high. No imports may come in below the fixed price; any difference between the E.E.C. price and a lower world-market price must be paid into the community budget and is used to finance the agricultural producers of the Community.[1] If the

[1] All this applies only to temperate agricultural products, of course.

TABLE 11.2

U.K. IMPORTS FROM THE WORLD AND FROM
LATIN AMERICA: TEMPERATE FOODSTUFFS[a]
(£ millions)

	1968	1969	1970
(011.1) Beef, fresh, chilled or frozen:			
Total	74·5	99·7	93·8
Brazil	(1·0)	(4·0)	3·4
Argentina	12·7	38·2	26·3
Uruguay	5·6	4·8	—
(013.81) Canned meat:			
Total	71·3	63·7	75·2
Brazil	1·1	1·1	0·8
Paraguay	2·1	1·6	1·6
Uruguay	0·7	0·1	—
Argentina	14·3	10·5	14·7
(041·0) Wheat:			
Total	117·8	132·4	140·6
Argentina	1·4	3·3	0·5
(044.0) Maize (corn):			
Total	88·2	78·4	88·0
Argentina	0·7	3·3	5·7

Source: Board of Trade, *Overseas Trade Statistics of the United Kingdom.*

[a] Numbers in brackets on the left refer to trade classification. Bracketed figures in the table are estimates; a dash indicates amount was less than £0·1 mil.

N.a. (see later tables) = not available.

price within the E.E.C. falls below a 'floor' or support price, which is a little below the price normally fixed for imports, then the E.E.C. steps in to purchase any surpluses at this price, dumping them on overseas markets if no other use is found for them, at any price they can fetch. The prices fixed by the community can be reviewed at a moment's notice, and apply even to shipments contracted for and already *en route*, say from Buenos Aires to London.

This has a negative effect on any 'outsiders', in several ways. Firstly, they cannot rationally plan their agriculture. How can (say) an Argentinian or Uruguayan *estancia* base calculations on sales to Europe, when the market could to all intents and purposes be closed to them at a moment's notice, and when no contracts which include prices would be valid if the E.E.C. altered the price at which imports are allowed to come in? Of course, the intention is to ensure that Europe is as self-sufficient as possible, or even if this is not the intention this has the effect of fixing import prices at a level at which the less efficient peasant holdings are rendered profitable. In one year, when harvests are poor or there is an inadequate output of meat, imports may be welcomed and be profitable. Similarly, the E.E.C. may decide actively to encourage imports of feeding stuffs for livestock. But this could be reversed the very next year if Europe's output rises. In a good year insult would be added to injury by dumping in third markets.

The high internal prices act as a stimulus to production and investment in agriculture, and naturally lead to a greater degree of self-sufficiency within the E.E.C. area. In the particular case of Britain, it must be expected that membership will lead to a switch towards European sources of supply, and also that the high prices will act as a stimulant to British agriculture, which is (by European standards) fairly low-cost and efficient, so domestic farm output, especially grain, is very likely to increase by a large percentage.

It is true that Dr Mansholt is advocating a plan to reduce the number of small peasant holdings, and to reduce gradually the very high farm prices now ruling. However, the strength of the farm lobby will make this a difficult and very slow matter – the United States price support scheme is similarly 'untouchable' politically – and the net result of transferring dwarf holdings to larger consolidated farms may increase Europe's farm output still further.

However, it is interesting to note that in 1969 Argentina sold far more cereals and feeding stuffs to the existing E.E.C. countries than to Great Britain (see Table, Appendix D), and so it must certainly not be assumed that prospects must be poor. Obviously, Great Britain's membership would enlarge the Community's deficit in many temperate agricultural products to which the policy applies. It is also worth mentioning that, in a period of inflation, it is unnecessary to reduce prices in order to reduce incentives and bring European prices closer to world levels; and it would be enough to hold them steady. However, experience suggests that it is very difficult indeed to resist pressure to increase farm prices.

Britain's role as a member will be to strengthen those who favour lower prices and better terms for imports, since this would accord with her economic interest. Realism compels one to state that moves in this direction are likely to encounter strong opposition, especially from the French but also from the Germans.

IMPORTS OF OTHER AGRICULTURAL PRODUCTS AND MATERIALS

(i) *Fruit and vegetables*

Latin America has contributed little here. Brazil has supplied about 1·5 per cent of the British market for oranges, Ecuador 1 per cent of the bananas, Brazil sells £1·7 million of nuts, Chile has a modest share under the heading of 'fresh fruit not elsewhere specified', and Mexico and Argentina have a tiny portion of the market for fruit juices. The only other item under this head of any significance for Latin America is £1·4 million of unspecified vegetables from Chile.

In this sector (and also in the case of coffee and cacao) membership of the E.E.C. would have extremely complex consequences, and this for a number of reasons. Firstly, there are a few instances where an E.E.C. country will be directly favoured, for instance Italy. Secondly, there are developing countries which are associates. The Yaoundé agreement gives reciprocal preferences to former French, Belgian and Italian colonies in Africa, and the Arusha convention affects Uganda, Kenya and Tanzania. These and other former British colonies in Africa are to be offered 'Yaoundé' terms of association. Britain is also negotiating special arrangements for the West Indies. If all concerned accept, then this could work to the disadvantage of outsiders. Thus, to take one example, West Indian bananas might gain in the existing E.E.C. countries, while Britain could buy more from former French or Italian colonies, which would be of no benefit to Latin America. Other countries (Turkey, Morocco, for instance) and other preferential trading agreements (e.g. with Israel and Yugoslavia) affect the fruit and vegetable picture, or could do so if negotiations are completed.

However, there are further complications. Thus, the dominance of Commonwealth suppliers in the British market is due partly to Commonwealth preference, but most of all to old-established trading and business links, reinforced in some instances by quota restrictions. One must also compare customs duties. All these factors play a role in assessing the future of banana imports. The trade is dominated by a very few firms. The E.E.C. countries have a 20 per cent tax on bananas from non-associated countries, while Great Britain admits them duty free from the Commonwealth, levies a small duty (£0·375 per cwt) on other countries, and imposes a quota on imports of bananas from the dollar area. Partly because of the quota, partly because of the buying habits of the importing firms, such countries as Ecuador are all but excluded from the British market – and it is not surprising that Ecuador therefore does not see why it should encourage British exports to that country. In such a situation, what effect would Britain's membership of the E.E.C. have? It is very unpredictable, but, in the case of bananas, not too hopeful. (It is even possible that the lucrative West German market will be adversely affected by the inclusion of British ex-colonies under the expanded Yaoundé agreement, but hitherto West Germany has made an exception for banana imports and allowed a special quota of non-E.E.C. and non-associated bananas.)

(ii) *Sugar and molasses*

The figures are given in Table 11.3. Here again, old Commonwealth links and preferences, administered by quotas rather than import duties, are very strong. In fact, the biggest single supplier of sugar to the British market is Mauritius, with Australia second and

TABLE 11.3

U.K. IMPORTS OF SUGAR AND MOLASSES
FROM THE WORLD AND FROM LATIN AMERICA
(£ million)

	1968	1969	1970
(061.1) Raw sugar, beet and cane:			
Total	92·3	100·2	95·0
West Indies*a*	(26·1)	(25·9)	(28·4)
British Honduras	n.a.	n.a.	(1·1)
Guyana	(7·2)	(9·7)	(9·3)
Cuba	0·3	0·3	0·8
Brazil	0·3	0·6	—
(061.5) Molasses:			
Total	5·7	5·5	7·3
Cuba	n.a.	n.a.	3·8
Mexico	n.a.	n.a.	0·7
Brazil	n.a.	n.a.	0·2

For source and other notes, see Table 11.2.

a Jamaica, Antigua, Barbados, Trinidad and Tobago.

Jamaica third. The 'world market' is a network of special arrangements, special prices and special quotas. One real menace is, of course, sugar-beet. Britain has long been a country which relies heavily on imports of cane sugar,[1] while the E.E.C. countries have large sugar-beet interests. In the negotiations for Britain's entry, much was made of the need to protect the interests of Britain's traditional suppliers of cane sugar. It is hoped that this will happen, at least for a while, but clearly the chances of other would-be exporters of sugar are poor, to put it mildly. However, the future depends also on the re-negotiation of the international Sugar Agreement, and the future of the Australian quota.

[1] Though Britain herself has farmers who grow sugar-beet, and who might so benefit from higher E.E.C. prices that they would expand production. However, it is thought likely that restrictions will be placed on the expansion of sugar-beet acreages not only in Britain but also in France, according to assurances given by Mr Rippon, Britain's chief negotiator.

Cuba remains a major supplier of molasses, and this is likely to be a sector where cane enjoys a great advantage.

(iii) *Coffee*

The British market has been transformed. In 1937 we imported a mere 370,000 cwt of coffee, and the masses of the people hardly ever drank it, preferring tea at all times. In 1970 the total imported was close to 2,000,000 cwt. Coffee drinking has spread to all classes. However, the share of Latin America in the market has declined very greatly. In 1937 Costa Rica was the largest supplier by value, and a close second to Kenya and Uganda by volume. Colombia and Brazil trailed far behind, but Latin America supplied almost half the market. After the war Uganda and Kenya soared ahead of everyone. Even as recently as 1968 the three Latin American countries named above together held a mere 12 per cent of the British market, as shown in Table 11.4. In the very last years, however, Brazil has moved up very sharply, as the table shows. This has been due to two causes, both connected with the dominance in the British market of soluble coffee powders: the direct sale in Britain of Brazilian-made powders, and an important deal between Brazilian producers and three British manufacturers of soluble coffee.

TABLE 11.4

U.K. IMPORTS OF COFEE FROM THE WORLD
AND FROM LATIN AMERICA
(£ million)

	1968	1969	1970
(0.71.1–0.71.3) Coffee beans, extracts, concentrates, etc.:			
Total	31·2	34·1	42·4
Costa Rica	n.a.	n.a.	0·2
Colombia	0·8	1·0	1·8
Brazil	3·6	7·3	13·3

Source and notes: see Table 11.2.

Until these Brazilian deals were made, the lower-quality but cheaper coffees (of the Robusta species) had dominated the market, because they are quite adequate for soluble coffee – and the British consumer has no coffee-drinking tradition which would enable him to judge quality (coffee consumption per head is still far below most European countries or the United States). This factor and established commercial ties have been far more important than Commonwealth preference in keeping Latin Americans out. Indeed the rate of duty (£0·315 per cwt) is now little over 1 per cent.

Membership of the E.E.C. would alter the picture, probably in an adverse direction. There is a common external tariff of 7 per cent. But 'Yaoundé' countries' coffee can enter duty free. If these rules are maintained after British entry, it would increase the extent of discrimination against Latin American coffees. There might also be the impact of Value Added Tax, if this applies to coffee (in Germany there is an internal tax in addition).

On the other hand, a glance at Appendix D will show how insignificant the British market is for Latin America, compared with the heavy coffee drinkers of the Continent of Europe. If U.K. membership increases coffee-drinking, and if firms which market Brazilian, Colombian and Costa Rican coffees can more easily invade the British market, this may well offset the negative aspects of membership, and sales in Britain may go up.

(iv) *Cacao*

Practically all British imports of beans (£27·8 million in 1970) come from the Commonwealth (Nigeria and Ghana). Presumably this must be expected to continue, and be reinforced by the logic of 'Yaoundé'. However, Brazil has acquired about 15 per cent of the British market for cacao butter (£2·5 million out of £15 million), and it is not clear how this would be affected by E.E.C. membership.

(v) *Feeding stuffs for animals*

Oil-seed cake from Argentina, and fish meal from Peru, each have a small (roughly 5 per cent) share of a market dominated by suppliers who are likely to benefit from E.E.C. membership or association. However, Latin American countries sell far more to existing members than to the United Kingdom (see Appendix D), so the future could be bright.

IMPORTS OF RAW MATERIALS

(i) *Timber and textile materials*

Brazil has a small share in the market for lumber. The situation is given in Table 11.5. Brazil also provides about 1·5 per cent of Britain's imports of plywood. For lumber and products the competition is almost wholly non-E.E.C. (U.S.S.R., Finland, Sweden, U.S.A., Poland, are the largest sources of supply), and so prospects would be quite good.

Latin America plays a bigger role in supplying wool, as shown in Table 11.6. Britain's principal suppliers are Commonwealth countries (Australia and New Zealand especially). It may be that membership of the E.E.C. will help to increase the Latin American share of the market.

The situation is also promising for cotton, in that Britain's present suppliers are 'outsiders'. The figures are given in Table 11.7. In addition, Brazil sells cotton linters and cotton waste, and, with Argentina, supplies hides, skins and furs, but with only a small share of the market.

TABLE 11.5

U.K. IMPORTS FROM THE WORLD AND FROM
LATIN AMERICA: TIMBER
(£ million)

	1968	1969	1970
(243.21) Sawn lumber, conifer:			
Total	175·2	166·3	184·0
Brazil	8·3	6·1	6·0

Source and notes: see Table 11.2.

TABLE 11.6

U.K. IMPORTS FROM THE WORLD AND FROM
LATIN AMERICA: WOOL
(£ million)

(262.1 and 262.2) Sheep's and lamb's wool:	1968	1969	1970
Total	98·7	99·3	79·5
Peru	1·0	0·8	0·25
Chile	0·5	0·9	0·6
Brazil	3·0	4·1	3·7
Uruguay	10·3	7·6	7·8
Argentina	7·5	6·8	4·4

Source and notes: see Table 11.2.

TABLE 11.7

U.K. IMPORTS FROM THE WORLD AND FROM
LATIN AMERICA: COTTON
(£ million)

	1968	1969	1970[a]
(263.1) Raw cotton:			
Total	50·7	43·4	43·7
Colombia	5·9	6·1	6·2
Brazil	n.a.	n.a.	2·0
Peru	2·3	2·1	n.a.
Mexico	1·0	1·1	n.a.

[a] A change of statistical coverage in 1970 makes the figures not perfectly comparable. Figures for countries for 1970 are not published: the two quoted were obtained from the Department of Trade and Industry.

For source and other notes, see Table 11.2.

(ii) *Imports of minerals and metal ores*

Mexico has been supplying about 10 per cent of the British market for sulphur, but the principal competitor is France. Iron ore is of greater importance; see Table 11.8. Britain's biggest supplier has been Canada, and membership of the E.E.C. could well increase Latin American opportunities, though of course much depends on the rate of expansion of the iron and steel industry.

TABLE 11.8

U.K. IMPORTS FROM THE WORLD AND FROM LATIN AMERICA: IRON ORE
(£ million)

	1968	1969	1970
(281.3) Iron ore and concentrates:			
Total	84·2	87·5	105·1
Venezuela	7·8	7·2	7·9
Brazil	2·8	4·9	7·7

Sources and notes, see Table 11.2.

Peru supplies half of Britain's imports of lead, and a small portion (5 per cent or so) of zinc ores. Tin has for long been dominated by the 'Latins'; see Table 11.9.

Brazil has some 20 per cent of the market for manganese, and Bolivia has a similar share of the tungsten. Mexico has a similar share of the important silver ore market. There is every prospect of progress in all these commodities, if Britain's economy grows.

Brazil has a dominant position as a supplier of castor oil (£2·3 million out of £2·4 million in 1970).

(iii) *Imports of oil*

Oil is a huge item. Imports of oil and oil products together amounted to £925 million in 1970, and have grown faster than any major commodity. Of this sum, Venezuela provided £42 million in 1970,

TABLE 11.9

U.K. IMPORTS FROM THE WORLD AND FROM LATIN AMERICA: TIN
(£ million)

	1968	1969	1970
(283.6) Tin ores and concentrates:			
Total	27·7	35·2	30·2
Bolivia	24·4	31·4	24·5
Argentina	n.a.	n.a.	1·5

Source and notes, see Table 11.2.

mostly in the form of crude, which happened to be a good deal less than the figure for £968 (£64 million), the fall being bigger still if price changes are allowed for. Despite its immense importance, there is little point in considering the future of the oil trade, dependent as it is on the policy of the oil companies and on unpredictable events in the Middle East.

A much smaller volume of a different kind of oil ('essential oils', i.e. perfume materials), worth £9·5 million in all, includes small quantities from Brazil (£0·45 million) and Paraguay (£0·16 million).

IMPORTS OF METAL SEMI-MANUFACTURES

Peru and Mexico provide about 7 per cent of the market for silver.

The importance of Chile as a supplier of copper is evident from Table 11.10. The two largest suppliers to the British market are

TABLE 11.10

U.K. IMPORTS FROM THE WORLD AND FROM
LATIN AMERICA: COPPER
(£ million)

	1968	1969	1970
(682.1) Copper and copper alloys:			
Total	235·0	279·4	272·4
Chile	51·7	66·9	58·2

Source and notes, see Table 11.2.

Zambia and the United States. Apart from small quantities of other non-ferrous metals from Peru and Mexico, no other country or item is at all significant under this head.

IMPORTS OF MANUFACTURES

The Latin American countries are conspicuous by their insignificance in all the categories of manufactured goods, as the table in Appendix A shows.

Prospects under this head may well be affected by the tariff preferences for developing countries, proposed by UNCTAD and now coming into operation. Both Great Britain and the E.E.C. countries are introducing duty-free entry for a wide range of manufactures and semi-manufactures, and also some processed foodstuffs. One effect is to improve the competitive position of non-Commonwealth developing countries, since those in the Commonwealth benefited from duty-free access in a number of cases. The E.E.C. proposals differ in some respects from the British ones: thus the list of duty-free commodities is more 'liberal' for manufactures, less so for processed foodstuffs. The duty-free provisions are modified by a quota ceiling based on a formula (the value of imports of the given product in 1968, plus 5 per cent of all imports from outside the Community), whereas the British proposals reserved the right to impose restrictions to avoid 'serious injury' to domestic producers.[1]

SOME CONCLUDING OBSERVATIONS ON IMPORTS

Clearly it is trade in manufactures which is growing most rapidly, and equally clearly the Latin American impact on British and other European markets is negligible. The right to duty-free access to developing countries in manufactured goods is a step forward, but this hardly solves the problem. Import duties on most manufactures are low anyway, and a few per cent preference as against Japan or the U.S.A., or equal terms with competitors from West Germany, Italy and France, will not really help, unless of course Latin American countries develop some original and competitive lines of their own.

The E.E.C. rules, which Britain will be adopting if she joins, can harm agricultural exports of every 'outsider', and Latin America along with Canada, the U.S.S.R., Australia and the U.S.A. will lose ground in the British market, in so far as they supply temperate foodstuffs. It is hard to defend the agricultural rules of the Community, save in terms of political necessity. But such necessity is a familiar fact of political life also in the United States and elsewhere.

Equally anomalous are the special arrangements made for ex-colonies. Originally designed to preserve special advantages for ex-colonies of the 'Six', mainly in Africa, and extended to some former British colonies by British membership, these arrangements divide the developing world into two categories: those which were colonies until recently and those which were not. This to some extent replaces special forms of preference (differing from product to product) granted, before the E.E.C. was formed, by Britain and by France for their colonies and ex-colonies, and so the difference made by British membership may not be great, but on balance the net effect on Latin America is likely to be negative.

It follows that the best chance of big expansion lies in the area of industrial raw materials, minerals, fuels and semi-manufactures, unless and until, possibly in partnership with Western firms, manufacturing for export to Europe progresses far beyond its present insignificant state.

[1] Details taken from *Trade and Industry* (24 March 1971), pp. 630–1.

TABLE 11.11

U.K. EXPORTS AND RE-EXPORTS TO LATIN AMERICA
BY COUNTRY
(f.o.b., £ million)

	1966	1967	1968	1969	1970	Imports from U.K. as Percentage of Total Imports[a]
Argentina	23·3	25·3	33·8	46·9	44·1	5·9 (ii)
Bolivia	1·7	1·7	2·3	2·6	2·2	4·6 (iii)
Brazil	17·1	19·9	44·7	43·7	60·8	4·5 (i)
Chile	11·0	13·4	15·0	17·6	20·5	5·7 (i)
Colombia	15·7	8·5	12·2	12·2	12·9	5·0 (i)
Costa Rica	2·6	3·7	2·7	5·8	4·7	6·2 (ii)
Cuba	8·1	8·7	12·5	13·2	20·6	2·9 (iii)
Dominican Republic	2·2	2·2	2·6	2·9	3·6	3·5 (i)
Ecuador	3·3	3·3	4·5	4·2	7·0	5·2 (i)
El Salvador	3·5	3·0	1·9	1·8	2·3	2·6 (iv)
Guatemala	3·7	3·1	4·1	3·5	4·2	3·1 (ii)
Haiti	0·6	0·5	0·7	0·8	1·0	—
Honduras	1·0	1·0	1·2	1·3	1·5	1·7 (ii)
Mexico	20·6	26·9	32·2	29·9	34·2	3·1 (ii)
Nicaragua	1·8	2·9	2·1	2·9	2·7	4·0 (ii)
Panama and Canal Zone	5·5	6·7	6·1	7·7	8·8	4·1 (ii)
Paraguay	1·3	1·3	2·0	2·5	2·2	8·9 (ii)
Peru	12·0	12·5	11·6	11·8	9·9	4·9 (i)
Uruguay	3·2	3·4	3·4	4·8	6·4	6·1 (ii)
Venezuela	23·9	21·7	32·8	31·7	33·7	5·4 (ii)
Total	162·3	169·7	228·4	247·9	283·2	
Percentage of total British exports	3·1	3·3	3·6	3·4	3·5	

[a] Figures in last column kindly provided by Department of Trade and Industry, London: (i) 1968; (ii) 1969; (iii) 1967; (iv) 1970.

Source and other notes, see Table 11.2.

U.K. EXPORTS OF GOODS

Recent trends in total British exports to Latin America are given in Table 11.11. These exports are concentrated in relatively few broad categories, as shown in Table 11.12. Exports of most consumers' goods are insignificant, due mainly to very high tariffs in the principal countries concerned. The two exceptions are whisky and, to a very limited extent, motor cars. Machinery alone accounts for over half the total.

TABLE 11.12

U.K. EXPORTS TO LATIN AMERICA AND TO
THE WORLD, BY COMPOSITION, 1970[a]
(£ million)

	To All Latin American Countries	Total Exports to All Countries
(11) Alcoholic beverages	15·0	224·9
(51 and 53) Chemicals and dyestuffs	17·7	291·8
(68) Iron and steel	15·3	350·2
(69) Metal goods, cables, tools, etc.	11·9	260·4
(71) Machinery, except electric	98·2	1,642·4
(72) Electrical machinery	24·0	579·1
(73) Vehicles, ships, aircraft	39·1	1,079·8
Total	221·2	

[a] 1970 is the first year in which trade statistics are arranged in this manner by sub-category, and so comparable figures for past years cannot be given for the above items.

Source and other notes, see Table 11.2

It is as well to stress again the small share of Latin America in British exports. Sales to Belgium in 1970 amounted to £228·6 million, more than to all twenty countries. Yet Belgium has about an eighth of the population of Mexico alone. The United States took £933 million of British exports.

While it appeared important to devote considerable space to discussing the prospects of Latin American exports to the United Kingdom, and the effects upon them of E.E.C. membership, it does not appear necessary in the present context to go at great length into the complex pattern of British exports to twenty countries, the more so as the list of types of machinery and equipment exported to each is formidable. It will, I hope, suffice if broad generalisations are accompanied by a detailed look at a few selected items of special interest.

The overwhelming importance of capital goods makes British exports greatly dependent on the investment policies of the Latin American countries, and so to some extent also on British investments in Latin America, since equipment often comes from the investing country. A good example is the export of aero engines and parts to Brazil, where Rolls Royce have a subsidiary. Most British exports are unlikely to be affected by Latin American integration, since they largely consist of machines not made by any of the countries, and the key problem will be competitiveness with other potential suppliers. This may well prove an incorrect statement, in the light of more detailed knowledge of development plans. Whatever one's scepticism about the future of LAFTA, when there are very high tariffs, a preferential rate for 'LAFTA' countries can make a big difference. Thus Argentina levies duties of 50–90 per cent and more on steel imports and charges half these rates to LAFTA countries, and this has given Brazil a sizeable part of the market. But the biggest threats to British exports of steel to Argentina were from the ambitious Argentine plan to increase domestic production 2·5 times by 1975 over 1970 levels, and from U.S. and Japanese competition.

TABLE 11.13

SPECIFIC EXPORTS TO LATIN AMERICAN
COUNTRIES, 1970
(£ million)

(531.01/533.1)	Synthetic dyestuffs and other colouring materials, Brazil	2·1
(711.41)	Aircraft engines, Brazil	2·4
(711.5)	Internal combustion engines, Mexico	6·0ᵃ
	Internal combustion engines, Argentina	1·7
(712.5)	Tractors, Venezuela	1·9
	Tractors, Colombia	1·9
	Tractors, Chile	1·2
(714.92)	Office machinery parts, Brazil	1·8
(715.1)	Machine-tools, Brazil	0·9
(717.1)	Textile machinery, Brazil	2·6
(718.3)	Food processing machines, Cuba	1·3
(718.42)	Excavators, Chile	0·6
	Excavators, Brazil	1·4
	Excavators, Argentina	1·5
(719.31)	Lifting and holding machinery, Mexico	1·9
(719.64)	Spraying machinery, Cuba	1·2
(719.8)	Miscellaneous machinery, Chile	0·8
	Miscellaneous machinery, Brazil	1·8
	Miscellaneous machinery, Argentina	0·8
(724.1)	Telecommunications apparatus, Brazil	4·6
	Telecommunications apparatus, Chile	1·6
	Telecommunications apparatus, Venezuela	1·6

ᵃ These are used mainly in mining, not cars.

Source and other notes, see Table 11.2.

Let us now look at some detailed examples of major British exports to particular countries, in Tables 11.13 and 11.14. The latter sets out the vehicles category in detail. This table illustrates the effect of protection, and also the important links between investment and trade. In the larger countries the import of cars is rendered virtually impossible by a high tariff wall,[1] and the export to these countries of

[1] Which, no doubt, is why exports of British cars to Jamaica alone are almost equal to the whole of Latin America put together.

TABLE 11.14

U.K. EXPORTS OF VEHICLES TO LATIN AMERICA, 1970
(£ million)

	Cars	Lorries	Motor Vehicle Parts	Aircraft
Total (to all the world)	330·5	128·0	288·5	133·2
Dominican Republic	0·5	0·3	0·3	—
Nicaragua	0·2	0·25	0·15	—
Costa Rica	0·6	0·6	0·3	—
Guatemala	—	0·6	0·3	—
El Salvador	—	0·2	0·1	—
Honduras	—	0·15	—	—
Panama	0·3	0·3	0·5	—
Venezuela	2·1	0·3	1·1	—
Ecuador	0·1	0·3	0·25	—
Peru	0·6	0·2	0·3	—
Chile	0·6	0·2	0·5	0·17
Brazil	—	0·2	0·4	3·2
Uruguay	—	0·8	0·7	—
Argentina	—	0·15	0·8	1·4
Cuba	—	—	1·0	—
Mexico	—	—	2·4	1·7
Colombia	—	—	0·5	0·14

Source and notes, see Table 11.2.

parts is associated with car factories, usually erected by or with the help of foreign capital. British car and lorry manufacturers have neglected their investment opportunities, as compared with the Germans in particular, as can be seen in Brazil and elsewhere. An effort in Argentina by the former B.M.C. (British Leyland) collapsed. As can be seen in Appendix B, British investments in the Latin American automobile industry are now almost zero.

In general, many British exporters find Latin America to be a distant and difficult market of which they know little. They have tended to concentrate their effort elsewhere, with, of course, honourable exceptions. To the remoteness of the market must be added its fragmentation, and some unfortunate experiences in receiving payments and 'navigating' the shoals of import and currency controls. However, there are some brighter spots. Thus an ambitious British exhibition in Buenos Aires produced an impressive list of orders, and licensing and joint venture agreements are being negotiated. Perhaps this is why, despite a recession in Argentinian business, British exports in the first half of 1971 (£25·7 million) look like being much higher than in 1970 (£44 million in the full year).

Opportunities exist and are sometimes being taken. The figures show rapid headway in the Brazilian market. There is interest in joint projects, in sale of know-how on a royalty basis, and in advanced equipment in connection with such projects. Perhaps in this way Britain could help to equip, for instance in Brazil, an industry capable of producing manufactures which can compete in foreign markets.

A recent example of a 'joint venture' type of agreement, which promises well, is one reported in the *Financial Times* (13 August 1971), concluded by Howard Rotavators. An Anglo-Brazilian company is being set up, jointly with the *Fabrica Nacional de Implementos*, to make rotary hoes. The British contribution includes some capital, some know-how and also some of the components.

In the first post-war years, the United Kingdom in common with other European countries was in very urgent need of imported food and raw materials, while being short of exportable commodities. There was therefore a very large Latin American surplus, spent largely on imports from the United States. Trade more nearly balances today. Some countries (Bolivia and Chile for instance) still purchase comparatively little in comparison with their sales to the United Kingdom, while others such as Mexico buy much more from the United Kingdom than they sell to us.

II. UNITED KINGDOM EXPORTS OF CAPITAL AND OTHER FINANCIAL RELATIONS

The whole issue of the role of foreign capital, the burden of repayments, profit remittances and foreign control over national assets, has been and is the subject of much controversy. This is not the place to argue such matters. I will confine myself to Britain's role as a source of investment and/or aid.

It is well known that before the First World War Britain was by far the largest investor in Latin America. Net investment was slight between the wars, while the United States' investment in the region rose rapidly. The war and its aftermath caused substantial U.K. disinvestment, and traditional ties of economic interest and personal knowledge were severed.

Statistical data are incomplete and elusive. The Inter-American Development Bank published a valuable survey, *European Financing of Latin America's Economic Development*. For some reason this is undated, but since the latest figures in it relate to 1964, it presumably appeared in 1966. Data on British investments appear annually in *Trade and Industry* and other publications of the Department of Trade and Industry. Statistics also appear from time to time in Latin American countries, and it is very unlikely that I have been able to track down even the majority of them. Consequently the figures given here will often be incomplete. None the less, the general pattern that emerges is fairly clear, and justifies the comments, explanations and generalisations, which will be offered.

Capital investment merges with trade credits of various kinds, and they must be treated together.

GOVERNMENT AID (EXCLUDING CREDIT GUARANTEES)

British aid (with grants and experts under official auspices) has been concentrated in the main within the sterling area, and comparatively little has gone to Latin America. According to the I.D.B. publication, in the years 1960–64 net disbursements of bilateral credits by the United Kingdom to all Latin American countries were only $11·54 million, compared with $119 million from West Germany and $53 million from Italy and £46 million from France.[1] (This excludes refinancing arrangements, mentioned below.) In grants and technical assistance contributions the United Kingdom was second to West Germany, but the sum involved was very small indeed.[2] In view of (until recently) a difficult balance of payments situation, it is hardly surprising that Britain has had little to spare, after supporting the developing countries of the Commonwealth. In the period 1960–64 only about 2 per cent of the United Kingdom's considerable 'official capital flows to less developed countries' went to Latin America.[3]

'Disbursement of bilateral loans' fell to zero in 1965, but picked up in more recent years. Thus in 1968 the amount was £905,000 ($2·2 million), in 1969 it was slightly lower. However, in 1966 Great Britain put £4·1 million into a trust fund through the I.D.B., tied to purchases in Britain for various projects, and half of this has already been disbursed. A further £2 million trust fund, untied, was made available to the I.D.B. in June 1971.

Technical assistance shows a marked upward trend, doubling in the years 1966–70 to reach a level of £1·2 million in the latter year. (Figures kindly provided by the Department of Trade and Industry.)

Britain was also involved in so-called refinancing operations, along with other creditor countries, which provided government credits and payments rescheduling in respect of both official and private commercial debt owed by Argentina, Brazil and Chile. These arrangements were made in 1956, 1961, 1962 and 1964. These were, however, in the nature of reliefs and postponements, rather than a capital flow or investment *sensu stricto*.

[1] I.D.B., *European Financing of Latin America's Economic Development*, p. 110.
[2] *Ibid.*, p. 108. [3] *Ibid.*, p. 234.

Britain also, of course, contributes to international agencies of various kinds.

CREDIT GUARANTEES

Latin America shares in a system which guarantees (insures) suppliers' credit, which plays such a vital role in transactions involving capital goods. The credit itself can be obtained from a number of sources: the big banks, the merchant banks and other finance houses. No doubt this important facility will increase with exports of capital goods. Undoubtedly, apart from adding to the competitiveness of British industry, it provides credits at interest rates lower than would otherwise be the case.

PRIVATE INVESTMENT

The total value of direct private investment in Latin America is given in Appendix B. Unfortunately, the figures exclude oil, and sometimes also insurance and banking. They show that in 1962 Latin America had only 4 per cent of all British investments abroad, and while the total increased in absolute terms (though not by much, when one allows for price changes and devaluation), this percentage had fallen in 1968 to 4·2 per cent. There is almost three times as much British investment in Canada as in all Latin American countries added together.

TABLE 11.15

U.K. NET PRIVATE INVESTMENT ABROAD[a]
(£ million)

	1961	1962	1963	1964	1965	1966	1967	1968	1969
Total, all countries	226·0	209·0	236·0	263·0	308·0	276·0	281·0	410·0	547·0
Latin America	21·5	13·9	15·7	18·1	18·0	11·2	8·3	17·4	21·3

[a] The figures exclude oil and include unremitted profits.

Source: *Board of Trade Journal*, 9 May 1969, p. 1310, and *Business Monitor*, 1971, Table 16.

Table 11.15 gives the net annual flow of U.K. private investments. It can be seen that the trend is, if anything, downwards. By contrast, West German investments, which were still modest in the early sixties, have been rising rapidly, no doubt buoyed up by favourable balance of payments and also by tax advantages, and have now moved ahead. This is reflected by a table prepared by F.I.R.C.E. in Brazil for foreign investments in that country as at 31 December 1970 (see Table 11.16). It is obvious from the table that Britain is lagging

TABLE 11.16

BRAZIL: FOREIGN PRIVATE INVESTMENTS
RECEIVED, BY SOURCE
($ million)

	Investments	Reinvestments	Total
U.S.A.	527	460	987
Canada*a*	220	40	260
West Germany	181	72	253
United Kingdom	71	137	208
Switzerland	114	18	132
Japan	102	3	105
Panama*a*	53	13	66
Neth. Antilles	38	21	59
Belgium	38	7	46
Sweden	26	13	39
France	32	2	34
Italy	28	4	32

a United States firms in the main.

Source: F.I.R.C.E. as cited in a report kindly supplied by the Department of Trade and Industry.

much further behind in new investments than in reinvestments, thus reinforcing the impression that the trend is not upwards.

Tables in Appendix B give the statistics of investment flow, earnings and total book value of investments. It must be borne in mind that the figures are neither complete nor altogether reliable. Thus oil is always excluded, insurance and banking sometimes excluded. Also such aggregates as 'book values' of investment are often distorted, which also affects the validity of rates-of-return statistics to be quoted later on. However, these figures are the best that we have, and do represent at least a rough order of magnitude.

Why is British private investment so modest in Latin America? There are several reasons, some of them not at all specific to the area.

The first is simply Britain's own balance of payments difficulties of post-war years. Far from wishing to encourage investments abroad, successive governments have subjected it to varying degrees of discouragement and restriction. The main exception was the sterling area. The latest rules were explained in the *Board of Trade Journal* of 26 April 1968. Prior permission for any investment outside the sterling area is required. Permission will be given if there is benefit to the U.K. balance of payments. The '*Journal*' goes on to divide investment projects into three:

(a) 'Supercriterion projects', which both benefit U.K. exports and provide benefits to the balance of payments (via additional exports and profits) which at least equal the total amount invested within 18 months 'and will continue hereafter'.

(b) 'Normal criterion projects'. These do not exceed £25,000 per project per year, or, if they exceed this sum, promise benefits for the balance of payments at least equal to the investment within 2 to 3 years 'and continuing hereafter'.

(c) 'Non-criterion projects': the rest.

All these come under the Exchange Control Act and have to be approved by the Treasury and the Bank of England. There are long and complex rules about what kind of financing is allowed for each category, including the procedures for applications and terms and exchange rates on which 'investment currency' can be obtained, with special provisions covering the use of foreign currency owned by non-residents in U.K. banks ('Euro-dollars', etc.). If one considers the uncertainties and delays in having to obtain permission, these rules of themselves do something to deter would-be investors. A diagrammatic representation of the rules appears as Appendix C.

Portfolio investments are, as a rule, made only out of a 'pool' of resources obtained through the sale of foreign securities already held by British residents. As such, they can scarcely lead to a net expansion of foreign investment.

A further disincentive is the British taxation system: British companies can offset foreign taxes against corporation tax, but not against income tax on dividends. The German tax system makes investment in developing countries more attractive.

If one adds problems of liquidity facing many British companies, high interest rates, unfamiliarity with remote markets and fairly good profit opportunities in more familiar areas, it is hardly surprising

TABLE 11.17

U.K. RATES OF RETURN ON OVERSEAS INVESTMENTS
(per cent, based on mid-year values)

	1965	1966	1967	1968
All areas	8·7	8·4	8·3	9·0
E.E.C.	4·8	5·7	4·9	10·3
U.S.A.	11·9	12·5	11·7	12·0
Developing countries	8·9	8·9	8·6	9·1
Latin America:				
Total	8·6	10·2	10·2	12·5
Argentina	8·0	6·9	4·1	10·0
Brazil	9·0	14·9	16·6	17·5
Chile	11·4	12·2	15·9	8·6

Source: *Business Monitor* (1971), Table 37.

that few British private investors have ventured into Latin America without their already having a base or well-developed interests there.

Rates of return vary widely. Table 11.17 gives average rates of return, after overseas tax (excluding oil, insurance and banking). It will be seen that in 1968 Latin America as a whole provided a higher rate of return than average, and in fact Brazil in that year had the highest figure for any country. However, if one takes the figures over four years, investments in the United States have yielded more, and have given greater security. (Note that these percentages, though 'official', may well be misleading, for conceptual as well as account-ancy reasons.)

Latin American conditions act as a considerable deterrent to investment. As I am writing these words I have before me the day's issue of *The Times* (23 July 1971). It contains the following on one of its financial pages:

> United Alcohol (Argentina), a subsidiary of Tate & Lyle's United Molasses Division, made a £2,600,000 trading loss, owing to 'mis-judgments' in trading, devaluation and Argentine government export restrictions, which left the company with large stocks of sunflower seeds. . . . Tate & Lyle has been sufficiently chastened by the experience to curtail Argentine activities severely.

Would-be investors suffer from lack of information, price control, currency problems, restrictions on the movement of goods. The strong feeling in many countries against foreign capital, the possibility of nationalisation, price controls, foreign exchange rules, compulsory participation of local citizens, plus the unpredictability of each of these factors, do not serve to encourage investors. The very large indebtedness, on both governmental and commercial accounts, of many Latin American countries gives rise to fears of default.

A few months ago the British financial press reported the interest of the Andean group in British investment. This may have been partially motivated by political dislike of American economic domination. However, investments are scarcely likely to be forth-coming after a careful reading of the '*Régimen común de trata-miento a los capitales extranjeros*', adopted as part of the Cartagena accord.

According to the strict letter of the rules, all foreign investments, new and already-existing, will have to be to all intents and purposes self-liquidating. There must be assured '*la participación progresiva de inversionistas nacionales*'. Within fifteen to twenty years a majority holding must be transferred to the nationals of the Andean republics, by stages. Foreign investments are barred from public utilities, banking, insurance, internal transport, advertising, commercial radio and TV transmissions, publications, etc. (Articles 28, 30, 31, 41, 42, 43 of the '*Régimen común*'). Any existing foreign enterprises which are allowed to continue to function without conforming to the above rules will not have extended to them the free-trade advantages of the Cartagena accord (Article 44).[1]

There are also restrictive provisions applying to 'transfers of technology and patents', to prevent or discourage member countries from acquiring these on conditions involving undertakings to acquire capital goods from any particular source (Article 20). Still another article (16) limits the interest payments on commercial credits.

The whole spirit of the '*Régimen común*' is of a negative, discouraging character, which is inherently unreasonable, unless the intention is not to have any private investment from overseas. It seems likely that the rules will have to be modified in practice.

This modification may vary considerably, however, according to the political situation in each of the Andean countries. Thus Chile under Allende is pressing ahead with nationalising foreign enterprises, and foreign private investment has ceased. Peru and Bolivia may or may not go as far, while Colombia could take a less restrictive line. There are many uncertainties, but this in itself is a negative influence.

Nationalism as a factor militating against foreign capital is certainly no monopoly of left-wing political forces. Argentinian generals are just as prone to keep foreign interests out of their country.

In view of this, the future for private investment in many of the Latin American countries looks bleak. Perhaps Brazil, Venezuela and Mexico are exceptions, despite the nationalisation of Venezuelan oil resources.

GOVERNMENT AND INVESTMENT IN LATIN AMERICA

For all the above reasons, it is difficult to visualise any major expansion of 'normal' private investment. From Britain's point of view, it is by no means obvious that it ought to be increased. One could argue that the slowness of Britain's growth, both recently and earlier in the century, was in some part due to export of capital, just as it has been pointed out that generations of potential industrial leaders and managers have been trained to govern colonies. In other words, imperialism (economic and political) has had a considerable cost in terms of industrial development of the metropolis, though a cost which, in the nature of things, cannot be computed. With so many artificialities in exchange rates and trade barriers of many kinds, it

[1] I am quoting from the '*Régimen común*' reprinted in *Suplemento de Comercio Exterior* (Mexico, February 1971).

can hardly be argued today that the highest profit necessarily represents the best use of investment capital. It may well be that export of capital goods is not always an unmixed blessing. By this I do not mean that we should go back to the early nineteenth century, when efforts were made to prevent sales of machines to potential competitors abroad. It is clear that much of foreign trade in general, and exports to Latin America in particular, consists and ought to consist of machinery and equipment. However, if one looks at the pattern of British production and exports, the encouragement of exports of capital goods (especially in the post-war years) tended to delay the modernisation of British industry. I well recall, when I was myself an official in the Board of Trade, playing a small part in administering regulations which restricted domestic investment largely to exporting industries. We then deliberately stimulated export of equipment and actually obstructed, through investment controls, the re-equipment of many of our factories. Until very recently, even after investment in Britain was freed from such controls as these, we saw anomalies: thus the acquisition of British-built ships was made financially attractive for the foreign purchaser, while British ship-owners found that it paid them to place orders abroad. The net effect of all this on the balance of payments could at best have been zero.

It therefore seems, at a time when Great Britain is firmly at the bottom of the international growth league, that there is no very good economic reason for the government to be more encouraging in respect of private investment overseas, save of course in cases where there is promise of a rapid return, in other words more or less on the conditions quoted from the *Board of Trade Journal* a few pages back. The fact that there has been a large overall payments surplus in the last two years should not greatly affect these policies, the more so as we now have a dangerous rise in unemployment.

However, it would be wrong to take too negative a view, wrong from the standpoint both of long-term export prospects and of the general policy with regard to developing countries. Indeed, the present government takes a more positive stand with regard to capital investment abroad.

Perhaps the way forward should be linked with the large and growing role of state industry and state-sponsored investment institutions in Latin American countries. They vary widely, of course. There have been nationalised industries operating for many years in Mexico, and a high proportion of new investment in that country is in the public sector, which is being extended in a number of other countries. Thus, the Inter-American Development Bank report, already cited, could speak of 'Peru's tradition of economic liberalism', and express doubts as to whether the public sector there would 'invade areas traditionally reserved for private enterprise'. Five years later the picture has changed radically.

Private industry is also dependent, in many countries, on credits and investment funds provided by a state development or industrial bank. However, opportunities should also be sought and taken in a variety of joint ventures with private firms, where circumstances are right.

Perhaps the biggest British contribution in this whole field of capital development might be for British firms and consortia to enter into some species of partnership with state-run or state-sponsored bodies responsible for the management or finance of investment schemes. These could be in the public sector (highways, electricity generators, minerals, water supply), or in developments to be run by local private enterprise in manufacturing. Consultancy services, technical know-how, equipment, would be linked with medium-term or long-term trade credits, with government guarantees on both sides. The 'taint' of foreign ownership would be avoided, a real contribution made to development, and both sides could and should gain. This would require some imagination and willingness to co-operate by both sides. British industry must surely take a more active interest in pursuing its trading opportunities in Latin America, with the blessing of the British government, and Latin American countries must appreciate that no large flow of 'developmental' credits can be expected without a sense of security and a reasonable share in the profits, even if ownership will ultimately reside in the country where the investment is made. There may be something to learn from East European experience. Plant has been erected in the Soviet Union in co-operation with British, French, Italian consortia. They are built with the help of nationals of the respective countries, who instal the plant (much of it supplied from the countries concerned), train the Soviet labour and management to operate it, and then in due course withdraw. The deals include purchase of designs and technique, and are financed by credits. No doubt such agreements have been concluded by Latin American countries also, but the fact that the Soviet government can do this, while retaining ownership and ultimate control, could reassure those 'economic nationalists' who fear that this would represent a threat to economic independence. Other examples include American-financed hotels in Budapest and Bucharest, and a new law in Roumania provides for the possibility of a 49 per cent foreign ownership of equity capital of mixed companies (though the details are as yet far from clear). Incidentally the Soviet Union and its allies have achieved over the years a very good record in punctual payment, which naturally helps them in obtaining credits.

Another possible line in co-operation involves the manufacture of components. A relatively small country is unlikely to develop its own machinery industry, but it can provide parts for assembly. No doubt this will occur within Latin America itself, but it can form the basis of long-term agreements with Western firms. Once again there are East European parallels: e.g., Hungary manufactures parts used by the Fiat company in Italy. This justifies investments or credits from the company which would utilise the components. There may be unutilised opportunities for such deals with British firms, but they too require confidence and security: failure of an essential part to arrive can seriously damage production. One cannot imagine the necessary confidence being present unless the government of the country concerned is directly or indirectly in on the deal.

CONCLUDING REMARKS

Plainly there is no likelihood of Great Britain ever again becoming a major trading and investment partner for Latin America. However, there is no reason why her interest in the area should remain at its present low levels (3·5 per cent of all exports, 2·5 per cent or so of all foreign investment). A more energetic and sustained effort to sell in Latin America, and a selective policy of investment, in co-operation with state agencies, could yield useful results and lead to an increase in Britain's contribution. Unfortunately, the negative effects of membership of the E.E.C. may well stand in the way of any substantial expansion of Latin American agricultural exports to Britain, and this could cause difficulties for some countries in paying off past loans and credits, let alone contracting large new obligations. Or is this too pessimistic? Membership could well have some unexpected results in the context of a more dynamic economy, and the Community's own policies are not unalterable.

APPENDIX A

U.K. IMPORTS FROM LATIN AMERICA, 1970[a, b]
(£ million)

Class No.	Category of Goods	Imports from Latin America	Imports from All Countries	Percentage from Latin America
Section 0: Food and animals				
00	Live animals	—	56·5	—
01	Meat products	51·1	438·2	11·7
02	Dairy products and eggs	—	185·5	—
03	Fish	1·2	74·2	1·6
04	Cereals and preparations	10·4	281·4	3·7
05	Fruit and vegetables	5·5	379·9	1·5
06	Sugar, etc.	6·0	117·5	5·1
07	Coffee, tea, cocoa, spices	20·8	209·7	9·9
08	Feeding stuffs for animals	4·0	88·2	4·5
09	Misc. food preparation	—	31·4	—
	Total	99·2	1,862·6	5·3
Section 1: Beverages and tobacco				
11	Beverages	0·5	79·0	0·6
12	Tobacco, tobacco mfres	0·8	110·3	0·7
	Total	1·3	189·4	0·7

[a] Owing to rounding, subtotals do not always add to totals. A dash means less than £0·1 million, or 0·5 per cent in the final column.

[b] No comprehensive and comparable figures were published for earlier years, since a new system of reporting went into operation in 1970. The reclassification then introduced is helpful in some respects. Thus exports to and imports from each trade area and country appear in full in summary tables, classified by divisions and sections of the international trade classifications (as given in the above table). However, this classification is not available for any previous year, and for the first time the trade statistics as published do not give the comparable figures for the previous year, in any table. For many purposes greater commodity detail is wanted (e.g. 26 covers *all* textile raw materials). In previous years there were country breakdowns also for sub-divisions (e.g. 262: wool and other animal hair). These have now disappeared, and in their place we have sub-sub-groups (e.g. 262.2: 'sheep's and lamb's wool degreased, whether or not bleached and dyed'). These sub-sub-groups omit some countries some of the time. As a result, it is sometimes hard to be sure whether country series carried through the years 1968–70 are quite comparable, and in some instances it is impossible to make the comparison at all. Finally, the distinction between exports of U.K. produce and re-exports has been eliminated.

It should further be explained that the term 'Latin America', in U.K. trade and investment statistics, *excludes* the former British, French and Dutch colonies in the Caribbean. This, and also the exclusion of oil from the investment statistics, explains certain discrepancies with figures quoted in the paper by Mr Schaeffer in this volume.

Appendix A (*continued*)

Class No.	Category of Goods	Imports from Latin America	Imports from All Countries	Percentage from Latin America
Section 2: Crude materials, inedible, excl. fuels				
21	Hides, skins, furs (undressed)	2·2	70·2	3·1
22	Oilseeds, oilnuts and kernels	0·3	41·7	0·7
23	Crude rubber (incl. synthetic)	0·3	57·7	0·5
24	Wood, lumber, cork	6·9	238·8	2·9
25	Pulp and waste paper	—	197·9	—
26	Textile fibres and waste	31·2	183·9	17·0
27	Crude fertilisers and crude minerals (excl. coal, oil and precious stones)	11·4	65·3	17·5
28	Metalliferous ores and scrap	54·7	346·6	15·8
29	Crude animal and vegetable matter n.e.s.	2·4	60·9	3·9
	Total	99·4	1,263·2	7·9
Section 3: Mineral fuels, lubricants, etc.				
32	Coal, coke, briquettes	—	3·4	—
33	Petroleum and products	44·0	925·4	4·8
34	Gas	0·3	15·3	2·0
35	Electric energy	—	1·6	—
	Total	44·3	945·7	4·7
Section 4: Animal and vegetable oils and fats				
41	Animal oils and fats	—	23·4	—
42	Fixed vegetable oils and fats	2·9	68·1	4·3
43	Processed oil, fats and waxes	0·5	9·1	5·5
	Total	3·5	100·7	3·5
Section 5: Chemicals				
51	Chemical elements and components	2·7	237·8	1·1
52	Mineral tar and crude chemicals (from coal, oil, gas)	0·1	5·5	—
53	Dyeing, tanning and colouring materials	0·2	33·4	0·6
54	Medicinal and pharmaceutical products	1·7	33·7	5·0
55	Essential oils, perfumes, toiletries, etc.	0·8	23·2	3·4
56	Fertilisers, manufactured	0·1	23·1	—
57	Explosives	—	1·0	—
58	Plastics, art. resins	− 0·1	110·9	—
59	Chemical materials n.e.s.	0·4	74·2	0·5
	Total	6·2	542·8	1·1

Appendix A (*continued*)

Class No.	Category of Goods	Imports from Latin America	Imports from All Countries	Percentage from Latin America
Section 6:	*Manufactured goods classified by material*			
61	Leather and fur and manufactures n.e.s.	1·0	32·5	3·1
62	Rubber manufactures n.e.s.	—	27·6	—
63	Wood and cork manufactures (excl. furniture)	1·1	108·5	1·0
64	Paper and manufactures	—	231·1	—
65	Textile yarn and fabrics	0·1	256·4	—
66	Non-metallic mineral mfres n.e.s.	1·1	382·3	—
67	Iron and steel	0·3	222·5	—
68	Non-ferrous metals	62·5	608·7	10·3
69	Metal manufactures n.e.s.	0·2	97·0	—
	Total	66·3	1,966·7	3·4
Section 7:	*Machinery, etc.*			
71	Machinery, excl. electric	2·4	855·7	—
72	Electric machinery and apparatus	0·5	342·2	—
73	Transport equipment	0·5	298·5	—
	Total	3·4	1,496·5	—
Section 8:	*Miscellaneous manufactures*			
81	Sanitary, plumbing, heating, lighting fittings	—	10·0	—
82	Furniture	—	15·6	—
83	Travel goods, handbags	—	5·7	—
84	Clothing and knitwear	—	129·4	—
85	Footwear	0·1	40·6	—
86	Instruments, optics, photographic goods, watches, etc.	0·2	141·5	—
89	Misc. manufactures n.e.s.	1·6	231·0	0·7
	Total	1·9	573·9	—
Section 9:	*Unclassified commodities*	0·5	110·0	0·5
Grand Total		325·9	9,051·5	3·6

APPENDIX B: U.K. OVERSEAS INVESTMENTS

TABLE I

VALUE OF U.K. DIRECT INVESTMENTS ABROAD
(Excluding oil, insurance, banking)
(£ million)

	1962	1963	1964	1965	1966	1967	1968
Total All Areas	3,405·0	3,635·0	3,905·0	4,210·0	4,402·0	5,187·0	5,585·0
Developing countries	1,274·0	1,313·0	1,363·0	1,432·0	1,395·0	1,589·0	1,668·0
Latin America	171·8	183·5	199·4	212·8	213·4	227·9	233·4
Argentina	49·3	53·5	60·5	64·6	59·8	60·5	67·6
Brazil	37·2	40·7	42·0	45·1	53·2	62·6	61·2
Chile	4·2	4·1	4·3	4·2	4·2	4·9	15·4
Mexico	28·0	31·1	35·0	41·0	41·2	48·1	48·6
Venezuela	10·2	10·6	11·9	11·8	12·7	12·9	12·4

Source: *Business Monitor* (1971), Table 34.

TABLE II

U.K. NET EARNINGS BY AREA AND COUNTRY ON DIRECT INVESTMENT[a]
(£ million)

	1963	1964	1965	1966	1967	1968	1969
Total All Areas	330·0	370·0	400·0	429·0	438·0	568·0	650·0
Total Latin America	16·3	19·4	20·3	24·7	23·8	34·2	32·7
Argentina	3·2	6·3	5·3	4·6	2·5	6·7	6·3
Brazil	4·2	3·3	4·1	7·5	9·2	11·8	12·6
Chile	0·6	0·9	0·7	0·6	0·7	0·9	0·9

[a] The figures exclude oil.

Source: *Business Monitor* (1971), Table 21.

TABLE III

U.K. NET EARNINGS IN 1969 ON DIRECT INVESTMENT
IN LATIN AMERICA[a]
(£ million)

(i) *By Sector*		(ii) *By Component*	
Total	32·7	Total	32·7
Agriculture	0·5	Net profits of branches	5·7
Mining	—	Net profits of subsidiaries	26·8
Vehicles and shipbuilding	0·1	Interest	0·1
Mechanical engineering	—		
Other manufactures	23·2		
Construction	0·1		
Distribution	2·4		
Transport and communication	0·5		
Shipping	—		
Other (incl. banking and insurance)	5·8		

[a] Excluding oil.

Source: *Business Monitor*, Tables 23 and 24.

TABLE IV

U.K. NET INVESTMENT ABROAD BY COMPONENT, 1969[a]
(£ million)

	Total	Argentina	Brazil	Chile	Mexico
Total	21·3	5·3	9·3	0·3	2·7
Unremitted profits of subsidiaries	17·3	3·6	9·0	0·4	2·4
Net acquisition of share and loan capital	1·9	0·2	0·9	—	—
Changes in indebtedness to parent company:					
by Branches	—	0·2	—	—	—
by Subsidiaries	2·1	1·3	0·7	0·2	0·4
Changes in related trade credit:					
Credit extended	4·3	3·5	0·4	—	0·2
Credit received	0·5	0·1	—	—	—
Provisions for depreciation	10·5	2·3	2·8	0·5	2·0

[a] Excluding oil.

Source: *Business Monitor* (1971), Table 18.

TABLE V

**U.K. INVESTMENT (FLOW) BY SECTOR
IN LATIN AMERICA**[a]
(£ million)

	1968	1969
Total	17·4	21·3
Agriculture	0·7	0·2
Mining	—	—
Electrical and mechanical engineering	1·0	0·2
Vehicles and shipbuilding	0·6	0·4
Other manufacturing	13·3	15·6
Construction	—	– 0·7
Distribution	0·8	2·8
Transport and communications	—	0·4
Shipping	—	—
Other (incl. insurance and banking)	2·5	3·2

[a] Excluding oil.

Source: *Business Monitor* (1971) Table 18.

APPENDIX C

The following diagrams illustrate the main rules governing overseas investments by British firms. The definitions of super-criterion, normal criterion and non-criterion investments were given on pp. 351–2 above.

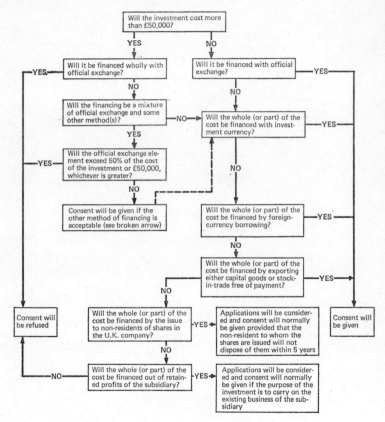

FIG. 11.1

Super-Criterion Investments

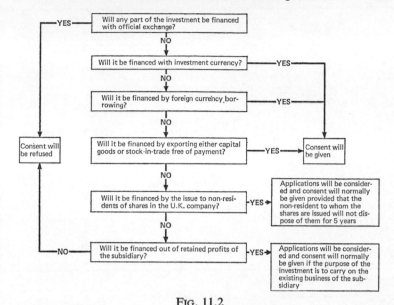

FIG. 11.2

Normal Criterion Investments
(Including Investments Costing £25,000 or less per Project per year)

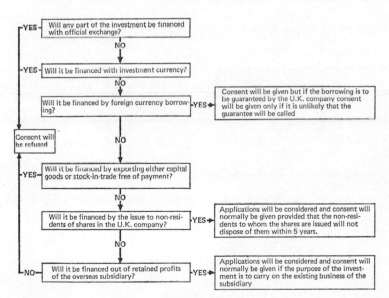

FIG. 11.3

Non-Criterion Investments
Source: *Board of Trade Journal* (26 April 1968).

APPENDIX D

E.E.C. AND U.K. IMPORTS FROM LATIN AMERICA: SOME SELECTED AGRICULTURAL PRODUCTS
JANUARY–DECEMBER, 1969
(1,000 U.S. dollars)

Exports To: From:	Bananas		Wool and Other Animal Hair		Textile Yarn and Thread		Meat, Fresh, Chilled or Frozen		Cereals and Cereal Preparations		Coffee		Feeding Stuff for Animals Excluding Unmilled Cereals	
	E.E.C.	U.K.	E.E.C.	U.K.	E.E.C.	U.K.	E.E.C.	U.K.	E.E.C.	U.K.	E.E.C.	U.K.	E.E.C.	U.K.
Mexico	—	—	346	79	941	—	8	—	6,172	—	7,817	415	3,106	16
Cuba	—	—	—	—	—	—	196	970	—	—	2,409	25	—	—
Haiti	36	—	9	—	—	—	—	—	—	—	8,413	3	10	—
Dominican Republic	1	—	—	—	—	—	—	—	—	—	2,910	33	—	—
Guatemala	8,487	68	—	—	—	5	—	—	—	—	26,947	872	19	—
Honduras	38,110	—	—	—	—	—	—	—	103	—	5,102	58	8	—
Nicaragua	—	—	—	—	—	—	34	—	—	—	12,756	149	45	—
Costa Rica	11 051	—	—	—	—	—	1	—	—	—	22,074	523	243	—
Panama	20,896	—	—	—	—	—	—	—	—	—	834	—	—	—
Colombia	15,244	79	37	4	33	—	2	—	119	—	108,283	2,509	121	—
Peru	—	—	1,712	3,709	239	—	—	—	—	—	4,446	192	483	—
Brazil	—	—	8,128	9,780	—	—	17,860	12,643	25,617	—	208,673	17,610	103,030	6,993
Paraguay	—	—	289	73	—	—	805	27	—	—	180	—	42,408	145
Argentina	—	—	32,068	16,922	286	—	121,390	97,144	229,852	—	119	—	1,982	6,652
Uruguay	—	—	20,479	18,345	—	—	13,522	11,659	686	20,497	—	—	97,458	62
El Salvador	5	—	—	—	—	—	—	—	271	123	57,389	112	3,391	—
Venezuela	—	—	—	—	—	—	—	—	1	—	953	6	73	—
Ecuador	39,184	360	42	—	—	—	—	—	—	—	9,547	—	136	—
Chile	—	—	3,773	2,127	—	—	—	—	—	—	—	—	—	699
Bolivia	—	—	—	—	—	—	—	—	—	—	309	38	10,832	—

Source: O.E.C.D., Series C, Trade by Commodities.

Discussion of the Papers by
Mr. Schaeffer and Professor Nove

Professor Lambert commented on the strongly contrasting impressions the two papers gave as to their respective authors' basic optimism or pessimism concerning the effect of a rapidly growing European Community on its economic relations with Latin America. On the one hand, Professor Nove saw the economic and financial ties between the United Kingdom and Latin America as having stabilised at a low level, with little prospect of stronger ties as a result of Britain's entry. On the other hand, Mr. Schaeffer focussed on the extent to which the possible effect on Latin America of Community preferences for African imports had in fact been offset by increasing overall reliance on imports and by special measures in favour of developing countries generally. He himself felt that the conflict was to some degree apparent rather than real: the basis of Mr. Schaeffer's case was one he fully supported, namely that in so far as trade grows very rapidly in an area which is going through a process of economic integration, the growth of intra-regional trade nevertheless leaves ample room for growth of trade with other partners. Professor Nove's discussions of the precise effects consequent on the entry of the United Kingdom in no way affected this basic argument.

Turning to the details of the arguments which Professor Nove used to present his case for the poor opportunities offered to Latin America by the United Kingdom's entry into the E.E.C., the first point he wanted to make was that the picture was obscured by statistical distortions.[1] The most important was concerned with trade in oil products and the relationships between European mother countries and their remaining dependencies in the Caribbean. The distortion was very obvious in the E.E.C. data on foreign aid, which was reduced by about one-quarter when French development assistance to the Antilles and Guyana was removed. By contrast, the United Kingdom considerably understated its trade and financial flows to Latin America in its statistics, which excluded both oil and related activities, and its trade and financial links with the Caribbean Free-Trade Area. It followed that the level of trade and commercial flows between the United Kingdom and Latin America was similar to that of the Common Market once the Caribbean was included, and the financial flows might even be higher if allowance was made for direct investment in the energy and banking sectors.

However, what could not be denied was the difference in the relevant rates of growth. Latin American exports to the Common Market had doubled over ten years (rising at the same rate as those from the associated African States, incidentally); by contrast, as Professor Nove showed, trade and financial flows between Latin America and the United Kingdom had been relatively stagnant. But he thought that in some respects at least the paper's assessment of such trade was unduly pessimistic.[2]

[1] The two authors have taken account of Professor Lambert's remarks in the revised versions of their papers.

[2] Editors' note: Professor Lambert presented his discussion of trade relations

First, in regard to temperate agricultural products, it was argued that Britain's entry to the E.E.C. would close its market still more, at the same time as Europe's new relations with the Commonwealth would close the Continental Market. But, in the first place, the British consumer would exert pressure for lower intervention prices, and in the second place, and most importantly, an enlarged Europe would remain a net importer. It was true, however, that productivity considerations favoured European agriculture: the European peasant had a better chance of making up lost ground in relation to his standard of living than did the Latin American rural inhabitant.

In regard to tropical and semi-tropical products, by contrast, he was in agreement that prospects were poor. The most serious competition was to be faced over coffee, cocoa and oilseeds. It should be noted, though, that after the signature of the Yaoundé Convention in 1963, Latin American exports to those members of the Six with whom links already existed were little affected (i.e. Germany, Italy and the Netherlands). The E.E.C. was, however, the world's largest consumer of cocoa, and the grant of preferences to English-speaking African states could have serious consequences for Latin America.

In regard to oil and mineral products, he again saw a basis for some optimism: the United Kingdom had always imported from a variety of supply sources, and this diversification was in the interest of Continental Europe, which was dependent on the Mediterranean Basin, the Middle East and Africa.

The real problem, however, would come with Latin American exports of manufactures. Whereas the French-speaking states of Africa had negligible industrial capacity, some of the nations with close ties to Britain were semi or fully industrialised. And more serious still, Britain's ties were to countries whose industrial policy was based on export-oriented products, particularly in South East Asia, in sharp contrast to the import substituting industrial strategy of Latin America. He would point out that the problem of the ability of poor countries to penetrate the markets of the rich was rarely envisaged in this framework. The Prebisch analysis looked at trade between Latin America and industrialised countries, especially the United States. But the analysis could also be applied at another level, that of competition between subgroups in the Third World. The sole buyer continued to be the developed world. But the comparative advantage which permitted penetration of this market was no longer, as in the original analysis, grounded in productivity gains incorporated in export prices by means of wage increases. Rather, when the competing suppliers were industrialising countries with relatively low living standards, comparative advantage was, it seemed to him, a question of ability to marshal labour resources and a low wage level. Obviously, industrial real wages in Bengal

---

to the conference in a detailed written report which it was not possible to present fully here. The reader is referred to Professor Lambert's series of articles on the subject in *Économie appliquée, tiers monde et monde en développement* and in *L'Amérique latine: économies et sociétés* (Colin, 1971).

or Taiwan were much lower than in Mexico or Bogota. Foreign trade between countries with unequal incomes strengthened the comparative advantage of the rich when the countries concerned were at opposite ends of the development scale, but among Third World countries the advantage often lay with the poorer country.

He thus conceded that there were some unfavourable aspects to Britain's entry in regard to trade: it was the more general picture presented by Professor Nove with which he disagreed most strongly. As seen by Professor Nove, membership of the Common Market implied such a degree of concentration of economic effort that Britain would have to abandon certain of her ambitions. Whatever safeguards were introduced, her 'new European destiny' would serve to loosen the ties inherited from her nineteenth-century expansion, and in particular her links with Latin America. The new trading bloc would represent the largest single trade flow in the Western world. This would represent a self-sufficient unit which could be protected in the event of a recession in international trade. But as he saw it this was too pessimistic. The market for Latin American goods in Europe had not in fact been whittled away by the arrival of African imports. The E.E.C. bought and sold much more in Latin America than it did in Africa. There would, further, be scope in Africa for a long time to come for the traditional exports of Europe, and especially of Britain. The European countries had taken a clear stance at UNCTAD in favour of eliminating special preferences. And since July 1971, when the first stage of dismantling of customs barriers on imports from developing countries was put into effect, the customs tariff of the E.E.C. had been the lowest of any group of industrialised nations.

The second half of Professor Nove's paper concerned investment flows. It certainly seemed a reasonable forecast that the U.K. balance of payments difficulties which had led to restrictions on capital export since 1968 would continue, at least until European monetary union was under way. In any case, British firms would be given incentives to invest in Europe, whereas investment in Latin America would remain a political risk. He did not agree, however, with Professor Nove's reasons for saying that the United Kingdom *should* not export capital. Exhaustion of rural manpower reserves, *à la* Kaldor, seemed a more likely explanation of slow growth. On the argument that to export capital was to divert resources required by British industry, there was no proof that these resources would have been employed productively. More importantly, both France and Germany had achieved very high growth rates in the post-war period by maintaining both a higher rate of domestic investment and of capital export than the United Kingdom. Most important of all, if Europe was to form a counter-weight to the multinational firms, overseas investment outside of former colonies had to be a fundamental bastion of its strategy.

He would fully support Professor Nove's positive suggestions as to reorganisations which might permit the expansion of financial and commercial relations in a framework that preserved the autonomy of host country governments. However, Professor Nove appeared to favour the creation of public corporations to achieve this end, so that private capital from abroad was associated with official funds of multinational origin and national capital resources, along lines similar to the contracts signed with Eastern European countries. His own view was that outside a collectivist economy, the public corporation involved management risks. A nationalised firm, or even a part-state-owned joint venture, was an 'immortal' entity: whatever its lack of profitability, it would not go under.

Finally, he would like to turn to the broader issue of whether an expansion of relations with Europe was or was not in Latin America's interest. The radical economists of Latin America might have reason for short-term self congratulation if Europe were to pull out of the sub-continent; and Europe would be clear of the accusation of domination. But one of the lessons of the 1930s and of the post-war recessionary periods was precisely that the economies of Latin America would be better able to resist the destabilising effects of foreign trade if they reduced the extent of their dependence on a single partner, namely the United States. Trade and even financial links with the United States had in fact already been reduced by turning to Europe and Japan, and even to Eastern Europe. The ten countries of an enlarged Europe were likely to become an even bigger trading unit than the United States, and Latin American vulnerability to the disruptive effects of foreign trade should therefore on balance decline. And the more diversified one's partners, the easier it was to preserve national autonomy.

Dr. Bacha, commenting on Mr. Schaeffer's paper, likewise stressed that the basic significance of the E.E.C. for Latin America was that it opened up a possibility of greater geographical diversification of sources of dependence. Yet precisely with respect to dependence, what concerned him most in the paper was the paternalistic attitude he found there; the approach was entirely in terms of what the E.E.C. could do to help Latin America, with no element of the *quid pro quo* essential to an 'independent' relationship. He foresaw an asymmetrical relation, where both economic gains for the E.E.C. and increased political dependence of Latin America on the E.E.C. were traded for an increase in trade and foreign capital flows for Latin America. It was in line with his whole approach that Mr. Schaeffer nowhere mentioned the difficulties Latin America would face as a result of the common agricultural policy – 'a monument to lack of logic'.

Mr. Macario found a serious incompatibility between the Community's intentions and its degree of imagination in finding new ways to implement its hopes. The E.E.C. appeared to see itself playing a world role – yet up to now its orientation had been inwards. Mr. Schaeffer's paper typified the Community's approach: concern on the one hand, yet a substantial part of the paper spent showing how little can be actually done. The kind of excuses given were unacceptable – for example that the field for action was limited while integration was incomplete, or while the entry of the United Kingdom was being negotiated. Such arguments would postpone action for ever. He also could not accept the historical justification of a special relationship with Africa; the only acceptable argument for a special relationship was economic need, and consistency would require that much of Latin America be included on the basis of such an argument.

Mr. Schaeffer had argued that the Community's commercial policy was favourable to Latin America. But, for example, the Kennedy Round concessions were given in exchange for others. He concurred with Dr. Bacha in finding the agricultural policy one of the most objectionable parts of E.E.C. policy; it seriously distorted international trade flows and hence was not legitimate.

Mr. Schaeffer also overstated the case for an optimistic view by failing to mention the effect of entry of the United Kingdom. Following this the E.E.C. would have associated to it some fifty less developed countries; in contrast to Professor Lambert, he saw this as a division of the world into areas of influence which would have serious repercussions for Latin America and would inevitably push her even more completely into the sphere of influence of the United States.

Dr. Krieger Vasena also deplored the E.E.C. agricultural policy, not for its goal but for the method chosen to maintain the income of European farmers. The French notion had been that their internal policy should be meshed with the organisation of markets on an international scale; as the case had been put to Argentina all were to benefit, in particular since price fluctuations would be smoothed out. The negotiations with Argentina had represented the first attempt to try out this notion. Argentina had gone with goodwill to negotiate, having put in five months of preparation. He himself had been a signatory to the agreement, which replaced the double levy system with indicative prices. Other countries such as Australia had not signed; in the event they were proved right not to have wasted time on it, for after the agreement had been ratified by GATT France had simply intervened to veto it.

As to the prospects for Latin American trade with the E.E.C., he was pessimistic as to the immediate future. The worst problem was not the size of the levy but its extreme variability. He would point out that to date the United Kingdom had secured no modification of the agricultural policy. The only possible ground for optimism was that the cost of the policy to the E.E.C. was so high that according to a recent study[1] it could not be maintained in the long run.

Mr. Wionczek considered the papers concealed more than they revealed by their failure to place the relationship between Europe and Latin America within the context of the whole system of international relations. It was only within this context, for example, that one could understand why the E.E.C. had not contributed to the I.D.B. Mr. Schaeffer's paper further clouded the real issues by discussing all trade and capital flows within the context of 'assistance' to Latin America. Professor Nove's paper was equally mystifying in criticising the Andean Pact countries for a tough attitude to foreign capital, which in fact was less tough than that embodied in the joint ventures between Western and Eastern European countries which he later applauded.

Dr. Ferrer questioned Mr. Schaeffer's description of the E.E.C. and

[1] *The Future for European Agriculture* (The Atlantic Institute, Paris 1970), Paper No. 4.

Latin America as complementary. In fact it was precisely between countries of similar high levels of industrialisation that one found a high degree of effective complementarity. It was the low level of Latin American development which had resulted in their very limited economic relationships with the E.E.C. Turning to Professor Nove's paper, he found in it a view that was common but incorrect, namely that the present wave of nationalism was an irrational thing. On the contrary, it was something which had deep roots in history and was fully in accord with Latin American development needs. It was not something that either would or was intended to keep foreign capital out totally – e.g. the Argentine approach had been one of *redirection* rather than elimination of foreign capital.

Mr. Urquidi commented that while the expansion of trade between the E.E.C. countries and Latin America was impressive, it derived mostly from the growth of G.N.P. in Western Europe rather than from a favourable tariff and commercial policy on the part of the Europeans. Too many protectionist and discriminatory elements remained which prevented Latin American countries from participating sufficiently in the growth of European consumption. Such remaining restrictions had to be removed if Europe, including the United Kingdom, was to play a significant role in furthering Latin American development through trade. In addition, Western Europe, which had managed to accumulate such a large share of international liquidity, would have to devise new machinery for increasing the investment of public capital, preferably through multilateral means, in Latin American development. It was in Europe's own interests to liberalise its trade and financial relations with Latin American countries. It was true that the policy of the E.E.C. was more favourable than it would have been if the pre-war protectionist policies of each individual country had prevailed. But it was also true that the objectives of the E.E.C. were not only economic, but also political and concerned with security; for these reasons not too much should perhaps be expected in the way of policies favourable to the less developed countries.

Professor Vernon saw the present lack of bargaining power on the part of the developing countries as following from their own post-war decision to opt out of the bargaining system as it developed. Thus both at Chapultepec in 1945 and at Havana in 1948 they insisted on recognition of their special problems, and were granted exemption from practically all the main provisions of GATT. This simply strengthened the preoccupation of the United States and United Kingdom with relations with advanced countries; in the years that followed the main activities of GATT involved relations between the E.E.C., United States, United Kingdom and Japan. The resulting activities and occasional violations certainly affected the developing countries, but there was no direct agreement. Hence, having by choice no commitments, the developing countries had had no bargaining power; psychologically they had to beg for scraps rather than negotiate for advantages. He saw this as a totally inappropriate policy for the present stage of Latin American development – what was needed was that the individual countries of Latin America should pool their resources for negotiating purposes, and understand that a willingness to enter into agreements and take on commitments was essential to the bargaining process.

He also saw the conference's preoccupation with agricultural policy and exports as typical of the Latin American tendency to concern itself with the problems of the past decade rather than the next. The concern today should be with penetration of the U.S. and European market in manufactured goods.

Mr. Schaeffer, replying, stressed that it was important not to confuse the long-term policies that might reasonably be imputed to the Community, once fully in existence, with the actual empirical situation of heterogeneous countries with specific structural characteristics and traditional commitments. Of course one could not abstract the Community from its members, but it was reasonable to think that given time it would achieve ever greater success in surmounting contradictions and in formulating true Community policies. Many of the criticisms emanating from Latin America so far really represented not the consequences of integration but the lack of it. In fact he would argue that one should view European integration as a phenomenon as yet fundamentally unaccomplished. It would be quite premature to expect immediate and extensive actions on behalf of all the developing countries from a Europe which had to concentrate its attention on its own birth and survival, if it was ever to possess the necessary instruments for co-operation with others. He himself considered that the Community should not be viewed with pessimism by the developing world; on the one hand it would acquire over the next few years a remarkable political weight and economic autonomy; on the other, integration was necessitating extensive modernisation and structural change in a context of a general awareness concerning development problems, while the high degree of exposure to which the Community's policy making was subject would itself lead such policy making to confront sincerely the needs of outsiders.

Professor Nove, replying in his turn, agreed with Mr. Macario that major disturbances in world trade were now occurring as more countries were added to an arrangement which initially was a compromise between countries which were already protecting their agriculture. One speaker had praised the British subsidy system; he would point out that its apparent virtues really sprang from the fact that Britain had such a large deficit in temperate foodstuffs. In response to Dr. Ferrer, he had not wished to argue that nationalism was irrational. Japan was a clear example of rational nationalism, where the presence of foreign enterprises was felt to interfere too greatly with the informal but successful Japanese system of industrial planning.

12 Japan's Economic Relations with Latin America: Prospects and Possible Lines of Action

Akio Hosono[1]

ECONOMIC COMMISSION FOR LATIN AMERICA (ECLA)

I. GENERAL FEATURES OF THE EVOLUTION OF TRADE AND FINANCIAL RELATIONS[2]

TRADE RELATIONS

During the last decade trade between Latin America and Japan has increased considerably. The annual value of exports from Latin America to Japan rose at a cumulative annual rate of over 9 per cent – almost 10 per cent in the last few years – leaving a trade surplus for Latin America. Thus, the total value of the region's exports, which in the fifties hardly reached U.S. $250 million, increased to $1,020 million in 1970; this figure corresponds now to almost 7 per cent of Latin America's total exports. This increase was larger than that of Latin American exports to other regions, except for the socialist area, which increased its imports from Latin America due mainly to sugar shipments from Cuba.

This favourable evolution of Latin American exports to Japan was due mainly to the extraordinary increase in the demand for the main export products of Latin America motivated by the rapid

[1] The author is a staff member of the Economic Commission for Latin America (ECLA), but the opinions expressed in this document are not necessarily those of ECLA. This report was prepared in anticipation of the announcement of new economic measures adopted by the United States in August 1971.

[2] The analysis in this chapter has the purpose of bringing out some salient features, and does not pretend to be an exhaustive description. The following publications contain more complete information on Japan's overall foreign trade, and the trade relations between Latin America and Japan:

1. A study on Japan's foreign trade that contains up-to-date information, was published by GATT: *Japan's Economic Expansion and Foreign Trade 1955 to 1970* (Geneva, July 1971).

2. Saburo Okita, *Japón y América Latina: Una Relación Económica en Cambio*, report presented at the Pacific Conference, October 1970, Vina del Mar, reprinted in *Comercio Exterior* (Mexico, February 1971).

3. A chapter in ECLA's *Economic Survey of Latin America: 1970*, April 1971: 'Latin American Exports to Japan: Trends and Prospects' includes an analysis at the product level and information on the tariff levels, quantitative restrictions and other trade barriers, as well as the main competitors in the Japanese market for the 58 main products of interest to Latin America.

growth of Japan, which has in *per capita* terms a meagre endowment of natural resources and arable land. The Japanese efforts to fulfil some commitments in the sphere of commercial policy have also been favourable elements; the elimination of restrictions on imports of tropical products is an example. In general terms, access to the Japanese market was considerably facilitated, which together with the extraordinary increase in demand in that market, opened up great possibilities for the growth of exports from Latin America to Japan.

However, these possibilities were not fully exploited. In spite of such a favourable evolution of Latin American exports to Japan, which was more dynamic than that of exports to other markets, it has not been enough to prevent the share of Latin America in the total of Japanese imports from falling; this share declined from 8·8 per cent (1956–8 average) to 6·2 per cent (1968–70 average).

In addition, the increase in exports occurred only in a small number of primary products, in spite of the great interest of Latin America in diversifying its exports, and above all in increasing the share of new products and manufactures.

The larger increases in Latin American exports to Japan correspond to food products (especially tropical and animal feeds) and mineral raw materials. In the last five-year period the first group of products almost tripled its value, while the second increased by 80 per cent. The following goods can be pointed out as relevant, among others: meat (the index was 225 during the period 1969–70 with respect to the base period 1964–5), fish and sea food (most of it lobster: 269), bananas (572), sugar (246), coffee (367), animal feed (mainly maize, bran, sorghum, fish-meal: 300), iron ore (165), non-ferrous metals (mainly copper and zinc: 227). In contrast with these products, one of the traditional Latin American exports to Japan, i.e. textile raw materials, decreased, or increased less: wool (103), cotton (97). These products accounted for 81 per cent of total exports from Latin America to Japan.

Thus the food group and mineral raw materials each accounted for more or less a third of overall exports from Latin America to Japan, while the share of textile raw materials, having reached 38 per cent of total exports to Japan, decreased to 16 per cent in 1970. There has been, naturally, an uneven evolution of exports from the different Latin American countries to Japan, the countries exporting the foregoing products having achieved an extraordinary increase.

On the other hand, Japanese exports to Latin American countries have also increased with similar intensity. The value of exports from Japan to Latin America in 1970 was U.S. $990 million, which represents 5·1 per cent of the total of Japanese exports and 6·6

per cent of the total of Latin American imports (in *f.o.b.* terms).
There was a notable change in the structure of Japanese exports to
Latin America: in the last five-year period, exports of heavy industrial and chemical products tripled, while those of light industry
products rose by only about 40 per cent. Therefore, these products,
which represented more than 30 per cent of Japanese exports to
Latin America at the beginning of the last decade, accounted for
approximately 15 per cent of the total in 1970. Meanwhile, heavy
industry and chemical products reached more than 80 per cent of
Japan's total exports to Latin America. Some products showed an
impressive increase: exports of heavy electrical machinery grew
eight and a half times between 1964–5 and 1969–70, precision instruments (watches, photographic and other optical devices) over
300 per cent, transportation equipment (mainly ships and motor
vehicles) more than 250 per cent, and other machinery over 300 per
cent. Some industrial materials such as chemical products (plastics,
etc.), steel and synthetic fibres, increased also very rapidly. In contrast, the exports of traditional textiles and other light industry
articles stagnated.

The composition of Japanese exports to Latin America has experienced great variations in the last decade, due to the new import
needs that have emerged in Latin America as a result of a sustained
industrialisation process, as well as to the evolution of Japanese
industry, where heavy industry and chemicals have gained in importance.

FINANCIAL AND TECHNICAL CO-OPERATION

Financial aid from Japan to developing countries grew very rapidly
in the last decade; its value reached U.S. $1,824 million in 1970,
against less than $400 million in the first years of the decade. This
increase was even faster than the rate of growth of Japan's gross
national product, and this is reflected in the fact that this country's
financial aid as a percentage share of G.N.P. has risen from less
than 0·6 per cent to 0·93 per cent in 1970.

However, a careful analysis of the composition of Japanese financial assistance brings out some characteristics that are not completely favourable to developing countries. In the first place, the
share of public assistance for development in the total value of
financial co-operation has always been smaller in Japan (34·5 per
cent in 1969) than in other countries which are members of the
Development Assistance Committee (D.A.C.) of the O.E.C.D. (the
average in 1969 was 49·7 per cent), although this share has consistently grown faster in Japan.

In the second place, in Japan the conditions on which assistance is offered continue to be inferior to those of other developed countries, in spite of the considerable improvements of the last few years; development aid in the form of donations given by the government represented 41·5 per cent of the total in comparison with 58·7 per cent, the average for all the D.A.C. countries in 1969. In direct government financing the average interest rate was 3·66 per cent per annum and a term of 19·5 years compared with 2·8 per cent and 27·8 years in the D.A.C. countries as a whole.

In the third place, the percentage of technical assistance is very low: barely 5·6 per cent of government development assistance, as against 24·8 per cent in France and 13·7 per cent in the United States.

Japanese aid is concentrated in Asian countries, which received, in 1969, 55·9 per cent of Japanese bilateral financial aid. However, this does not result from the same causes that stimulate some European countries to direct aid to their former colonies or to countries with which they have preferential relations.[1] The aid given to Latin America is much lower than that granted to Asian countries. For instance, Japan's bilateral aid to Latin America in 1969 was only 6·7 per cent (10·3 per cent in 1968), of the total amount of this type of aid granted by that country to the developing world.

Another characteristic of Japanese aid to Latin America is the lower proportion of direct government aid. In net terms, this element of assistance was negative from 1967 to 1969, that is, the aid granted was lower than the sum paid by Latin America to Japan as payment for amortisation and interest; however, this was partly due to special factors: in these years three Latin American countries had to pay amortisations due on re-financing loans granted by Japan in 1965.

This tendency in governmental aid contrasts with the dynamic evolution of private financing to Latin America. This has consisted chiefly of medium and long-term financing for imports (U.S. $173 million[2] for the fiscal year 1968) used mainly to buy capital goods such as industrial machinery, communications equipment, ships, etc.; the remainder was direct investment.

Japan's private investment in foreign countries increased rapidly in the last decade, especially in the last few years (U.S. $551 million in the fiscal year 1968 and £668 million in 1969), and reached a total of U.S. $2,683 million in March 1970. It is estimated that the value

---

[1] In the case of France, in 1968, 86 per cent of public aid and 37 per cent of private assistance went to 14 countries that were former French territories, and to the provinces and territories overseas. Also in 1968, the United Kingdom directed more than 92 per cent of its aid to the countries within the Commonwealth.

[2] This includes U.S. $52 million used for ships flying the Panamanian flag.

of Japanese investments in Latin America will have surpassed the assets of Great Britain and Western Germany by 1971. However, Latin America, which used to be one of the most important areas for Japanese investment, absorbed this investment at a lower rate in the last few years than other regions such as Asia. The value of Japanese private investments in the post-war period (from 1951 until March 1970) in Latin America reached a cumulative total of U.S. $513 million, a figure slightly lower than investments in South and East Asia (U.S. $604 million), and in the United States and Canada ($720 million). The proportion of these Japanese investments in Latin America going to manufacturing (47 per cent) was higher than in any other region, developed or developing. In the case of Asia, for example, investments in manufacturing were 33 per cent of total Japanese investment. In Latin America a substantial proportion of the Japanese funds invested in industry was channelled into textiles, transportation equipment and non-electrical machinery.

It is worth pointing out that more than half of Japanese investments are concentrated in Brazil, particularly in the steel industry, shipbuilding, textiles, etc.

II. THE PROSPECTS OF EXPANSION IN RECIPROCAL TRADE AND FINANCIAL CO-OPERATION

TRADE PROSPECTS

The prospects for the expansion of reciprocal trade, particularly of exports from Latin America to Japan, are extremely favourable. The possibilities of increasing financial and technical co-operation are very large, which is also a favourable factor for mutual trade.

The rate of growth of the Japanese economy is forecast to be higher than that of other industrialised countries, according to projections for the near future. According to the new official Economic and Social Development Plan of Japan for the quinquennium 1970–5, the cumulative annual rate of growth of the gross national product in current dollars will be 14·7 per cent, which is equivalent to 10·6 per cent in real terms. All the projections coincide in suggesting that at least in the next few years the dynamism of the Japanese economy will continue and that, in general, the rate of growth of its gross domestic product will be double the average of industrialised nations, so long as unforeseen factors such as the monetary measures taken recently by the United States do not damage the Japanese economy.

Further, the import elasticity of the gross national product is higher in Japan than in the more industrialised countries, especially for products of major interest for the Latin American countries. The elasticity of food imports in Japan with respect to the gross national product was 1·29 (average, 1960/61 to 1966/7) which compares favourably with that of other countries: 0·35 in the United Kingdom, 0·74 in the United States, 0·79 in France, etc.[1] The high Japanese elasticity of food imports is due to special factors: (1) the increase in the consumption of food in view of its still relatively low level compared with that of Western countries (2,206 calories *per capita* per day in 1966, which is 30 or 40 per cent below Western countries); (2) a change in the traditional diet based on fish, rice, local fruits and beverages towards a larger consumption of bread, meat, imported fruits and beverages. Both factors are a response to Western influence and the larger purchasing power of the public. In Japan, a very high proportion of food based on cereals is still consumed. The percentage of carbohydrates in total consumption is 60 per cent, as compared with around 30 per cent in Western countries. The *per capita* annual domestic consumption of beef is increasing at an annual rate of 10 to 15 per cent and imports represent at present 15 per cent of domestic consumption. However, annual *per capita* consumption, 10 kilograms in the latter years of the last decade, is still very much below the level of consumption in Western countries, where, in some of them, it reaches 100 kilograms. If Japanese consumption reached half the level of present consumption in the United States, this would mean an increase of 4 million tons of meat or 50 million tons of animal feed.

The same is happening in the case of sugar, fruits and tropical beverages. The consumption of bananas, pineapples, coffee, cocoa, etc., has increased extraordinarily in the last few years, although it has not reached the level of consumption of Western countries.

Moreover, the Japanese elasticity of imports of raw materials is also very high as compared with that of other industrialised countries, since the figure corresponding to Japan is around 0·60, while the figure for other countries fluctuates around 0·40. This high percentage is due in the first place to the extreme scarcity of natural resources in Japan in comparison with other countries, and to the considerable contribution of the manufacturing sector to the increase of Japan's gross national product. The scarcity of natural resources will be even more acute in the future. As the relative supply of domestic resources diminishes, Japan's dependence on overseas resources and the elasticity of demand for imports with respect to output rise. According to the Ministry of International Trade and Industry (M.I.T.I.), the demand for iron ore will reach

[1] Economic Planning Agency (Japan). *Economic Survey of Japan, 1968–69* (Tokyo, 1969).

200 million tons in 1975 as compared with 97 million in 1969, which is an increase of external dependence from 86 per cent to 91 per cent. Regarding petroleum, dependence, which is already very high, will rise to almost 100 per cent in 1975. In the same way, copper will come from abroad in an increasingly higher proportion, and this will augment external dependence from 72 per cent to 89 per cent between 1969 and 1975. In the case of zinc, it will rise from 49 to 57 per cent in the same period. For the rest, external dependence in the case of bauxite and nickel will continue to be total.

These factors lead to a very favourable conclusion with respect to the prospects offered by the Japanese market to the main Latin American products. If the rate of growth of the gross national product projected for the next five years is combined with the elasticity of imports given above, an estimated rate of growth of imports of food products of 19 per cent per annum is obtained, of 9 per cent for industrial raw materials, and of 16 per cent for mineral fuels. Now, if it is assumed that the increase in Latin American exports to the world will continue at the same rate as in the last few years, and the rate of growth of Japanese imports given by the new Official Plan (15 per cent) is applied, imports could reach some U.S. $2,000 million in 1975 and absorb 12 per cent of total Latin American exports. Even when the average growth rate of Latin American exports to Japan in the last ten years is applied (9·2 per cent), the corresponding percentage would still be 9 per cent. This shows the importance of the Japanese market for Latin America.

The prospects for trade in manufactures are also favourable. The industrialisation process in Latin America, increased by the regional and sub-regional integration under way, will have important implications for mutual trade in manufactures. This process requires a larger volume of more complex or higher quality capital goods and intermediate products. At the same time, an increase in competitive capacity will improve export possibilities of manufactures produced by Latin American industry. In a parallel way, in Japan various forces are at work towards a restructuring of its industry, which will induce a shift towards the importation of certain classes of manufactures and increased exports of products of the heavy and chemical industries. There exists, then, the prospect of a dynamic process of industrial complementation between Latin America and Japan.

THE NEW ORIENTATION OF TRADE POLICY

Japanese trade policy is characterised by a growing liberalisation and diversification of trade, which is determined by the following factors:

(a) the need to prevent an excessive accumulation of foreign exchange due to the trade surplus and other factors;
(b) the need to control the inflationary process which started some years ago;
(c) the need to obtain a more secure and stable supply of basic materials for industrial production and food production;
(d) the need to solve the problems derived from excessive concentration of productive capacity, such as pollution of the environment, etc.

The problem of an excess of foreign exchange reserves in Japan is well known, and reached its peak in August 1971 as a consequence of the monetary measures adopted by the United States. The gold and foreign exchange reserves (largely in dollars) were U.S. $4,500 million in January 1971 and rose by August to U.S. $12,000 million. This contrasts with the very vulnerable position of Japan's balance of payments during a long period after the war, and is due in part to the extraordinary increase in exports in the last few years (25 per cent in 1968, 22 per cent in 1969, and 21 per cent in 1970) as compared with a smaller rate of increase in imports.

Although it is not easy to foresee the effects of the monetary and other measures adopted in August and September, the concern of the Japanese authorities over foreign exchange reserves will continue to be one of the main factors that will determine the characteristics of Japan's foreign policy. Two kinds of measures designed to solve this problem are of interest to Latin America: those measures that aim at increasing imports, and those that seek to widen financial and technical co-operation with developing countries.

Another factor that has recently had great influence in the determination of Japanese trade policy is the inflationary process. This has been due fundamentally to the relative scarcity of labour, but import restrictions imposed to protect some sectors, particularly the agricultural sector, have also had an influence. According to the *Economic Survey of Japan, 1969*, agricultural products accounted for 44 per cent of the rise in the cost of living in 1968 and for 54 per cent in 1967. It is to be expected that the decrease in the various restrictions on agricultural products will have an important anti-inflationary effect. The reduction in the customs tariff, on agricultural products as well as on manufactures, is also considered an effective measure to mitigate the inflationary process.

Several measures have been taken already to liberalise and increase Japanese imports; among others, the most significant are:

(a) The anticipated application of concessions in the Kennedy Round negotiations. The 50 per cent reduction in the tariff on the majority of manufactured products and some agricultural goods was to be applied gradually until its completion by January 1972, but had been put into effect eight months before that date.

(b) Likewise, the general system of preferences for manufactured products of developing countries was implemented in August 1971, well in advance of its implementation in most other countries, including the United States.

(c) The programme of liberalisation of quantitative restrictions is being carried out. Until recently (the end of 1969) about 120 products were subject to these restrictions, a greater number than in European countries.

In April 1971, the number of products was reduced to 60 and to 40 in October, and it is expected that it will go down to 30 before April 1972. Among the products liberated before October are several of great interest to Latin America, such as fish-meal.

(d) The importation of any product has been authorised up to 3 per cent of its domestic consumption, which could have important effects on the imports of the items subject to quantitative restrictions such as meat, some fish and sea-food, meat products, dairy products, etc.

(e) Furthermore, the lowering of tariffs is being carried out on about 40 products, mutton, goat and horse meat (until they reach zero). The application of a seasonal tariff on bananas has been adopted also to favour imports for the period from April to September. According to official calculations the average tariff (customs revenue divided by the total value of imports) will decrease from 6·9 per cent in the fiscal year 1970 to 6·2 per cent in the fiscal year 1971, thanks to the tariff reductions; the level is approaching that of European countries (United States 6·2 per cent, Western Germany 3·9 per cent, France 4·0 per cent, Italy 7·3 per cent, as of 1968).

(f) Changes and enlargements are being made to the Bank of Japan's system of financing of imports (more favourable conditions) and that of the Export and Import Bank (special financing for a larger number of products, metals and minerals among others).

Finally, a few comments are in order on pollution in Japan, and some of its consequences for the country's foreign trade. The fact that pollution of the environment is increasingly more serious in Japan as compared with other countries is easily understood if it is recalled that, in this country, industry has been built much more densely, in relation to the availability of plainland, than in other industrial countries. At present, the gross national product per habitable hectare is over one million dollars (1967); this is 5·5 times larger than the corresponding figure for the United States. Therefore, Japan has to face, at an earlier stage than other countries, the problem of pollution and others deriving from high industrial density. All available means will have to be used to solve or mitigate these problems, according to the Japanese government's statements.

The effect of this new element on Japan's foreign trade, particularly on imports, cannot be evaluated quantitatively yet, but some probable consequences are already anticipated. In the first place, the anti-pollution campaign would favour imports of more highly processed products. For example, the importation of refined metals, instead of metallic minerals, would increase more than before. It is obvious that one of the main causes of pollution would be eliminated if the refining process were carried out in deserts such as, say, Chuquicamata, Chile, instead of in very agglomerated industrial areas in Japan. The replacement of minerals by refined metals will occur for two reasons. In the first place, the pressure of public opinion will force the government to lower the tariff on imports of refined metals, which face a high effective rate in comparison with duty-free entry for metallic minerals. On the other hand, it is also probable that government demands on industrial enterprises to take efficient measures to prevent pollution will be more rigorous; this will raise costs in some production processes such as, for instance, the refining of some metals, and this will discourage domestic production.

Another probable consequence for imports is the change in the source of some basic products. For example, the importation of raw materials with a lower content of sulphur would be required. In this sense, Japan would favour imports of oil from the Andean countries (Colombia, Ecuador and Peru). On the other hand, with respect to iron ore imports, those from Brazil and Australia would be preferred, for instance, over those from Peru. The possibility of carrying out some process to reduce the sulphur content in Peruvian ores before shipment is already being considered.

PROSPECTS FOR FINANCIAL AND TECHNICAL CO-OPERATION

Great possibilities exist for increasing financial and technical co-operation between the developing countries and Japan. Its larger availability of foreign exchange permits Japan to lend financial and technical assistance and to increase its investments abroad.

The Japanese government pointed out, in May 1970, in a

statement made before a meeting of Ministers of the O.E.C.D., the following indicative goals for foreign aid:

(1) the total value of Japanese foreign aid should reach 1 per cent of its gross national product before 1975, and

(2) Japan's public foreign aid should be increased to the equivalent of 0·7 per cent of its gross national product before 1980.

Furthermore at the meeting of the Development Assistance Committee (D.A.C.) of the O.E.C.D. in September 1970, the Japanese government announced its support of the principle that public financial assistance to developing countries shall not be tied, whether granted directly or through the international organisations.

Since it is estimated that Japan's gross national product will reach U.S. $400,000 million in 1975, according to the new official plan, if the proposed indicative goals are accomplished, Japan's foreign aid will grow from U.S. $1,824 million in 1970, to $4,000 million in 1975, which is an amount comparable to the United States overall foreign aid: U.S. $4,645 million in 1969.

This prospect has special significance for Latin America. Even if the relatively low share corresponding to Latin America with respect to the total of Japanese foreign aid (about 10 per cent on average in the last three years) is maintained, the overall figure estimated for 1975 of U.S. $400 million as the approximate value of assistance for Latin America in that year will be four times larger than that of 1968. If the structure of Japanese aid is modified to achieve a larger geographical diversification, the figure could be much larger; for example, if aid were distributed according to the respective proportion of Japanese exports to the region (13·5 per cent at the present), Japanese aid to Latin America would grow to U.S. $530 million per annum in 1975.

In addition, the effort required to raise the percentage of government aid might constitute a very favourable factor for Latin America. The small Latin American share of this assistance will be corrected as the available amount of direct government assistance grows.

An important amount of Japanese aid will be employed in combined projects of 'development and trade', that is to say, projects that not only foster development and the exploitation of resources but also their marketing and, particularly, their exportation to the Japanese market. In other words, these are financial and technical co-operation projects oriented to increase Japanese imports.

Some of these projects are being carried out already under the name of 'development and imports' (*kaihatsu yunyu*) and four semi-state organisations collaborate in them. The Export–Import Bank of Japan and the Economic Co-operation Fund finance, among others, production and transportation projects; the Overseas Technical Co-operation Agency (OTCA) sends experts and engineers in technical aid and receives foreign technicians for training, and the Japan External Trade Organization (JETRO) has created a special fund to encourage the importation of products from the developing nations and, among other activities, primary and industrial products of those countries are exhibited in Tokyo. Furthermore, in 1970 the Japan Overseas Development Corporation was created to finance the construction of the necessary infra-structure for the production of primary products, as well as the importation from the developing countries of primary products when their price is higher than the international price. There are also private sector projects, which are supported and stimulated by the Government, such as the activities of the International Development Centre of Japan, which is in charge of assistance on projects of a broader nature, such as regional development, pre-investment studies, and other forms of aid.

Some other semi-official organisations with specific aims, such as the Corporation for the Development of Metallic Minerals Prospecting, the Corporation for the Development of Petroleum, etc., have also helped to foster co-operation with the developing nations.

Likewise, it is estimated that Japanese investment abroad will expand. The liberalisation of private investments abroad has been achieved in Japan. The campaign for 'development and imports', together with the measures mentioned above and the broader public financing, has allowed Japanese firms to carry out a larger number of projects abroad in the last few years. For example, by the end of 1969, Japanese investments had been made in about 50 mines in the non-ferrous metals sector alone, and in the next few years more than 40 exploration and production projects amounting to at least U.S. $500 million will be implemented.

Although a considerable part of Japanese investments will be dedicated to the exploitation of foreign natural resources, given the great potential demand and the urgent need to secure a stable supply, investments will be made also in the development of agriculture and livestock, fishing and manufacturing, with a view to exports to Japan and other countries.

III. TOWARDS THE EXPANSION OF MUTUAL TRADE AND TECHNICAL AND FINANCIAL CO-OPERATION: POSSIBLE LINES OF ACTION

JOINT ACTION IN INTERNATIONAL TRADE POLICY

In the last few years, strong resistance has emerged in large trading centres to the liberalisation of international trade. It suffices to recall the imposition of a 10 per cent tax on imported products adopted by the United States in August 1971, as well as the initiatives submitted to the Congress of this country, in order to issue laws to apply restrictions on imports of several products. The same tendency is observed in the European Economic Community, in its special preferential agreements with the associated African countries and the Mediterranean. A deep concern has been expressed regarding these trends, since the increasing adoption of new protectionist measures and the proliferation of preferential trade agreements could start a process of reprisals, and the countries most affected by this would be the developing nations and those which are highly dependent on foreign trade, in spite of the fact that these nations are not necessarily responsible for the aggravation of such tendencies.

In the face of this situation, Latin American countries have made important efforts, particularly through CECLA (Special Committee on Latin American Co-ordination), with respect to their relationships with the E.E.C. and the United States. Japan, given its high dependence on external supply of basic products and fuels and its exports of some industrial products, has always been conscious of the importance of widening and liberalising international trade and has participated positively in international efforts towards liberalisation. Japan has not had special preferences, with respect to any country, that discriminate against imports from third countries. Further, besides fulfilling its international commitments in the context of the Kennedy Round in advance of schedule, Japan is carrying out, without demanding reciprocity, the liberalisation of quantitative restrictions and a unilateral reduction of tariffs and is imposing voluntary restrictions on its own exports to other countries, while some European nations continue the application of a series of discriminatory restrictions against Japan.

This background suggests the possibility of joint action on the part of Latin America and Japan aimed at defending the achievements of the last twenty years in liberalising international trade.

The joint action of both parties would also be very important in certain products such as sugar, wheat, textile raw materials, nonferrous metals, etc., since Japan has become the major or one of the most important buyers of these products in the world,[1] and Latin

---

[1] According to the GATT study cited above, Japan has now become the world's largest national market for raw materials and fuels, as well as a number of foodstuffs entering world trade. The growth of Japan's imports accounted for about one-third of the total increment between 1961 and 1969 in the value of world imports of raw materials, cereals and oilseeds. It explains very largely why the forecasts of a sluggish growth of exports of primary products made in the early 1960s proved to be incorrect for the most important commodities. Japan took 34·5 per cent of total purchases of iron ore by O.E.C.D. countries (average

America obviously continues to be one of the main suppliers. Through co-ordinated action, they could contribute to the stabilisation of prices and supplies of these products in the world market.

THE EXPANSION OF MUTUAL TRADE AND TECHNICAL AND FINANCIAL CO-OPERATION BETWEEN LATIN AMERICA AND JAPAN

(a) *General remarks*

Although between Latin America and Japan there exist no problems similar to those between Latin America and the United States or between Latin America and the EEC, since the relationships have been rather favourable, there is a wide field for more intense and harmonious action aimed at the expansion of trade and economic co-operation between Latin America and Japan.

The propositions as to the possible lines of action aimed at the expansion of mutual trade and economic co-operation must be formulated on the basis of very clearly established objectives, such as (1) preventing a decrease in the share of Latin America in the Japanese market by taking proper advantage of the possibilities of expansion of mutual trade; (2) diversifying the exportation of products from Latin America, with a larger share of manufactures, through a dynamic process of industrial complementarity between both economies; and (3) establishing more adequate formulas for the expansion of financial and technical co-operation between Latin America and Japan, taking the foregoing goals into account.

(b) *The improvement in access to the Japanese market*

First, in relation to quantitative restrictions, Latin American countries would benefit if Japan achieved the liberalisation of those restrictions that may remain even after the completion of the liberalisation programme since various products of interest to Latin America, particularly beef, some foodstuffs such as those prepared on the basis of meat, some fish, sea-weed, some fruits and fruit preparations, dairy products, etc., will remain restricted. Meanwhile increasingly larger quotas should be authorised for those products which remain subject to quantitative restrictions, for instance up to more than 5 per cent of internal consumption, rather than 3 per cent.

1966 to 1968); in the same way, 24·2 per cent of non-ferrous metals, 31·2 per cent of cotton, 21·5 per cent of wool, 24·6 per cent of oilseeds (chapter 22 in the S.I.T.C.). It can be pointed out also that Japan has become the largest buyer of sugar in the free market, that is, not subject to special purchasing agreements such as those applied by the United States, the United Kingdom, etc.

Second, in regard to tariffs, in spite of tax reductions through the Kennedy Round and favourable treatment in the general preference system, the customs tariffs on many products of interest to Latin America remain quite high, particularly in processed foodstuffs. Processed meat products received practically no favourable treatment in the general system of preferences. It should be pointed out that some primary products are also still subject to a high rate of custom tariffs, among others bananas, sugar, pineapples, beef, roasted coffee, etc. Moreover, processed foodstuffs in general did not obtain more favourable access, and the relatively high effective domestic protection rate remains unaltered. Given the great potential demand for the Western-type food products that the Japanese people increasingly prefer, the reduction of tariffs on these products, and the consequent lowering of consumer prices, together with certain measures to foster consumption through advertising and diffusion, would permit a greater expansion of Latin American exports to Japan.

Although manufactured products, with rare exceptions, were included in the general preference system, several products of interest to Latin America received only 50 per cent, not 100 per cent, exemption from customs tariffs; this was true of several textile products, some leather products, and some non-ferrous metals. It would be very beneficial to Latin America to obtain better treatment in this respect, and constitutes one of the most urgent actions to be taken concerning exports to Japan.

Besides increasing the number of products to which the system applies, it seems important to enlarge the preference quotas since, according to available information, the imports of some products from developing countries rapidly reached the quota ceiling in 1971.

In the long run it is also necessary to reduce custom tariffs on several industrial goods, for they are very high in Japan as compared with other industrialised nations and constitute a relatively high effective protection rate. These products are mainly those made with raw materials exported by Latin America to Japan, such as textiles, leather products, metals and alloys, besides the processed food products referred to above. Some other manufactured items that require a higher technological level should also have better access to the Japanese market, so they can be exported by Latin America, but other complementary measures would also be required, such as Japanese financial and technical co-operation.

(c) *Financial and technical co-operation*

It is indispensable to establish an integral programme of financial and technical co-operation between Latin America and Japan. In such a programme more emphasis should be placed on technical aid and public assistance for development, which has been very limited until now. In the matter of financial aid, although Latin American countries have already reached a more advanced level of development than Asian countries, this does not imply that the former have less need for foreign financing. In fact the reverse is true, since these countries are experiencing large social and economic changes and their industrialisation process is in a more advanced stage implying higher costs. On the other hand, financing conditions should be improved so they do not increase the burden of interest due. In shaping the integral co-operation programme, a higher priority should be given, both in the amount and in the conditions of assistance, to the relatively less developed countries such as Ecuador, Bolivia, Paraguay, and the Central American countries, instead of strictly applying the efficiency formulas.

The special needs of Latin American countries should also be considered: economic integration, industrialisation, the promotion of exports, particularly manufactures, etc. In this sense a higher priority should be given to export and production projects.

One of the advantages of these projects is that, since they are for exports, the payments on interest and amortisation of aid can be financed with part of the income from exports of the articles produced by the projects within the assistance programme. Given the accumulating financial commitments of the Latin American nations and the excellent possibilities of increasing exports to Japan, projects of such a nature could have extensive advantages. Obviously this does not prevent the development of co-operation in other fields such as assistance in communications, in which Japan has some experience in Latin America, and in other infrastructure projects, as well as in purely technical aid.

Further, the study of special aid for small enterprises would be worth undertaking. The credit lines given by Japan to Argentina and Chile had precisely the purpose of facilitating imports of machinery and equipment for those industries. However, the lines established have not been fully utilised up to now. This experience shows the need to elaborate a more efficient and wider formula for these enterprises, in which technical assistance should be included in a co-ordinated manner, in addition to financial assistance.

Finally, the role of regional or sub-regional financial organisations, such as the Inter-American Development Bank, the Central American Bank for Economic Integration and the Andean Development Corporation could also be of great importance. The financing granted by Japan to these institutions has been very limited, above all when it is compared to the financing given by Japan to the Asian

Development Bank. The establishment of greater contacts and better formulas for collaboration are to be expected between the Japanese organisations and the Latin American institutions mentioned above, so as to intensify multilateral co-operation between Latin America and Japan.

In the case of technical assistance, a very important factor that should be kept in mind is the fact that Japan has achieved very rapid technological progress based on a relatively greater availability of labour than characterises other industrialised nations, basically through the introduction, adaptation or modification of foreign technologies.[1] It would be convenient to introduce in Latin America some of the technological processes adopted and developed in Japan. By a 'process' is understood here not only the patents, but also the set or combination of techniques used in Japanese industry and adapted to the needs of the country, besides a wide range of knowledge and practices that have contributed to increase productivity, above all in the field of research, the acquisition of machinery, administration of production, quality control, etc.

The Japanese government has made important efforts in the field of technical assistance. It has established thirty centres in developing countries. In view of the comments made above, it is strongly to be recommended that Japan intensify these efforts, taking advantage of its valuable experience in technological progress, with the aim of introducing and spreading Japanese methods.

A combination of technical assistance in pre-investment and other studies, and financial assistance in development projects could also be very beneficial, particularly in regard to those sectors which in Japan have reached a more advanced technological level, such as some manufacturing industries (namely, electronics, ship-building, precision manufactures, metals, textiles), communications, fishing and agriculture.

It is very important to widen the Japanese programme of technical assistance in a systematic way, according to these and other criteria, since the value of Japanese technical assistance has been very limited until now. In 1969 it reached U.S. $19 million compared with $637 million in the United States, $432 million in France, and $149 million in Western Germany.

(d) *Co-operation in production and exports*

(*i*) *Animal feeds.* For these there is no problem of access to the Japanese market since most of them, maize, sorghum, oilseed cake and fish-meal among others, are not subject to quantitative restric-

---

[1] See 'Export Promotion in Japan and its application to Latin America', *Economic Bulletin for Latin America* (ECLA) first semester, 1970.

tions or to tariffs. A definite increase will be achieved if production under competitive conditions is increased, which could be attained through Japanese financial and technical aid. As an example of immediate action, Latin America could propose several joint projects[1] in the field: Japan has particularly wide experience in the 'development and importation' of maize in Asian countries.

(*ii*) *Industrial raw materials and fuels.* Given the good demand prospects and free access to the market, the main field of action rests on the creation of competitive conditions of supply as against other exporters, particularly those of developed countries such as Australia, the United States, Canada and South Africa, who have an advantage in terms of financial resources and experience. Certain disadvantages in Latin America with respect to these countries could be overcome through the formula 'development and importation' proposed by Japan; such a formula could be adjusted to the different conditions of each country, and could be a means to solve problems such as the lack of an infrastructure, the high cost of transportation, etc.

On the basis of these considerations, more intensive action is necessary to establish long-term contracts between Latin America and Japan, similar to those between Australia and Japan, for example. Brazil has already had favourable results in this field, such as the exploitation of iron ore and its exportation to Japan, with the active participation of Britain in state enterprises. Any Latin American initiatives would be positively welcomed by Japan, since this country needs a more stable and secure supply of industrial raw materials and fuels and shows its preference for obtaining these resources through direct participation in production, in co-operation with the country owning the resources, rather than buying them from the multinational corporations specialised in the exploitation of such resources. The most promising possibilities of co-operation in production and exports are in non-ferrous metals. Chile and Peru have considerably increased their exports of copper and alloys in the last few years, contributing over 80 per cent of Japanese imports from Latin America. In addition to other minerals such as tin, zinc and lead which Latin American countries export in large volumes, Japan is also interested in aluminium and nickel which could be produced under good competitive conditions in countries that have inexpensive electricity, such as Venezuela. Copper manufactures, such as wires and plate, and zinc alloys, etc., and metallic manufactures will then have better export projects in Japan, as long as the

---

[1] For this purpose, the projects of integral development of unpopulated rural areas, such as those in the North of Argentina, some areas in Brazil, Bolivia, Paraguay, Colombia, etc., could be of use. The Rio Bermejo Plan is a concrete case.

tariff reductions mentioned before are implemented and other complementary measures are taken.

Petroleum exports from Latin America to Japan have been very limited until now, but have very favourable prospects. The development of oil resources in countries like Colombia, Ecuador and Peru offers great advantages to Japan, in view of the diversification of supply sources it represents, as well as the lower sulphur content in this oil.

(*iii*) *Manufactures.* Latin America could propose new forms of direct investment or financial and technical co-operation in manufactures. One of the ways to proceed could be the association of Latin American firms with Japanese industrial processes through joint ventures or through purely technical assistance. Japanese firms could entrust specific Latin American enterprises with the production of certain production line components, full elaboration of which is difficult in Latin America. Industries in which Japan enjoys the advantage of a high technological level such as electronics, precision instruments, machinery, automobile parts, ship-building, etc., would have extensive possibilities. Not only is such technology more labour intensive than that of the United States or most European countries, as was pointed out above, but Japan also has experience in this form of co-operation with its neighbouring countries.

(*iv*) *Transportation and marketing.* In the first place, measures should be taken to overcome certain geographical disadvantages, such as the distance between Latin America and Japan. Although efforts have been made to solve this problem through the building of large capacity ships, it is essential to continue this effort. Fortunately, Japan is one of the major shipbuilding countries, so is in an excellent position to contribute to the solution of the problem. Special ships are already being successfully used to carry iron ore and oil between Japan, the Middle East and Brazil. Furthermore, a mixed Brazilian–Japanese enterprise has plans to build in Brazil in the near future ships with similar characteristics for reciprocal trade.

It is also important to establish a larger number of regular shipping lines between Latin America and Japan. More joint venture initiatives of the kind which have created shipping lines between Argentina and Japan, and Brazil and Japan are of great importance in view of the fact that a large proportion of mutual trade is carried in ships owned by third countries. A greater collaboration in the administration of lines would also facilitate the solution of various problems such as that of ships returning empty.

The improvement of port services and equipment is equally important, since the high cost of transportation is the result of this as well as of the expenses incurred in loading and unloading, and in some cases in land transportation. Mexico and some Central American countries have better ports on the Atlantic coast than on the Pacific since most of their trade is with Europe and the East and South of the United States. The delays and the lack of installations in some ports are part of the reason why some Mexican products are exported indirectly to Japan through the United States. It is indispensable, then, to explore possibilities of co-operation with Japan in this field also.

Co-operation between Latin America and Japan could include marketing also, through technical assistance in the promotion of exports, the financing of Japanese imports and other means. Japanese experience in the promotion of exports could be of great use to Latin America, and direct technical assistance would have an immediate effect in this field. This type of co-operation would be needed particularly for the exportation of manufactures, since Latin American firms in general have a very limited experience in this area and a very reduced financial capacity.

In this respect, collaboration with Japanese trading companies would be very valuable;[1] the Japanese government could assign a fund to these firms for its utilisation in financing the export of certain Latin American manufactures to Japan, taking advantage of the great trading experience of this country and of the trading channels maintained by these companies. The initiative of the United States Export–Import Bank is very interesting in this respect. It is being carried out under an agreement with the main Japanese trading firms entrusting them with the promotion of exports of certain manufactures of small and medium-size United States industries, with funds provided by the Bank.

An increase of funds to finance Japanese imports by the Export–Import Bank of Japan could be very useful, particularly the funds for the importation of products of interest to Latin America.[2]

Japan is not a very well-known market in Latin America, and thus there is a need for special measures. It is important to carry out research to discover new exportable products for the Japanese market. Some examples, such as Argentinian sorghum, agar-agar

---

[1] CEPAL, *Las empresas de comercialización integrada en el Japón*, ST/ECLA/ Conf. 37/L.20, July 20, 1971; reprinted in *Comercio Exterior* (Mexico, February, 1972).

[2] Other means of co-operation could be explored, one of which might be the triangular trading system. Through a special agreement, Latin American countries could take advantage of the possibilities of increasing their exports to Socialist countries, regardless of their permanent trade surpluses and Japan in turn could increase its imports from countries like the Soviet Union, in spite of its large trade deficit with that country.

from Chile and Argentina, etc., suggest the need to carry out that type of research, since the Japanese market is characterised by a structure of demand which is still quite different from that of the Western countries, in spite of the marked influence of the latter on Japan during the last few years. For the same reason, there is a need to adapt some export products to the characteristics of the Japanese market. The *Cavendish* Ecuadorian banana has been better accepted by Japanese consumers than the *Gros Michel*.

Research of this nature could be carried out by combined groups of Latin American and Japanese experts, with possible financing by Japan.

(e) *Some institutional arrangements*

Another field of action for Latin America might be the establishment of some institutional framework for consultation and negotiation.

Until now, no regional mechanism has been established for the interchange of information and the formulation of possible measures to be taken jointly to improve trade and mutual co-operation, in spite of the fact that both of these aspects have become more and more important, and that it is estimated that exports from Latin America to Japan will reach 10 per cent of the region's total exports within five years. At the moment, annual conferences of joint committees are being held, between industrial and commercial business men from Japan and both Mexico and Argentina, and between Brazil and Japan at governmental level.

It would be very timely if meetings similar to the former were established with the countries of the Andean Group and the Central American Common Market. Latin American countries could perhaps suggest the creation of a regional meeting between Latin America and Japan, since these countries have various common interests regarding trade and co-operation. The convenience of a meeting of such a nature could be discussed in CECLA, since the mission of this body is that of 'co-ordinating and drawing together the interests of its members and to propose mutual actions'.

In view of its valuable experience in the setting up of measures for the expansion of exports to the industrialised countries such as the United States and the E.E.C., CECLA could establish a definition of the common Latin American position, based on consensus, with respect to trading and economic co-operation with Japan, with a view to the meeting suggested, if the Latin American countries considered it convenient.

All the subjects discussed previously, such as international trade policy, the improvement of access to the Japanese market, and financial and technical co-operation, could become elements for consultation and negotiation in the meetings thus established.

Finally, Latin America should be interested in participating in some of the initiatives regarding trade and co-operation that are being discussed in Japan. The creation of the Organisation for Economic Co-operation in the Pacific Area, which implies various forms of co-operation, could be one of the possible channels. It might be convenient perhaps to formulate long-term strategies regarding the relationships between Latin America and the whole group of Pacific countries, since these relationships will be more intense every day. For example, while Latin American exports of textile raw materials to Japan tend to decrease, there exist great possibilities of increasing exports of these products to the countries neighbouring Japan. The Asian countries, in turn, will have products of the same kind that Japan previously exported to Latin America. Latin America could participate actively in a wide trading and economic co-operation system in the Pacific area.

Discussion of the Paper by Mr. Hosono

Mr. Bazdresch opened the debate, suggesting that the author's analysis of trade prospects given by Japan's growing need for raw materials, plus his statement that Japan was anxious to invest both in the development of such resources and in the infrastructure necessary to their exportation, really amounted to proposing the same role for Latin America as had been handed out so often in the past by other industrialised countries. It was of course true in general that Japanese growth would provide opportunities for natural resource development which Latin America should take advantage of. However, decisions to invest must take all costs and benefits into account; in the case of natural resources there were three aspects which had to be given particular attention: first, the implicit risk in an often irreversible specialisation of resources in primary goods production, given a history of both long-run inelastic demand and elastic supply; second, the effect on comparative advantage of using prices corresponding to marginal social productivity; third, the terms of external financing and other conditions. On the first, the problem was to find a way of sharing the risk among the participants; Japan appeared willing to take her share but it would be tricky to negotiate. The second was a question in part of balancing the immediate need for foreign exchange, the possibilities of industrial development, and so forth. The third raised not only the problem of the various balance of payments effects, but also the question of the distribution among nations of the gains from the investment: given the monopoly elements typically present, Latin American governments could not leave this to the market but should exert their bargaining power.

Without doubt Mr. Hosono's proposal would arouse strong opposition. But what he particularly liked was his suggestion that all these problems should be discussed collectively between Latin America and Japan. Perhaps the greatest merit of the paper was that it reopened questions which might, this time, find a better solution than that of import substitution.

Mr. Macario was less pessimistic than Mr. Bazdresch on the question of direct foreign investment: there was one very interesting characteristic of Japanese investment, which was their insistence on participation as a minority stockholder only. He of course shared Mr. Bazdresch's criticism of their concentration on primary products; in fact there were excellent opportunities for expansion in manufacturing, especially in electronics which being relatively labour intensive was ideally suited to Latin America. And Japan must develop new markets by some means, given first the danger of awakening distrust of her imperialistic pretensions by too great an expansion in Asia, and second, the increasing resistance and concern she was meeting in the markets of Europe and the U.S.A.

Mr. Wionczek also saw grounds for optimism. In questions of direct investment it appeared that global political considerations played a greater and more rational role in Japan than in other countries. There was full awareness of the danger of continued investment in developed zones, and conscious decisions had been taken to diversify into the Middle East, South East Asia, even Africa, as well as Latin America. Investment in natural resources represented only the first stage of this process; in the second stage, just begun, there would be much more investment in manufactures.

Turning to the question of adaptation of technology, he was inclined to think that Japan would prove more successful than others in scaling down processes, if only because she had herself initially had to scale down foreign technology for her own market. M.I.T.I. had in fact requested a study of Japanese plants in less developed countries which had shown that in the majority of cases there was a possibility of adapting technology to smaller scale production – something that might, he suspected, be more generally true than people realised. The problem was often that the size of plant was decided on beforehand and there was no real search for an alternative. He quoted the example of Dupont, which had insisted for years that the small market size made production in Mexico impossible. Yet when Swiss and German firms entered and showed it was possible, Dupont found in its own files similar processes which had been filed away as not useful for the U.S. market. Dupont was then able to pull out and use the systems it had rejected and forgotten.

Dr. Ferrer, however, agreed with Mr. Bazdresch that the paper appeared to reproduce a pattern very similar to Latin American–United Kingdom relations in the nineteenth century. He saw industrial complementarity agreements as the key both to successful integration within the Andean Pact framework and to the establishment of links with Japan that would be really beneficial to both parties.

Professor Sunkel also wished to underline the point Dr. Bazdresch had made. Trade expansion was not necessarily something good in itself. The paper made it clear that Japan's own long-run interest was in the expansion of a kind of trade Latin America wanted to escape from. Yet he also agreed with Dr. Bazdresch that the opportunity to expand raw material production could not be neglected. The fact that eight or ten large corporations handled the vast majority of Japanese trade surely opened the way for a bargaining process that could secure for Latin American technology, market access *and*, most importantly, a rising share of value added within Latin America.

Professor Vernon took up the question of bargaining: if one viewed Latin America's trade relations as a question of strategy, then it was probably true that the more sources of technology and markets she confronted the greater the possibilities of a successful bargaining outcome; in this sense Japan's entry into the field could only be welcomed. The task was now to delineate the nature of the game. Certain characteristics of the new adversary were rather clear: first, the degree of co-ordination of policy *vis-à-vis* her external position was greater than was true either of Western Europe or the U.S.A. Then some 70 per cent of imports were handled by six or seven firms, who were deeply involved in the internal market. And thirdly, Latin America confronted a rather centralised and clear-cut policy designed to maximise the long-run interest of Japan, an interest which had to be different from that of Latin America.

Professor Machlup said he was puzzled at the implicit assumption Professor Vernon appeared to be making that the Japanese 'successfully' intervened to co-ordinate policy. His own understanding was that such intervention in the United States typically strengthened cartellisation and resulted in a further departure from the competitive position. *Professor Vernon* replied to this that M.I.T.I. most probably did not produce a result closer to the competitive norm. But the Japanese perceived that most of the situations in which they were involved were *oligopoly* situations where the outcome of negotiations by M.I.T.I. plus trading enterprises was both different from the outcome of independent negotiations – and closer to the Japanese national interest, since they were typically confronting situations where goods were not available at 'competitive prices'.

Professor Eastman agreed with Professor Vernon that the entrance of Japan decreased the problems national governments in Latin America might have in negotiating appropriate agreements with foreign investors and other purchasers of national resources. Japan reduced the oligopoly power of potential purchasers and raised rents in countries possessing the natural resources. Indeed it might be that the U.S. measures of 15 August were partly intended to apply a brake on Japanese expansion and competition which was raising world rents.

But would this not simply worsen what he understood to be one of the main preoccupations of the conference? This was that Latin American countries engaged in too much trade, in the sense that exports of raw materials earned foreign exchange, which pushed down the rate of exchange and so the price of import-substituting manufactured goods, so depressing their development. The question then arose as to why this increased difficulty in developing import competing manufactures was a loss exceeding the gains from trade. The answer presumably had to do with the importance of manufacturing in raising the productivity of labour or in creating a more desirable distribution of income.

Dr. Arndt commented that the division of the future we should be concerned about was not so much that into 'Centre' and 'Periphery' as into clean and polluted nations, following Mr. Hosono's suggestion that the danger of pollution might lead to increased processing in the less developed nations. Here there was clear potential for conflict between the targets of growth and of environmental preservation.

Mr. Hosono, replying, agreed that the lack of prospects for Latin American manufacturing exports in Japan was a legitimate concern, and that there was a danger of a return to a Centre–Periphery situation. But we had to face the realities of balance of payments difficulties; in this light Japan offered positive opportunities. Also, the very fact of expansion of trade with a country like Japan with many special characteristics represented valuable diversification of Latin American trade relations. He also thought there was scope for expansion of exports of manufactures and had mentioned measures which could be taken in his paper. He could not accept the view which saw Japan as a new 'Centre'; apart from the real possibilities of expanding trade in manufactures, Japan was still marginal to Latin America's trade relations. And there would be much investment in transport and infrastructure which fell outside the traditional pattern. The Andean group had been mentioned; Japan was indeed very conscious of the opportunities this offered, and he agreed that Japan's freedom to manoeuvre, because of a lack of existing trade and investment relations, was an important characteristic which would be helpful in this context.

He also agreed with Professor Sunkel's stress on the significance of the large trading corporations. He felt specifically that their size and the breadth of their business might provide a way of taking account of Latin America's need to expand her exports of manufactures. On the role of M.I.T.I. itself, he found it difficult to comment, but did feel strongly that M.I.T.I. had in fact struggled against the large corporations, and had said they were a major reason for the problems Japan was having in trade with the U.S.

13 Eastern European Trade and Financial Relations with Latin America

Vladimir Pertot

UNIVERSITY OF LJUBLJANA, YUGOSLAVIA

Geographically the term 'Eastern Europe' is relatively simple to define. The term has, however, often been misused or misinterpreted in political terminology. It is sometimes used as a synonym for the so-called 'S.E.V.' or 'COMECON' group of countries. Very often it includes all European communist countries. It has been used to designate simply the eastern political block of countries, and it may even stand for that group of European countries with centrally planned economies.[1]

Since our primary concern here will be with methods of economic planning and their influence on international trade and finance, we shall make this our criterion. The term 'Eastern Europe' will in this paper designate the following centrally planned economies: the U.S.S.R., Poland, the German Democratic Republic, Czechoslovakia, Hungary, Romania and Bulgaria. This corresponds to the COMECON countries, excluding Mongolia. Of the European communist countries we have excluded Albania, although its economy is centrally planned, an omission justified by its negligible participation in world trade. Yugoslavia could logically be excluded also on the grounds that it does not belong to the eastern political block and is not a member of the COMECON centrally planned group of countries; in fact it will be treated here separately as an example of a workers' council market economy, i.e. as an intermediate case between the centrally planned Eastern European countries and western market economies. Yugoslavia represents the only example of a communist country heavily involved in the international division of labour.

[1] None of the above denominations covers the same number of countries. Thus, the COMECON organisation includes Czechoslovakia, which is a Central rather than Eastern European country, as well as Mongolia, which is in Asia, as is the greater part of the U.S.S.R. It does not include either Yugoslavia or Albania, both geographically belonging to the southern part of Eastern Europe. The identification of Eastern Europe with the eastern political block would leave the present position of Romania uncertain. The block certainly does not include the non-aligned Yugoslavia or the Mao-oriented Albania. All these countries belong, however, to the group of countries with communist constitutions, though they do not all have central economic planning. Yugoslavia, for one, has a market economy.

Given the centrally planned nature of the economies in question, one might expect to find that Latin American trade with Eastern Europe was low, not only absolutely but even relative to the general low level of Latin American trade with the world. This is because the opinion is often expressed that, all other things being equal, the foreign trade of a centrally planned economy will be lower than that of a free market economy. By definition central planning apparently tends to be antagonistic to the development of foreign economic relations, even as between countries belonging to the same social system. The aversion of a centrally administered economy to foreign trade is based on the fact that it is impossible completely to plan the foreign trade sector: it is only in the exchange of goods and services with other countries that the central administration lacks the power to direct both sides of the economic process, supply and demand. The smaller the percentage of foreign trade in G.N.P., the smaller the degree of uncertainty the central administration faces over accomplishing its target. Any unforeseen development in foreign demand in relation to planned exports, any unforeseen development in foreign supply of planned imports endanger the chances of a complete realisation of the plan. Such a development in foreign demand or supply need not necessarily be the result of oscillations in world markets; it can equally be the result of other centrally planned economies incompletely fulfilling their own targets. This supposed antagonism of central planning to foreign trade is then not only the consequence of a political aversion to tying one's economic development to that of countries with different social or economic systems. It is also a direct consequence of the inevitable risk of not accomplishing targets of economic policy whenever scope is given to the influence of foreign demand and supply. It is true – and present intra-Eastern European trade seems to confirm this – that special efforts to enforce a balanced development of trade between centrally administered economics can in fact yield an exceptionally high level of trade. Trade can develop between such countries in size, directions and items that would be unthinkable under circumstances other than central planning. But this seems to be possible only in the context of such extraordinary efforts and again only between centrally planned economies. For the rest of the world we may still assume that central planning does not favour the development of foreign trade.

Can we, however, simply assume that *ceteris paribus* Latin American trade with an Eastern European country will always be relatively smaller than that with a country without centrally planned trade? We have to consider that the bias against foreign trade in centrally planned economies has its natural limits. It exists only so long as there is a choice between foreign trade and expansion of internal production. When there is no such choice and indispensable commodities can be obtained only by imports then the level of imports may have to exceed the point which from the planning point of view may be considered desirable. In such a case exports too have to be planned so as to provide for the necessary foreign exchange. The scarcer the national resources of a centrally planned economy the less weight the country can give to the planning risk involved in the expansion of foreign trade. Because of this the level of foreign trade per head of the population between similarly developed centrally planned economies varies as it does between any two countries.[1]

We may thus approach an analysis of Latin American–Eastern European trade with a certain presupposition that in the past the level of trade between these two regions will, because of this planning risk, have been lower than trade between Latin America and the rest of the world. This does not, of course, mean that there might not also be other factors affecting Latin American–Eastern European trade with similarly adverse results.

It is impossible to determine what the trade between two regions or two countries would have been without the existence of the mentioned planning risk. But to compare Latin American trade with different regions or continents over long periods may be revealing nevertheless. If the long-term trend and short-term oscillations of Latin American–Eastern European trade are found to reflect the characteristics of the bulk of Eastern European trade with the whole world or even of intra-Eastern European trade, it may be argued that in Latin America the level of trade has been predominantly influenced by the mechanism of central planning. On the other hand, if the tendencies and oscillations of Latin American–Eastern European trade correlate positively with the general tendencies of Latin America's international trade as a whole one may assume that Latin America has imposed its own rhythm of trade on Eastern Europe and that the trade relationship with Eastern Europe has been poor because of the inability of Latin America to adapt itself commercially to the needs of Eastern Europe.

It would not be surprising to find that an analysis of Latin Ameri-

[1] Given that an Eastern European country needs certain imports and has to increase its planned exports, it will still try to diminish the resulting uncertainty as much as possible. It will try to enforce the use of trade instruments which will automatically balance bilaterally external demand and supply with internal planned demand and supply. The imposition of bilateral trade agreements represents the use of such an instrument. They have not been readily accepted by Latin American countries. But even where they have been accepted, in the case of Latin America they have not functioned as automatically as they must in order to eliminate the planning risk.

can trade with Eastern Europe since 1958 gave no direct confirmation of either of the two extreme assumptions. The bulk of trade usually lies somewhere between extremes. However, interestingly enough, it will be seen that in fact Latin American–Eastern European trade developed according to a pattern quite distinct from that of either Latin American or Eastern European trade in general.

This specific character of Latin American–Eastern European trade is easier to illustrate in aggregate than in detail. The more we split this inter-regional trade into its national components the less the specific trends are intelligible; they disappear completely if we analyse trade in individual commodities between individual pairs of countries. Surprisingly, however, the characteristic pattern does not disappear once we eliminate Cuba from the total of Latin American–Eastern European trade. Cuba is the only Latin American country that has been in a position to eliminate the element of planning risk from this inter-regional trade; thus, it would not have been surprising if Cuba's trade had had much in common with the general tendencies of Eastern European trade.

Turning now to Fig. 13.1, Latin American trade is here defined as the trade of the two American subcontinents without the U.S.A. and Canada. It will be seen that this trade compared with total trade of other regions in the world represents a small section of world trade. In the last twelve years the nominal value of world trade has risen almost exponentially (Fig. 13.1, item (1)). This very high rate of increase has resulted in recent years from an above average rate of increase in the trade of the group of developed market economies (2) and a below average increase in the trade of both the developing market economies (3) and the centrally planned economies (4). Comparing (3) and (4), we see that the graph which shows the slowing down of trade of the developing countries is concave in shape when compared with the trend of world trade, while by contrast the graph for the centrally planned economies is convex. But if we deduct the total trade of Latin America from the trade of all developing countries (3a), in the case of imports the concave shape vanishes almost completely and the rate of growth appears much steadier. The reverse effect is achieved, however, when we deduct from the trade figures of the centrally planned economies the trade of the Asiatic members of this group. The resulting curves of Eastern European trade (5) reflect an even higher convexity when compared with world trade, particularly in imports.

Thus there exists in the pattern of development of Eastern European trade and Latin American trade (6) at once an interesting similarity and dissimilarity. Both groups reflect a similarly irregularly oscillating retardation of the rate of increase of their trade when

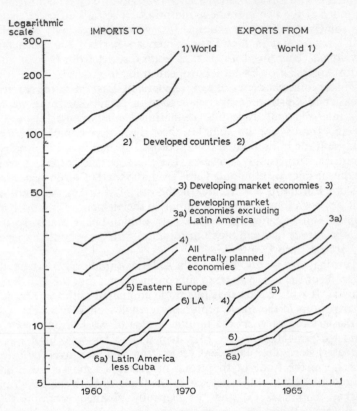

FIG. 13.1 Trends and composition of world trade 1958–69, billions of U.S. dollars, current prices. Source: Data from the U.N. Statistical Yearbooks, processed for the needs of this analysis. The U.N. statistics include in the group of developed market economies: the U.S.A., Western Europe, Australia, New Zealand, South Africa and Japan. Western Europe is every country that is not Eastern Europe (in the above-mentioned sense). Yugoslavia and Turkey are thus included, although they are located in South East Europe and neither is developed. This inaccuracy need not be corrected here, the share of both Yugoslavia and Turkey in world trade being so low that no visible modification of the curves presented here would be noticeable. Besides, the role of Yugoslavia will be discussed in more detail later. The group of centrally planned economies comprises Eastern Europe as defined earlier with the addition of the centrally planned Asiatic economies such as China, Mongolia, Democratic People's Republic of Korea and Democratic Republic of Vietnam. The developing market economies are taken to be all the countries that do not belong to either of the other two groups.

compared with world events, while the yearly fluctuations in trade of the two groups show, if anything, inverse tendencies: the years of slowest growth of Eastern European trade are years of relatively rapid growth for Latin American trade, and *vice versa*. The reasons for the retardation of trade in both cases would seem to be of a fundamentally different origin.

The dissimilarity of the deviations from world trends in the two groups of countries is practically unchanged if we deduct Cuban from Latin American trade (6a). The only effect is to make the resulting Latin American export curve somewhat less smooth.

Such diversity in trends in the total trade of the two regions does not, of course, necessarily exclude the existence of parallel movements within the much smaller sector of pure Latin American–Eastern European trade. We therefore turn now to look at Eastern European trade specifically (Fig. 13.2). First, there can be no doubt that Eastern Europe's total trade is overwhelmingly determined by the requirements of centrally planned economic policies. This is shown by the near identity between the graph of total Eastern European trade (7, equal to 5 in Fig. 13.1) and the graph of Eastern European intraregional exchange (9). Roughly three-fifths of total Eastern European trade consists of planned intraregional exchange, and only two-fifths are exposed to the risk of external influences. Second, both kinds of Eastern European trade are absolutely low if compared with trade levels of the rest of the world, be it developed (2) or developing (3), and taking into account the political, economic, geographic and demographic importance of this particular region. It is strikingly low if one takes into consideration the degree of technological development that some of these countries (U.S.S.R., C.S.R., or G.D.R.) have achieved. The picture does not substantially change when we add to intra-Eastern European trade all the trade with the non-European planned economies such as China (8). Thus, this identity of the level and pattern of intraregional trade with the trends of total Eastern European trade suggests that, other things equal, central administrative planning generally does lead to relatively lower levels of international trade and to a below-average dynamism in trade in the long run.

The share of both developed market economies and developing market economies in Eastern European trade is also relatively and absolutely low. But Eastern Europe's trade with both groups reveals a dynamism which is much greater than that of intra-Eastern European trade itself (11 and 12). Moreover, by about 1965 the share of developed market economies in total Eastern European trade had reached the same level as the total share of the U.S.S.R. in Eastern European trade (10). It should further be stated that from a

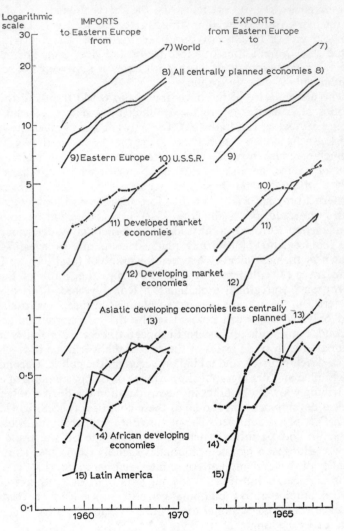

FIG. 13.2. Trends and composition of trade of Eastern Europe, billions of U.S. dollars, current prices.

Source: see Fig. 13.1.

long-term point of view the share of the developed market economies in Eastern European trade is increasing at a faster rate than total Eastern European trade (and, of course, Eastern European intra-regional trade). Non-economic circumstances in the past decade cannot be described as particularly favourable to the development of Eastern European trade with the developed market economies. Just because of that, one cannot overlook the fact that during this decade the rate of increase of Eastern European trade with the developed market economies (11) surpassed even the rate of increase of total trade of market economies (2). This suggests that it is at least possible that under certain conditions free market forces can overcome the antagonism to trade of central planning.

It seems only logical that developed market economies should show more vitality in such penetration into the centrally planned economies than the developing market economies. So one would expect to find that the exports and imports of the developing market economies with Eastern Europe had increased less than the trade of developed market economies with Eastern Europe. But again even this slower rate of increase was still faster than the rate of increase of total Eastern European trade (7) and of intra–Eastern European trade.

The developing market economies represent, of course, a mixture of policies and belong geographically to different continents. Once we turn to an analysis by continent, however, it is necessary to qualify the general statement made above about the role of all developing countries in Eastern European trade. Trade between Eastern Europe and Africa (14) shows an above average rate of increase compared with the group of all developing countries trading with Eastern Europe. The trade of Eastern Europe with Asian developing countries (13) lies approximately on trend. Only Latin America (15) shows a fluctuating but usually below average rate of increase in trade with Eastern Europe. This comparatively slow increase in Latin American–Eastern European trade remains whether we compare it with the trade of other developing continents, with the total trade of Eastern Europe, or with intra-Eastern European trade. If aggressive trade policies of market economies, developed or developing, have something to do with the high rate of increase in trade with the centrally planned economies and with the successes in breaking the general resistance of Eastern Europe to unregulated foreign trade, evidently this is less true of Latin American commercial policies than of anywhere else.

To clarify further the general pattern of Latin American–Eastern European trade, we must divide the past twelve years into two sub-periods, before and after 1961. Before 1961 and the Cuban crisis the trade of Eastern Europe with Latin America was at such a low level that the steep increase around 1961 can be characterised as a movement to a level rather nearer that which would normally pertain between two regions of their size. But the Cuban crisis constituted a once-and-for-all boost which was not repeated: even after the

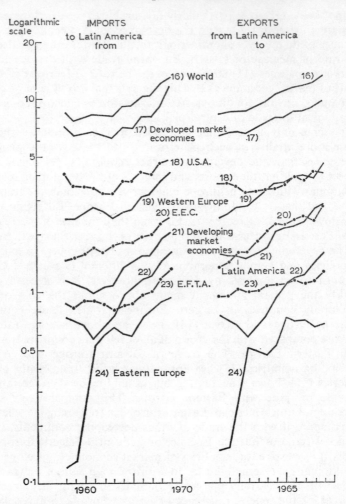

FIG. 13.3. Trends and composition of Latin American trade 1958–69, billions of U.S. dollars at current prices.

Source: Dinar figures of the Yugoslav official foreign trade statistics (Savezni Zavod za Statistiku: Statistika Spoljne Trgovine S.F.R. Jugoslavije, Beograd) for the corresponding year, converted into U.S.A. dollars at the corresponding official rate.

establishment of closer trade relationships between Cuba and Eastern Europe the rate of increase of Latin American–Eastern European trade remained low, and well below the average rates of the rest of the world.

Turning now to Fig. 13.3 we see that not only does Latin American–Eastern European trade have little in common with the general pattern of Eastern European trade, but it also bears little resemblance to the general pattern of other Latin American trade.

The main difference between total Latin American trade and trade of other regions is that exports and imports do not fluctuate together (16). This may be the consequence of the typical nature of economic policies, and particularly foreign trade policies, in Latin American countries. Restrictive measures on imports and incentives to exports are typically not synchronised. This is not a consequence of excessively liberal economic policies. Latin America is the classic continent of differential exchange rate practices and has by no means abandoned this tradition. On the contrary, there are probably few restrictive measures in foreign trade used anywhere in the world that have not been applied in some Latin American country. The point is that in practice the intensive interventionism in Latin American foreign trade in many countries does not seem to affect imports to the same degree and in the same manner as exports. Intervention is rarely used to help exports through import policy, or vice versa. Export policy in general seems to be more closely connected with internal production policy and exports are directly exposed to the influence of oscillations on the world market. Import policies are, on the contrary, much more a result of developments in domestic consumption, of the availability of imports of capital and of foreign exchange arising from export sales in previous periods which in turn were the product of independent export policies.

On the whole, trends in Latin American exports are dominated by exports to the developed market economies (17), which follow, with a slightly slower rate of increase, the rapid and unbroken trend of imports of the developed market economies (2). Imports into Latin America on the other hand stagnate until about 1965 and then grow slowly (16). Their pattern seems to have been imposed upon them by developments in imports into Latin America from developed market economies (17) and particularly by imports from the U.S.A. (18). Exports to the U.S.A. over this period were growing very slowly, and the extent to which the dollar inflow could be overdrawn has been increasingly restricted by the decreasing import of U.S.A. capital during the past twelve years. There was a similar stagnation in Latin American imports from the EFTA countries (23) because of the failure of Latin American exports to this region to grow and an increasing limitation on the export of capital to Latin America, particularly from the United Kingdom. In contrast to this stagnation of Latin American imports from the U.S.A. and the United Kingdom caused mainly by a change in traditional financial ties with Latin

America, trade with the E.E.C. showed a quite rapid rate of growth The level and the increasing rate of Latin American exports to this region (20) permitted a similarly steady rate of increase of Latin American imports from the E.E.C.

But the best illustration of how far the development of Latin American trade has been influenced by external financial factors is given by the totally contrasting trends in Latin American trade with the developing market economies. Exports to these regions are as a rule higher than imports (21), so no currency obstacles stood in the way of Latin American imports from such regions. The consequence is that while Latin American exports to developing countries increased more rapidly than to any other area, Latin American imports from the same regions increased at an even higher rate. Thus, trade with other developing market economies outstripped even Latin American intraregional trade (22), which one might have expected to show the highest rate of increase (as was true within the E.E.C.), since it was the only trade which was carried out on a reciprocal basis.

One might think, then, that the surplus of Latin American trade with the developing countries indicates where the possibilities for increasing Latin American imports lie. But this would be overlooking two important facts. First, Latin America needs a positive balance of trade with at least some of the world regions, since she has to be able to fulfil her most urgent debt payments obligations. In the second instance, even if these financial considerations were omitted, there would remain the question of how far Latin America can import from developing markets the commodities that she needs. Few of today's developing countries can supply the equipment and highly processed commodities Latin America is so badly lacking.

One would expect it to be precisely at this point that Eastern European trade with Latin America should enter on the scene. Nothing of the kind can be remarked, at least at present, in the trade between Latin America and Eastern Europe (24). This trade is low in absolute level, and in its annual fluctuations is quite atypical of any other items of Latin American trade. Since the development of Latin American trade with the rest of the world seems favourable to the expansion of Latin American–Eastern European trade, the general constellation of Latin American trade policies must be rather unfavourable to such an expansion to account for this failure. Very roughly, one may try to sum up the diverse situations in different Latin American countries as one in which Latin America cannot count on a substantial increase in exports to Eastern European countries unless such additional purchases have been previously included in their plans. However, such purchases will not be provided for in Eastern European countries unless their planners have reasonable confidence that such imports from Latin America will be realisable on time and at planned prices. But Latin American export policies are often non-existent and rarely regionally oriented, so there is practically no security for the Eastern European planners, and they will turn in preference to other sources that can by chance offer more security. Of course, as we know, a very strong political reason may from time to time override the risks. But on the whole even such exceptions have not much increased the level of Latin American–Eastern European trade.

If, very generally speaking, Latin American trade policies became more regionally conscious, if exports were directed to regions or countries where the probability of obtaining determined imports are higher, it would certainly represent a step towards improving Latin American–Eastern European trade. It might at least mean that it would increase at a rate similar to the rate of increase of intra-Eastern European trade (9). This would still not represent a high rate of growth, but it would at least be close to the rate of increase of trade between Latin America and Western Europe (19). This would not solve Latin America's trade problems, but it would restore a more normal trade relation with Eastern Europe. As it is (24), except for the increase in 1961, trade with Eastern Europe develops more slowly than any other part of trade, and more slowly than any other part of Eastern European trade (15). Being at present a residual for both parties, the trends in trade reflect the characteristics of trade of neither party, and result in fact from inactive trade policy on both sides.

How far could trade be increased if Eastern Europe alone altered its passive attitude? To answer this, it will be helpful to look at an intermediate case, namely Yugoslavia. She does not play a particularly important role in Latin American trade; rather, her interest lies first in the fact that while she is socialist she is free of the particular constraints on foreign trade which as we have shown hamper general Eastern European foreign trade, since being a market economy she does not need to consider the problem of planning risks, and second in the fact that to exist between two political blocks she has to pursue an active trade policy all over the world, including Latin America. Yugoslav internal trade mechanisms do not require any adaptation by foreign trading partners to any internal institutions.

We turn then to Fig. 13.4. During the period under discussion, the average annual rate of increase of Yugoslav trade (25, 26) was very close to that of developed market economies (2), especially in the case of imports. The dynamism of Yugoslav trade thus exceeded that of the developing market economies (3) and that of the centrally planned economies (4). Since only about one fifth of Yugoslav total

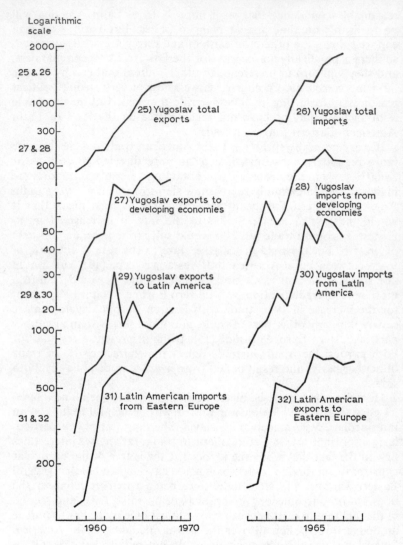

FIG. 13.4. Yugoslav trade figures as compared with Latin American–Eastern European trade, 1958–69, millions of U.S. dollars, current prices. Source: See Fig. 13.3.

trade is with the developing market economies the rapid rate of increase of Yugoslav total trade results principally from trade with developed market economies and with Eastern Europe. Yugoslav foreign trade interventionism was elastic enough to permit an increasing trade with countries of any politico-economic system. The rigidities of the Eastern European central planning system, while representing technically a difficulty, were never in practice a brake on the development of trade. Yugoslavia was able to adopt a policy of directing exports in any direction in which she could expect to obtain needed imports. The country adopted the same policy also with regard to all developing countries (27 and 28), with the result that the rate of growth of exports and imports in trade with developing countries remained high, not as high as the rate of increase of trade with developed economies, but still higher than the average rate of increase of the whole group of developing countries (3). Only in the last few years is there noticeable a slight slowing down in the rate of increase of Yugoslav trade with the developing countries. Perhaps this is again the result of a failure to meet with responsiveness in the trade policies of developing countries. The worsening of Yugoslav's trade balance with the developing economies may be part of the explanation for the recession.

What is interesting about the figures is the near identity in trends and yearly oscillations between Yugoslav exports (27) and imports (28) with the developing world, which reflects Yugoslavia's trade policy, which actively directs exports to the source of prospective imports. By contrast, less coincidence in trends and oscillations can be found when one considers Yugoslav trade with Latin America alone (29, 30). The implication of this is confirmed by common experience: it is widely known that in practice in trade with Latin America Yugoslav initiative is often halted by local policies unaccustomed to adapting to the requirements of bilateral trade. Yugoslav trade with Latin America is too small to be entitled to adaptations of local policies. But would such policies be more adaptable if the trade in question were greater?

Such a failure of local policy to adapt may explain at least in part why the pattern of Yugoslav trade with Latin America is much closer to that of Latin American–Eastern European trade (29–32), particularly in the last ten years, than to that of Yugoslav trade with developing countries in general, or even of Yugoslav total trade.

The rather haphazard response of Latin American trade to initiatives coming from outside may be even better illustrated – again from the Yugoslav example – in Fig. 13.5. Figures of Yugoslav total trade with Latin America (33) may correlate rather badly with other Yugoslav trade, but they still do represent the result of Yugoslav's more or less active efforts to establish trade with Latin America. But there is no similarity between these total curves and the development of trade between Yugoslavia and any of the more important Latin American countries. With very strong yearly fluctuations, in the

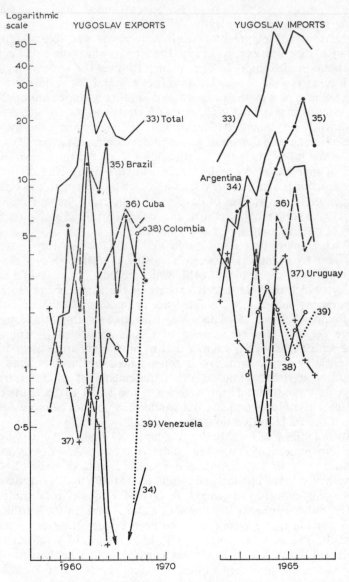

FIG. 13.5. Yugoslav trade with Latin America, 1958–69, in millions of U.S. dollars.

Source: See Fig. 13.3.

early sixties Argentina and Brazil (34, 35) were the most important countries for Yugoslav exports, while in the late sixties Cuba, Colombia and Venezuela (36, 38, 39) took the lead. Meanwhile, the importance of other countries increased or became nil. To cover her needs for imports, Yugoslav policy pushed exports to Latin America to a certain necessary level. These exports went to the countries where they could best be sold at a given moment. There would not have been such enormous oscillations in Yugoslav exports to individual countries if any given penetration of a Latin American market by Yugoslav commodities had met with a bilateral response in foreign trade policy. This is shown conclusively by the composition of Yugoslav imports from Latin America. The generation of these imports is the exclusive result of Yugoslav initiative and policy. The yearly oscillations of this trade are smaller with individual countries than in total, and the order of importance in trade, corresponding to the commodities Yugoslavia needed, became fairly consistently Argentina, Brazil, Cuba, Uruguay, Colombia. Yugoslav imports from these countries would certainly have increased further if Yugoslav exports to the same countries oscillated less.

A parallel argument can be made also in regard to Latin American–Eastern European trade. By using the same method of illustration and considering the national distribution of Latin American–Eastern European trade, we obtain a similar picture of trade instability (Table 13.1).

However, this general picture is distorted by the development of Eastern European trade with Cuba. But the sudden importance of Cuba in Latin American–Eastern European trade is less an example of increased trade volume than a politically caused shift from an existing trade partner, the U.S.A., to the new partners in Eastern Europe. This shift was accomplished the more easily since at the same moment Cuba moved over to become a centrally planned economy. But Cuban trade after 1961 did not increase more than the trade of most other Latin American countries. The change in the economic system enabled Cuba to reorient existing trade to the advantage of Eastern Europe, but it did not help Cuba achieve a better rate of growth in foreign trade. Thus, once this shift was accomplished, the new higher level of Latin American–Eastern European trade showed no more dynamism than before. Given present trends, with trade initiatives remaining firmly on the Eastern European side, we have no reason to expect Latin American–Eastern European trade to increase in the near future at a higher rate than in the past, unless as a result of the structural changes that political events might always bring.

This does not, of course, mean that on the Latin American side

TABLE 13.1

TRADE OF EASTERN EUROPE WITH SOME
LATIN AMERICAN ECONOMIES 1958/68

	Argentina		Brazil		Colombia		Cuba		Mexico		Uruguay	
	Exp.	Imp.	Exp.	Imp.	Exp.	Imp.	Exp.	Imp.	Exp.	Imp.	Exp.	Imp.
U.S.S.R. (millions of rubles)												
1958	16	14	—	1				14	1		5	22
1959	15	25	1	4				7		1	8	14
1960	13	20	14	8			64	93	1	3	1	1
1961	10	18	17	22			248	281				4
1963	1	17	27	39			360	148		7		5
1964	4	18	22	33			331	260		2		1
1965	18	65	25	30			338	308	1			3
1966	7	97	25	28			432	257	1	9	1	8
1967	21	11	31	1			507	336	1	8		3
1968	3	26	12	25			562	250	2	8	1	1
C.S.R. (millions of Kcs)												
1960	79	103	137	122								
1961	71	97	109	158								
1962	32	131	115	85								
1963	29	65	72	94								
1964	19	50	80	93								
1965	27	69	51	99								
1966	27	61	87	93								
Poland (millions of zloty)												
1960	35	78	80	105			16	39	1		2	7
1961	29	55	46	66			90	98	1	1	1	6
1962	6	78	20	24			81	76	1	1	1	7
1963	2	75	53	49	2	6	97	69	1	1	1	8
1964	8	58	22	33	4	6	55	31	3	39	2	25
1965	10	53	18	29	6	14	21	17	3	278	2	5
1966	13	93	47	26	7	17	31	54	2	28	3	24
1967	9	57	49	56	11	15	27	30	3	4	3	10
German D.R. (millions of Marks)												
1960			51	51	6	7	11	19	2			
1961			68	63	9	14	116	14	3	1		
1962			36	37	11	16	96	18	2			
1963			25	49	13	14	130	12	1			
1964			53	63	24	22	138	9	1			
1965			31	59	24	22	101	14	3	1		
1966			40	59	30	43	154	13	3	3		
1967			111	80	22	38	186	20	3	11		
1968			113	76	18	50	151	23	4	1		
Hungary (millions of forint)												
1960	117	102	47	50	9	14	13				3	7
1966	7	158	14	156	3	3	60	32			1	12
1967	4	122	164	114	3	12	37	51			1	12

Table 13.1 (*continued*)

	Argentina		Brazil		Columbia		Cuba		Mexico		Uruguay	
	Exp.	Imp.	Exp.	Imp.	Exp.	Imp.	Exp.	Imp.	Exp.	Imp.	Exp.	Imp.
Romania (millions of lei)												
1960	13	10	18	7							1	1
1961	20	7	13	9			69	3	18			2
1962	9	28	19	18			34	36				
1963	4	14	11	33			73	47				
1964	6	18	15	27			36					
1965	7	7	27	31			15					
1966	20	2	5	13			17					
1967	8	4	16	7			7					

Source: Figures are taken from the following sources (and for the corresponding year): U.S.S.R., Vnješnjaja torgovlija S.S.S.R., Statističeskij obzor; C.S.R., Statni statisticky Ufd, Statistická Ročenka Ceskoslovenské Socialistické Republiky; Poland, Glówny Urzad Statystyczny: Rocznik Statystyczny; GDR, Statistisches Jahrbuch der Deutschen Demokratischen Republik; Hungary, Központi Statistikai Hivatal, Statisztikai Erkönyr; Romania, Republica Socialista România, Anuarul Statistical Republicii Socialiste România.

there do not exist possibilities of improving interventionist techniques and foreign trade policies. But this is again probably less a problem of improving Latin American–Eastern European relations than a more fundamental problem of activating Latin American foreign trade policies in general and in all directions, as the Yugoslav example showed.

Even when Latin American–Eastern European trade is further broken down into trade of individual countries in individual items, it keeps its oscillating and mostly incidental character. Eastern Europe buys in Latin America the raw materials that at a given moment can be obtained there most cheaply or at the right moment. In payment, except in the case of Cuba, Eastern Europe exports there whatever accidental surpluses can be best placed there at the time. This is shown for instance by the structure of trade of the U.S.S.R. with its most important partners in Latin America (Table 13.2). To pay for the wool, hides, coffee, cocoa butter, sugar or minerals delivered from different Latin American countries, the U.S.S.R. supplies, mostly to Cuba, Argentina and Brazil, corresponding amounts of machines and parts, or preferably oil and oil derivatives. Only in the case of Cuba is the planned export list of the U.S.S.R. longer, including exports of steel, non-ferrous metals, chemicals, cellulose and paper, wheat and flour, canned meat and vegetables, etc. Many of these items are not goods in which the U.S.S.R. has a competitive position. But it is the import of capital to Cuba from Eastern Europe that facilitates such trade.

In conclusion, to summarise what has been said about Latin

TABLE 13.2

TRADE OF THE U.S.S.R. WITH SOME LATIN AMERICAN
COUNTRIES 1967 AND 1968
(millions of rubles at current prices)

	Argentina 1967	Argentina 1968	Brazil 1967	Brazil 1968	Cuba 1967	Cuba 1968
Exports from U.S.S.R.						
Machines and parts	1·4	0·5	1·1	0·9	145·6	205·2
Oil and derivatives	1·4	2·3	5·2	4·8	61·8	62·6
Raw steel					13·0	13·1
Processed steel					7·7	9·3
Non-ferrous metals (including processed)					9·5	11·4
Chemicals					53·9	32·1
Cellulose and paper					10·5	9·5
Wheat and flour			3·0	4·5	54·9	54·1
Canned meat					12·5	14·7
Vegetable oils					16·2	9·9
Total	4·3	2·9	10·8	12·4	506·7	561·8
Imports to U.S.S.R.						
Wool	4·9	12·2				
Hides	11·6	9·4	2·1	0·8		
Coffee			8·3	8·4		
Cocoa butter			4·7	6·0		
Sugar					302·3	212·7
Minerals and concentrates					24·5	25·0
Total	20·2	25·8	31·2	25·2	335·5	250·0

Source: See Table 13.1.

American–Eastern European trade, the lack of positive foreign trade policies has been stressed relative to other factors determining the rather low rate of growth of Latin American trade. The case may have been overstated, but the importance of this factor lies in the fact that while other causal elements may be beyond the reach of Latin America, the shaping of national trade policies is something well within the sphere of possibilities of any country. Even if it may not in fact effect the largest changes, it is the first thing that can be done by Latin American countries themselves.

Latin America by itself can exert less influence on the fundamental problem of capital imports. Anyone not convinced of the importance of capital imports to the growth of Latin American trade has only to consider why Latin American imports from the U.S.A. (18), or from the United Kingdom (EFTA, 23) stagnated when, as shown above, the trade of other developing continents did much better. Of course, Latin American–Eastern European trade did not stagnate because capital flows declined, since none of much importance ever existed. But this is an indication of one means whereby trade between Latin America and Eastern Europe could really be improved. However, this is a matter where Latin America has much less say than in the question of her own trade policies.

The third and not the least important factor which we encountered in the analysis is the political one. Leaving aside here the question of major political blocks, which would take us far beyond the reach of economic reasoning, there is still much that could be said about the political possibilities of improving Latin American trade. We cannot neglect the fact that, once organisations like LAFTA or the Central American Common Market embarked on the political organisation of intra-regional trade, such trade developed an extraordinary impetus, although remaining at a low absolute level (22). There is no reason why other political actions of the same type could not increase Latin American trade in inter-regional organisations. The development of such organised forms of trade expansion may with time even help to make national foreign trade policies of Latin American countries more expansionist.

Discussion of the Paper by Professor Pertot

Dr. von Gleich said that the importance of Eastern Europe as a potential trading partner for Latin America contrasted sharply with her very limited participation to date in the increasing trade between Eastern Europe and Western countries in general. The importance was rooted in Latin America's desire to reduce her dependence on a few markets and to find new markets, especially for manufactures. It was hoped that given the stage of industrial development of Eastern Europe there could be opportunities for Latin American manufactures both in terms of aggregate demand and of competitiveness. As against this there were great problems involved in trade relations with Eastern Europe. The tool used to reduce the planning risk described by Professor Pertot was the bilateral agreement; this brought in its train problems such as what price should be used and what should be done with surpluses in favour of Latin American countries which were unusable because of supply difficulties in Eastern Europe. A further problem that had arisen was the distortion which occurred when Latin American goods passed through an Eastern Europe country into a traditional market. Also, the lack of stable commercial and business organisations made it very difficult to establish new markets in industrial goods.

Turning to prospects for future trade, he was not optimistic. He did not agree with Professor Pertot's statement that the increasing trade between centrally planned and market economies was due mainly to the commercial aggressiveness of the latter; it arose rather from the growing complementarity between the industrialised economies of Western and Eastern Europe. Such complementarity was possible for Latin America but would only be achieved by serious medium- and long-range planning, of a kind that appeared unlikely in most Latin American countries.

Circumstances would of course be quite different if more Latin American countries were to opt for a Socialist system, whereupon they would undoubtedly divert trade. The question would then be whether economic dependence would have been reduced – or merely shifted.

Dr. Mayobre took up the question of 'planning risk' which Professor Pertot had presented as a reason impeding foreign trade in centrally planned economies. He suggested that while the argument was valid for large and well endowed countries such as the U.S.S.R., for small countries like those of Central Europe there was a real need to increase trade in order to get essential equipment and materials. He thought that some of the most important reasons for the low level of trade with Latin America were the following: First, equipment formed an important part of Latin American imports, coming from the U.S.A. and Western Europe; it was not easy to change one's supplier in this field, and there were problems over servicing and spares with Eastern European suppliers. Second, Eastern European countries did not have an adequate commercial system; official missions came and made approaches to state enterprises, but this was not enough. It was necessary to get directly to the private sector. The Japanese selling techniques were a good example of what was necessary. And third, the financial infrastructure played a crucial role in trade; this existed for present markets but was lacking in respect of Eastern Europe.

Mr. Macario agreed with Dr. Mayobre that the central problems were those of expanding trade between countries with little or no trade at present. He thought that the promotion of trade with Eastern Europe was one of the most important accomplishments of the E.E.C., by, for example, promoting direct contacts between businessmen. He suggested that the purchase of whole factories – i.e. vertically integrated processes – could reduce the problem of dependence on parts. He commented on the change in attitude in Latin American countries. Until recently they had been afraid of Western retaliation; now even Brazil and Argentina were willing to establish trade relations with Eastern Europe.

Both Mr. Macario and *Professor Nove* stressed that bureaucracy was a serious hindrance to trade. Mr. Macario concurred with other speakers in blaming in part the bilateral system, but Professor Nove pointed out that this was an obstacle also encountered and apparently overcome in trading with other than Eastern European countries. He saw lack of information and interest as hindrances and added that a further problem was that credit given by Eastern European countries was typically not generous.

Mr. Hosono took up the same question of financial infrastructure: one solution could be the creation of a financial institution whose task was to purchase the inconvertible balance held by Latin American countries in favour of socialist countries and to sell it to developed countries such as Japan or Western Europe, who could use it to pay for imports they typically were anxious to make from the Socialist Bloc. Such an arrangement had in fact been made in the case of India: the surplus currency was deposited with a Bulgarian bank and was used by Western European countries for making purchases from Eastern Europe. There could also be scope for special triangular trade agreements on specific products. Socialist countries had not made effective concessions to developing countries in the way that the developed market economies had via trade preferences: such three-cornered arrangements could form an important contribution.

Mr. Urquidi praised Professor Pertot for an illuminating paper. It appeared, however, that trade between Latin America and Eastern Europe was not at all large. It amounted to some U.S. $ 600–800 million, including some U.S. $ 20–40 million with Yugoslavia. Most of this trade seemed to take place with Cuba. Looking to possible solutions for the difficulties other speakers had mentioned, Mr. Urquidi felt that, contrary to Professor Pertot's suggestion that Latin American trade policies should be activated in this direction, the initiative should be taken by the Eastern European countries by purchasing larger amounts of Latin American basic products, thus creating a trade balance in favour of Latin America that should serve as an inducement to find practical ways of developing exports of Eastern machinery and equipment to Latin America, on a commercial basis, over a medium-term range, not on a year-to-year bilateral balancing of trade. Efforts should be made in particular to identify specific areas of technology where Eastern European equipment was designed for more labour-intensive operations appropriate to Latin American labour surplus conditions.

This last suggestion was challenged, however, by *Mrs. Warman*. She thought that Cuba was the perfect illustration of why it was misguided to think of a low capital–labour ratio as something desirable in itself. A typical labour surplus economy before the Revolution, Cuba had taken major decisions on how to utilise the economic surplus, as a result of which the problem of excess labour had disappeared.

Dr. Lang made a number of comments which illuminated the potential importance of Eastern Europe for Latin America's foreign trade. First, Eastern European countries in general had a high rate of growth which would continue, and were undergoing deep structural changes in their economies. The definite interest in trade with countries with different socio-economic systems was part of their adjustment to a higher level of economic development and would endure. But economic relations with industrially developed countries and even with Africa and Asia were developing much more rapidly than with Latin America. More rapid development of such relations could, he felt, contribute to necessary structural changes in Latin American economies. Diversification of international economic relations had important effects on one's bargaining power and on choice of options. Trade with Eastern Europe gave the opportunity of long-term arrangements – particularly important for developing countries suffering from unstable revenues.

He agreed with other participants that possibilities for increased trade were not being adequately explored. In particular he thought industrial co-operation offered possibilities. Research on this in his own institute in Yugoslavia suggested that while such joint ventures were few in number at present, their strengths were that they were possible between countries at different levels of development and with different socio-economic systems, they were not linked to the promotion of the *status quo* (in contrast to private foreign investment), and they promoted structural change and rational industrialisation by facilitating greater specialisation and economies of scale. He saw industrial co-operation as blurring the distinction between 'active' and 'passive' partners in international economic relations by requiring a common effort from all; this had important consequences in terms of economic power.

Professor Sunkel asked if he might turn to the general topic of the conference. He said that the gap between the views he had tried to express in his paper and the views people had been expressing since was so great as to suggest a serious communication problem, and he wished to restate his case. The topics with which people had been concerned were short-term and medium-term in nature (trade, exchange etc.). For him the crucial concern was the longer run, and it appeared that such short-run policies had important implications for the long run. It might well be that the aims of short-term policy and of long-run development conflicted. For example, it was clear that trade could be increased by increasing foreign investment. But the maximisation of trade could only be an end in itself in a world of perfect markets; hence it became crucial to attempt to understand the long-run effects of such a policy.

The framework he was proposing for such an examination was an analysis of the generation and use of surplus (i.e. the surplus which provided access to the essential ingredient for development – technology). To understand why countries which had generated huge surpluses in their primary goods sectors had yet failed to become developed, it was essential to analyse who obtained the surplus and for what purpose – i.e. the social structure must enter explicitly into the analysis. At this point we found the surplus held by *élite* upper groups and by foreigners. The latter had no responsibility for our development; the former did and had not shouldered it. And these *élite* groups had been able to lean for support on the international structure.

Professor Vernon responded by saying that Professor Sunkel had beyond doubt identified a major problem. He would quarrel only with his choice of a solution – the substantial diminution of ties with the foreigner – as if it were self evident. One could find evidence in plenty both of countries which had opted for such a solution and failed to develop, and of countries which had achieved development with no such break, a paramount example being Mexico itself, where today he saw the degree of independence of the foreigner in terms of ability to make internal choices as greater than ever before.

Professor Pertot said that he too would like to make the opportunity of elaborating a little on his own understanding of the question of dependency. It had been persuasively stressed, notably in Professor Sunkel's paper, that active economic policy to increase the industrial exports of Latin America, while it might sometimes increase trade in some specific product, often led simultaneously to increased economic and political dependency on the developed countries with whom industrial co-operation was taking place. For himself, he could not share this pessimism. He was convinced that a clear-cut economic policy aiming at the development of closer industrial connections must remain a target; if economic dependence resulted, then that could only be because policy was inadequate in some way. The first goal for each developed country was to shape as early as possible her own concept of economic development and a corresponding well thought out system of economic policy. However, despite the wide range of interventionist policies open to them, it was still the case that very few countries, and in particular very few developing countries, did more than attempt to reduce, by short-term policies constituting more or less instinctive reactions, the harmful aspects of situations which only arose because of the lack of a clear conception of long-run policy.

He did not in fact believe that any of the cases of economic dependence which had been mentioned in the course of the conference would have occurred if the situations had been part of a previously thought up policy of development. He could illustrate this by an example which he was familiar with in Yugoslavia: motor vehicle assembly. This was clearly not begun either in Yugoslavia or in Latin America as a result of a long-term policy and careful study of comparative advantage. In fact, he was fairly sure such a study would have led to the rejection of the idea of any such factory. The end of the Second World War had surprised the developing countries with an enormously rich inventory of policy instruments at their disposal, but found them at the same time lacking in real initiatives to form a development policy to be implemented by the use of the wide range of policies which had only just become either known or admissible. While the developed countries succeeded in defining both short-term and long-term targets quite quickly, the developing world remained rather on the defensive, using instruments of restriction only to neutralise successive imbalances in international payments.

Instead of a long-term policy of tariff protection of selected branches of industry, developing countries thus tended to forget the protective and utilise the distributive function of tariffs. To offset the effect of large imports of cars, it seemed easier to impose high tariffs on imports or introduce differential rates, than to raise internal sales taxes. In due course such tariffs rose to the point where external capital became interested in the profits such high protection was offering. If small countries were now complaining about the 'dependence' such co-operation had brought (on imports of parts, or even more through the identification of the interest of the national assembly units with that of the foreign metropolitan-based parent plant), he thought this was seriously misguided. Such characteristics were unavoidable because of the nature of the industry in question, which resulted from the initial lack of a development policy.

However, it was quite wrong to generalise from this to the undesirability of any kind of industrial co-operation policy. On the contrary, to him it indicated the imperative need for any developing country to concentrate her efforts on shaping her own development policy. This would avoid the use of inadequate instruments of policy and the state or sense of dependency their application might directly or indirectly cause. This, incidentally, would then greatly facilitate trade with Eastern Europe. Once Latin American countries had clearly defined their own policy targets, then many of the political and other prejudices that were today preventing them from increasing trade with Eastern Europe would disappear. Furthermore, planning long-term bilateral obligations would become possible.

It was not of course ignorance of such considerations which prevented Latin American countries changing their own policies. It was rather the difficulty of agreeing on a given long-term policy. But he was optimistic since it seemed to him that the very pace of technological development would soon force countries to agree more rapidly on long-term policy. The real problem would be for each country to manage to choose in time that policy which was in its own best interest.

Turning to reply to other participants, he took up Dr. von Gleich, who had asked him to say more on the institutional background to Eastern European trade. There were two chief aspects to this, the first being the foreign trade fund and the second the bilateral agreement. The former worked in the same way as any tariff or other interventionist trade measure would work. The latter's form was obvious; in response to the criticisms which had been made of it, he pointed out that in one respect it was actually a very flexible instrument: such agreements could be easily adapted just because they were bilateral.

In reply to Mr. Urquidi, he agreed that changes were of course necessary also in Eastern European policies; he had, however, interpreted the Conference's concern as being with Latin America and therefore with aspects of the question that were within the reach of Latin American economic policy.

Lastly, in reply to Mr. Macario's suggestion that the purchase of whole factories would avert dependence on parts, he would like to point out how this again reinforced the centrality of industrial co-operation policy, since the purchase and successful operation of an entire factory would require even more knowledge and even closer technical co-operation.

Index

Entries marked in **bold type** indicate papers given by participants; entries in *italic* indicate contributions by participants to discussions.